Keats · Ausgewählte Werke

John Keats

Werke und Briefe

Lyrik

(Englisch/Deutsch)

Verserzählungen · Drama

Briefe

Ausgewählt und übertragen
von Mirko Bonné
unter Verwendung der Briefübersetzungen
von Christa Schuenke

Nachwort
von Hermann Fischer

Reclam

RECLAMS UNIVERSAL-BIBLIOTHEK Nr. 9403
1995 Philipp Reclam jun. GmbH & Co. KG,
Siemensstraße 32, 71254 Ditzingen
Druck und Bindung: Eberl & Koesel GmbH & Co. KG,
Am Buchweg 1, 87452 Altusried-Krugzell
Printed in Germany 2022
RECLAM, UNIVERSAL-BIBLIOTHEK und
RECLAMS UNIVERSAL-BIBLIOTHEK sind eingetragene Marken
der Philipp Reclam jun. GmbH & Co. KG, Stuttgart
ISBN 978-3-15-009403-7
www.reclam.de

Inhalt

Lyrik

Poems

Imitation of Spenser

Now Morning from her orient chamber came,
And her first footsteps touched a verdant hill;
Crowning its lawny crest with amber flame,
Silv'ring the untainted gushes of its rill;
Which, pure from mossy beds, did down distill,
And after parting beds of simple flowers,
By many streams a little lake did fill,
Which round its marge reflected woven bowers,
And, in its middle space, a sky that never lowers.

There the king-fisher saw his plumage bright
Vying with fish of brilliant dye below;
Whose silken fins, and golden scalès light
Cast upward, through the waves, a ruby glow:
There saw the swan his neck of archèd snow,
And oared himself along with majesty;
Sparkled his jetty eyes; his feet did show
Beneath the waves like Afric's ebony,
And on his back a fay reclined voluptuously.

Ah! could I tell the wonders of an isle
That in that fairest lake had placèd been,
I could e'en Dido of her grief beguile;
Or rob from aged Lear his bitter teen:
For sure so fair a place was never seen,
Of all that ever charmed romantic eye:
It seemed an emerald in the silver sheen
Of the bright waters; or as when on high,
Through clouds of fleecy white, laughs the cerulean sky.

Gedichte

Spenser-Imitation

Nun trat der Morgen aus dem Orientsaal,
Und grünen Hügeln galt sein erster Schritt –
Krönend den Graskamm mit gelbgoldnem Strahl,
Silbernd den klaren Guß des Quells damit,
Der, durch sein Moosbett rein, herniederglitt
Und, als er Beete schlichten Flors durchwand,
In Rinnsaln einen kleinen See erstritt,
Der Rankenlauben spiegelte am Rand
Und, wo die Mitte war, ein stetes Himmelsband.

Dort sah der Eisvogel sein Federkleid
Wetteifern mit Glanz des Fischs um ihn,
Die seidnen Flossen, goldnen Schuppen weit
Die Flut durchstrahln, ein glühender Rubin –
Dort sah der Schwan Schnee seinen Hals umziehn
Und glitt dahin in königlichem Maß;
Funkeln sein schwarzes Aug – im Wasser schien
Sein Fuß aus Ebenhölzern Afrikas,
Indessen eine Fee voll Wollust auf ihm saß.

Ah! könnt ich schildern jenes Inselreich,
Hineingesetzt in diesen schönsten See –
Ich nähm selbst Dido ihren Gram sogleich
Und raubt dem greisen Lear sein bittres Weh:
Keinen so schönen Fleck sah man wohl je,
Der solch romantisches Gefühl entfacht;
Er schien ein Edelstein im Silberschnee
Des hellen Wassers; als ob seiner Pracht,
Durch wolliges Gewölk, azurner Himmel lacht.

And all around it dipped luxuriously
Slopings of verdure through the glossy tide,
Which, as it were in gentle amity,
Rippled delighted up the flowery side;
As if to glean the ruddy tears, it tried,
Which fell profusely from the rose-tree stem!
Haply it was the workings of its pride,
In strife to throw upon the shore a gem
Outvying all the buds in Flora's diadem.

To Hope

When by my solitary hearth I sit,
And hateful thoughts enwrap my soul in gloom;
When no fair dreams before my 'mind's eye' flit,
And the bare heath of life presents no bloom;
Sweet Hope, ethereal balm upon me shed,
And wave thy silver pinions o'er my head.

Whene'er I wander, at the fall of night,
Where woven boughs shut out the moon's bright ray,
Should sad Despondency my musings fright,
And frown, to drive fair Cheerfulness away,
Peep with the moon-beams through the leafy roof,
And keep that fiend Despondence far aloof.

Should Disappointment, parent of Despair,
Strive for her son to seize my careless heart;
When, like a cloud, he sits upon the air,
Preparing on his spell-bound prey to dart:
Chase him away, sweet Hope, with visage bright,
And fright him as the morning frightens night!

Und ringsher tauchten dieser Pracht geweiht
Ergrünte Hänge durch die lichte Flut,
Die, als wär es aus sanfter Freundlichkeit,
Beglückt auf Blumenufer Plätschern lud –
Sie kam zu sammeln Tränen rot wie Blut,
Die von den Rosen fielen voller Glanz!
Am Werk war hier vielleicht ihr stolzer Mut,
Gemmen zu spüln aufs Gras des Uferrands,
Schöner als all der Flor in Floras Blumenkranz.

An die Hoffnung

Wenn ich stumm dasitz am verlaßnen Herd
Und Haß die Seele in sein Dunkel zieht;
Wenn mir kein Traum vors ›Aug des Geistes‹ fährt
Und nichts im brachen Feld des Lebens blüht –
Dann, Hoffnung, gieß aus Ätherbalsam hier
Und schwing die Silberflügel über mir.

Wenn ich umherstreif, in der Dämmerung,
Wo Zweigwerk aussperrt hellen Mondenschein;
Ängstigt mein Sinnen da Verzweifelung,
Schreckt es, verscheucht das holde Fröhlichsein –
Lug du durchs Dach aus Laub mit Mond und Stern
Und halt den Feind Verzweiflung von mir fern.

Der Vater der Verzagtheit, der Verdruß,
Sucht er in meinem ruhigen Herz den Sohn;
Sitzt, wolkengleich, er in der Luft, zum Schuß
Bereit auf den gebannten Beutelohn –
Verscheuch ihn, Hoffnung, hell die Stirn entfacht,
Und schreck ihn wie der Morgen schreckt die Nacht!

Whene'er the fate of those I hold most dear
  Tells to my fearful breast a tale of sorrow,
O bright-eyed Hope, my morbid fancy cheer;
  Let me awhile thy sweetest comforts borrow:
    Thy heaven-born radiance around me shed,
    And wave thy silver pinions o'er my head!

Should e'er unhappy love my bosom pain,
  From cruel parents, or relentless fair;
O let me think it is not quite in vain
  To sigh out sonnets to the midnight air!
    Sweet Hope, ethereal balm upon me shed,
    And wave thy silver pinions o'er my head!

In the long vista of the years to roll,
  Let me not see our country's honour fade:
O let me see our land retain her soul,
  Her pride, her freedom; and not freedom's shade.
    From thy bright eyes unusual brightness shed –
    Beneath thy pinions canopy my head!

Let me not see the patriot's high bequest,
  Great Liberty! how great in plain attire!
With the base purple of a court oppressed,
  Bowing her head, and ready to expire:
    But let me see thee stoop from heaven on wings
    That fill the skies with silver glitterings!

And as, in sparkling majesty, a star
  Gilds the bright summit of some gloomy cloud;
Brightening the half-veiled face of heaven afar:
  So, when dark thoughts my boding spirit shroud,
    Sweet Hope, celestial influence round me shed,
    Waving thy silver pinions o'er my head.

Wenn mir das Schicksal derer, die ich lieb,
  Die Brust schnürt mit Geschichten ihrer Sorgen –
O Hoffnung, glänzend, lös den kranken Trieb;
  Laß eine Weile mildsten Trost mich borgen;
    Dein Himmelsstrahlen gieß rings um mich hier
    Und schwing die Silberflügel über mir!

Schmerzt bittre Liebe meinen Busen je,
  Da Eltern hart sind, da die Schöne lacht –
O laß mich denken, nicht vergebens fleh
  Ich mit Sonetten an die Mitternacht!
    Dann, Hoffnung, gieß aus Ätherbalsam hier
    Und schwing die Silberflügel über mir!

Vom Ausguck auf die Wogen nahender Zeit
  Laß unser Land mich niemals ruhmlos sehn –
O laß mich sehn, was Seele ihm verleiht,
  Stolz, Freiheit – nicht auf Freiheitsschemen spähn.
    Dein glänzend Aug gieß neuen Glanz aus hier –
    Ein Kissen sei dein Silberflügel mir!

Laß mich, wofür die Patrioten stehn,
  Die große Freiheit! groß in schlichtem Kleid!
Nicht unterm Joch höfischen Purpurs sehn,
  Gesenkt ihr Haupt, zum Abdanken bereit –
    Doch laß mich sehn, wie du vom Himmel schießt,
    Auf Flügeln silbern glitzernd ihn begießt!

Und wie, mit sprühender Majestät, ein Stern
  Sein Gold in Scheitel düstrer Wolken mengt,
Den Himmelsschleier aufhellt nah und fern –
  So, wenn mein Geist nur Dunkles ahnt und denkt,
    Gieß, Hoffnung, aus himmlischen Einfluß hier,
    Schwingend die Silberflügel über mir.

Give me Women, Wine, and Snuff
Until I cry out, 'Hold, enough!'
You may do so sans objection
Till the day of resurrection;
For, bless my beard, they aye shall be
My belovèd Trinity.

To my Brother George

Full many a dreary hour have I passed,
My brain bewildered, and my mind o'ercast
With heaviness; in seasons when I've thought
No sphery strains by me could e'er be caught
From the blue dome, though I to dimness gaze
On the far depth where sheeted lightning plays;
Or, on the wavy grass outstretched supinely,
Pry 'mong the stars, to strive to think divinely:
That I should never hear Apollo's song,
Though feathery clouds were floating all along
The purple west, and, two bright streaks between,
The golden lyre itself were dimly seen:
That the still murmur of the honey bee
Would never teach a rural song to me:
That the bright glance from beauty's eyelids slanting
Would never make a lay of mine enchanting,
Or warm my breast with ardour to unfold
Some tale of love and arms in time of old.
But there are times, when those that love the bay,
Fly from all sorrowing far, far away;
A sudden glow comes on them, naught they see
In water, earth, or air, but poesy.
It has been said, dear George, and true I hold it,
(For knightly Spenser to Libertas told it,)
That when a Poet is in such a trance,

Gebt mir Frauen, Schnupfkraut, Wein,
Bis ich ausruf »Haltet ein!«
Ihr hört dabei keine Klage
Bis zum Auferstehungstage –
Denn sie, von meinem Bart geweiht,
Lieb ich als Dreieinigkeit.

An meinen Bruder George

Manch öde Stunden habe ich verbracht,
Mein Hirn durchwühlt, den Geist mit schwerer Fracht
Verfinstert; Zeiten, die mich glauben ließen,
Kein Sphärenton würd sich mir je erschließen
Am blauen Dom, und starr ich bis zum Schielen
Tief in den Raum, wo weithin Blitze spielen,
Oder, rücklings gestreckt in wehendes Ried,
Die Sterne an, zu denken wie ein Gott bemüht –
Daß nie ich hören sollt Apolls Gesang,
Trieben auch Wolken federleicht entlang
Im Purpurwest und wär, zwei helle Bahnen,
Die goldne Leier selbst schwach zu erahnen –
Daß mir der Murmellaut der Honigbiene
Nie als ein ländlicher Gesang erschiene –
Daß nie die hellen Lider einer Schönen
Je zaubrisch ließen meine Lieder tönen
Oder die Brust durchglühn, um auszubreiten
Die Mär von Krieg und Liebe wie vorzeiten.
Doch kommt die Zeit, da die um Ruhm sich mühn
All ihrer Kümmernis weit, weit entfliehn;
Ein Glühn tritt sie jäh an, nichts sehen sie
In Wasser, Erde, Luft als Poesie.
Es heißt, George, und ist wahr, wenn man mich fragte
(Da Ritter Spenser es Libertas sagte),
Wenn Dichter einen solchen Rausch verspüren,

In air he sees white coursers paw, and prance,
Bestridden of gay knights, in gay apparel,
Who at each other tilt in playful quarrel,
And what we, ignorantly, sheet-lightning call,
Is the swift opening of their wide portal,
When the bright warder blows his trumpet clear,
Whose tones reach naught on earth but Poet's ear.
When these enchanted portals open wide,
And through the light the horsemen swiftly glide,
The Poet's eye can reach those golden halls,
And view the glory of their festivals:
Their ladies fair, that in the distance seem
Fit for the silvering of a seraph's dream;
Their rich brimmed goblets, that incessant run
Like the bright spots that move about the sun;
And, when upheld, the wine from each bright jar
Pours with the lustre of a falling star.
Yet further off, are dimly seen their bowers,
Of which, no mortal eye can reach the flowers –
And 'tis right just, for well Apollo knows
'Twould make the Poet quarrel with the rose.
All that's revealed from that far seat of blisses,
Is, the clear fountains' interchanging kisses,
As gracefully descending, light and thin,
Like silver streaks across a dolphin's fin,
When he upswimmeth from the coral caves,
And sports with half his tail above the waves.

These wonders strange he sees, and many more,
Whose head is pregnant with poetic lore.
Should he upon an evening ramble fare
With forehead to the soothing breezes bare,
Would he naught see but the dark, silent blue
With all its diamonds trembling through and through?
Or the coy moon, when in the waviness
Of whitest clouds she does her beauty dress,

Dann sehn sie Schimmel luftwärts scharrn, stolzieren
Mit bunten Rittern, bunt in ihrem Kleid,
Die nach sich stoßen in gespieltem Streit,
Und was wir arglos Wetterleuchten heißen,
Ist 's Öffnen ihres breiten Tors, ein Gleißen,
Zu dem der Wächter bläst ins helle Horn,
Hörbar auf Erden nur den Dichterohrn.
Wenn diese Zaubertore sich so weiten
Und rasch durchs Licht heraus die Reiter gleiten,
Kann 's Dichteraug in goldne Hallen spähn
Und ihrer Feste Herrlichkeiten sehn:
Die Damen, schön, daß sie von fern im Raum
Wie Silber scheinen in des Seraphs Traum;
Die Becher, die, gefüllt, stets weiter gehen
Wie Flecken hell sich um die Sonne drehen;
Und, hoch erhoben jeder Krug, strömt Wein
Herab mit eines fallenden Sternes Schein.
Entfernter sieht man schwach auch Lager dann,
Flor, den kein Sterblicher beschreiben kann –
Und 's ist nur recht so, weiß Apoll doch gut,
Die Rose reizte sonst des Dichters Wut.
Zu sehn vom fernen Thronsitz der Genüsse
Sind klarer Quellen ausgetauschte Küsse,
So voller Anmut fallend, licht und dünn
Wie silbern Flossenstreifen beim Delphin,
Wenn er emportaucht von Korallenschnellen
Und hineilt, seinen Schwanz halb auf den Wellen.

Dies Wunderwerk und viele mehr sehn die,
Die schwangergehn im Kopf mit Poesie.
Der, den ein Abend durch die Felder führt
Und dessen Stirn besänftigt Brisen spürt,
Wird der nichts sehn als stilles, blaues Schweben,
Das Diamanten durch und durch durchbeben?
Die scheue Mondin, wenn die Welligkeit
Weißester Wolken ihr die Schönheit leiht,

And staidly paces higher up, and higher,
Like a sweet nun in holy-day attire?
Ah, yes! much more would start into his sight –
The revelries, and mysteries of night:
And should I ever see them, I will tell you
Such tales as needs must with amazement spell you.

These are the living pleasures of the bard:
But richer far posterity's award.
What does he murmur with his latest breath,
While his proud eye looks through the film of death?
'What though I leave this dull, and earthly mould,
Yet shall my spirit lofty converse hold
With after times. The patriot shall feel
My stern alarum, and unsheathe his steel;
Or, in the senate thunder out my numbers
To startle princes from their easy slumbers.
The sage will mingle with each moral theme
My happy thoughts sententious; he will teem
With lofty periods when my verses fire him,
And then I'll stoop from heaven to inspire him.
Lays have I left of such a dear delight
That maids will sing them on their bridal night.
Gay villagers, upon a morn of May,
When they have tired their gentle limbs with play,
And formed a snowy circle on the grass,
And placed in midst of all that lovely lass
Who chosen is their queen – with her fine head
Crownèd with flowers purple, white, and red:
For there the lily, and the musk-rose, sighing,
Are emblems true of hapless lovers dying.
Between her breasts, that never yet felt trouble,
A bunch of violets full blown, and double,
Serenely sleep: she from a casket takes
A little book and then a joy awakes
About each youthful heart, with stifled cries,

Steigt sie ruhig höher, höher in die Nacht
Wie eine Nonne in der Festtagstracht?
Ah, ja! er schaut weit mehr, als ich erdächte:
Die Lockungen, Mysterien der Nächte –
Seh ich sie je, werd ich Dir Dinge schreiben,
Die Dich verzaubernd ins Erstaunen treiben.

Reich sind des Barden Lebensfreuden schon –
Weit reicher aber noch der Nachwelt Lohn.
Was murmelt er mit seinem letzten Hauch,
Durchblickt sein Aug den Film des Todes auch?
»Muß ich mit dumpfer Erdenhülle brechen,
Soll fortan doch mein Geist erhaben sprechen
Zur Nachwelt; soll mein Waffenruf durchglühn
Den Patrioten, er den Degen ziehn;
Soll den Senat mit seinen Silben wecken,
Ja, Fürsten dort aus seichtem Schlummer schrecken.
Mit dem, was glücklich ich gedacht, schmeckt ab
Der Weise die Moral; er fleht herab
Die hehre Zeit, Glut meiner Dichtung spürend,
Und schon schöß ich herab, ihn inspirierend.
Lieder ließ ich zurück, die Freuden bringen,
Daß Jungfraun sie in ihrer Brautnacht singen;
Menschen im Dorf, an einem Maienmorgen,
Die müde sind vom Spielen ohne Sorgen,
Deshalb im Gras zum schneeigen Zirkel rücken
Und in der Mitte auf das Mädchen blicken,
Das sie zur Fürstin ausersahn – sein Haupt
Von Blumen purpurn, weiß und rot umlaubt:
Denn Lilien, Moschusrosen, dunkle Farben
Sind Zeichen dort, daß zwei vor Kummer starben.
Auf ihren Brüsten, nie von Gram erfaßt,
Ruht ein Bund Veilchen, blühend jeder Last
Wie jene bar; aus einem Kästchen nimmt sie
Ein kleines Buch, und schon zur Freude stimmt sie
Ein jedes junges Herz, gespanntes Munkeln,

And rubbing of white hands, and sparkling eyes –
For she's to read a tale of hopes, and fears,
One that I fostered in my youthful years.
The pearls, that on each glistening circlet sleep,
Gush ever and anon with silent creep,
Lured by the innocent dimples. To sweet rest
Shall the dear babe, upon its mother's breast,
Be lulled with songs of mine. Fair world, adieu!
Thy dales, and hills, are fading from my view:
Swiftly I mount, upon wide spreading pinions,
Far from the narrow bounds of thy dominions.
Full joy I feel, while thus I cleave the air,
That my soft verse will charm thy daughters fair,
And warm thy sons!' Ah, my dear friend and brother,
Could I, at once, my mad ambition smother,
For tasting joys like these, sure I should be
Happier, and dearer to society.
At times, 'tis true, I've felt relief from pain
When some bright thought has darted through my brain:
Through all that day I've felt a greater pleasure
Than if I'd brought to light a hidden treasure.
As to my sonnets, though none else should heed them,
I feel delighted, still, that you should read them.
Of late, too, I have had much calm enjoyment,
Stretched on the grass at my best loved employment
Of scribbling lines for you. These things I thought
While, in my face, the freshest breeze I caught.
E'en now I'm pillowed on a bed of flowers
That crowns a lofty clift, which proudly towers
Above the ocean-waves. The stalks, and blades,
Chequer my tablet with their quivering shades.
On one side is a field of drooping oats,
Through which the poppies show their scarlet coats,
So pert and useless, that they bring to mind
The scarlet coats that pester human-kind.
And on the other side, outspread, is seen

Das Reiben weißer Hände, Augenfunkeln –
Sie liest ein Werk voll Hoffnung, Bangigkeit,
Eins, das ich schrieb in meiner Jugendzeit.
Die Perlen, die auf jedem Haarreif liegen,
Ergießen sich stets neu mit stillem Wiegen,
Gelockt von keuschen Grübchen. Süße Ruh
Am Mutterbusen schenkt dem Kind im Nu
Eins meiner Lieder. Schöne Welt, adieu!
Aus meinem Blick entschwinden Tal und Höh;
Rasch steig ich auf, auf weit gespreiztem Flügel,
Hinweg aus engen Tälern deiner Hügel.
Beglückt fühl ich, da ich die Luft durcheil,
Bezaubern deine Töchter wird mein Teil
Und wärmen deine Söhne!« Ah, mein Lieber,
Könnt ich ersticken, jetzt, dies Ehrgeizfieber,
Solch Glück zu kosten – froher sicherlich
Und der Gesellschaft nützlicher wär ich.
Manchmal, 's ist wahr, fühlt ich mich frei von Wirrn,
Schoß glänzend ein Gedanke durch mein Hirn:
Solch Tag hat mir ein größres Glück vermacht,
Als hätt ich einen Schatz ans Licht gebracht.
Und mein Sonettwerk, schätzt man es auch nicht –
Noch immer freut mich, daß es Dir entspricht.
Auch jüngst empfand ich jene stille Freud,
Gestreckt ins Gras zur Lieblingstätigkeit:
An Dich zu kritteln. Dies hier dachte ich,
Da mein Gesicht der frischste Wind umstrich.
Auch jetzt lieg ich, von Blumen ganz umschirmt,
Auf einem hohen Kliff, stolz aufgetürmt
Über den Meereswogen. Blatt und Stiel
Mustern die Tafeln mir mit Schattenspiel.
Dort liegt ein Feld voll Hafer, der sich neigt
Und durch den Mohn die roten Röcke zeigt,
So frech und nutzlos ganz, daß man sich fragt
Nach jenem Rotrock, der die Menschheit plagt.
Dort breitet sich des Meeres Mantel, schau,

Ocean's blue mantle streaked with purple, and green.
Now 'tis I see a canvassed ship, and now
Mark the bright silver curling round her prow.
I see the lark down-dropping to his nest
And the broad winged sea-gull never at rest;
For when no more he spreads his feathers free,
His breast is dancing on the restless sea.
Now I direct my eyes into the west,
Which at this moment is in sunbeams dressed:
Why westward turn? 'Twas but to say adieu!
'Twas but to kiss my hand, dear George, to you!

Stanzas

I

You say you love; but with a voice
  Chaster than a nun's, who singeth
The soft Vespers to herself
  While the chime-bell ringeth –
    O love me truly!

II

You say you love; but with a smile
  Cold as sunrise in September,
As you were Saint Cupid's nun,
  And kept his weeks of Ember.
    O love me truly!

Purpurn und grün durchwirkt sein Blau.
Ich seh ein Schiff vorm Wind, ich seh den Flug
Des hellen Silberschaums um seinen Bug.
Zum Nest die Lerche stürzen seh ich nun,
Seh breit beschwingt die Möwe niemals ruhn;
Denn segelt sie nicht länger hin und her,
Tanzt ihre Brust im ruhelosen Meer.
Nunmehr gehört der Westen meinen Blicken,
Den augenblicklich Sonnenstrahlen schmücken –
Warum der Westen? Um Adieu zu sagen!
Den Handkuß, lieber George, zu Dir zu tragen!

Strophen

I

Du sagst, du liebst; es klingt jedoch
  Keuscher als die Nonne könnte,
Die für sich die Vesper liest,
  Da die Glocke tönte –
    O lieb mich wirklich!

II

Du sagst, du liebst; doch lächelst du
  Kalt wie die Septembersonne,
Als hieltst du grad Fastenzeit
  Als Sankt Cupidos Nonne,
    O lieb mich wirklich!

III

You say you love – but then your lips
Coral tinted teach no blisses
More than coral in the sea –
They never pout for kisses –
O love me truly!

IV

You say you love; but then your hand
No soft squeeze for squeeze returneth,
It is like a statue's, dead –
While mine for passion burneth –
O love me truly!

V

O breathe a word or two of fire!
Smile, as if those words should burn me,
Squeeze as lovers should – O kiss
And in thy heart inurn me!
O love me truly!

Lines Rhymed in a Letter Received (by J.H. Reynolds) From Oxford

The Gothic looks solemn –
The plain Doric column
Supports an old Bishop and crosier;
The mouldering arch,
Shaded o'er by a larch
Stands next door to Wilson the Hosier.

III

Du sagst, du liebst – dein Mund jedoch
  Lehrt korallenrot Genüsse
Wie's Korallenriff im Meer –
  Nie spitzt er sich zum Küssen –
    O lieb mich wirklich!

IV

Du sagst, du liebst; doch deiner Hand
  Ist kein zartes Drücken lieber,
Wie die der Statue ist sie, tot –
  Nur meine brennt im Fieber –
    O lieb mich wirklich!

V

O hauche ein, zwei Wort' voll Feuer!
  Lächle, und das Wort durchglüh mich,
Drück, ganz Liebende – o küß
  Und in dein Herzgrab zieh mich!
    O lieb mich wirklich!

Gereimte Zeilen in einem Brief, erhalten (von J.H. Reynolds) aus Oxford

Wie gotisch euphorisch –
Die Säule ist dorisch,
Trägt glatt einen Bischof samt Krummstock;
Die Wölbung verlattet,
Von Lärchen beschattet,
Wo nebenan »Wilson – Ihr Strumpf« hockt.

Vicè – that is, by turns –
O'er pale faces mourns
The black-tassled trencher and common hat;
The chantry boy sings,
The steeple bell rings,
And as for the Chancellor – *dominat.*

There are plenty of trees,
And plenty of ease,
And plenty of fat deer for parsons;
And when it is venison,
Short is the benison –
Then each on a leg or thigh fastens.

I

In drear-nighted December,
Too happy, happy tree,
Thy branches ne'er remember
Their green felicity:
The north cannot undo them,
With a sleety whistle through them,
Nor frozen thawings glue them
From budding at the prime.

II

In drear-nighted December,
Too happy, happy brook,
Thy bubblings ne'er remember
Apollo's summer look;
But with a sweet forgetting,
They stay their crystal fretting,
Never, never petting
About the frozen time.

Vice – sprich: mal und mal nicht –
Klagt blaß ein Gesicht,
Wenn's Hut oder schwarz seine Bommeln hat;
Der Chorknabe singt,
Die Turmglocke klingt
Und ja, der Kanzöller – *dominat.*

Es gibt vieles an Bäumen
Und viel zu verträumen
Und viel fetten Hirsch für die Pfaffen;
Und geht's ans Zerlegen,
Macht man kurz diesen Segen –
Dann sich an Schenkel und Lende zu schaffen.

I

Im nacht-dunklen Dezember,
Zu froher, froher Baum,
Wird deinen Zweigen fremder
Ihr glücklich grüner Traum –
Der Nord kann sie nicht greifen,
Nur eisig durch sie pfeifen,
Wird Frost sie auch bereifen,
Sie knospen schon im Keim.

II

Im nacht-dunklen Dezember,
Zu froher, froher Bach,
Wird deinem Schäumen fremder
Apollos Sommerpracht –
Doch trotz süßem Entfallen,
Sein Kräuseln bleibt kristallen,
Nie ist's, nie ein Wallen,
Sucht Kälte es jetzt heim.

III

Ah! would 'twere so with many
A gentle girl and boy!
But were there ever any
Writhed not of passèd joy?
The feel of not to feel it,
When there is none to heal it,
Nor numbèd sense to steel it,
Was never said in rhyme.

Apollo to the Graces

APOLLO
Which of the fairest three
Today will ride with me?
My steeds are all pawing on the thresholds of Morn:
Which of the fairest three
Today will ride with me
Across the gold Autumn's whole kingdoms of corn?

THE GRACES *all answer*
I will, I – I – I –
O young Apollo let me fly along with thee,
I will, I – I – I,
The many, many wonders see –
I – I – I – I –
And thy lyre shall never have a slackened string.
I – I – I – I
Thro' the whole day will sing.

III

Ah! ging's manch jungen Frauen
  Und Herren ebenso!
Doch wen hier packt nicht Grauen,
  Wenn ihm das Glück entfloh?
 Zu spüren, nichts zu spüren,
 Und keiner wird's kurieren,
 Kein tauber Sinn sich rühren,
  Nie sagte das ein Reim.

Apollo zu den Grazien

APOLLO
  Wer der drei Schönsten hier
  Wohl reitet heut mit mir?
Es scharrn meine Rösser auf den Schwellen zum Tag –
  Wer der drei Schönsten hier
  Wohl reitet heut mit mir,
Wenn ich durch des Herbsts goldnes Erntereich jag?

DIE GRAZIEN *antworten alle*
  Ich will, ich – ich – ich –
  O hör, Apoll, laß mich dahinfliegen mit dir,
  Ich will, ich – ich – ich,
   Mich zu all, all den Wundern führ –
  Ich – ich – ich – ich –
Und niemals soll deine Leier schwächer klingen.
   Ich – ich – ich – ich –
Will tagelang nur singen.

I

O blush not so! O blush not so!
  Or I shall think you knowing;
And if you smile the blushing while,
  Then maidenheads are going.

II

There's a blush for won't, and a blush for shan't,
  And a blush for having done it:
There's a blush for thought, and a blush for naught,
  And a blush for just begun it.

III

O sigh not so! O sigh not so!
  For it sounds of Eve's sweet pippin;
By those loosened hips you have tasted the pips
  And fought in an amorous nipping.

IV

Will you play once more at nice-cut-core,
  For it only will last our youth out?
And we have the prime of the kissing time,
  We have not one sweet tooth out.

V

There's a sigh for yes, and a sigh for no,
  And a sigh for I can't bear it!
O what can be done, shall we stay or run?
  O, cut the sweet apple and share it!

I

O werd nicht rot! o werd nicht rot!
  Sonst denk ich, du wirst's wissen,
Und lächelst du so rot dazu,
  Auch deine Unschuld missen.

II

Man wird rot fürs Noch und wird rot fürs Jedoch
  Und wird rot für längst Erfahrnes;
Man wird rot und denkt und wird rot und verdrängt
  Und wird rot für just Getanes.

III

O stöhn nicht so! O stöhn nicht so!
  Als würd's Evas Apfel zerreißen;
Um die Hüften nackt, hast du Kerne geknackt
  Und fochtest ein liebendes Beißen.

IV

Willst du nochmals gern solch fein runden Kern,
  Der nicht über die Jugend hinaus hält?
Und wir sind doch bereit für die Küssenszeit,
  Kein süßer Zahn, der ausfällt.

V

Und man stöhnt fürs Ja und man stöhnt fürs Nein
  Und fürs *Du mußt dich beeilen!*
O was nur jetzt tun, was machen wir nun?
  O laß uns den Apfel jetzt teilen!

Hence Burgundy, Claret, and Port,
  Away with old Hock and Madeira,
Too couthly ye are for my sport;
  There's a beverage brighter and clearer.
Instead of a pitiful rummer,
My wine overbrims a whole summer;
  My bowl is the sky,
  And I drink at my eye,
  Till I feel in the brain
  A Delphian pain –
Then follow, my Caius! then follow!
  On the green of the hill
  We will drink our fill
  Of golden sunshine,
  Till our brains intertwine
With the glory and grace of Apollo!

God of the meridian,
And of the East and West,
To thee my soul is flown,
And my body is earthward pressed.
It is an awful mission,
A terrible division,
And leaves a gulf austere
To be filled with worldly fear.
Ay, when the soul is fled
To high above our head,
Affrighted do we gaze
After its airy maze,
As doth a mother wild,
When her young infant child
Is in an eagle's claws –
And is not this the cause

Klarett fort, Burgunder und Port,
  Madeira und Hochheimer Keller –
Zu lieblich seid ihr mir als Sport;
  Einen Trunk gibt's, viel klarer und heller.
Statt ihn nur in Römer zu gießen,
Wird mein Wein den Sommer lang fließen:
  Den Himmel als Krug,
  Trinkt mein Auge im Flug,
  Bis sich delphisch verwirrn
  Ich spüre mein Hirn –
Dann folge, mein Cajus, dem Pfade!
  Auf dem Hang vor der Stadt
  Trinken wir zwei uns satt
  Am goldenen Licht,
  Bis uns die Hirne umflicht
Apollinische Glorie und Gnade!

Dir Gott des Meridians
Und Gott von Ost und West
Folgt meine Seele ganz –
Meinen Leib hält die Erde fest.
Welch ehrfurchtsvolle Haltung,
Welch fürchterliche Spaltung,
Von der ein Abgrund bleibt,
In den Lebensangst uns treibt.
Ja, wenn die Seele so
Hoch übers Haupt entfloh,
Verfolgt man nur verwirrt,
Daß sie die Luft durchirrt,
Wird wie die Mutter wild,
Die hört, ihr Säugling brüllt
In eines Adlers Klauen –
Und ist nicht dieses Grauen

Of madness? – God of Song,
Thou bearest me along
Through sights I scarce can bear:
O let me, let me share
With the hot lyre and thee,
The staid Philosophy.
Temper my lonely hours,
And let me see thy bowers
More unalarmed!

Robin Hood

To a friend

No! those days are gone away,
And their hours are old and grey,
And their minutes buried all
Under the down-trodden pall
Of the leaves of many years;
Many times have winter's shears,
Frozen North, and chilling East,
Sounded tempests to the feast
Of the forest's whispering fleeces,
Since men knew nor rent nor leases.

No, the bugle sounds no more,
And the twanging bow no more;
Silent is the ivory shrill
Past the heath and up the hill;
There is no mid-forest laugh,
Where lone Echo gives the half
To some wight, amazed to hear
Jesting, deep in forest drear.

Schon Wahn? – Sehn läßt du mich,
Gott des Gesangs, was ich
Zu sehen kaum ertrag;
O gib, daß mich mein Tag
Zur heißen Leier, dir
Und Lebensweisheit führ.
Stimm mich Einsamen mild,
Laß nicht mehr angsterfüllt
Mich deine Schätze sehn!

Robin Hood

An einen Freund

Nein! *die* Tage warn einmal,
Alt die Stunden jetzt und fahl,
Staub ein jeglicher Moment,
Unterm Tuch längst abgetrennt
All des Laubs aus all der Zeit;
Winters Scher'n warn oft bereit,
Frostig' Nord und eisig Ost,
Lauter Sturm zur Festtagskost,
Der die stillen Vliese spannte,
Da man Lehn und Pacht nicht kannte.

Nein, das Horn ertönt nicht mehr,
Und der Bogen schwirrt nicht mehr,
Stumm ist aller Waldhornklang
Längs der Heide und am Hang;
Niemand lacht da tief im Wald,
Wo ein Echo dumpf verhallt
Und den Wicht der Mut verläßt,
Hört er Scherze im Geäst.

On the fairest time of June
You may go, with sun or moon,
Or the seven stars to light you,
Or the polar ray to right you;
But you never may behold
Little John, or Robin bold;
Never one, of all the clan,
Thrumming on an empty can
Some old hunting ditty, while
He doth his green way beguile
To fair hostess Merriment,
Down beside the pasture Trent;
For he left the merry tale
Messenger for spicy ale.

Gone, the merry morris din;
Gone, the song of Gamelyn;
Gone, the tough-belted outlaw
Idling in the 'grenè shawe';
All are gone away and past!
And if Robin should be cast
Sudden from his turfèd grave,
And if Marian should have
Once again her forest days,
She would weep, and he would craze.
He would swear, for all his oaks,
Fallen beneath the dockyard strokes,
Have rotted on the briny seas;
She would weep that her wild bees
Sang not to her – strange! that honey
Can't be got without hard money!

So it is – yet let us sing,
Honour to the old bow-string!
Honour to the bugle-horn!
Honour to the woods unshorn!

Geh, mag schönster Juni sein,
Geh im Mond- und Sonnenschein,
Leuchten dir die sieben Sterne,
Der Polarstrahl in die Ferne –
Du wirst nie, nach allem Gehn,
Little John und Robin sehn;
Keiner, nie, aus dieser Schar,
Singt ein altes Jagdlied gar,
Schwingt den Becher, während er
Kaum die grüne Trift, doch mehr
Wirtin Lustigkeit nun kennt,
Unten, bei der Weide Trent;
Denn die Mär verließ er hier,
Eilkurier für dunkles Bier.

Fort, der Morris-Lärm dahin;
Fort das Lied von Gamelyn;
Fort der Schuft, den Gurt gelöst,
Der »im grünen Strauche« döst –
Alles aus und weit weit fort!
Und stieg Robin plötzlich dort
Aus dem Grab im Gras herauf,
Tauchte Marian nochmals auf –
Dann, wenn sie den Wald erblickt',
Weinte sie, würd er verrückt.
Er schrie, jede Eiche sei,
Fällte sie die Werft nahbei,
Längst verfault am Salz im Meer;
Sie jedoch vermißte sehr
Ihre Bienen: aus den Waben –
Seltsam! – kann, wer Geld hat, haben!

Ja, so ist's – doch singen wir:
Ehr dem Bogen, daß er schwirr!
Ehr dem Horn, so laut und alt!
Ehr dem ungeschornen Wald!

Honour to the Lincoln green!
Honour to the archer keen!
Honour to tight little John,
And the horse he rode upon!
Honour to bold Robin Hood,
Sleeping in the underwood!
Honour to maid Marian,
And to all the Sherwood-clan!
Though their days have hurried by
Let us two a burden try.

Lines on the Mermaid Tavern

Souls of Poets dead and gone,
What Elysium have ye known,
Happy field or mossy cavern,
Choicer than the Mermaid Tavern?
Have ye tippled drink more fine
Than mine host's Canary wine?
Or are fruits of Paradise
Sweeter than those dainty pies
Of venison? O generous food!
Dressed as though bold Robin Hood
Would, with his maid Marian,
Sup and bowse from horn and can.

I have heard that on a day
Mine host's sign-board flew away,
Nobody knew whither, till
An astrologer's old quill
To a sheepskin gave the story,
Said he saw you in your glory,

Ehr dem satten Lincoln-Grün!
Ehr dem Bogenschützenmühn!
Ehr dem schweren Little John
Und dem Pferd, so müd davon!
Ehre Robin Hood, so stolz
Schlafend tief im Unterholz!
Ehr dem Mädchen Marian
Und dem ganzen Sherwood-Clan!
Ist auch ihre Zeit vorbei,
Komm, besingen sie wir zwei.

Zeilen auf die Meerfrauschenke

Seelen der Dichter, tot und stumm,
Saht ihr ein Elysium,
Mooswandhöhle, heitre Senke,
Edler als die Meerfrauschenke?
Habt ihr feinern Wein geschmeckt
Als hier ich Kanariensekt?
Ist das Obst im Paradies
Süßer als solch leckrer Spieß
Aus Wild? O Speisen, köstlich gut!
Grad als ob Held Robin Hood
Mit dem Mädchen Marian
Schlürft und säuft aus Horn und Kann'.

Ich hört, eines Tags flog dort
Meinem Wirt das Schankschild fort,
Keiner wußte, wo es blieb,
Bis ein Astrologe schrieb
Und auf Schafleder gebracht,
Daß er euch in eurer Pracht

Underneath a new-old sign
Sipping beverage divine,
And pledging with contented smack
The Mermaid in the Zodiac.

Souls of Poets dead and gone,
What Elysium have ye known,
Happy field or mossy cavern,
Choicer than the Mermaid Tavern?

Extracts from an Opera

I

O! were I one of the Olympian twelve,
Their godships should pass this into a law –
That when a man doth set himself in toil
After some beauty veilèd far away,
Each step he took should make his lady's hand
More soft, more white, and her fair cheek more fair;
And for each briar-berry he might eat,
A kiss should bud upon the tree of love,
And pulp and ripen richer every hour,
To melt away upon the traveller's lips.

II Daisy's Song

1

The sun, with his great eye,
Sees not so much as I;
And the moon, all silver-proud,
Might as well be in a cloud.

Unter dem neu-alten Schild
Mit dem Himmelstrank gefüllt
Und zuprosten sah voll Genuß
Der Meerfrau im Zodiakus.

Seelen der Dichter, tot und stumm,
Saht ihr ein Elysium,
Mooswandhöhle, heitre Senke,
Edler als die Meerfrauschenke?

Auszüge aus einer Oper

I

Oh! wär ich einer der olympischen Zwölf –
Gesetz sein sollte dies kraft Göttermacht:
Daß wenn ein Mann sich vorwärtsmühen muß
Zu einer Schönen, weit entfernt verhüllt,
Ein jeder Schritt die Hand der Frau nochmal
So sanft, weiß und so hold die Wange mache;
Und jede Beere, die er äß vom Strauch,
Sollt als ein Kuß am Baum der Liebe blühn
Und stündlich reicher reif und fleischig sein,
Um zu zerschmelzen auf des Wandrers Lippen.

II Lied des Gänseblümchens

I

Die Sonne, Aug an sich,
Sieht nicht soviel wie ich;
Und der Mond, ganz Silberstrahl,
Wär umwölkt genauso fahl.

2

And O the spring – the spring!
I lead the life of a king!
Couched in the teeming grass,
I spy each pretty lass.

3

I look where no one dares,
And I stare where no one stares,
And when the night is nigh,
Lambs bleat my lullaby.

III Folly's Song

When wedding fiddles are a-playing,
    Huzza for folly O!
And when maidens go a-maying,
    Huzza, etc.
When a milk-pail is upset,
    Huzza, etc.
And the clothes left in the wet,
    Huzza, etc.
When the barrel's set abroach,
    Huzza, etc.
When Kate Eyebrow keeps a coach,
    Huzza, etc.
When the pig is over-roasted,
    Huzza, etc.
And the cheese is over-toasted,
    Huzza, etc.
When Sir Snap is with his lawyer,
    Huzza, etc.
And Miss Chip has kissed the sawyer,
    Huzza, etc.

2

Und oh, der Mai – der Mai!
Ich bin ein König und frei!
Wenn ich im Gras voll Klee
Nach jedem Mädchen späh.

3

Wohin man sich nicht traut,
Schau ich, wie man nicht schaut,
Und sinkt die Nacht herein,
Lullt Lammgeblök mich ein.

III Lied der Tollheit

Wenn Hochzeitsfiedeln endlich geigen,
Heißa, die Tollheit oh!
Und dem Mai sich Mädchen zeigen,
Heißa, usw.
Wenn im Hof die Milch verläuft,
Heißa, usw.
Und im Zuber Wäsche träuft,
Heißa, usw.
Ist der Hahn ins Faß gekloppt,
Heißa, usw.
Wenn Kates Auge Kutschen stoppt,
Heißa, usw.
Wurd das Schwein zu lang begossen,
Heißa, usw.
Ist der Käse lang zerflossen,
Heißa, usw.
Wenn Sir Snap zum Anwalt müßte,
Heißa, usw.
Und Miss Chip den Säger küßte,
Heißa, usw.

IV

O, I am frightened with most hateful thoughts!
Perhaps her voice is not a nightingale's,
Perhaps her teeth are not the fairest pearl;
Her eye-lashes may be, for aught I know,
Not longer than the may-fly's small fan-horns;
There may not be one dimple on her hand –
And freckles many. Ah! a careless nurse,
In haste to teach the little thing to walk,
May have crumped up a pair of Dian's legs
And warped the ivory of a Juno's neck.

V Song

1

The stranger lighted from his steed,
  And ere he spake a word,
He seized my lady's lily hand,
  And kissed it all unheard.

2

The stranger walked into the hall,
  And ere he spake a word,
He kissed my lady's cherry lips,
  And kissed 'em all unheard.

3

The stranger walked into the bower –
  But my lady first did go:
Ay, hand in hand into the bower,
  Where my lord's roses blow.

IV

O häßlichste Gedanken plagen mich!
Vielleicht singt sie nicht wie die Nachtigall,
Vielleicht sind ihre Zähne keine Perlen,
Sind ihre Wimpern doch, soviel ich weiß,
Wie Fühler kleiner Eintagsfliegen lang;
Kann sein, kein Grübchen ist auf ihrer Hand –
Nur Sommersprossen. Ah! ein Kindermädchen,
Voll Hast dem kleinen Ding das Gehn zu lehrn,
Hat zwei Dianabeine eingeschrumpft
Und einen edlen Junohals verkrümmt.

V Lied

1

Der Fremde stieg von seinem Roß
  Und, ehe ein Wort fiel,
Griff meiner Herrin Lilienhand
  Und küßte sie ganz still.

2

Der Fremde trat ein in den Saal
  Und, ehe ein Wort fiel,
Küßt' meiner Herrin Kirschenmund
  Und küßte ihn ganz still.

3

Der Fremde trat ein in die Laube –
  Doch die Herrin führte ihn:
Ja, Hand in Hand, wo an der Laube
  Des Herren Rosen blühn.

4

My lady's maid had a silken scarf,
  And a golden ring had she,
And a kiss from the stranger, as off he went
  Again on his fair palfrey.

VI

Asleep! O sleep a little while, white pearl!
And let me kneel, and let me pray to thee,
And let me call Heaven's blessing on thine eyes,
And let me breathe into the happy air,
That doth enfold and touch thee all about,
Vows of my slavery, my giving up,
My sudden adoration, my great love!

Over the hill and over the dale,
And over the bourn to Dawlish –
Where gingerbread wives have a scanty sale
And gingerbread nuts are smallish.

Rantipole Betty she ran down a hill
And kicked up her petticoats fairly.
Says I, 'I'll be Jack if you will be Jill.'
So she sat on the grass debonairly.

'Here's somebody coming, here's somebody coming!'
Says I, ''Tis the wind at a parley.'
So without any fuss, any hawing and humming,
She lay on the grass debonairly.

'Here's somebody here, and here's somebody *there*!'
Says I, 'Hold your tongue, you young gipsy.'
So she held her tongue and lay plump and fair,
And dead as a Venus tipsy.

4

Der Herrin Magd hatt' ein Seidentuch,
  Hatte einen goldnen Ring
Und den Kuß jenes Fremden, als der zurück
  Zu dem schönen Zelter ging.

VI

Jetzt schlaf! O weiße Perle, schlaf ruhig ein!
Und laß mich knien, und laß mich zu dir beten
Und Himmelssegen rufen auf dein Aug,
Und laß mich hauchen in die heitre Luft,
Die dich umhüllt und überall berührt,
Gelübde meiner Knechtschaft, Hörigkeit,
Heißen Verehrung, meiner großen Liebe!

Über den Hügel, über das Tal
Und über die Dawlischen Flüsse –
Wo Lebkuchenweiber-Einkünfte schmal
Und klein sind die Lebkuchennüsse.

Betty, der Wildfang, die rannte dort weg
Und ließ ihren Unterrock schießen.
Sag ich, »Bist du Jill, dann bin ich dein Jack«.
Und so saß sie fein brav in den Wiesen.

»Da kommt wer gelaufen, da kommt wer gelaufen!«
Sag ich, »'s ist's Geplauder der Brisen.«
Und so ließ sie den Lärm, alles Stottern und Schnaufen,
Und lag so fein brav in den Wiesen.

»Da ist jemand dort, und da ist jemand hier!«
Sag ich, »Wildes Ding, laß das Unken.«
So ließ sie es sein und lag drall vor mir
Wie eine »Venus«, zu Tode trunken.

O who wouldn't hie to Dawlish fair,
O who wouldn't stop in a meadow?
O [who] would not rumple the daisies there,
And make the wild fern for a bed do?

To J.H. Reynolds, Esq.

Dear Reynolds, as last night I lay in bed,
There came before my eyes that wonted thread
Of shapes, and shadows, and remembrances,
That every other minute vex and please:
Things all disjointed come from North and South –
Two witch's eyes above a cherub's mouth,
Voltaire with casque and shield and habergeon,
And Alexander with his nightcap on,
Old Socrates a-tying his cravat,
And Hazlitt playing with Miss Edgeworth's cat,
And Junius Brutus, pretty well so so,
Making the best of's way towards Soho.

Few are there who escape these visitings –
Perhaps one or two whose lives have patient wings,
And through whose curtains peeps no hellish nose,
No wild-boar tushes, and no mermaid's toes;
But flowers bursting out with lusty pride,
And young Aeolian harps personified,
Some, Titian colours touched into real life –
The sacrifice goes on; the pontiff knife
Gloams in the sun, the milk-white heifer lows,
The pipes go shrilly, the libation flows;
A white sail shows above the green-head cliff,
Moves round the point, and throws her anchor stiff.
The mariners join hymn with those on land.

O wer eilte nicht nach Dawlish fort,
O wer hielt nicht an in den Auen?
O wer drückte nicht diese Blüten dort
Und würd sich kein Farnlager bauen?

An J. H. Reynolds, Esq.

Mein lieber Reynolds, ich lag wach die Nacht,
Da zogen vor mein Aug mit alter Macht
Gestalten, Schemen und Erinnerungen,
Voll Qual und Wonne jedem Nu entsprungen –
In Fetzen kamen sie aus Nord und Süd:
Zwei Hexenaugen unterm Cherublid,
Voltaire, der Helm und Schild und Halsberg' trug,
Und Alexander, schon im Schlafanzug;
Dann Sokrates, sich die Krawatte streckend,
Auch Hazlitt, Fräulein Edgeworths Katze neckend,
Und Junius Brutus, hübsch mal so, mal so,
Wie er sich wacker durchschlägt nach Soho.

Nur wenige entgehen dieser Schar –
Zwei, drei mit einem ruhigen Flügelpaar,
Durch deren Vorhang keine Nasen spähen,
Kein Eberhauer, keine Meerfrauzehen;
Nur Knospen, die sich in die Blüte warfen,
Und junge, körperliche Äolsharfen,
Ein paar nah Titians Farben, oder besser –
Das Opfern schreitet fort; das Priestermesser
Wird fahl im Licht, die weiße Färse brüllt,
Die Pfeifen schrillen, Spendentrank entquillt;
Ein Segel zeigt sich überm grünen Kap,
Umsteuert es und läßt den Anker ab.
Die Mannschaft fällt ins Lied derer an Land.

You know the Enchanted Castle – it doth stand
Upon a rock, on the border of a lake,
Nested in trees, which all do seem to shake
From some old magic-like Urganda's sword.
O Phoebus! that I had thy sacred word
To show this castle, in fair dreaming wise,
Unto my friend, while sick and ill he lies!

You know it well enough, where it doth seem
A mossy place, a Merlin's Hall, a dream.
You know the clear lake, and the little isles,
The mountains blue, and cold near-neighbour rills,
All which elsewhere are but half animate;
Here do they look alive to love and hate,
To smiles and frowns; they seem a lifted mound
Above some giant, pulsing underground.

Part of the building was a chosen see,
Built by a banished santon of Chaldee;
The other part, two thousand years from him,
Was built by Cuthbert de Saint Aldebrim;
Then there's a little wing, far from the sun,
Built by a Lapland witch turned maudlin nun;
And many other juts of agèd stone
Founded with many a mason-devil's groan.

The doors all look as if they oped themselves,
The windows as if latched by fays and elves,
And from them comes a silver flash of light,
As from the westward of a summer's night;
Or like a beauteous woman's large blue eyes
Gone mad through olden songs and poesies –

See! what is coming from the distance dim!
A golden galley all in silken trim!
Three rows of oars are lightening, moment-whiles,
Into the verdurous bosoms of those isles.

Du kennst das Märchenschloß – es steht am Rand
Eines Seeufers, wird auf Felsgesteinen
Umsäumt von Bäumen, die zu zittern scheinen
Vom alten Zauber des Urgandaschwerts.
O Phöbus! dein geweihtes Wort, im Schmerz
Dies Schloß zu zeigen, träumend noch verschönt,
Dem Freund, da schwach und krank er stöhnt!

Du kennst es gut genug, wo es ein Raum
Aus Moos, ein Festsaal Merlins scheint, ein Traum.
Du kennst die kleinen Inseln, klaren Wellen,
Die blauen Berge, nahgelegnen Quellen,
Halb so lebendig anderswo und trübe;
Hier sehn sie offen aus für Haß und Liebe,
Für Zorn und Freude; scheinen wie ein Mund
Zu einem riesigen pulsiernden Grund.

Teil des Gebäudes war ein Sitz, benannt
Nach einem Derwisch, aus Chaldäa verbannt;
Den zweiten, zwei Jahrtausende nach ihm,
Erbaute Cuthbert de St. Aldebrim;
In einem schmalen Flügel, fern der Sonne,
Ward eine Lapplandhexe weinend Nonne;
Und noch manch andre Flucht aus alten Steinen
Entstand mit manches Maurerteufels Greinen.

Von selbst scheint jede Tür hier aufzugehn,
Als schlöß ein Elf die Fenster, oder Feen,
Und silbern leuchtend sind sie hell entfacht
Ähnlich dem Westen einer Sommernacht,
Dem blauen Aug der Schönen aus dem Norden,
Die irr an altem Lied und Sang geworden. –

Schau! was daherkommt von der trüben Kimm!
Eine goldne Galeer' in seidnem Trimm!
Drei Ruderreihn blitzen, nur einen Nu,
Aufs grüne Innre jener Inseln zu.

Towards the shade, under the castle wall,
It comes in silence – now 'tis hidden all.
The clarion sounds, and from a postern-grate
An echo of sweet music doth create
A fear in the poor herdsman, who doth bring
His beasts to trouble the enchanted spring.
He tells of the sweet music, and the spot,
To all his friends – and they believe him not.

O that our dreamings all, of sleep or wake,
Would all their colours from the sunset take,
From something of material sublime,
Rather than shadow our own soul's daytime
In the dark void of night. For in the world
We jostle – but my flag is not unfurled
On the admiral staff – and to philosophize
I dare not yet! O, never will the prize,
High reason, and the lore of good and ill,
Be my award! Things cannot to the will
Be settled, but they tease us out of thought.
Or is it that imagination brought
Beyond its proper bound, yet still confined,
Lost in a sort of purgatory blind,
Cannot refer to any standard law
Of either earth or heaven? It is a flaw
In happiness, to see beyond our bourne –
It forces us in summer skies to mourn;
It spoils the singing of the nightingale.

Dear Reynolds, I have a mysterious tale,
And cannot speak it. The first page I read
Upon a lampit rock of green seaweed
Among the breakers. 'Twas a quiet eve;
The rocks were silent, the wide sea did weave
An untumultuous fringe of silver foam
Along the flat brown sand. I was at home

Den Schatten unter der verstärkten Wehr
Steuert sie an – nun sieht man sie nicht mehr.
Die Zinke tönt, und aus verborgnen Gittern
Erweckt ein Echo süßen Klangs ein Zittern
Der Furcht im Hirten, der mit seinen Tieren
Zum Zauberquell geht, um ihn aufzurühren.
Den Freunden von dem süßen Klang, dem Ort
Erzählt er – doch sie glauben ihm kein Wort.

O daß ein Traum, der wach, der schlafend käme,
Vom Sonnenuntergang die Farben nähme,
Von etwas stofflicher Erhabenheit,
Nicht schwärzte unsrer Seele Tageszeit
Im dunklen Raum der Nacht. Denn in der Welt
Stoßen wir an – doch meine Flagge fehlt
Am Topp des Flaggschiffs – und Philosophie
Wag ich noch nicht! O mein Ertrag wird nie
Erkenntnis sein, der Schluß auf Gut und Schlecht
Mein Lohn! Den Dingen wird man nicht gerecht
Nach Wunsch, sie schrecken uns nur aus dem Denken.
Oder ist's so, daß Phantasie, Versenken
Ins Jenseits ihrer Grenzen, neu gefesselt,
In blindem Fegefeuer eingekesselt,
Sich an kein Richtmaß halten kann, gewiß
Auf Erden und im Himmel? 's ist ein Riß
Im Glück, ins Jenseits sehn zu wagen –
Er zwingt uns, in der Sommerluft zu klagen;
Er macht das Lied der Nachtigall zunichte.

John, ich kenn eine seltsame Geschichte
Und kann sie nicht erzähln. Die erste Seite
Las ich auf einem Felsen in der Weite
Voll Tang und Schnecken. Ruhiger Abend war's;
Die Felsen still, die weite See durchmaß
Mit einem glatten Saum des Silberblaus
Den flachen braunen Sand. Ich war zu Haus

And should have been most happy – but I saw
Too far into the sea, where every maw
The greater on the less feeds evermore. –
But I saw too distinct into the core
Of an eternal fierce destruction,
And so from happiness I far was gone.
Still am I sick of it; and though, today,
I've gathered young spring-leaves, and flowers gay
Of periwinkle and wild strawberry,
Still do I that most fierce destruction see –
The shark at savage prey, the hawk at pounce,
The gentle robin, like a pard or ounce,
Ravening a worm. – Away, ye horrid moods!
Moods of one's mind! You know I hate them well,
You know I'd sooner be a clapping bell
To some Kamchatkan missionary church,
Than with these horrid moods be left in lurch.
Do you get health – and Tom the same – I'll dance,
And from detested moods in new romance
Take refuge. Of bad lines a centaine dose
Is sure enough – and so 'here follows prose' ...

Sweet, sweet is the greeting of eyes,
And sweet is the voice in its greeting,
When adieus have grown old and goodbyes
Fade away where old Time is retreating.
Warm the nerve of a welcoming hand,
And earnest a kiss on the brow,
When we meet over sea and o'er land
Where furrows are new to the plough.

Und wär sehr froh gewesen – doch sah ich
Zu weit ins Meer, wo alle Mäuler sich
Als größre stets von kleineren ernährn –
Doch blickte ich zu tief in diesen Kern
Der wilden ewigen Zerstörungswut,
War deshalb weit entfernt von frohem Mut.
Und noch krank ich daran; auch wenn ich, heute,
An Frühlingsblättern, buntem Flor mich freute,
Am Immergrün und an den Walderdbeeren –
Ich seh doch noch dies schreckliche Verheeren:
Der Hai auf Raubzug, Falken stürzend Sieger,
Das Rotkehlchen, wie Jaguar und Tiger,
Zerreißend einen Wurm. – Fort, Schreckenswahn!
Wahn eines Geists! Du weißt, ich haß nichts mehr,
Weißt, eine Bimmelglocke wär ich eher,
Würd am Missionshaus in Kamtschatka kleben,
Als diesem Schreckenswahn mich zu ergeben.
Werd du gesund – Tom gleichfalls – und ich tanze
Und such vom Wahn bei einer neuen Romanze
Zuflucht. An schlechten Zeilen hundert Strich
Tun's wohl – und so »folgt Prosa hier« für dich ...

Süß, süß ist ein Auge, das grüßt,
Und süß eine Stimme im Grüßen,
Sind Lebwohls schon uralt und Adieus
Schon entschwunden, wo Zeiten zerfließen.
Warm der Druck der willkommnenden Hand
Und ernsthaft ein Kuß auf die Stirn,
Komm ich zu euch übers Meer und das Land,
Dem neu ist der Pflug an Geschirrn.

Old Meg she was a gipsy,
  And lived upon the moors,
Her bed it was the brown heath turf,
  And her house was out of doors.

Her apples were swart blackberries,
  Her currants pods o' broom,
Her wine was dew o' the wild white rose,
  Her book a churchyard tomb.

Her brothers were the craggy hills,
  Her sisters larchen trees –
Alone with her great family
  She lived as she did please.

No breakfast had she many a morn,
  No dinner many a noon,
And 'stead of supper she would stare
  Full hard against the moon.

But every morn of woodbine fresh
  She made her garlanding,
And every night the dark glen yew
  She wove, and she would sing.

And with her fingers old and brown
  She plaited mats o' rushes,
And gave them to the cottagers
  She met among the bushes.

Old Meg was brave as Margaret Queen
  And tall as Amazon,
An old red blanket cloak she wore,
  A chip-hat had she on.
God rest her agèd bones somewhere –
  She died full long agone!

Old Meg, die war Zigeunerin
  Und lebte tief im Moor,
Ihr Bett war brauner Heidetorf
  Und ihr Haus die Luft davor.

Ihr Apfelbaum der Brombeerstrauch,
  Der Ginster Beerenhain,
Ihr Wein war Heckenrosentau,
  Ihr Buch ein Grabmalstein.

Wie Brüder sah sie schroffe Höhn,
  Wie Schwestern Lärchen an –
Sie lebte, wie es ihr gefiel,
  Allein mit ihrem Clan.

Wie oft hat sie kein Mahl in der Früh
  Und nichts zum Mittag belohnt,
Und oft war noch ihr Abendbrot
  Ein Starren in den Mond.

Doch stets war morgens frisch ein Kranz
  Aus Geißblatt um ihr Haupt,
Und stets flocht nachts sie mit Gesang
  Der Schluchten Eibenlaub.

Und braun und alt war ihre Hand,
  Die Binsenmatten webte
Und an das Häuslervolk vergab,
  Das in den Wäldern lebte.

Old Meg war amazonengroß,
  Besaß Queen Margarets Mut,
Sie trug ein altes rotes Cape
  Und einen Bastschlapphut.
Schon lang liegt ihr Gebein im Grund –
  Gib Gott, daß es dort ruht!

A Song about Myself

I

There was a naughty boy,
A naughty boy was he,
He would not stop at home,
He could not quiet be –
He took
In his knapsack
A book
Full of vowels
And a shirt
With some towels –
A slight cap
For night-cap –
A hair brush,
Comb ditto,
New stockings,
For old ones
Would split O!
This knapsack
Tight at's back
He rivetted close
And followed his nose
To the North,
To the North,
And followed his nose
To the North.

Ein Lied über mich selbst

I

Es war ein frecher Kerl,
Ein frecher Kerl war der,
Den hielt's nicht lang zu Haus,
Nie still war's um ihn her –
Er nahm
In den Rucksack
An Kram
Selbstlautbücher
Und ein Hemd,
Ein paar Tücher,
'ne Prachtmütz
Als Nachtmütz
Und Bürste,
Kamm dito,
Frisch Socken,
Denn alte,
Da sieht – O!
Den Rucksack
Im Huckpack,
So ging es hinaus,
Die Nase voraus,
In den Norden,
In den Norden,
Die Nase voraus,
In den Norden.

II

There was a naughty boy
  And a naughty boy was he,
For nothing would he do
  But scribble poetry –
    He took
    An inkstand
    In his hand
    And a pen
    Big as ten
    In the other
    And away
    In a pother
    He ran
    To the mountains
    And fountains
    And ghostès
    And postès
    And witches
    And ditches,
    And wrote
    In his coat
    When the weather
    Was cool –
    Fear of gout –
    And without
    When the weather
    Was warm.
    Och, the charm
    When we choose
  To follow one's nose
    To the North,
    To the North,
  To follow one's nose
    To the North!

II

Es war ein frecher Kerl,
  Ein frecher Kerl war der,
Denn niemals tat er was,
  Nur Verse schmierte er –
    Er nahm
    Sich Tinte
    In die Linke
    Und den Stift
    Für viel Schrift
    In die Zweite,
    Staubumwölkt
    In die Weite,
    Lief er
    Zu den Bergen
    Und Zwergen
    Und Quellen
    Und Schnellen
    Und Briefen
    Und Tiefen
    Und schrieb,
    Aber blieb
    Schön im Mantel,
    Wenn's fror –
    Angst vor Gicht –
    Und blieb's nicht,
    War's im Mantel
    Zu heiß.
    Ach, der Reiz,
    Ging's hinaus,
  Die Nase voraus,
    In den Norden,
    In den Norden,
  Die Nase voraus,
    In den Norden!

III

There was a naughty boy
  And a naughty boy was he,
He kept little fishes
  In washing tubs three
    In spite
    Of the might
    Of the maid,
    Nor afraid
    Of his granny-good,
    He often would
    Hurly burly
    Get up early
    And go,
    By hook or crook,
    To the brook
    And bring home
    Miller's thumb,
    Tittlebat
    Not over fat,
    Minnows small
    As the stall
    Of a glove,
    Not above
    The size
    Of a nice
    Little baby's
    Little finger –
    O he made
    ('Twas his trade)
  Of fish a pretty kettle,
    A kettle –
    A kettle,
  Of fish a pretty kettle,
    A kettle!

III

Es war ein frecher Kerl,
  Und ein frecher Kerl war der,
Er räumte für Fische
  Drei Waschzuber leer,
    Die Magd
    Nicht gefragt,
    Ohne Angst,
    Daß du bangst,
    Vor dem Omilein
    Wurde er fein
    Mit Ach und Krach
    Früh morgens wach
    Und ging
    Auf Biegen und Brechen
    Zu den Bächen
    Und trug dort
    Kaulkopf fort,
    Stichling und,
    Nicht grade rund,
    Kleinen Aal,
    Däumlingsschmal
    Wie die Hand,
    Auch entspannt
    So groß
    Wie des bloß
    Kleinen Babys
    Kleiner Finger –
    O er schuf
    (Sein Beruf)
  'ne schöne Fischgeschichte,
    Geschichte,
    Geschichte,
  'ne schöne Fischgeschichte,
    Geschichte!

IV

There was a naughty boy,
  And a naughty boy was he,
He ran away to Scotland
  The people for to see –
    The re he found
    That the ground
    Was as hard,
    That a yard
    Was as long,
    That a song
    Was as merry,
    That a cherry,
    Was as red,
    That lead
    Was as weighty,
    That fourscore
    Was as eighty,
    That a door
    Was as wooden
    As in England –
  So he stood in his shoes
    And he wondered,
    He wondered,
  He stood in his
    Shoes and he wondered.

IV

Es war ein frecher Kerl,
  Und ein frecher Kerl war der,
Er rannte fort nach Schottland,
  Die Leute sehn wollt er –
    Doch errr fand,
    Ein Stück Land
    War so hart
    Und ein Yard
    War so lang
    Und Gesang
    Ohne Schwere
    Und die Beere
    War so rot,
    Das Lot
    So gewichtig,
    Für fourscore
    Achtzig richtig
    Und ein Tor
    War so hölzern
    Wie in England –
  Da stand er mit zwei Schuhn
    Ganz verwundert,
    Verwundert,
  Er stand da mit zwei
    Schuhn ganz verwundert.

Under the flag
Of each his faction, they to battle bring
Their embryon atoms.
Milton

Welcome joy, and welcome sorrow,
  Lethe's weed and Hermes' feather;
Come today, and come tomorrow,
  I do love you both together!
  I love to mark sad faces in fair weather,
And hear a merry laugh amid the thunder.
  Fair and foul I love together:
  Meadows sweet where flames burn under,
  And a giggle at a wonder;
  Visage sage at pantomime;
  Funeral, and steeple-chime;
  Infant playing with a skull;
  Morning fair, and stormwrecked hull;
  Nightshade with the woodbine kissing;
  Serpents in red roses hissing;
  Cleopatra regal-dressed
  With the aspics at her breast
  Dancing music, music sad,
  Both together, sane and mad;
  Muses bright and Muses pale;
  Sombre Saturn, Momus hale.
  Laugh and sigh, and laugh again –
  O the sweetness of the pain!
  Muses bright, and Muses pale,
  Bare your faces of the veil!
  Let me see! and let me write
  Of the day and of the night –
  Both together. Let me slake
  All my thirst for sweet heart-ache!
  Let my bower be of yew,
  Interwreathed with myrtles new,
  Pines and lime-trees full in bloom,
  And my couch a low grass tomb.

Unter den Fahnen
All seiner Gruppen werfen sie ins Feld
Die keimenden Atome.
Milton

Willkommen Glück, willkommen Sorgen,
Hermes' Federn, Lethes Weiden;
Kommt ihr heute, kommt ihr morgen,
Ich mag jeden von euch beiden!
Ich mag bei Sonne trübe Mienen leiden
Und heitres Lachen hören während Blitzen.
Schund und Schönheit mag ich leiden:
Wiesen, drunter Flammen schwitzen,
Reizt ein Wunder wen zu Witzen;
Blickt der Pantomime klug;
Turmgeläut und Leichenzug;
Kleinkind, Schädel in der Hand;
Schöner Morgen, Wrack am Strand;
Nachtschatten, das Geißblatt küssend;
Schlangen in den Rosen zischend;
Reich geschmückt Kleopatra,
An der Brust das Aspispaar;
Lieder froh und kummervoll,
Ob bei Sinnen oder toll;
Musen bleich und Musen licht;
Momus' Heil, Saturns Gericht.
Lach und seufz und lach nochmal –
O die Süße aller Qual!
Musen bleich und Musen licht,
Nehmt den Schleier vom Gesicht!
Laßt mich sehn! auf daß ich dann
Tag und Nacht beschreiben kann –
Beides. Löschen laß mein Herz
Seinen Durst auf süßen Schmerz!
Laß mein Haus aus Eiben sein,
Flechtet junge Myrten ein,
Kiefern, Linden, voll erblüht,
Und mein Bett ein Grab im Ried.

Where's the Poet? Show him! show him,
Muses nine, that I may know him!
'Tis the man who with a man
  Is an equal, be he king,
Or poorest of the beggar-clan,
  Or any other wondrous thing
A man may be 'twixt ape and Plato.
  'Tis the man who with a bird,
Wren or eagle, finds his way to
  All its instincts. He hath heard
The lion's roaring, and can tell
  What his horny throat expresseth,
And to him the tiger's yell
  Comes articulate and presseth
On his ear like mother-tongue.

Fancy

Ever let the Fancy roam,
Pleasure never is at home:
At a touch sweet Pleasure melteth,
Like to bubbles when rain pelteth.
Then let wingèd Fancy wander
Through the thought still spread beyond her:
Open wide the mind's cage-door,
She'll dart forth, and cloudward soar.
O sweet Fancy! let her loose –
Summer's joys are spoilt by use,
And the enjoying of the Spring
Fades as does its blossoming;
Autumn's red-lipped fruitage too,
Blushing through the mist and dew,
Cloys with tasting. What do then?
Sit thee by the ingle, when

Wer ist Dichter? Wer hier, wer hier?
Mir, neun Musen, zeigt, welch Herr hier!
's ist der Mann, der einem Mann
  Gleichgestellt ist, sei er reich,
Sei wie der ärmste Bettler dran
  Oder dem Wunderlichsten gleich,
Und sei es auch ein Affenplato.
  's ist der Mann, der kennen kann
Adler, Sperling, beide grad so
  Wie sie selbst sich. Er vernahm,
Wie Löwen brüllen, weiß dabei,
  Was die Schwielenrachen sagen,
Und ihm ist der Tigerschrei
  So verständlich und ein Plagen
Seines Ohrs wie Muttersprache.

Phantasie

Schweifen laß stets Phantasie,
Denn daheim sind Wonnen nie:
Kaum berührt, sind süße Wonnen
Wie ein Regenguß zerronnen.
Drum laß die Beschwingte streifen,
Wo Gedanken nicht mehr greifen:
Sperr dem Hirn das Tor weit auf,
Schon steigt sie pfeilschnell hinauf.
Phantasie! o laß sie frei –
Schal geht Sommerglück vorbei,
Es schwinden in der Frühlingszeit
Freuden wie ihr Blütenkleid;
Herbstobst, rot geschminkt, hat auch,
Glühend durch den Dunst und Rauch,
Viel zuviel Geschmack. Was dann?
Rück an den Kamin heran,

The sere faggot blazes bright,
Spirit of a winter's night;
When the soundless earth is muffled,
And the cakèd snow is shuffled
From the ploughboy's heavy shoon;
When the Night doth meet the Noon
In a dark conspiracy
To banish Even from her sky.
Sit thee there, and send abroad,
With a mind self-overawed,
Fancy, high-commissioned – send her!
She has vassals to attend her:
She will bring, in spite of frost,
Beauties that the earth hath lost;
She will bring thee, all together,
All delights of summer weather;
All the buds and bells of May,
From dewy sward or thorny spray;
All the heapèd Autumn's wealth,
With a still, mysterious stealth:
She will mix these pleasures up
Like three fit wines in a cup,
And thou shalt quaff it – thou shalt hear
Distant harvest-carols clear;
Rustle of the reapèd corn;
Sweet birds antheming the morn:
And, in the same moment – hark!
'Tis the early April lark,
Or the rooks, with busy caw,
Foraging for sticks and straw.
Thou shalt, at one glance, behold
The daisy and the marigold;
White-plumed lilies, and the first
Hedge-grown primrose that hath burst;
Shaded hyacinth, alway
Sapphire queen of the mid-May;

Wenn das Scheit hell lodernd kracht,
Geist in einer Winternacht;
Wenn die Erde still umschmiegt ist
Und der Ackerharsch durchpflügt ist
Von des Jungknechts schweren Schuhn;
Wenn die Nacht die Mittnacht nun
Dunkles planend trifft und gleich
Den Abend bannt aus ihrem Reich.
Setz dich dort und send ins Land,
Durch ein Hirn, selbst-übermannt,
Phantasie, höchst eilig, send sie!
Aufmerksame Diener kennt sie:
Statt des Frosts bringt sie hervor
Schönheit, die das Land verlor;
Bringt dir her, mit allen Düften,
All das Glück aus Sommerlüften;
All den Flor und Flaum des Mais,
Von feuchtem Gras und Dornenreis;
All die Pracht der Erntezeit,
Still und voller Heimlichkeit:
Sie mischt diese Wonnen klug
Wie drei Weine in den Krug,
Und du sollst saufen – sollst von fern
Klar die Erntelieder hörn;
Garben rauschen durch den Wind;
Vögel, da der Tag beginnt;
Und, zur selben Zeit – sei still!
Schon die Lerche des April
Oder emsig Krähngekrächz,
Lärm des Stroh- und Stockgefechts;
Sollst, auf einen Blick gleich, sehn
Calendula und Tausendschön;
Weiß-zart Lilien und verfrüht
Heckenprimeln, schon erblüht;
Schattenhyazinthen, ganz
Mittmais Königinnenglanz;

And every leaf, and every flower
Pearlèd with the self-same shower.
Thou shalt see the field-mouse peep
Meagre from its cellèd sleep;
And the snake all winter-thin
Cast on sunny bank its skin;
Freckled nest-eggs thou shalt see
Hatching in the hawthorn-tree,
When the hen-bird's wing doth rest
Quiet on her mossy nest;
Then the hurry and alarm
When the bee-hive casts its swarm;
Acorns ripe down-pattering,
While the autumn breezes sing.

O, sweet Fancy! let her loose;
Every thing is spoilt by use:
Where's the cheek that doth not fade,
Too much gazed at? Where's the maid
Whose lip mature is ever new?
Where's the eye, however blue,
Doth not weary? Where's the face
One would meet in every place?
Where's the voice, however soft,
One would hear so very oft?
At a touch sweet Pleasure melteth
Like to bubbles when rain pelteth.
Let, then, wingèd Fancy find
Thee a mistress to thy mind:
Dulcet-eyed as Ceres' daughter,
Ere the God of Torment taught her
How to frown and how to chide;
With a waist and with a side
White as Hebe's, when her zone
Slipped its golden clasp, and down

Und jede Blume, jedes Blatt
Von demselben Schauer satt;
Sehn die Feldmaus, mager noch
Nach dem Schlaf in ihrem Loch;
Und die Schlange, winterschlank
Sich häuten auf der heißen Bank;
Fleckige Gelege auch,
In der Brut im Weißdornstrauch,
Wenn des Rebhuhns Flügel gut
Auf dem Nest aus Moosen ruht;
Dann die Hast und den Alarm,
Stürzt vom Korb der Bienenschwarm;
Wie die Eichel prasselnd reift,
Während schon der Herbstwind pfeift.

Phantasie! o laß sie frei;
Alles geht so schal vorbei:
Welche Wange wird nicht grau
Durchs Bestarren? Welcher Frau
Gereifte Lippen sind stets neu?
Wo ist's Auge, noch so treu,
Das nicht langweilt? Das Gesicht,
Das man ständig treffen möcht?
Wo die Stimme, noch so sacht,
Die dich stets neu lauschen macht?
Kaum berührt, sind süße Wonnen
Wie ein Regenguß zerronnen.
Drum laß Phantasie auf Schwingen
Deinem Hirn die Herrin bringen:
Ceres' Tochter gleich an Zärte,
Eh der Martergott sie lehrte,
Wie man zürnt und rast wie er;
Weiß um Leib und Lenden her
Ganz wie Hebe, als ihr Kleid,
Vom Verschluß aus Gold befreit,

Fell her kirtle to her feet,
While she held the goblet sweet,
And Jove grew languid. – Break the mesh
Of the Fancy's silken leash;
Quickly break her prison-string
And such joys as these she'll bring.
Let the wingèd Fancy roam,
Pleasure never is at home.

Faery Bird's Song

Shed no tear – O, shed no tear!
The flower will bloom another year.
Weep no more! O! weep no more!
Young buds sleep in the root's white core.
Dry your eyes! O! dry your eyes,
For I was taught in Paradise
To ease my breast of melodies –
    Shed no tear.

Overhead! look overhead!
'Mong the blossoms white and red –
Look up, look up. I flutter now
On this flush pomegranate bough.
See me! 'tis this silvery bill
Ever cures the good man's ill.
Shed no tear! O shed no tear!
The flower will bloom another year.
Adieu, adieu – I fly, adieu,
I vanish in the heaven's blue –
    Adieu, adieu!

Ihr auf ihre Füße sank,
Während sie vom Weinkelch trank
Und schwach ward Zeus. – Zerreiße nur
Phantasiens Seidenschnur;
Schneid rasch ihre Fesseln auf,
Und sie bringt solch Glück zuhauf.
Fliegen laß die Phantasie,
Denn daheim sind Wonnen nie.

Lied des Märchenvogels

Weint doch nicht – O weint doch nicht!
Die Blume lockt bald neues Licht.
Laßt den Schmerz! O! laßt den Schmerz!
Der Keim schläft weiß im Wurzelherz.
Hebt den Blick! O! hebt den Blick –
Im Paradies erfuhr ich's Glück,
Die Brust zu lindern mit Musik –
    Weint doch nicht.

Über euch! seht über euch!
Im weiß-roten Blattgesträuch –
Seht auf, seht auf. Ich hab mich jetzt
Auf den Granatapfel gesetzt.
Schaut! mein Schnabel heilt allzeit
Silbern jedes Guten Leid.
Weint doch nicht! O weint doch nicht!
Die Blume lockt bald neues Licht.
Adieu, adieu – ich flieg, adieu,
Ich schwinde in die blaue Höh –
    Adieu, adieu!

La Belle Dame sans Merci

A Ballad

I

O what can ail thee, knight-at-arms,
  Alone and palely loitering?
The sedge has withered from the lake,
  And no birds sing.

II

O what can ail thee, knight-at-arms,
  So haggard and so woe-begone?
The squirrel's granary is full,
  And the harvest's done.

III

I see a lily on thy brow,
  With anguish moist and fever-dew,
And on thy cheeks a fading rose
  Fast withereth too.

IV

I met a lady in the meads,
  Full beautiful – a faery's child,
Her hair was long, her foot was light,
  And her eyes were wild.

V

I made a garland for her head,
  And bracelets too, and fragrant zone;
She looked at me as she did love,
  And made sweet moan.

La Belle Dame sans Merci

Eine Ballade

I

O was nur fehlt dir, Rittersmann,
Streifst du allein und schwach umher?
Längst welkt das Schilf am See und singt
Kein Vogel mehr.

II

O was nur fehlt dir, Rittersmann,
So abgezehrt und schmerzensbleich?
Des Eichhorns Vorratsbau ist voll
Und die Ernte reich.

III

Ich seh die Lilie deiner Stirn
Vor Angstschweiß feucht und fiebernaß
Und deiner Wangen Rose welk,
Auch sie rasch blaß.

IV

Ich traf im Feld auf eine Frau,
Vollkommen schön – ein Feenbild:
Ihr Haar war lang, ihr Fuß war leicht
Und ihr Auge wild.

V

Ich flocht ihr einen Kranz ums Haupt,
Flocht Reife, Gürtel überdies;
Sie sah mich an, als liebte sie,
Und klagte süß.

VI

I set her on my pacing steed,
  And nothing else saw all day long,
For sidelong would she bend, and sing
  A faery's song.

VII

She found me roots of relish sweet,
  And honey wild, and manna-dew,
And sure in language strange she said –
  'I love thee true'.

VIII

She took me to her elfin grot,
  And there she wept and sighed full sore,
And there I shut her wild wild eyes
  With kisses four.

IX

And there she lullèd me asleep
  And there I dreamed – Ah! woe betide! –
The latest dream I ever dreamt
  On the cold hill side.

X

I saw pale kings and princes too,
  Pale warriors, death-pale were they all;
They cried – 'La Belle Dame sans Merci
  Thee hath in thrall!'

VI

Ich hob sie auf mein schreitend Roß
  Und sah nicht mehr, was rings geschieht,
Denn seitwärts lehnte sie und sang
  Ein Feenlied.

VII

Saftsüße Wurzeln, Honigseim
  Und Mannatau fand sie für mich,
Und sicher fremdländisch sprach sie –
  »Treu lieb ich dich«.

VIII

Zu ihrer Elfengrotte ging's,
  Da weinte sie und stöhnte schier,
Da schloß ich ihr wild wildes Aug
  Mit Küssen vier.

IX

Da lullte sie mich in den Schlaf,
  Da träumte ich – Ah! weh, so lang! –
Den letzten Traum, den ich je träumt
  Auf dem kalten Hang.

X

Ich sah Monarchen, Fürsten bleich,
  Bleich Krieger, todbleich alle Mann;
Sie schrien – »La Belle Dame sans Merci
  Hält dich in Bann!«

XI

I saw their starved lips in the gloam,
  With horrid warnings gapèd wide,
And I awoke and found me here,
  On the cold hill's side.

XII

And this is why I sojourn here
  Alone and palely loitering,
Though the sedge is withered from the lake,
  And no birds sing.

Two or three posies
With two or three simples –
Two or three noses
With two or three pimples –
Two or three wise men
And two or three ninnies –
Two or three purses
And two or three guineas –
Two or three raps
At two or three doors –
Two or three naps
Of two or three hours –
Two or three cats
And two or three mice –
Two or three sprats
At a very great price –
Two or three sandies
And two or three tabbies –
Two or three dandies
And two Mrs — mum!

XI

Sah Lippen klaffen, schmal im Dunst,
  Aus denen Fluch und Warnen drang,
Und wachte auf und fand mich hier,
  Auf dem kalten Hang.

XII

Und deshalb harre ich hier aus,
  Streif ich allein und schwach umher,
Ist auch welk das Schilf am See und singt
  Kein Vogel mehr.

Zwei bis drei Vasen
Mit zwei bis drei Mitteln –
Zwei bis drei Nasen
Mit zwei bis drei Pickeln –
Zwei bis drei Köpfe
Und zwei, drei Ideen –
Zwei bis drei Börsen
Und zwei, drei Guineen –
Zwei, drei Portale
Zwei-, dreimal bewummern –
Zwei bis drei Male
Von zwei bis drei schlummern –
Zwei bis drei Pfoten
Auf zwei bis drei Mäusen –
Zwei bis drei Sprotten
Zu gesalzenen Preisen –
Zwei bis drei Sandys
Und zwei bis drei Emmis –
Zwei bis drei Dandys
Und zwei Mrs — pst!

Two or three smiles
And two or three frowns –
Two or three miles
To two or three towns –
Two or three pegs
For two or three bonnets –
Two or three dove's eggs
To hatch into sonnets.

What can I do to drive away
Remembrance from my eyes? for they have seen,
Ay, an hour ago, my brilliant Queen!
Touch has a memory. O say, love, say,
What can I do to kill it and be free
In my old liberty?
When every fair one that I saw was fair,
Enough to catch me in but half a snare,
Not keep me there;
When, howe'er poor or parti-coloured things,
My muse had wings,
And ever ready was to take her course
Whither I bent her force,
Unintellectual, yet divine to me –
Divine, I say! What sea-bird o'er the sea
Is a philosopher the while he goes
Winging along where the great water throes?

  How shall I do
  To get anew
Those moulted feathers, and so mount once more
  Above, above
  The reach of fluttering Love,
And make him cower lowly while I soar?

Zwei bis drei Lächeln
Auf zwei, drei böse Worte –
Zwei-, dreimal hecheln
An zwei bis drei Orte –
Zwei bis drei Nägel
Für zwei, drei Bonnette –
Zwei, drei Gelege
Als Brut für Sonette.

Wie kann ich die Erinnrung fort
Aus meinen Augen wischen? sahn sie doch,
Ja, das Strahlen meiner Königin grad noch!
Die Haut vergißt nicht. Liebes, sag ein Wort –
Wie kann ich sie nur töten, mich befrein
Und frei wie früher sein?
Als mich die Schöne, die ich sah, durchfuhr,
Und sie mich fing, doch bloß mit halber Schnur,
Ein Weilchen nur;
Als mich, ein noch so quergefärbter Spuk,
Die Muse trug,
Die stets bereit nach Kräften den Kurs flog,
Zu dem ich sie bewog,
Und nicht hoch geistig war, doch göttlich mir –
Ja, göttlich! Welcher Meeresvogel hier
Ist auch ein Philosoph, wenn er erfüllt
Dahinfliegt, wo das große Wasser brüllt?

Was soll ich tun,
Daß neu ihm nun
Solch Fittich wächst, er mich so nochmals hebt
Hinein, hinein
Ins Reich der Liebelein
Und flach sich kauert, da er mit mir schwebt?

Shall I gulp wine? No, that is vulgarism,
A heresy and schism,
  Foisted into the canon law of love;
No – wine is only sweet to happy men;
  More dismal cares
  Seize on me unawares –
Where shall I learn to get my peace again?
To banish thoughts of that most hateful land,
Dungeoner of my friends, that wicked strand
Where they were wrecked and live a wreckèd life;
That monstrous region, whose dull rivers pour,
Ever from their sordid urns into the shore,
Unowned of any weedy-hairèd gods;
Whose winds, all zephyrless, hold scourging rods,
Iced in the great lakes, to afflict mankind;
Whose rank-grown forests, frosted, black, and blind,
Would fright a Dryad; whose harsh-herbaged meads
Make lean and lank the starved ox while he feeds;
There flowers have no scent, birds no sweet song,
And great unerring Nature once seems wrong.

O, for some sunny spell
To dissipate the shadows of this hell!
Say they are gone – with the new dawning light
Steps forth my lady bright!
O, let me once more rest
My soul upon that dazzling breast!
Let once again these aching arms be placed,
The tender gaolers of thy waist!
And let me feel that warm breath here and there
To spread a rapture in my very hair –
O, the sweetness of the pain!
Give me those lips again!
Enough! Enough! It is enough for me
To dream of thee!

Wein schlucken soll ich? Nein, es wär blasphemisch,
Wär abtrünnig und hämisch,
    Schlich dies sich in den Liebeskanon ein;
Nein – Wein verspricht nur frohen Menschen Glück;
    Ein tiefrer Stich
    Fährt unversehns durch mich –
Wo hol ich meinen Frieden mir zurück?
Und denk nicht mehr an dies verhaßte Land,
Kerker der Freunde, der verruchte Strand
Fürs Schiffbruchleben nach dem Schiffbruch dort;
Monströse Gegend, deren Wasser zäh
Stets aus verdreckten Urnen strömt zur See
Und keinem tangbehaarten Gott gefällt;
Wo Wind, nie Zephyr, geißelnd Peitschen hält,
Vereist in großen Seen, zur Menschenqual;
Wo Riesenwälder, frostig, schwarz und fahl,
Dryaden schreckten; Gras so kärglich ist,
Daß dünn und dürr das Vieh wird, das es frißt;
Blumen geruchlos sind, kein Vogel girrt
Und die Natur, stets klar, auf einmal irrt.

Oh, einen Spruch aus Licht,
Der in die Schatten dieser Hölle bricht!
Sag, sie sind fort – in neuem Dämmerschein
Tritt hell mein Mädchen ein!
Oh, laß erneut voll Lust
Die Seele ruhn auf jener Brust!
Laß nochmals diesem wehen Arm die Macht,
Die zärtlich deinen Leib bewacht!
Und jenen heißen Atem hier und da
Als Feuer spüren noch in meinem Haar –
Oh, die Süße aller Qual!
Gib diesen Mund nochmal!
Genug! Genug! Genug ist mir
Ein Traum von dir.

This living hand, now warm and capable
Of earnest grasping, would, if it were cold
And in the icy silence of the tomb,
So haunt thy days and chill thy dreaming nights
That thou would wish thine own heart dry of blood
So in my veins red life might stream again,
And thou be conscience-calmed – see here it is –
I hold it towards you.

Die Hand hier, lebenswarm und fähig jetzt
Fest zuzugreifen, würd dich, wär sie kalt
Und in der Eisesstille ihres Grabs,
So plagen tags und schaudern nachts im Traum,
Daß blutleer wünschtest du dein eignes Herz,
Damit in mir neu rotes Leben ström
Und dein Gewissen ruhig sei – hier, sieh her –
Ich halte sie dir hin.

Sonnets

On Peace

O Peace! and dost thou with thy presence bless
  The dwellings of this war-surrounded Isle;
Soothing with placid brow our late distress,
  Making the triple kingdom brightly smile?
Joyful I hail thy presence; and I hail
  The sweet companions that await on thee;
Complete my joy – let not my first wish fail,
  Let the sweet mountain nymph thy favourite be,
With England's happiness proclaim Europa's liberty.
O Europe! let not sceptred tyrants see
  That thou must shelter in thy former state;
Keep thy chains burst, and boldly say thou art free;
  Give thy kings law – leave not uncurbed the great;
  So with the horrors past thou'lt win thy happier fate!

Written on the Day that Mr Leigh Hunt left Prison

What though, for showing truth to flattered state,
  Kind Hunt was shut in prison, yet has he,
  In his immortal spirit, been as free
As the sky-searching lark, and as elate.
Minion of grandeur! think you he did wait?
  Think you he naught but prison walls did see,
  Till, so unwilling, thou unturned'st the key?
Ah, no! far happier, nobler was his fate!
In Spenser's halls he strayed, and bowers fair,
  Culling enchanted flowers; and he flew

Sonette

Auf den Frieden

O Frieden! segnest du mit deiner Zeit
  Die Schwellen dieses kriegumtobten Lands,
Nimmst uns mit milder Stirn das jüngste Leid,
  Und schenkst der Dreierkrone heitern Glanz?
Freudig begrüß ich dich; grüß auch die Schar
  Der Kameraden, wartend nur auf dich;
Erfreu mich ganz – mein erster Wunsch werd wahr,
  Laß dir die Bergnymphe das Höchste sein,
Mit Englands Freude läute du Europas Freiheit ein.
Europa! zeigen wieder Zepter sich,
  Such du nicht Schutz bei frühren Tyrannein;
Zersprengt laß Ketten, sag tapfer, frei bin ich;
  Gib Königen Gesetze – bind sie ein,
  Und nach den Grauen wird dein Los ein frohres sein!

Geschrieben am Tag, als Mr. Leigh Hunt das Gefängnis verließ

Was tut's, die Wahrheit war's, kein Schmeicheln bloß,
  Wofür der Staat Hunt eingesperrt, doch er,
  Im unsterblichen Geist, strich frei umher
Wie himmelwärts die Lerche, frei und groß.
Lakai des Adels! Er die Hand im Schoß?
  Glaubst du, er sah die Kerkerwand, nicht mehr,
  Bis du den Schlüssel umdreht'st, fiel's auch schwer?
Ah, nein! weit froher, edler war sein Los!
In Spensers Saal schritt er, im Laubenduft
  Bezaubert Blumen pflückend; voller Mut

With daring Milton through the fields of air:
To regions of his own his genius true
Took happy flights. Who shall his fame impair
When thou art dead, and all thy wretched crew?

O Solitude! if I must with thee dwell,
Let it not be among the jumbled heap
Of murky buildings; climb with me the steep –
Nature's observatory – whence the dell,
Its flowery slopes, its river's crystal swell,
May seem a span; let me thy vigils keep
'Mongst boughs pavilioned, where the deer's swift leap
Startles the wild bee from the foxglove bell.
But though I'll gladly trace these scenes with thee,
Yet the sweet converse of an innocent mind,
Whose words are images of thoughts refined,
Is my soul's pleasure; and it sure must be
Almost the highest bliss of human-kind,
When to thy haunts two kindred spirits flee.

To one who has been long in city pent,
'Tis very sweet to look into the fair
And open face of heaven – to breathe a prayer
Full in the smile of the blue firmament.
Who is more happy, when, with heart's content,
Fatigued he sinks into some pleasant lair
Of wavy grass, and reads a debonair
And gentle tale of love and languishment?
Returning home at evening, with an ear
Catching the notes of Philomel – an eye

Flog er mit Milton durch das Reich der Luft:
  Und treu hob ihn sein Genius ausgeruht
Ins eigne Reich. Wer sagt, er sei ein Schuft,
  Wenn du erst stirbst und deine ganze Brut?

O Einsamkeit! Hast du mich heimgesucht,
  Dann wohne nicht mit mir im wirren Hauf
  Des Häusergraus; den Fels steig mit hinauf –
Sternwarte der Natur – von wo aus Schlucht
Und Blumenhang, Fluß und kristallne Bucht
  Spannbreit erscheinen; ich paß für dich auf
  Im Zelt aus Laub, schlägt Wild im raschen Lauf
Vom Fingerhutkelch Bienen in die Flucht.
Folg ich auch froh mit dir den Szenen hier,
  Ist doch Gespräch, süß und von freiem Geist,
  Der Bilder reifen Denkens klar umreißt,
Mein Seelenglück; und sicher bin ich mir,
  Die höchste Seligkeit der Menschheit heißt,
Zwei gleichgesinnte Geister fliehn zu dir.

Für einen, lange von der Stadt erdrückt,
  Ist's süß, wenn er ins Himmelsantlitz späht,
  Das hell und offen – wenn er ein Gebet
Voll in das Lächeln blauer Lüfte schickt.
Wer freut sich mehr, wenn er, im Herz beglückt,
  Erschöpft ein weiches Lager suchen geht
  Im wehenden Gras und Verse liest, beredt
Und fein mit Lust und Liebe ausgeschmückt?
Kehrt er am Abend heim, fängt mit dem Ohr
  Das Tönen Philomelas auf und sieht

Watching the sailing cloudlet's bright career,
He mourns that day so soon has glided by:
E'en like the passage of an angel's tear
That falls through the clear ether silently.

O! how I love, on a fair summer's eve,
When streams of light pour down the golden west,
And on the balmy zephyrs tranquil rest
The silver clouds, far – far away to leave
All meaner thoughts, and take a sweet reprieve
From little cares; to find, with easy quest,
A fragrant wild, with Nature's beauty dressed,
And there into delight my soul deceive.
There warm my breast with patriotic lore,
Musing on Milton's fate – on Sidney's bier –
Till their stern forms before my mind arise:
Perhaps on the wing of Poesy upsoar,
Full often dropping a delicious tear,
When some melodious sorrow spells mine eyes.

To my Brother George

Many the wonders I this day have seen:
The sun, when first he kissed away the tears
That filled the eyes of morn – the laurelled peers
Who from the feathery gold of evening lean –
The ocean with its vastness, its blue green,
Its ships, its rocks, its caves, its hopes, its fears –
Its voice mysterious, which whoso hears
Must think on what will be, and what has been.
E'en now, dear George, while this for you I write,
Cynthia is from her silken curtains peeping

Zum schönen Gleitflug des Gewölks empor –
  Dann klagt er, daß der Tag so bald schon schied:
Er kommt ihm wie die Engelsträne vor,
  Die lautlos durch den klaren Äther zieht.

O! wie ich's lieb, im Sommerabendschein,
  Wenn Licht in Strömen golden westwärts fuhr
  Und auf den linden Zephyrn ausruhn nur
Die Silberwolken, weit – weit zu zerstreun
Niedre Gedanken und mich zu erfreun
  An Sorgenpausen; Wildnis auf der Spur
  Zu sein, duftend im Festkleid der Natur,
Und lustvoll dort mein Herz dem Trug zu weihn.
Dort warmer Brust von heimatlicher Mär
  Nachsinnen Miltons Schicksal, Sidneys Sarg
    Bis ernst mein Denken sie heraufbeschwört:
Vielleicht, daß Poesie mein Flügel wär,
  Auf dem ich oft genüßlich weinen mag,
    Wenn meine Augen klangvoll Schmerz betört.

An meinen Bruder George

Mancherlei Wunder hab ich heut gesehn:
  Die Sonne, die im Aug des Morgens ruht
  Und Tränen fortküßt – der Bekränzten Glut,
Die aus dem Federngold des Abends wehn –
Den Ozean, seine Weite, sein Blaugrün,
  Die Schiffe, Felsen, Grotten, Angst und Mut –
  Den ungeheuren Ton, der eine Flut
Gedanken lenkt auf Werden und Vergehn.
Da ich dir, lieber George, dies schreibe hier,
  Lugt Cynthia aus ihrem Seidenschleier

So scantly, that it seems her bridal night,
  And she her half-discovered revels keeping.
But what, without the social thought of thee,
Would be the wonders of the sky and sea?

How many bards gild the lapses of time!
  A few of them have ever been the food
  Of my delighted fancy – I could brood
Over their beauties, earthly, or sublime:
And often, when I sit me down to rhyme,
  These will in throngs before my mind intrude:
  But no confusion, no disturbance rude
Do they occasion; 'tis a pleasing chime.
So the unnumbered sounds that evening store;
The songs of birds, the whispering of the leaves,
  The voice of waters, the great bell that heaves
With solemn sound, and thousand others more,
  That distance of recognizance bereaves,
Make pleasing music, and not wild uproar.

On First Looking into Chapman's Homer

Much have I travelled in the realms of gold,
  And many goodly states and kingdoms seen;
  Round many western islands have I been
Which bards in fealty to Apollo hold.
Oft of one wide expanse had I been told
  That deep-browed Homer ruled as his demesne;
  Yet did I never breathe its pure serene
Till I heard Chapman speak out loud and bold:

So scheu wie in der Hochzeitsnacht, scheint mir,
  Da sie's beläßt bei halb-gezeigtem Feuer.
Was aber wären, dächt' ich nicht an dich,
Die Wunder Meer und Himmel schon für mich?

Wie viele Barden vergolden die Zeit!
  Mit manchen nähr ich meine Phantasie
  Schon immer – brütend über der Magie,
Ob irdisch oder voll Erhabenheit;
Und setz ich mich, ganz einem Reim geweiht,
  Drängen in Scharen in die Sinne sie:
  Doch Wirrnis, rüde Unruh ist es nie,
Was sie verbreiten; lieblich ist's Geläut.
So auch Geräusch, des Abends zahllos wach;
Die Vogellieder, Laub, das wispernd bebt,
  Der Wasserlaut, die Glocke, die sich hebt
Mit ernstem Ton und mehr, das tausendfach
  Und fern aller Erkennbarkeit entschwebt,
Sind liebliche Musik, kein wilder Krach.

Aufs erste Hineinschauen in Chapmans Homer

Die goldnen Reiche hab ich viel durchreist
  Und manches Land und Königtum gesehn;
  Manch Insel westwärts, die in treuem Lehn
Apolls ein Barde hält, hab ich umkreist.
Oft hörte ich, wie es von Weiten heißt,
  Breitstirnig war Homer ihr Souverän;
  Doch atmete ich nie ihr reines Wehn,
Bis ich vernahm, wie Chapman es laut preist:

Then felt I like some watcher of the skies
  When a new planet swims into his ken;
Or like stout Cortez when with eagle eyes
  He stared at the Pacific – and all his men
Looked at each other with a wild surmise –
  Silent, upon a peak in Darien.

To a Young Lady
who sent me a Laurel Crown

Fresh morning gusts have blown away all fear
  From my glad bosom: now from gloominess
  I mount for ever – not an atom less
Than the proud laurel shall content my bier.
No! by the eternal stars! or why sit here
  In the Sun's eye, and 'gainst my temples press
  Apollo's very leaves, woven to bless
By thy white fingers and thy spirit clear.
Lo! who dares say, 'Do this'? Who dares call down
  My will from its high purpose? Who say, 'Stand',
Or 'Go'? This very moment I would frown
  On abject Caesars – not the stoutest band
Of mailèd heroes should tear off my crown:
  Yet would I kneel and kiss thy gentle hand!

Wie einem Astronom erging's mir da,
  Schwimmt ihn ein neuer Stern im Fernrohr an;
Wie Cortez, als sein Adlerblick ganz nah
  Auf den Pazifik fiel – und jeder Mann
Wild rätselnd ins Gesicht des Nachbarn sah –
  Auf einem Pik Dariéns nur schweigend sann.

An eine junge Dame, die mir einen Lorbeerkranz sandte

All meine Furcht blies frischer Morgenwind
  Vom frohen Busen: Trübsal laß ich jetzt
  Für alle Zeit – auf daß im Sarg zuletzt
Nichts als nur stolzer Lorbeer sich befind.
Nein! bei den ewigen Sternen! was beginnt
  Man sonst im Aug der Sonne, aufgesetzt
  Das Laub Apolls, von hellem Geist geschätzt
Und wanden weiße Finger dies Gebind.
Seht! wer sagt dreist »Tu dies«? Wer bringt mich ab
  Von meinen hohen Zielen? Wer sagt »Los«,
Wer »Halt«? Schon blickte finster ich hinab
  Auf elende Cäsarn – mir riß kein Stoß
Der kühnsten Helden meinen Kranz herab:
    Doch kniet' ich und küßt' Eure Hand im Schoß!

Keen, fitful gusts are whispering here and there
  Among the bushes half leafless, and dry;
  The stars look very cold about the sky,
And I have many miles on foot to fare.
Yet feel I little of the cool bleak air,
  Or of the dead leaves rustling drearily,
  Or of those silver lamps that burn on high,
Or of the distance from home's pleasant lair:
For I am brimful of the friendliness
  That in a little cottage I have found;
Of fair-haired Milton's eloquent distress,
  And all his love for gentle Lycid drowned;
Of lovely Laura in her light green dress,
  And faithful Petrarch gloriously crowned.

To my Brothers

Small, busy flames play through the fresh-laid coals,
  And their faint cracklings o'er our silence creep
  Like whispers of the household gods that keep
A gentle empire o'er fraternal souls.
And while, for rhymes, I search around the poles,
  Your eyes are fixed, as in poetic sleep,
  Upon the lore so voluble and deep,
That aye at fall of night our care condoles.
This is your birth-day Tom, and I rejoice
  That thus it passes smoothly, quietly.
Many such eves of gently whispering noise
  May we together pass, and calmly try
What are this world's true joys – ere the great voice,
  From its fair face, shall bid our spirits fly.

Scharf wechseln Böen und wispern hier und dort
  In den Gebüschen, trocken und halb kahl;
  Am Himmel stehn die Sterne kalt und fahl,
Und ich muß manche Meil zu Fuß noch fort.
Doch fühl ich kaum, daß kühler Wind rumort
  Und tote Blätter rascheln ohne Zahl
  Und droben dieser Silberlampen Strahl
Und wie weit 's ist zum warmen Bett im Ort:
Denn noch bin ich randvoll von Freundlichkeit,
  Die mich in einem Landhaus hat verwöhnt;
Von Blondschopf Miltons sanft beredtem Leid,
  Das den ertrunknen Lycidas umtönt;
Von Laura, hübsch im leichten grünen Kleid,
  Und von Petrarca, treu und ruhmgekrönt.

An meine Brüder

Schmal züngeln Flammen, frisch im Herd geschürt,
  Umgleiten knisternd unsre Schweigsamkeit
  Und wispern leise wie die Hausgottheit,
Die brüderliche Seelen sanft regiert.
Und da manch Reim mich um die Pole führt,
  Ruhn eure Augen, traumversunken weit,
  Auf jener Mär, so reich an Wort und Leid,
Die trostreich stets zur Nacht das Herz uns rührt.
Du hast Geburtstag, Tom, und mir gefällt,
  Wie friedlich er verstreicht, wie unbeschwert.
Lieg manch solch Abend wispernd sanft erhellt
  Noch vor uns und sehn wir, was wahrer Wert
Auf dieser Welt – eh fliehn ihr holdes Feld
  Die große Stimme unsre Seelen lehrt.

Written in Disgust of Vulgar Superstition

The church bells toll a melancholy round,
  Calling the people to some other prayers,
  Some other gloominess, more dreadful cares,
More hearkening to the sermon's horrid sound.
Surely the mind of man is closely bound
  In some black spell; seeing that each one tears
  Himself from fireside joys, and Lydian airs,
And converse high of those with glory crowned.
Still, still they toll, and I should feel a damp –
  A chill as from a tomb – did I not know
That they are dying like an outburnt lamp;
  That 'tis their sighing, wailing ere they go
  Into oblivion – that fresh flowers will grow,
And many glories of immortal stamp.

On the Grasshopper and Cricket

The poetry of earth is never dead:
  When all the birds are faint with the hot sun,
  And hide in cooling trees, a voice will run
From hedge to hedge about the new-mown mead –
That is the Grasshopper's. He takes the lead
  In summer luxury; he has never done
  With his delights, for when tired out with fun
He rests at ease beneath some pleasant weed.
The poetry of earth is ceasing never:
  On a lone winter evening, when the frost
    Has wrought a silence, from the stove there shrills
The Cricket's song, in warmth increasing ever,
  And seems to one in drowsiness half lost,
    The Grasshopper's among some grassy hills.

Geschrieben aus Ekel vor volkstümlichem Aberglauben

Die Glocke, die so melancholisch tönt,
Ruft Volk zu weiteren Gebeten her,
Zu weitrer Trübsal, daß es sorgenschwer
Noch mehr im Lärm der Schreckenspredigt stöhnt.
Der Geist des Menschen hat sich wohl gewöhnt
An faulen Zauber; fliehn doch immer mehr
Familie, Lydiens Lüfte und Verkehr
Mit Werken derer, die der Ruhm stolz krönt.
Noch tönt sie, noch, und schaudern sollt's mich kalt –
Ein Hauch wie aus dem Grab – wenn ich nicht wüßt,
Daß sie, so wie ein Licht erlischt, verhallt;
Daß sie hier seufzt, bloß heult, eh man vergißt,
Wie sie einst klang – daß frischer Flor bald ist
Und Herrlichkeit von ewiger Gestalt.

Auf Grashüpfer und Heimchen

Die Poesie der Erde ist nie tot:
Sucht jeder Vogel schwach im Sonnenlicht
Ein kühles Baumversteck, läuft das Gerücht
Die Hecken lang, das Feld sei frisch gemäht –
Es ist des Grashüpfers. Sein Singen steht
Für Sommerwohligkeit; nichts unterbricht
Sein Glück, denn schwärmt er einmal nicht,
Ruht er bequem auf einem weichen Beet.
Die Erde wird an Poesie nie ärmer:
Am Winterabend, wenn der Frost zuvor
Ein Schweigen sponn, da schrillt vom Herd der Klang
Des Heimchenlieds, wird warm und immer wärmer
Und scheint dem, der sich dösend halb verlor,
Des Grashüpfers auf einem grünen Hang.

To G. A. W.

Nymph of the downward smile, and sidelong glance,
  In what diviner moments of the day
  Art thou most lovely? – When gone far astray
Into the labyrinths of sweet utterance?
Or when serenely wandering in a trance
  Of sober thought? – Or when starting away,
  With careless robe, to meet the morning ray,
Thou spar'st the flowers in thy mazy dance?
Haply 'tis when thy ruby lips part sweetly,
  And so remain, because thou listenest:
But thou to please wert nurtured so completely
  That I can never tell what mood is best.
I shall as soon pronounce which Grace more neatly
  Trips it before Apollo than the rest.

Happy is England! I could be content
  To see no other verdure than its own;
  To feel no other breezes than are blown
Through its tall woods with high romances blent:
Yet do I sometimes feel a languishment
  For skies Italian, and an inward groan
  To sit upon an Alp as on a throne,
And half forget what world or worldling meant.
Happy is England, sweet her artless daughters;
  Enough their simple loveliness for me,
    Enough their whitest arms in silence clinging:
Yet do I often warmly burn to see
    Beauties of deeper glance, and hear their singing,
And float with them about the summer waters.

An G. A. W.

Nymphe, die du verschmitzt zu Boden blickst,
Zu welcher himmlischeren Tageszeit
Bist du am lieblichsten? – wenn du befreit
Ein Labyrinth aus süßen Worten strickst?
Wenn du dich wandelnd wie im Rausch beglückst
An ernsten Dingen? – wenn du Helligkeit
Und Morgenstrahl begrüßt im losen Kleid
Und wirbelnd tanzend keine Blume knickst?
Vielleicht, wenn deine Lippen süß sich trennen,
Die du zu schließen, weil du lauschst, vergißt:
Nein, daß du ganz gefällst, würd ich verkennen,
Wüßt ich, wann du am allerschönsten bist.
Dann könnt ich ja Apoll die Grazie nennen,
Die tanzend hübscher als die andren ist.

Glücklich ist England! Mir wär es genug,
Nur dies ihm eigne satte Grün zu sehn,
Nur diesen Wind zu spüren, dessen Wehn
Stets Märchen durch die hohen Wälder trug:
Doch manchmal spürt ein sehnsuchtsvoller Zug
Italiens Himmel in mir, tief ein Flehn,
Auf einer Alpe wie ein Fürst zu stehn
Und zu vergessen Welt und Weltenspuk.
Glücklich ist England, seine Töchter bleiben
Voll schlichtem Liebreiz süß genug für mich,
Genug die Arme, die mich weiß umschlingen:
Doch oft verzehrt es mich und wünschte ich,
Daß Schöne tiefern Glanzes vor mir singen
Und wir auf sommerlichen Wassern treiben.

After dark vapours have oppressed our plains
  For a long dreary season, comes a day
  Born of the gentle South, and clears away
From the sick heavens all unseemly stains.
The anxious month, relieving from its pains,
  Takes as a long-lost right the feel of May,
  The eyelids with the passing coolness play,
Like rose leaves with the drip of summer rains.
And calmest thoughts come round us – as of leaves
  Budding – fruit ripening in stillness – autumn suns
Smiling at eve upon the quiet sheaves –
Sweet Sappho's cheek – a sleeping infant's breath –
  The gradual sand that through an hour-glass runs –
A woodland rivulet – a Poet's death.

To Leigh Hunt, Esq.

Glory and loveliness have passed away;
  For if we wander out in early morn,
  No wreathèd incense do we see upborne
Into the east, to meet the smiling day:
No crowd of nymphs soft voiced and young, and gay,
  In woven baskets bringing ears of corn,
  Roses, and pinks, and violets, to adorn
The shrine of Flora in her early May.
But there are left delights as high as these,
  And I shall ever bless my destiny,
That in a time, when under pleasant trees
  Pan is no longer sought, I feel a free,
A leafy luxury, seeing I could please
  With these poor offerings, a man like thee.

Nachdem von trübem Dunst die Flurn bedeckt
  Für lange öde Zeit warn, kommt mit Wind
  Von Süden sanfter Tag und fegt geschwind
Vom kranken Himmel fort, was ihn befleckt.
Der scheue Monat, schmerzfrei auferweckt,
  Nimmt sich sein Recht und wird als Mai nun lind,
  Die Lider spielen mit dem Tau und sind
Wie Rosen, die ein Sommerregen leckt.
Und ruhiger denken wir – wie Obst still reift –
  Wie Blätter knospen – Herbstlicht sich ergießt
Und abends heiter stumme Garben streift –
An Kinderschlaf – an Sapphos Wangenrot –
  Den Sand, der nach und nach durchs Uhrglas fließt –
Den Bach im Waldland – eines Dichters Tod.

An Leigh Hunt, Esq.

Die Glorie und der Liebreiz sind vorbei;
  Denn wandern wir in aller Früh hinaus,
  So sehn wir keinen Weihrauchqualm, der kraus
Gen Osten stieg, wo lächelnd Morgen sei:
Kein Nymphenschwarm, weich sprechend, jung und frei,
  Trägt in geflochtnen Körben Ähren aus,
  Die Rosen, Nelken und den Veilchenstrauß,
Zu zieren Floras Schrein im frühen Mai.
Doch Wonnen, groß wie diese, halten an,
  Und Dank sei meinem Schicksal ewiglich,
Denn während man bei kühlen Bäumen Pan
  Nicht länger sucht, blüht frei in mir, fühl ich,
Das Glück zu sehn, es freuten dann und wann
  Solch kleine Gaben einen Mann wie dich.

On Seeing the Elgin Marbles

My spirit is too weak – mortality
  Weighs heavily on me like unwilling sleep,
  And each imagined pinnacle and steep
Of godlike hardship, tells me I must die
Like a sick Eagle looking at the sky.
  Yet 'tis a gentle luxury to weep
  That I have not the cloudy winds to keep
Fresh for the opening of the morning's eye.
Such dim-conceivèd glories of the brain
  Bring round the heart an undescribable feud;
So do these wonders a most dizzy pain,
  That mingles Grecian grandeur with the rude
Wasting of old Time – with a billowy main –
  A sun – a shadow of a magnitude.

On a Leander Gem which Miss Reynolds, my Kind Friend, Gave Me

Come hither all sweet maidens soberly,
  Down-looking – ay, and with a chastened light
  Hid in the fringes of your eyelids white,
And meekly let your fair hands joinèd be,
Are ye so gentle that ye could not see,
  Untouched, a victim of your beauty bright –
  Sinking away to his young spirit's night,
Sinking bewildered 'mid the dreary sea:
'Tis young Leander toiling to his death.
  Nigh swooning, he doth purse his weary lips
    For Hero's cheek, and smiles against her smile.
  O horrid dream! see how his body dips
    Dead-heavy; arms and shoulders gleam awhile:
He's gone: up bubbles all his amorous breath!

Auf den Anblick der »Elgin Marbles«

Mein Geist versagt – so sterblich hier zu stehn,
Wiegt schwer, als hätte Schlaf mich übermannt,
Und jedes Bild von Gipfel, Felsenwand
Gottgleicher Müh sagt mir, ich muß vergehn
Wie kranke Adler, die zum Himmel spähn.
Doch still genieß ich, daß ich Tränen fand,
Weil düstren Wind zu blähn in meiner Hand
Nicht liegt, damit des Morgens Augen sehn.
Solch trüb-erahnte Glorien des Verstands
Bringen dem Herzen unbeschreiblichen Streit;
So nimmt ein Wunder teil am Schmerzenstanz,
Der griechisch Großes mischt mit alter Zeit
Grober Verschwendung – einem Meer im Glanz –
Der Sonne – Schatten einer Riesigkeit.

Auf eine Leander-Gemme, die Miss Reynolds, meine liebe Freundin, mir gab

Kommt her, ihr süßen Mädchen, kommt brav her,
Senkt euren Blick – ja, und auf keusche Pracht
Am Rand der weißen Lider seid bedacht,
Die zarten Hände reicht euch fromm nunmehr,
So sanft rührt euch doch wohl der Anblick sehr,
Den dort ein Opfer eurer Schönheit macht –
Sinkend zu seiner jungen Seele Nacht,
Verzweifelt sinkend auf dem öden Meer:
Leander ist's, der ringt mit seinem Tod.
Der Ohnmacht nah, sucht sein erschöpfter Mund
Noch Heros Wange, lacht ihr Lächeln nach.
O Alptraum! seht, wie totenschwer zum Grund
Sein Leib taucht; Arm und Schultern schimmern schwach –
Fort ist er: hochperlt Hauch voll Liebesnot!

On the Sea

It keeps eternal whisperings around
Desolate shores, and with its mighty swell
Gluts twice ten thousand caverns, till the spell
Of Hecate leaves them their old shadowy sound.
Often 'tis in such gentle temper found,
That scarcely will the very smallest shell
Be moved for days from where it sometime fell,
When last the winds of Heaven were unbound.
Oh ye! who have your eye-balls vexed and tired,
Feast them upon the wideness of the Sea –
Oh ye! whose ears are dinned with uproar rude,
Or fed too much with cloying melody –
Sit ye near some old cavern's mouth and brood,
Until ye start, as if the sea-nymphs quired!

On Sitting Down to Read "King Lear" Once Again

O golden-tongued Romance, with serene lute!
Fair plumèd Syren, Queen of far-away!
Leave melodizing on this wintry day,
Shut up thine olden pages, and be mute:
Adieu! for, once again, the fierce dispute
Betwixt damnation and impassioned clay
Must I burn through, once more humbly assay,
The bitter-sweet of this Shakespearian fruit:
Chief Poet! and ye clouds of Albion,
Begetters of our deep eternal theme!
When through the old oak forest I am gone,
Let me not wander in a barren dream,
But, when I am consumèd in the fire,
Give me new Phoenix wings to fly at my desire.

Auf das Meer

Es hält sich ewig flüsternd auf entlang
Verlaßner Küsten, und sein Brandungspflug
Füllt zwanzigtausend Höhlen, bald im Spuk
Der Hekate ganz alter düstrer Klang.
So mild gestimmt ist dann sein Wellengang,
Daß es die kleinste Muschel oft genug
Für Tage läßt, wo es sie hinverschlug,
Als sich der Wind zuletzt vom Himmel schwang.
Oh ihr! mit müden Augen, Zorn gewöhnten,
Am Meer und seiner Weite weidet sie –
Oh ihr! mit Ohren, von Tumult umdrängt,
Satt zuviel übersüße Melodie –
Setzt euch an einen Höhlenmund und denkt,
Bis euch's durchfährt, als ob die Nymphen tönten!

Auf das Sich-Hinsetzen, um nochmals »King Lear« zu lesen

O goldzüngige Dichtung, heitres Spiel!
Federnsirene, Fernenkönigin!
Leg diesen Wintertag die Laute hin,
Schließ deine alten Bände und sei still.
Adieu! Ich muß nochmals ins Streitgebrüll,
Verdammnis und erregten Staub darin
Durchrasen, kosten muß erneut mein Sinn
Vom bitter-süßen shakespeareschen Gefühl:
Höchster Poet! und Albions Wolkenmeer,
Ihr Stifter tiefen Stoffs von Ewigkeit!
Hab ich den alten Eichenwald durchquert,
Gebt, daß ich nicht durch öde Träume schreit,
Doch, wenn ich ganz dem Feuer unterliege,
Auf Phönixschwingen gen mein Sehnen fliege.

When I have fears that I may cease to be
  Before my pen has gleaned my teeming brain,
Before high-pilèd books, in charactery,
  Hold like rich garners the full-ripened grain;
When I behold, upon the night's starred face,
  Huge cloudy symbols of a high romance,
And think that I may never live to trace
  Their shadows, with the magic hand of chance;
And when I feel, fair creature of an hour!
  That I shall never look upon thee more,
Never have relish in the faery power
  Of unreflecting love! – then on the shore
Of the wide world I stand alone, and think
Till love and fame to nothingness do sink.

To —

Time's sea hath been five years at its slow ebb,
  Long hours have to and fro let creep the sand,
Since I was tangled in thy beauty's web,
  And snared by the ungloving of thy hand.
And yet I never look on midnight sky,
  But I behold thine eyes' well memoried light;
I cannot look upon the rose's dye,
  But to thy cheek my soul doth take its flight;
I cannot look on any budding flower,
  But my fond ear, in fancy at thy lips,
And hearkening for a love-sound, doth devour
  Its sweets in the wrong sense: – Thou dost eclipse
Every delight with sweet remembering,
And grief unto my darling joys dost bring.

Wenn Furcht mir kommt, ich hörte auf zu sein,
  Bevor mein Stift mein volles Hirn ablas,
Bevor Buch über Buch, in Letternreihn,
  Wie reiche Speicher reifes Korn besaß;
Wenn ich, auf der gestirnten Nacht Gesicht,
  Düstre Symbole hoher Kunst erblick
Und denk, vielleicht fließt mir ihr Schatten nicht
  Im Leben von der Zauberhand voll Glück;
Und wenn, Geschöpf für eine Stunde Zeit!,
  Ich fühl, ich soll nie wieder schaun auf dich,
Nie kosten Kraft und Märchenhaftigkeit
  Nicht reflektiernder Liebe! – dann steh ich
Am Strand der Welt allein und in Gedanken,
Bis Liebe, Ruhm zur Nichtigkeit versanken.

An —

Fünf Jahre sind verebbt im Meer der Zeit,
  Träg krochen lange Stunden durch den Sand,
Seit ich im Fangnetz deiner Lieblichkeit
  Umgarnt war vom Entblößen deiner Hand.
Und doch, ich seh nur in die Mitternacht,
  Schon strahlt dein unvergeßnes Auge dort;
Ich muß nur Rosen sehn in voller Pracht,
  Schon fliegt mein Herz zu deiner Wange fort;
Ich muß nur eine Knospe sehn, die sproßt,
  Schon horcht mein Ohr, im Geist an deinem Mund,
Auf einen Liebeslaut und schluckt die süße Kost
  Verkehrten Sinns: – Du nimmst mir jeden Grund
Zur Freude, denk ich süß an dich zurück,
Und bringst den Kummer meinem Herzensglück.

Spenser! a jealous honourer of thine,
  A forester deep in thy midmost trees,
Did last eve ask my promise to refine
  Some English that might strive thine ear to please.
But, Elfin Poet, 'tis impossible
  For an inhabitant of wintry earth
To rise like Phoebus with a golden quell,
  Fire-winged, and make a morning in his mirth.
It is impossible to escape from toil
  O' the sudden and receive thy spiriting:
The flower must drink the nature of the soil
  Before it can put forth its blossoming.
Be with me in the summer days and I
Will for thine honour and his pleasure try.

O thou whose face hath felt the Winter's wind,
  Whose eye has seen the snow-clouds hung in mist,
  And the black elm tops, 'mong the freezing stars,
  To thee the spring will be a harvest-time.
O thou, whose only book has been the light
  Of supreme darkness which thou feddest on
  Night after night when Phoebus was away,
  To thee the Spring shall be a triple morn.
O fret not after knowledge – I have none,
  And yet my song comes native with the warmth.
O fret not after knowledge – I have none,
  And yet the Evening listens. He who saddens
At thought of idleness cannot be idle,
And he's awake who thinks himself asleep.

Spenser! Jemandem, der dich heiß verehrt,
Einem Bewohner tief in deinem Wald,
Versprach ich gestern abend etwas, wert
Dem Englisch, das in deinem Ohr süß schallt.
Doch, Elfendichter, ganz unmöglich schafft,
Wer auf der Wintererde lebt, es so
Wie Phöbus aufzugehn mit goldner Kraft,
Feuer-beschwingt und frischen Morgens froh.
Es ist unmöglich, scheut man alle Mühn,
Daß einem jäh dein Geisterspuk gelingt:
Die Blume fährt erst fort in ihrem Blühn,
Wenn sie von der Natur des Bodens trinkt.
Bleib mir an Sommertagen treu, und ich,
Dich ehrend und ihn freuend, wage mich.

O du, des Antlitz Winterwind gespürt,
Des Aug durch Nebel Schneegewölk gesehn
Und Ulmenwipfel, schwarz im Sternenfrost,
Dir wird der Frühling eine Erntezeit.
O du, der Licht von größter Finsternis
Als einzig Buch besaß, das dich erhielt
Von Nacht zu Nacht, wenn Phöbus ferne war,
Dir soll der Frühling dreimal Morgen sein.
O plag dich nicht nach Wissen – ich hab keins,
Doch mit der Wärme kommt mein Lied von selbst.
O plag dich nicht nach Wissen – ich hab keins,
Und doch lauscht mir der Abend. Wen sein Denken
An Trägheit traurig stimmt, der kann nicht träg sein,
Und wach ist jener, der sich schlafend wähnt.

The Human Seasons

Four seasons fill the measure of the year;
  There are four seasons in the mind of man.
He has his lusty Spring, when fancy clear
  Takes in all beauty with an easy span.
He has his Summer, when luxuriously
  Spring's honeyed cud of youthful thought he loves
To ruminate, and by such dreaming nigh
  His nearest unto heaven. Quiet coves
His soul has in its Autumn, when his wings
  He furleth close; contented so to look
On mists in idleness – to let fair things
  Pass by unheeded as a threshold brook.
He has his Winter too of pale misfeature,
Or else he would forego his mortal nature.

To J.R.

O that a week could be an age, and we
  Felt parting and warm meeting every week,
Then one poor year a thousand years would be,
  The flush of welcome ever on the cheek:
So could we live long life in little space,
  So time itself would be annihilate,
So a day's journey in oblivious haze
  To serve our joys would lengthen and dilate.
O to arrive each Monday morn from Ind!
  To land each Tuesday from the rich Levant!
In little time a host of joys to bind,
  And keep our souls in one eternal pant!
This morn, my friend, and yester-evening taught
Me how to harbour such a happy thought.

Die menschlichen Jahreszeiten

Vier Zeiten füllen eines Jahres Maß;
  Es gibt vier Zeiten in des Menschen Geist.
Er steht im satten Frühling seines Jahrs,
  Wenn Phantasie das Schöne klar umreißt.
Er steht im Sommer, wenn er nochmals spürt,
  Wie honigsüß der Frühling, jugendlich
Sein Denken war und, nur vom Traum geführt,
  Wie nah dem Himmel. Schlupfwinkel für sich
Hat seine Seele dann im Herbst und rollt
  Die Flügel ein; beruhigt so, schaut er aus
Nach Nebeln – lässig läßt er alles Gold
  Vorbeiziehn, achtlos wie den Bach vorm Haus.
Auch ist sein Winter bleich voll Mißgestalten,
Sonst würde er sich für unsterblich halten.

An J.R.

O währten Wochen ewig, fühlten wir
  Begegnung, Abschied jede Woche neu –
Ein bloßes Jahr wär ein Jahrtausend hier,
  Stets auf der Wange die Willkommensscheu:
So lebten wir ein langes Leben schnell,
  So höbe sie sich selbst auf, alle Zeit,
Die Tagesreise im Vergessensgrell,
  Uns zum Gefallen würd sie lang und weit.
O stets aus Indien kommen montagfrüh!
  Von der Levante jeden Dienstag reich!
Ein Heer von Freuden sammeln ohne Müh,
  Das Sehnen unsrer Seelen ewiggleich!
Heut früh, mein Freund, und gestern abend legt
Mir nah, wie man solch Glücksgedanken hegt.

To Homer

Standing aloof in giant ignorance,
  Of thee I hear and of the Cyclades,
As one who sits ashore and longs perchance
  To visit dolphin-coral in deep seas.
So wast thou blind! – but then the veil was rent,
  For Jove uncurtained Heaven to let thee live,
And Neptune made for thee a spumy tent,
  And Pan made sing for thee his forest-hive;
Ay, on the shores of darkness there is light,
  And precipices show untrodden green;
There is a budding morrow in midnight;
  There is a triple sight in blindness keen;
Such seeing hadst thou, as it once befell
To Dian, Queen of Earth, and Heaven, and Hell.

On Visiting the Tomb of Burns

The town, the churchyard, and the setting sun,
  The clouds, the trees, the rounded hills all seem,
  Though beautiful, cold – strange – as in a dream
I dreamèd long ago. Now new begun
The short-lived, paly summer is but won
  From winter's ague, for one hour's gleam;
  Through sapphire-warm, their stars do never beam –
All is cold Beauty; pain is never done
For who has mind to relish, Minos-wise,
  The real of Beauty, free from that dead hue
    Fickly imagination and sick pride
  Cast wan upon it! Burns! with honour due
    I have oft honoured thee. Great shadow, hide
Thy face! I sin against thy native skies.

An Homer

Im Abseits riesiger Unwissenheit
Hör ich von den Kykladen und von dir,
Wie einer, der am Meer sitzt, sich wohl weit
Hinabsehnt zu Delphin-Korallen hier.
So warst du blind! – doch riß der Vorhang dann,
Denn dir zum Wohl schob Zeus den Himmel frei
Und schäumte auch Neptun ein Zelt heran
Und sang der ganze Waldschwarm Pans dabei.
Ja, auf des Dunkels Strand ist Licht entfacht,
Und Klippen deckt ein unbetretnes Grün;
Ein blühndes Morgen birgt die Mitternacht;
Ein dreifach Sehen birgt das blinde Mühn.
Dies sahest du, warst so Diana gleich
In ihrem Himmel-, Erd- und Höllenreich.

Auf einen Besuch an Burns' Grab

Stadt, Kirchhof und der Sonnenuntergang,
Gewölk, der Wald, der runde Hügelsaum,
All das scheint schön, doch – seltsam – kalt, ein Traum,
Geträumt vor langer Zeit. Mit neuem Drang
Lebt kurz der blasse Sommer auf, ein Klang
Des Winterfrosts nur, eine Stunde kaum.
Saphirn und warm glänzt nie ihr Stern im Raum –
Bloß kalte Schönheit; Schmerz währt endlos lang
Für den, der merkt, an Weisheit Minos gleich,
Wie wahrhaft Schönes schmeckt, nicht Leichenweiß,
Das Trugbilder und kranker Stolz so feist
Drauf werfen! Burns! ich ehrte dich oft heiß
Mit Ehrfurcht nach Gebühr. Birg, großer Geist,
Dein Antlitz! Ich beschmutz dein Heimatreich.

This mortal body of a thousand days
  Now fills, O Burns, a space in thine own room,
Where thou didst dream alone on budded bays,
  Happy and thoughtless of thy day of doom!
My pulse is warm with thine own barley-bree,
  My head is light with pledging a great soul,
My eyes are wandering, and I cannot see,
  Fancy is dead and drunken at its goal:
Yet can I stamp my foot upon thy floor,
  Yet can I ope thy window-sash to find
The meadow thou hast trampèd o'er and o'er,
  Yet can I think of thee till thought is blind,
Yet can I gulp a bumper to thy name –
O smile among the shades, for this is fame!

Translated from Ronsard

Nature withheld Cassandra in the skies,
  For more adornment, a full thousand years;
She took their cream of Beauty, fairest dyes,
  And shaped and tinted her above all peers:
Meanwhile Love kept her dearly with his wings,
  And underneath their shadow filled her eyes
With such a richness that the cloudy Kings
  Of high Olympus uttered slavish sighs.
When from the Heavens I saw her first descend,
  My heart took fire, and only burning pains …
They were my pleasures – they my Life's sad end;
  Love poured her beauty into my warm veins. …

Ein Leib von tausend Tagen Sterblichkeit
  Macht nun, o Burns, sich breit in deinem Raum –
Hier hast du dich dem Lorbeerkranz geweiht,
  Arglos und froh war dir dein Tod ein Traum!
Mein Blut pulst warm von deinem Malzlikör,
  Mein Kopf ist leicht und trinkt auf ein Genie,
Mein Auge wandert, und ich seh nicht mehr,
  Am Ziel bleibt tote, trunkne Phantasie –
Doch kann mein Fuß auf deinen Dielen stehn,
  Doch kann ich, hebe ich dein Fenster an,
Die Wiesen, wo du auf und ab gingst, sehn,
  Kann an dich denken, bis auch das zerrann,
Kann einen Becher deinem Namen weihn –
O lächle, Schatten, so berühmt zu sein!

Übersetzt aus dem Ronsard

Im Himmel hielt Kassandra die Natur
  Für tausend Jahre zu noch größrer Zier;
Nahm ihrer Schönheit holdste Farben nur,
  Gab keinem Farbe und Gestalt wie ihr.
Sanft hielt der Liebe Flügel sie derweil
  Und füllten seine Schatten ihren Blick
Mit solchem Glanz, daß knechtisches Geheul
  Olympus' Wolkenkönigen entstieg.
Als ich sie sah, wie sie vom Himmel kam,
  Fing mein Herz Feuer, aller Schmerzen Glut …
Sie warn mein Glück – mein Ende voller Gram;
  Schön goß mir Liebe sie ins warme Blut. …

Why did I laugh tonight? No voice will tell:
  No God, no Demon of severe response,
Deigns to reply from Heaven or from Hell.
  Then to my human heart I turn at once –
Heart! thou and I are here sad and alone;
  Say, wherefore did I laugh! O mortal pain!
O Darkness! Darkness! ever must I moan,
  To question Heaven and Hell and Heart in vain.
Why did I laugh? I know this being's lease
  My fancy to its utmost blisses spreads;
Yet could I on this very midnight cease,
  And the world's gaudy ensigns see in shreds.
Verse, Fame, and Beauty are intense indeed,
  But Death intenser – Death is Life's high meed.

The House of Mourning written by Mr Scott,
  A sermon at the Magdalen, a tear
  Dropped on a greasy novel, want of cheer
After a walk uphill to a friend's cot,
Tea with a maiden lady, a cursed lot
  Of worthy poems with the author near,
  A patron lord, a drunkenness from beer,
Haydon's great picture, a cold coffee pot
At midnight when the Muse is ripe for labour,
  The voice of Mr Coleridge, a French bonnet
Before you in the pit, a pipe and tabour,
A damned inseparable flute and neighbour –
  All these are vile, but viler Wordsworth's sonnet
On Dover. Dover! – who *could* write upon it?

Was lachte ich heut nacht? Niemand, der spricht:
  Ein Gott, ein Dämon, der erwidern kann
Aus Himmel oder Hölle, regt sich nicht.
  Dann rufe schnell mein Menschenherz ich an –
Herz! wir zwei sind hier traurig und allein;
  Sag, weshalb lachte ich? O Sterbensschmerz!
O Dunkel! Dunkel! ewig klag ich ein,
  Umsonst zu fragen Himmel, Hölle, Herz.
Was lachte ich? Des Daseins Ziel hat Macht,
  Die meinen Geist ins höchste Glück versetzt;
Doch könnt ich scheiden diese Mitternacht
  Und sehn, wie 's der Welt Wimpelputz zerfetzt.
Schönheit, Dichtung und Ruhm sind Großes schon,
  Tod mehr – Tod ist des Lebens hoher Lohn.

Das Haus der Trauer, von Mr. Scott verfaßt,
  Ein Magdalensermon, ein Tränchen Leid
  Getropft auf Schmierwerk, Wunsch nach Heiterkeit
Nach einem Hügelmarsch beim Freund zu Gast,
Mit einem Dämchen Tee, Fluch einer Last
  Wertvoller Verse, ihr Autor nicht weit,
  Ein Lord-Patron, 'ne Bierbetrunkenheit,
Groß Haydons Bild, Kaffee, kalt und verpaßt,
Um mitternachts die Muse noch zu greifen,
  Die Stimme Coleridges, der Franzosen Sorte
Von Haube bettwärts vor dir, Trommeln, Pfeifen,
Verflucht untrennbar Flöten, Nachbarskeifen –
  All dies taugt nichts, doch mehr als Wordsworths Worte
Auf Dover. Dover! – wer *beschreibt* solch Orte?

A Dream, after reading Dante's Episode of Paolo and Francesca

As Hermes once took to his feathers light,
  When lullèd Argus, baffled, swooned and slept,
So on a Delphic reed, my idle spright
  So played, so charmed, so conquered, so bereft
The dragon-world of all its hundred eyes;
  And, seeing it asleep, so fled away –
Not to pure Ida with its snow-cold skies,
  Nor unto Tempe where Jove grieved that day;
But to that second circle of sad hell,
  Where in the gust, the whirlwind, and the flaw
Of rain and hail-stones, lovers need not tell
  Their sorrows. Pale were the sweet lips I saw,
Pale were the lips I kissed, and fair the form
I floated with, about that melancholy storm.

To Sleep

O soft embalmer of the still midnight,
  Shutting, with careful fingers and benign,
Our gloom-pleased eyes, embowered from the light,
  Enshaded in forgetfulness divine:
O soothest Sleep! if so it please thee, close
  In midst of this thine hymn, my willing eyes,
Or wait the 'Amen', ere the poppy throws
  Around my bed its lulling charities.
Then save me, or the passèd day will shine
Upon my pillow, breeding many woes;
  Save me from curious conscience, that still hoards
Its strength for darkness, burrowing like the mole;
  Turn the key deftly in the oilèd wards,
And seal the hushèd casket of my soul.

Ein Traum, nachdem ich Dantes Episode von Paolo und Francesca gelesen hatte

Wie Hermes einst die leichten Federn schwang,
  Da Argus hinsank, eingelullt, und schlief,
So delphisch flötend, ganz im Müßiggang,
  So narrte, so bezwang mein Geist im Spiel
Die hundert Augen dieser Drachenwelt;
  Und als er sah, sie schläft, floh er so fort –
Nicht in den Schnee, der rein auf Ida fällt,
  Und nicht gen Tempe, Jovis Trauerort:
Zum zweiten düstren Höllenkreis flog er,
  Wo im Geheul aus Wirbeln, Regen, Hagelböen
Und Wind, wer liebt, nicht sagen muß, was mehr
  Ihn schmerzt. Bleich war der Mund, den ich gesehn,
Bleich, den ich küßte, und der Körper süß,
Mit dem mich's durch solch Sturm von Schwermut blies.

An den Schlaf

O zarter Salber stiller Mitternacht,
  Der mit so milder Hand und Sorgsamkeit
Ohnmächtig-frohe Augen schließt, vor Licht bewacht,
  Im Schatten göttlicher Vergessenheit –
O sänftigendster Schlaf! willst du, dann schließ
  Mein Aug zu dieser deiner Hymne schon
Oder wart noch aufs Amen, und dann gieß
  Rings um mein Bett als Wiegengabe Mohn.
Beschütz mich dann, daß nicht der Tag erneut
Aufs Kissen scheint, der mich so leiden ließ;
  Schütz mich, daß nicht Gewissensneugier noch
Im Dunkeln Kraft schöpf', maulwurfgleich dort quäle;
  Dreh rasch den Schlüssel im geölten Loch
Und schließ das stumme Kästchen meiner Seele.

If by dull rhymes our English must be chained,
And, like Andromeda, the Sonnet sweet
Fettered, in spite of painèd loveliness,
Let us find out, if we must be constrained,
Sandals more interwoven and complete
To fit the naked foot of Poesy:
Let us inspect the lyre, and weigh the stress
Of every chord; and see what may be gained
By ear industrious, and attention meet;
Misers of sound and syllable, no less
Than Midas of his coinage, let us be
Jealous of dead leaves in the bay wreath crown;
So, if we may not let the Muse be free,
She will be bound with garlands of her own.

On Fame

You cannot eat your cake
and have it too
Proverb

How fevered is the man who cannot look
  Upon his mortal days with temperate blood,
Who vexes all the leaves of his life's book,
  And robs his fair name of its maidenhood;
It is as if the rose should pluck herself,
  Or the ripe plum finger its misty bloom,
As if a Naiad, like a meddling elf,
  Should darken her pure grot with muddy gloom:
But the rose leaves herself upon the briar,
  For winds to kiss and grateful bees to feed,
And the ripe plum sill wears its dim attire,
    The undisturbèd lake has crystal space;
    Why then should man, teasing the world for grace,
  Spoil his salvation for a fierce miscreed?

Wenn Reimwerk unser Englisch fesseln muß
Und, wie Andromeda, süß das Sonett
Knebeln trotz schmerzerfüllter Lieblichkeit,
Laßt uns, da man uns zwingt zu dem Entschluß,
Verflochtnere Sandalen schaun, komplett
Dem nackten Fuß der Dichtung angepaßt –
Laßt uns die Leier prüfen, sehn, wie weit
Ein jeder Ton trägt und was an Genuß
Ein reges Ohr und rechte Wartung hätt;
Knicker mit Sang und Klang wie seinerzeit
Mit Münzen Midas, voller Argwohn laßt
Für totes Laub im Lorbeerkranz uns sein;
So, wird die Muse schon nicht frei erfaßt,
Fängt man sie mit den eignen Schlingen ein.

Auf den Ruhm

Keiner kann einen Kuchen essen
und zugleich behalten.
Sprichwort

Wie fiebert doch, wer nicht mit ruhigem Blut
  Zu schaun vermag auf seine Erdenfrist,
Wer seines Lebens Buch durchwühlt vor Wut
  Und seinem Namen raubt, was kindlich ist:
Als ob die Rose selbst sich pflücken soll,
  Die reife Pflaume reiben ihren Hauch
Und die Najade, täppisch wie ein Troll,
  Die reine Grotte schwärzen soll mit Rauch –
Die Rose aber läßt sich stehn am Stock,
  Küßt Wind und nimmt sich dankbarn Bienen an,
Es trägt die Pflaume ihren matten Rock
    Und bleibt der stille See kristalln erhellt –
    Was soll der Mensch, buhlend ums Lob der Welt,
  Sein Heil zerstörn für einen bösen Wahn?

The day is gone, and all its sweets are gone!
  Sweet voice, sweet lips, soft hand, and softer breast,
Warm breath, light whisper, tender semi-tone,
  Bright eyes, accomplished shape, and languorous waist!
Faded the flower and all its budded charms,
  Faded the sight of beauty from my eyes,
Faded the shape of beauty from my arms,
  Faded the voice, warmth, whiteness, paradise –
Vanished unseasonably at shut of eve,
  When the dusk holiday – or holinight –
Of fragrant-curtained love begins to weave
  The woof of darkness thick, for hid delight;
But, as I've read love's missal through today,
He'll let me sleep, seeing I fast and pray.

I cry your mercy, pity, love – ay, love!
  Merciful love that tantalizes not,
One-thoughted, never-wandering, guileless love,
  Unmasked, and being seen – without a blot!
O! let me have thee whole, – all, all, be mine!
  That shape, that fairness, that sweet minor zest
Of love, your kiss – those hands, those eyes divine,
  That warm, white, lucent, million-pleasured breast –
Yourself – your soul – in pity give me all,
  Withhold no atom's atom or I die;
Or living on perhaps, your wretched thrall,
  Forget, in the mist of idle misery,
Life's purposes – the palate of my mind
Losing its gust, and my ambition blind!

Der Tag ist fort, mit aller Süße fort!
  Mund, Stimme, weiche Hand und weichre Brust,
Das Hauchen, Flüstern, zarter Halbakkord,
  Blick und vollkommner Leib, voll matter Lust!
Vorbei die Blume und ihr blühnder Tag,
  Vorbei, was schön in meinen Augen hieß,
Vorbei, was schön in meinen Armen lag,
  Fort Stimme, Wärme, Weiße, Paradies –
Verschwunden noch, bevor der Abend geht
  Und Feiertag – nein, Feiernacht sein muß,
Die duft-umhüllte Liebe dicht vernäht
  Zum dunklen Zelt für heimlichen Genuß –
Doch wie in Amors Meßbuch ich heut seh,
Läßt er mich schlafen, da ich fast' und fleh.

Ich fleh dich an um Gnade, Mitleid, Liebe! –
  Ja, Liebe voller Gnade, die nicht quält,
Einhellige, stets feste, offne Liebe,
  Nie Maske, makellos – die nichts verhehlt!
O! gib dich mir ganz hin – sei ganz, ganz mein!
  Mit Schönheit, Leib, der süßen kleinen Lust
Davor, dem Kuß – die Hand, den Blick so rein,
  Die warme, weiße, endlos-weiche Brust –
Dich selbst – die Seele – gib und sei gerecht,
  Behalt kein kleinstes Stück, sonst sterbe ich;
Und leb ich doch, dein jämmerlicher Knecht,
  Verließ im Nebel eitlen Elends mich
Mein Lebenssinn – mein Geist geschmacklos, stumpf
Sein Gaumen, und mein Ehrgeiz nur mehr dumpf!

Bright star! would I were steadfast as thou art –
  Not in lone splendour hung aloft the night
And watching, with eternal lids apart,
  Like nature's patient, sleepless Eremite,
The moving waters at their priestlike task
  Of pure ablution round earth's human shores,
Or gazing on the new soft-fallen mask
  Of snow upon the mountains and the moors –
No – yet still steadfast, still unchangeable,
  Pillowed upon my fair love's ripening breast,
To feel for ever its soft swell and fall,
  Awake for ever in a sweet unrest,
Still, still to hear her tender-taken breath,
And so live ever – or else swoon to death.

Glänzender Stern! wär ich doch stet wie du –
 Nicht Schimmern, einsam aufgehängt zur Nacht,
Und schlaflos, offnen Lides immerzu,
 Einsiedler der Natur, der duldsam wacht,
Wie sich das Meer bewegt, das priestergleich
 Die Menschenküsten reinwäscht auf der Welt,
Und auf den Schnee blickt, dessen Maske weich
 Auf Heideland und Hügel niederfällt –
Nein – und doch stetig, stets unwandelbar,
 Gebettet auf der Liebsten junger Brust,
Dem sanften Auf und Ab für immer nah,
 Für immer wach in ruheloser Lust,
Stets, stets im Ohr den zarten Atemzug,
Und wär so ewig – sonst nie tot genug.

Odes

Ode to May

Fragment

Mother of Hermes! and still youthful Maia!
    May I sing to thee
As thou wast hymnèd on the shores of Baiae?
    Or may I woo thee
In earlier Sicilian? or thy smiles
Seek as they once were sought, in Grecian isles,
By bards who died content in pleasant sward,
  Leaving great verse unto a little clan?
O, give me their old vigour, and unheard
  Save of the quiet primrose, and the span
    Of Heaven and few ears,
Rounded by thee, my song should die away
    Content as theirs,
Rich in the simple worship of a day.

Ode to Psyche

O Goddess! hear these tuneless numbers, wrung
  By sweet enforcement and remembrance dear,
And pardon that thy secrets should be sung
  Even into thine own soft-conchèd ear:
Surely I dreamt to-day, or did I see
  The wingèd Psyche with awakened eyes?
I wandered in a forest thoughtlessly,
  And, on the sudden, fainting with surprise,
Saw two fair creatures, couchèd side by side
  In deepest grass, beneath the whispering roof

Oden

Ode an den Mai

Fragment

Mutter des Hermes! und stets junge Maja!
    Darf ich dich preisen
Wie du besungen wardst am Strand von Bajä?
    Gunst dir erweisen
In älterm Sizilianisch? suchen ganz
Dein Lächeln wie auf Inseln Griechenlands
Einst Barden, starben heiter sie im Gras
  Als große Dichter einer kleinen Schar?
O, meinem Lied gib deren altes Maß,
  Und hörbar Primeln, Himmelsrund, fürwahr
    Nur wenig Ohren so,
Vollkommen erst durch dich, verkläng es gleich
    Dem ihren froh,
Im schlichten Loben eines Tages reich.

Ode an Psyche

O Göttin! hör dies Versgeklingel, bracht
  Doch süßer Zwang zur Rückschau es hervor,
Vergib auch, sing ich dein Geheimnis sacht
  Noch in dein eignes zart-muschliges Ohr:
Ich träumt heut sicher, oder hab ich doch
  Die Flügel Psyches wachen Augs gesehn?
Durch einen Wald strich ich nichtsahnend noch,
  Da sah ich, blieb verwundert stehn,
Zwei holde Wesen, Leib an Leib gestreckt
  Ins tiefste Gras, wo unterm Flüsterdach

Of leaves and tremblèd blossoms, where there ran
A brooklet, scarce espied:
'Mid hushed, cool-rooted flowers, fragrant-eyed,
Blue, silver-white, and budded Tyrian,
They lay calm-breathing on the bedded grass;
Their arms embraced, and their pinions too;
Their lips touched not, but had not bade adieu,
As if disjoinèd by soft-handed slumber,
And ready still past kisses to outnumber
At tender eye-dawn of aurorean love:
The wingèd boy I knew;
But who wast thou, O happy, happy dove?
His Psyche true!

O latest born and loveliest vision far
Of all Olympus' faded hierarchy!
Fairer than Phoebe's sapphire-regioned star,
Or Vesper, amorous glow-worm of the sky;
Fairer than these, though temple thou hast none,
Nor altar heaped with flowers;
Nor virgin-choir to make delicious moan
Upon the midnight hours;
No voice, no lute, no pipe, no incense sweet
From chain-swung censer teeming;
No shrine, no grove, no oracle, no heat
Of pale-mouthed prophet dreaming.

O brightest! though too late for antique vows,
Too, too late for the fond believing lyre,
When holy were the haunted forest boughs,
Holy the air, the water, and the fire;
Yet even in these days so far retired
From happy pieties, thy lucent fans,
Fluttering among the faint Olympians,
I see, and sing, by my own eyes inspired.

Aus Blättern Blüten bebten und ein Quell
Dahinfloß, kaum entdeckt:
Auf Blumen, stumm, kühl wurzelnd, blau gescheckt,
Duftäugig, purpurn knospend, silberhell,
Da lagen sie ruhig atmend weich im Gras;
Ihr Arm- und Flügelpaar umschlang sie dicht;
Sie küßten und sie lösten sich auch nicht,
Gleichwie vom Schlaf getrennt mit sanften Händen
Und so bereit, ihr Küssen zu vollenden
Beim zarten Liebesmorgenrot des Blicks –
Den Flügelknaben dort erkannte ich;
Doch wen in dir, o Taube heitern Glücks?
Treu, Psyche, dich!

O letztgeborne, lieblichste Vision
Der vom Olymp verschwundnen Göttermacht!
Schöner als Phöbes Stern, Saphirregion
Und Hesp'rus, Liebesglühwurm in der Nacht;
Schöner, obgleich du weder Tempel hast,
Altar aus Blumenlagen
Noch Jungfraunchor, um selig und gefaßt
Zur Mitternacht zu klagen;
Nicht Stimme, Laute, Flöte, Weihrauchfaß,
Geschwungen zu Gebeten;
Nicht Schrein, Orakel, Hain noch inbrunstblaß
Die träumenden Propheten.

O Strahlendste! zu spät für Schwüre zwar,
Zu spät für die antike treue Leier,
Als heilig der bewohnte Haingrund war,
Heilig die Luft, das Wasser und das Feuer;
Doch selbst in unsrer Zeit, so unberührt
Vom Frommen, kann ich deine Schwingen schön
Um schwächliche Olympiern flattern sehn
Und sing, vom eignen Auge inspiriert.

So let me be thy choir, and make a moan
Upon the midnight hours;
Thy voice, thy lute, thy pipe, thy incense sweet
From swingèd censer teeming –
Thy shrine, thy grove, thy oracle, thy heat
Of pale-mouthed prophet dreaming.

Yes, I will be thy priest, and build a fane
In some untrodden region of my mind,
Where branchèd thoughts, new grown with pleasant pain,
Instead of pines shall murmur in the wind:
Far, far around shall those dark-clustered trees
Fledge the wild-ridgèd mountains steep by steep;
And there by zephyrs, streams, and birds, and bees,
The moss-lain Dryads shall be lulled to sleep;
And in the midst of this wide quietness
A rosy sanctuary will I dress
With the wreathed trellis of a working brain,
With buds, and bells, and stars without a name,
With all the gardener Fancy e'er could feign,
Who breeding flowers, will never breed the same:
And there shall be for thee all soft delight
That shadowy thought can win,
A bright torch, and a casement ope at night,
To let the warm Love in!

Ode on a Grecian Urn

I

Thou still unravished bride of quietness,
Thou foster-child of silence and slow time,
Sylvan historian, who canst thus express
A flowery tale more sweetly than our rhyme:

Darum laß mich dein Chor sein und gefaßt
Zur Mitternachtszeit klagen;
Mich Stimme, Laute, Flöte, Rauch im Faß,
Geschwungen zu Gebeten –
Dein Schrein, Orakel, Hain und inbrunstblaß
Die träumenden Propheten.

Ja, ich will Priester deines Tempels sein,
Wo Geist und Seele unbetreten sind
Und ein Gedankenwald, Sproß süßer Pein,
Anstatt von Kiefern murmeln soll im Wind:
Weit, weit rings soll ihr dunkel-dichtes Dach
Fiedern wild-schroffe Berge, Saum für Saum;
Dort sollen Zephyr, Vögel, Bienen, Bach
Im Moos Dryaden lullen in den Traum;
Und in dies weite schweigende Gebiet
Bau ich ein Heiligtum, das rosig blüht,
Aus eines tätigen Gehirns Geflecht,
Aus Knospen, Kelchen, Sternen ohne Zahl,
Was auch der Gärtner Phantasie erdächt,
Der züchtend Neues züchtet jedes Mal –
Und dort soll alle Wonne für dich sein,
Die Denken träumrisch kennt,
Ein Fenster, offen nachts, wo Fackelschein
Für heiße Liebe brennt!

Ode auf eine griechische Urne

I

Du gänzlich unberührte Braut der Ruh,
Langsamer Zeit und Stille Pflegekind,
Des Walds Chronistin, wieviel süßer du
Geschichten ausschmückst als ein Vers ersinnt:

What leaf-fringed legend haunts about thy shape
  Of deities or mortals, or of both,
    In Tempe or the dales of Arcady?
  What men or gods are these? What maidens loth?
What mad pursuit? What struggle to escape?
    What pipes and timbrels? What wild ecstasy?

II

Heard melodies are sweet, but those unheard
  Are sweeter; therefore, ye soft pipes, play on;
Not to the sensual ear, but, more endeared,
  Pipe to the spirit ditties of no tone:
Fair youth, beneath the trees, thou canst not leave
  Thy song, nor ever can those trees be bare;
    Bold Lover, never, never canst thou kiss,
Though winning near the goal – yet, do not grieve:
  She cannot fade, though thou hast not thy bliss,
    For ever wilt thou love, and she be fair!

III

Ah, happy, happy boughs! that cannot shed
  Your leaves, nor ever bid the Spring adieu;
And, happy melodist, unwearièd,
  For ever piping songs for ever new;
More happy love! more happy, happy love!
  For ever warm and still to be enjoyed,
    For ever panting, and for ever young –
All breathing human passion far above,
  That leaves a heart high-sorrowful and cloyed,
    A burning forehead, and a parching tongue.

Welch Sage wird dich laubumsäumt umziehn,
  Die Götter, Menschen oder beide zeigt,
    In Tempe oder in Arkadiens Tal?
  Welch Wesen sind's? Welch Mädchen, abgeneigt?
Welch irre Jagd? Welch Kampf, um zu entfliehn?
    Welch Pfeifen, Trommeln? Welches Bacchanal?

II

Gehört sind Klänge süß, doch ungehört
  Noch süßer; drum spielt, Pfeifen, fort im Chor;
Nicht dem Gehörsinn, nein, von größrem Wert,
  Dem Geist pfeift Lieder keiner Töne vor –
Du Jüngling, unterm Baum, kannst vom Gesang
  Nicht lassen, noch kann je dies Laub verwehn;
    Kühn Liebender, nie, nie gelingt dein Kuß,
Bist du dem Ziel auch nah – doch sei nicht bang:
  Sie kann nicht gehn, und wird dir kein Genuß,
    Liebst du doch ewig und bleibt sie so schön!

III

Ah! Glücks-, du Glücksgezweig, das nie verblüht,
  Nie gilbt, noch je dem Frühling sich empfiehlt;
Und glücklicher Flötist, der, nimmermüd,
  Für immer immerneue Lieder spielt –
Mehr Liebesglück! mehr Liebes-, Liebesglück!
  Für immer zu genießen und stets warm,
    Für immer keuchend und für immer jung –
Fern allem atmend menschlichen Geschick,
  Dem Herzen voller Überdruß und Gram,
    Der heißen Stirn und der verdörrten Zung.

IV

Who are these coming to the sacrifice?
  To what green altar, O mysterious priest,
Lead'st thou that heifer lowing at the skies,
  And all her silken flanks with garlands dressed?
What little town by river or sea shore,
  Or mountain-built with peaceful citadel,
    Is emptied of this folk, this pious morn?
And, little town, thy streets for evermore
  Will silent be; and not a soul to tell
    Why thou art desolate, can e'er return.

V

O Attic shape! Fair attitude! with brede
  Of marble men and maidens overwrought,
With forest branches and the trodden weed;
  Thou, silent form, dost tease us out of thought
As doth eternity: Cold Pastoral!
  When old age shall this generation waste,
    Thou shalt remain, in midst of other woe
Than ours, a friend to man, to whom thou say'st,
  'Beauty is truth, truth beauty, – that is all
    Ye know on earth, and all ye need to know.'

Ode to a Nightingale

I

My heart aches, and a drowsy numbness pains
  My sense, as though of hemlock I had drunk,
Or emptied some dull opiate to the drains
  One minute past, and Lethe-wards had sunk:

IV

Wer sind die, um den Moosaltar gereiht?
  Geheimnisvoller Priester, welchem Stein
Führst du die Färse zu, die aufwärts schreit
  Und deren seidne Flanken Kränze weihn?
Welch kleine Stadt am Fluß oder am Meer,
  Mit friedlichem Kastell am Berg erbaut,
    Verließ dies Volk zu dieser frommen Stund?
Und, Städtchen, deine Straßen bleiben leer
  Für immer – keiner, der uns anvertraut,
    Weshalb, kehrt je zurück und nennt den Grund.

V

O Attische! Form schöner Art! im Bund
  Mit Männern, Mädchen marmorn überdeckt,
Mit festgetretnem Laubgezweig im Rund;
  Du Stille, die uns aus dem Denken schreckt
Wie Ewigkeit: Du kaltes Hirtenspiel!
  Wenn uns das Alter fortrafft eines Tags,
    Sollst du bestehn, von Leid, dem hier nichts gleicht,
Umringt, ein Freund dem Menschen, dem du sagst:
  »Schönheit ist Wahrheit, Wahrheit schön – soviel
    Wißt ihr auf Erden, und dies Wissen reicht.«

Ode an eine Nachtigall

I

Mein Herz schmerzt, und ein tauber Krampf durchfährt
  Mein Hirn, als ob ich Schierling angerührt
Oder ein trübes Opiat vollends geleert
  Grad hätte und zur Lethe sinken würd:

'Tis not through envy of thy happy lot,
But being too happy in thine happiness –
  That thou, light-wingèd Dryad of the trees,
    In some melodious plot
  Of beechen green, and shadows numberless,
   Singest of summer in full-throated ease.

II

O, for a draught of vintage! that hath been
  Cooled a long age in the deep-delvèd earth,
Tasting of Flora and the country green,
  Dance, and Provençal song, and sunburnt mirth!
O for a beaker full of the warm South,
  Full of the true, the blushful Hippocrene,
   With beaded bubbles winking at the brim,
    And purple-stainèd mouth,
  That I might drink, and leave the world unseen,
   And with thee fade away into the forest dim –

III

Fade far away, dissolve, and quite forget
  What thou among the leaves hast never known,
The weariness, the fever, and the fret
  Here, where men sit and hear each other groan;
Where palsy shakes a few, sad, last grey hairs,
  Where youth grows pale, and spectre-thin, and dies;
   Where but to think is to be full of sorrow
    And leaden-eyed despairs;
Where Beauty cannot keep her lustrous eyes,
   Or new Love pine at them beyond to-morrow.

Nicht Neid ist's auf dein glückliches Geschick,
Vielmehr des Glücks in deinem Glück zuviel –
Daß du, Dryas des Walds, dich leicht beschwingst
Am melodienreichen Knick
Aus Buchengrün und lauter Schattenspiel
Und ruhig aus vollem Hals vom Sommer singst.

II

O einen Schluck des Weins!, der lang versteckt
Kühl im tief-ausgehöhlten Erdreich lag,
Nach Flora und den grünen Weiten schmeckt,
Tanz, Liedern der Provence, nach heißem Tag!
O einen Becher Süden, warm und rund,
Voll echter Hippokrene, rosigblaß,
Der blinkt am Rand, wo Perlenbläschen sind
Vorm rotgefleckten Mund,
Daß ich die Welt so ungesehn verlaß
Und mit dir fort, hinein ins Walddunkel verschwind –

III

Sich auflösen, verschwinden, und am Schluß
Vergessen, was im Laubwerk dich nie stört,
Die Qual, das Fieber und den Überdruß
Hier, wo ein jeder jeden stöhnen hört;
Wo letztes graues Haar vom Schlagfluß bebt,
Wo Jugend bleich und schemen-dürr verfällt;
Wo denken heißt, daß man vor Gram und Sorgen
Bleierne Lider hebt;
Wo Schönheit ihren Augenglanz nicht hält
Und neue Liebe dies nur schmerzt bis morgen.

IV

Away! away! for I will fly to thee,
  Not charioted by Bacchus and his pards,
But on the viewless wings of Poesy,
  Though the dull brain perplexes and retards.
Already with thee! tender is the night,
  And haply the Queen-Moon is on her throne,
    Clustered around by all her starry Fays;
      But here there is no light,
  Save what from heaven is with the breezes blown
    Through verdurous glooms and winding mossy ways.

V

I cannot see what flowers are at my feet,
  Nor what soft incense hangs upon the boughs,
But, in embalmèd darkness, guess each sweet
  Wherewith the seasonable month endows
The grass, the thicket, and the fruit-tree wild –
  White hawthorn, and the pastoral eglantine;
    Fast fading violets covered up in leaves;
      And mid-May's eldest child,
  The coming musk-rose, full of dewy wine,
    The murmurous haunt of flies on summer eves.

VI

Darkling I listen; and, for many a time
  I have been half in love with easeful Death,
Called him soft names in many a musèd rhyme,
  To take into the air my quiet breath;
Now more than ever seems it rich to die,
  To cease upon the midnight with no pain,
    While thou art pouring forth thy soul abroad
      In such an ecstasy!
  Still wouldst thou sing, and I have ears in vain –
    To thy high requiem become a sod.

IV

Fort! fort! fliegen zu dir will ich fürwahr,
  Nicht, daß mich Bacchus' Parderwagen trägt,
Nein Poesiens unsichtbares Flügelpaar,
  Auch wenn das Hirn sich wirr und schleppend regt.
Und bin schon bei dir! Zärtlich ist die Nacht
  Und thront vielleicht die Mondenkönigin
    Im Haufen aller ihrer Sternenfeen;
      Nur Licht scheint keines sacht
  Als jenes, das vom Himmel Brisen dünn
    Durchs dunkle Grün und Moos der Wege wehn.

V

Ich kann nicht sehn, was mir zu Füßen sprießt,
  Noch welch Geruch mild auf den Ästen hängt,
Doch ich erahn, im Duft des Dunkels süßt
  Der Monat alles zeitig und beschenkt
Das Gras, das Dickicht und den Obstbaum lind –
  Läßt Weißdorn neben Heiderosen sein;
    Rasch welke Veilchen ganz von Laub vermummt;
      Und Mittmais ältstes Kind,
  Die Moschusrose, bald voll Tau und Wein,
    Den Ort, der sommernachts vor Fliegen brummt.

VI

Umdunkelt lausch ich; ich hab manches Mal
  Mich halbwegs in den leichten Tod verguckt,
Gab ihm erträumte Namen ohne Zahl,
  Damit die Luft mein ruhiges Atmen schluckt;
Jetzt merk ich erst, wie köstlich Sterben ist,
  Wenn mitternachts sich aller Schmerz verlor,
    Da du dein Herz verströmst und ungehemmt
      In solch Ekstase bist!
  Du sängest weiter, und wär taub mein Ohr –
    Ich ein Stück Rasen für dein Requiem.

VII

Thou wast not born for death, immortal Bird!
No hungry generations tread thee down;
The voice I hear this passing night was heard
In ancient days by emperor and clown:
Perhaps the self-same song that found a path
Through the sad heart of Ruth, when, sick for home,
She stood in tears amid the alien corn;
The same that oft-times hath
Charmed magic casements, opening on the foam
Of perilous seas, in faery lands forlorn.

VIII

Forlorn! the very word is like a bell
To toll me back from thee to my sole self!
Adieu! the fancy cannot cheat so well
As she is famed to do, deceiving elf.
Adieu! adieu! thy plaintive anthem fades
Past the near meadows, over the still stream,
Up the hill-side; and now 'tis buried deep
In the next valley-glades:
Was it a vision, or a waking dream?
Fled is that music – Do I wake or sleep?

Ode on Melancholy

I

No, no, go not to Lethe, neither twist
Wolf's-bane, tight-rooted, for its poisonous wine:
Nor suffer thy pale forehead to be kissed
By nightshade, ruby grape of Proserpine;

VII

Du stirbst nicht, Vogel, du lebst ewiglich!
Nein, dich zertritt kein hungriges Geschlecht;
Wie ich dich heute nacht, so hörten dich
In alten Tagen Kaiser schon und Knecht:
Vielleicht das gleiche Lied, das unverhofft
Ruth durch ihr Herz fuhr, als sie, ohne Trost,
Vor Heimweh, in dem fremden Kornfeld stand;
Das gleiche, das so oft
Magie in Zauberfenster trug, umtost
Vom Sturmmeer, im verlornen Märchenland.

VIII

Verlorn! – das Wort schon ruft wie Glockenklang
Zurück von dir mein einsam Ich mir jäh!
Adieu! – die Phantasie täuscht nicht so lang
Wie man ihr nachrühmt, trügerische Fee.
Adieu! adieu! – dein Klagelied verklingt
Jenseits nahn Wiesen, überm stillen Bach,
Hangaufwärts; und ins nächste Tal gräbt's sich
Tief ein jetzt und versinkt:
War es Vision? Ein Traum und ich doch wach?
Fort die Musik – Wach oder schlafe ich?

Ode auf die Melancholie

I

Nein, nein, geh nicht zur Lethe, preß dir nicht
Vom Eisenhut, zähwurzlig, Gift ins Glas –
Wenn Nachtschatten dein bläßliches Gesicht
Auch küßt, die Purpurfrucht Proserpinas;

Make not your rosary of yew-berries,
  Nor let the beetle, nor the death-moth be
    Your mournful Psyche, nor the downy owl
A partner in your sorrow's mysteries;
  For shade to shade will come too drowsily,
    And drown the wakeful anguish of the soul.

II

But when the melancholy fit shall fall
  Sudden from heaven like a weeping cloud,
That fosters the droop-headed flowers all,
  And hides the green hill in an April shroud;
Then glut thy sorrow on a morning rose,
  Or on the rainbow of the salt sand-wave,
    Or on the wealth of globèd peonies;
Or if thy mistress some rich anger shows,
  Emprison her soft hand, and let her rave,
    And feed deep, deep upon her peerless eyes.

III

She dwells with Beauty – Beauty that must die;
  And Joy, whose hand is ever at his lips
Bidding adieu; and aching Pleasure nigh,
  Turning to poison while the bee-mouth sips:
Ay, in the very temple of Delight
  Veiled Melancholy has her sovran shrine,
    Though seen of none save him whose strenuous tongue
  Can burst Joy's grape against his palate fine;
His soul shall taste the sadness of her might,
    And be among her cloudy trophies hung.

Flicht keine Eibenbeern zum Rosenkranz,
  Auch Totenuhr und Totenkopf laß sein
    Als Klagepsyche, und als Freund im Leid
Trau der zerzausten Eule niemals ganz:
  Der Schattenzug stellt sich zu schleppend ein
    Und schluckt der Seele wache Ängstlichkeit.

II

Doch wenn Melancholie vom Himmel fährt
  Wie eine Wolke plötzlich tränen will,
Die alle schlaffen Blütenkelche nährt
  Und Hügel hüllt ins Grabtuch des April –
Dann schöpf von Morgenrosen neuen Mut,
  Von Regenbogen, Dünen, Salz und Sand
    Und reichem, kugligem Päonienflor;
Und zeigt die Herrin köstlich ihre Wut,
  Laß sie nur rasen, fang die zarte Hand
    Und dring tief, tief in diese Augen vor.

III

Sie lebt mit Schönheit – Schönheit, die bald stirbt;
  Mit Freude, deren Kußhand ewig winkt
Und sagt Adieu – und Wonnen nah verdirbt,
  Schon Gift wird, da der Bienenmund noch trinkt.
Ja, selbst im Tempel höchsten Glücks versteckt
  Melancholie noch ihren Hochaltar,
    Nimmt, wessen Zunge des Glücks Traube sprengt
  Am feinen Gaumen, ihn auch einzig wahr;
Sein Geist wird, ihre Trauermacht geschmeckt,
    Zu ihren düsteren Trophäen gehängt.

Ode on Indolence

They toil not, neither do they spin

I

One morn before me were three figures seen,
  With bowèd necks, and joinèd hands, side-faced;
And one behind the other stepped serene,
  In placid sandals, and in white robes graced;
They passed, like figures on a marble urn,
  When shifted round to see the other side;
    They came again; as when the urn once more
Is shifted round, the first seen shades return;
  And they were strange to me, as may betide
    With vases, to one deep in Phidian lore.

II

How is it, Shadows! that I knew ye not?
  How came ye muffled in so hush a masque?
Was it a silent deep-disguisèd plot
  To steal away, and leave without a task
My idle days? Ripe was the drowsy hour;
  The blissful cloud of summer-indolence
    Benumbed my eyes; my pulse grew less and less;
Pain had no sting, and pleasure's wreath no flower:
  O, why did ye not melt, and leave my sense
    Unhaunted quite of all but – nothingness?

III

A third time passed they by, and, passing, turned
  Each one the face a moment whiles to me;
Then faded, and to follow them I burned
  And ached for wings because I knew the three;

Ode auf die Lässigkeit

Sie arbeiten nicht, auch spinnen sie nicht

I

Drei Wesen konnt ich eines Morgens sehn,
Gebeugt, halb abgekehrt und Hand in Hand,
Und heiter nach und nach vorübergehn,
In leichten Schuhn und weißem Schmuckgewand;
Sie schwanden, wie Figurn im Marmorglanz
Auf Urnen, die man vor den Augen dreht;
Sie kamen neu – als sei das Drehn vollführt
Und zeige die Gestalten wieder ganz;
Und fremd warn sie mir, wie's wohl dem ergeht
Mit Vasen, der an Phidias' Künsten rührt.

II

Was hab ich, Schatten! euch nur nicht erkannt?
Was kamt ihr so maskiert und stumm verhüllt?
Habt ihr im stillen tief-verkappt geplant,
Ihr stehlt euch fort, daß meinen Tag nichts füllt
Als Trägheit? Reif war diese Stunde Schlaf;
Vor selger Sommerlässigkeit mein Blick
Ganz starr; mein Puls verflachte mehr und mehr;
Kein Schmerz, der stach, kein Glück, das Blumen warf:
O, warum wicht ihr nicht, ließt mich zurück
Und meinen Sinn, erfüllt von Nichts nur – leer?

III

Ein drittes Mal noch zogen sie vorbei
Und wandten sich mir zu in dem Moment;
Da brannte ich auf Flügel, diesen drei
Zu folgen, denn sie waren mir nicht fremd:

The first was a fair Maid, and Love her name;
  The second was Ambition, pale of cheek,
    And ever watchful with fatiguèd eye;
The last, whom I love more, the more of blame
  Is heaped upon her, maiden most unmeek –
    I knew to be my demon Poesy.

IV

They faded, and, forsooth! I wanted wings.
  O folly! What is love! and where is it?
And, for that poor Ambition – it springs
  From a man's little heart's short fever-fit.
For Poesy! – no, she has not a joy –
  At least for me – so sweet as drowsy noons,
    And evenings steeped in honeyed indolence.
O, for an age so sheltered from annoy,
  That I may never know how change the moons,
    Or hear the voice of busy common-sense!

V

A third time came they by – alas! wherefore?
  My sleep had been embroidered with dim dreams;
My soul had been a lawn besprinkled o'er
  With flowers, and stirring shades, and baffled beams:
The morn was clouded, but no shower fell,
  Though in her lids hung the sweet tears of May;
    The open casement pressed a new-leaved vine,
  Let in the budding warmth and throstle's lay;
O Shadows! 'twas a time to bid farewell!
    Upon your skirts had fallen no tears of mine.

Erst kam das hübsche Kind, das Liebe heißt;
  Dann kam der Ehrgeiz, blaß und abgezehrt
    Und müden Augs, doch schlafend nie;
Zuletzt, mir mehr lieb, je mehr Schmach ihr Geist
  Erträgt, Elfe am ehesten entehrt –
    Sah ich meine Dämonin Poesie.

IV

Sie schwanden – wahrlich! Flügel wollte ich.
  O Torheit! Liebe – was ist sie! und wo?
Und Ehrgeiz – dieser kurze Fieberstich,
  Der eines Menschen kleinem Herz entfloh.
Dann Poesie! – nein, nichts, das sie besitzt –
  Für mich niemals – vom Schlaf im Mittagslicht,
    Vom Abend, süß durchtränkt mit Lässigkeit.
O, eine Zeit, vor Plagen so geschützt –
  Ich wüßte, wie die Monde wechseln, nicht
    Und wäre taub für rege Nüchternheit!

V

Ein drittes Mal kamen sie – ach! warum?
  Mit trüben Träumen war mein Schlaf bestickt;
Der Rasen meiner Seele war rundum
  Mit Blumen, Licht und Schattenspiel geschmückt;
Bewölkt der Morgen, doch nicht regennaß,
  Nur seine Augen tränten süß vom Mai;
    Durchs Fenster, in das knospend Wein sich brach,
  Kam warmer Duft und Drossels Lied herbei –
O Schatten! Zeit, Lebwohl zu sagen, war's!
    Nicht eine Träne weinte ich euch nach.

VI

So, ye three Ghosts, adieu! Ye cannot raise
  My head cool-bedded in the flowery grass;
For I would not be dieted with praise,
  A pet-lamb in a sentimental farce!
Fade softly from my eyes, and be once more
  In masque-like figures on the dreamy urn.
    Farewell! I yet have visions for the night,
And for the day faint visions there is store.
    Vanish, ye Phantoms! from my idle sprite,
  Into the clouds, and never more return!

To Autumn

I

Season of mists and mellow fruitfulness,
  Close bosom-friend of the maturing sun,
Conspiring with him how to load and bless
  With fruit the vines that round the thatch-eves run;
To bend with apples the mossed cottage-trees,
  And fill all fruit with ripeness to the core;
    To swell the gourd, and plump the hazel shells
  With a sweet kernel; to set budding more,
And still more, later flowers for the bees,
Until they think warm days will never cease,
    For Summer has o'er-brimmed their clammy cells.

VI

Darum adieu, ihr Geister! Für euch fährt
  Mein Haupt nicht auf vom kühlen Bett im Gras;
Denn ich will nicht, daß man mit Lob mich nährt,
  Ein Schoßlamm in einer gefühlvollen Farce!
Weicht meinem Blick und setzt ein weitres Mal
  Das Maskenspiel auf diesem Traumkrug fort.
    Lebt wohl! Visionen nachts hab ich schon meist
Und zarte für den Tag in großer Zahl.
    Verlaßt, Phantome! meinen trägen Geist,
  Fort in die Wolken, und bleibt ewig dort!

An den Herbst

I

Neblige Zeit, die weiche Früchte häuft,
  Busenfreundin reifenden Sonnenscheins
Im Plan, die Rebe, die ums Strohdach läuft,
  Zu segnen mit der Traubenfracht des Weins;
Mit schweren Äpfeln, noch am Kern voll Saft,
  Bemooste Landhausbäume zu bemühn;
    Den Kürbis prall, die Haselnuß gesüßt
  Vorm Fall zu runden; Knospen aufzublühn,
Was Bienen mehr und noch mehr Blumen schafft,
Bis jede glaubt, nie ende diese Kraft,
    Weil Sommer ihre Waben überfließt.

II

Who hath not seen thee oft amid thy store?
  Sometimes whoever seeks abroad may find
Thee sitting careless on a granary floor,
  Thy hair soft-lifted by the winnowing wind;
Or on a half-reaped furrow sound asleep,
  Drowsed with the fume of poppies, while thy hook
    Spares the next swath and all its twinèd flowers;
And sometimes like a gleaner thou dost keep
  Steady thy laden head across a brook;
  Or by a cider-press, with patient look,
    Thou watchest the last oozings hours by hours.

III

Where are the songs of Spring? Ay, where are they?
  Think not of them, thou hast thy music too –
While barrèd clouds bloom the soft-dying day,
  And touch the stubble-plains with rosy hue:
Then in a wailful choir the small gnats mourn
  Among the river sallows, borne aloft
    Or sinking as the light wind lives or dies;
And full-grown lambs loud bleat from hilly bourn;
  Hedge-crickets sing; and now with treble soft
  The red-breast whistles from a garden-croft;
    And gathering swallows twitter in the skies.

II

Wer sah dich nicht schon oft in deinem Schatz?
  Man findet dich, wenn man ins Freie geht,
Nimmst du am Speicherboden sorglos Platz,
  Dein Haar vom Worfelwind weich aufgeweht;
Oder, wenn du in halbgemähter Bahn,
  Betäubt vom Mohnstaub, fest geschlafen hast
    Und deine Sichel Korn und Blumen schont;
Und Ährenlesern gleich trägt ab und an
  Dein Kopf ruhig über Bäche seine Last;
  Und preßt man Apfelmost, bist du der Gast,
    Den letztes Rieseln stundenlang belohnt.

III

Wo sind die Frühlingslieder? Ja, wohin?
  Denk nicht an sie, Musik besitzt auch du –
Da welken Tagen Streifenwolken blühn
  Und deckt ein Rot-Ton Stoppelfelder zu:
Dann jammern Mücken ihren Wehgesang
  In Uferweiden, steigen, um sogleich
    Zu sinken, stirbt, lebt auf der leichte Wind;
Und Lämmer blöken laut vom Bach am Hang;
  Busch-Heimchen singen; und nun zittert weich
  Der Pfiff des Rotkehlchens im Gartenreich,
    Da zwitschernd Schwalben in den Lüften sind.

To Fanny

I

Physician Nature! let my spirit blood!
  O ease my heart of verse and let me rest;
Throw me upon thy tripod till the flood
  Of stifling numbers ebbs from my full breast.
A theme! a theme! Great Nature! give a theme;
    Let me begin my dream.
I come – I see thee, as thou standest there,
Beckon me out into the wintry air.

II

Ah! dearest love, sweet home of all my fears,
  And hopes, and joys, and panting miseries,
Tonight, if I may guess, thy beauty wears
    A smile of such delight,
    As brilliant and as bright,
  As when with ravished, aching, vassal eyes,
    Lost in a soft amaze,
    I gaze, I gaze!

III

Who now, with greedy looks, eats up my feast?
  What stare outfaces now my silver moon!
Ah! keep that hand unravished at the least;
    Let, let, the amorous burn –
    But, prithee, do not turn
  The current of your heart from me so soon.
    O save, in charity,
    The quickest pulse for me!

An Fanny

I

Heilendes Wesen! nimm dem Geist sein Blut!
O ruhn mein Herz laß, das an Versen schleppt;
Wirf mich auf deinen Dreifuß, bis die Flut
Von Würgejamben mir vom Brustkorb ebbt.
Ein Thema! Wesen! gib ein Thema ein –
Laß mich ein Träumer sein.
Ich komme – sehe dich, die nach mir ruft,
Dir nachzufolgen in die Winterluft.

II

Ah! Liebste, Heimat meiner Ängstlichkeit,
Von Hoffnung, atemloser Pein und Glück –
Heut abend trägt dein Liebreiz wohl als Kleid
Ein Lächeln derart froh,
Glänzend und leuchtend so,
Als hätt mein knechtisch scheu geschundner Blick,
Der leicht erstaunt verharrt,
Gestarrt, gestarrt!

III

Wer giert, mit Blicken, nun nach meinem Fest?
Wer starrt dich nun verlegen, Silbermond!
Ah! laß zumindest diese Hand als Rest;
Laß, laß, das Brandmal sticht –
Doch, bitte, wend noch nicht
Den Herzstrom ab von mir, den ich gewohnt.
Bewahre, fürsorglich,
Den schnellsten Puls für mich!

IV

Save it for me, sweet love! though music breathe
  Voluptuous visions into the warm air,
Though swimming through the dance's dangerous wreath,]
    Be like an April day,
    Smiling and cold and gay,
  A temperate lily, temperate as fair;
    Then, Heaven! there will be
    A warmer June for me.

V

Why, this – you'll say, my Fanny! – is not true:
  Put your soft hand upon your snowy side,
Where the heart beats; confess – 'tis nothing new –
    Must not a woman be
    A feather on the sea,
  Swayed to and fro by every wind and tide?
    Of as uncertain speed
    As blow-ball from the mead?

VI

I know it – and to know it is despair
  To one who loves you as I love, sweet Fanny!
Whose heart goes fluttering for you everywhere,
    Nor, when away you roam,
    Dare keep its wretched home.
  Love, Love alone, has pains severe and many:
    Then, loveliest! keep me free
    From torturing jealousy.

IV

Bewahr ihn, Liebes! und weht auch ein Lied
Berauschend Bilder in die warme Luft,
Lockt Tanz, in dem man schwindelnd Kreise zieht,
Sei doch apriltaggleich,
Lächelnd und kühl und reich,
Lilie in Maßen, maßvoll wie voll Duft;
Dann, Himmel! spürte ich
Wärmren Juni um mich.

V

Weshalb ich irr, sagst – meine Fanny! – du:
Leg deine Hand auf deinen Leib wie Schnee,
Sanft wo das Herz schlägt; neu ist's nicht – gib zu,
Gleicht eine Frau nicht sehr
Der Feder auf dem Meer,
Wird hin und her gespült von Wind und See?
Eilt ungewiß im Raum
Wie Pusteblumenflaum?

VI

Ich weiß – und weiß er es, verzweifelt der,
Der dich liebt, süße Fanny, wie ich liebe!
Stets schlägt sein Herz dir flatternd hinterher
Und bleibt doch, schweifst du fort,
An seinem dumpfen Ort.
Es schmerzt schon stark und oft genug die Liebe –
Erspar mir, Lieb! zumal
Der Eifersüchte Qual.

VII

Ah! if you prize my subdued soul above
  The poor, the fading, brief, pride of an hour,
Let none profane my Holy See of Love,
    Or with a rude hand break
    The sacramental cake;
  Let none else touch the just new-budded flower;
    If not – may my eyes close,
    Love! on their last repose.

VII

Ah! soll mein Seelensiechen teurer sein
  Als Stolz, der hingeht, kümmerlich, kaum währt,
Laß nichts der Heilgen Liebe Stuhl entweihn
    Noch eine Hand brutal
    Das süße Abendmahl;
  Laß die erst blühende Knospe unversehrt;
    Sonst – geh mein Auge zu,
    Liebes! zur letzten Ruh.

Verserzählungen

Schlaf und Dichtung

Als ich im Bette lag, da wollt der Schlaf
Mir nicht gefallen, doch warum ich nicht
Schlief, wußt ich nicht: war keinem irdschen Wicht
(Wie es mich dünkt) doch leichter noch ums Herz
Denn mir, der ich spürt weder Leid noch Schmerz.
Chaucer

Was ist noch sanfter als ein Wind im Sommer?
Was stimmt noch milder als der hübsche Brummer,
Der kurz in einer offnen Blume weilt
Und froh von Laube fort zu Laube eilt?
Was blüht wie eine Moschusrose leis
Auf einer Insel, von der kein Mensch weiß?
Was ist noch heilsamer als Laub im Tal?
Geheimer als das Nest der Nachtigall?
Noch heitrer als Cordelias Gesicht?
Visionenreicher als ein Mär-Gedicht?
Was, Schlaf, als du? der sanfte Lidersenker!
Der Murmler, zarte Wiegenliederdenker!
Der leicht um unsre selgen Kissen schwebt!
Der Mohn- und Trauerweidenkränze webt!
Verschwiegner Haarverwirrer einer Schönen!
Glücklichster Lauscher! auf des Morgens Tönen,
Des Auge du belebt hast, das beglückt
So hell zum neuen Sonnenaufgang blickt.

Was ist undenkbar höher noch jedoch?
Frischer als Beeren eines Bergbaums noch?
Seltsamer, schöner, glatter, fürstlich edler
Als Schwanenschwingen, Tauben, ferne Adler?
Was ist es? Womit soll ich es vergleichen?
Es strahlt vor Ruhm, und nichts kann es erreichen:
Gedanken an es, heilig, süß, voll Klarheit,
Vertreiben alle Weltlichkeit und Narrheit;

Es kommt beizeiten her wie Donnergrollen,
Dann wie ein unterirdisch leises Rollen;
Und manchmal wie Geflüster rings
Von dem Geheimnis eines Wunderdings,
Das uns in der doch leeren Luft umweht,
So daß man schaut und voller Neugier späht,
Um Formen, licht, aus Luft gemalt, zu sehn
Und flutend schwache Hymnen zu verstehn,
Sich zu dem Lorbeerkranz hoch droben wendet,
Der unsre Namen krönt, wenn's Leben endet.
Auch adelt es die Stimme, daß man singt
Und »Freut euch! Freuet euch!« dem Herz entspringt –
Klang, der den Bildner allen Stoffs erreicht
Und voller Inbrunst murmelnd so verstreicht.

Wer einmal die ruhmreiche Sonne sah
Und alle Wolken und im Busen da
Den Schöpfer spürte, der weiß ohne Mühn,
Was ich hier mein, und fühlt sein Wesen glühn –
Drum stell ich seinen Geist auch nicht in Frage,
Indem ich, was er selbstverdient sieht, sage.

O Poesie! für dich schreib ich dies hin,
Der ich noch kein ruhmreicher Bürger bin
In deinem Himmel. – Sollt ich lieber knien
Auf einem Berggipfel, bis ich ein Glühn
Und Glänzen schweben spüre überall
Und deine eigne Stimme widerhall?
O Poesie! für dich geb ich mich hin,
Der ich noch kein ruhmreicher Bürger bin
In deinem Himmel; doch mir heißem Beter
Gib deines Heiligtumes klaren Äther,
Zur Trunkenheit besänftigt durch den Kuß
Erblühten Lorbeers, daß mein Tod Genuß
Am Tod sei und mein junger Geist mit Wonne,
Dem frischen Opfer gleich, der Morgensonne

Zu Apollon folg; und ertrag ich hier
Das übermannend Süße, bringt sie mir
Visionen allen Orts: ein Fleck nicht weit
Wird zum Elysium – Buch für alle Zeit,
Um manch lieblichen Spruch draus abzuschreiben
Von Blättern und von Blumen, von dem Treiben
Der Wald- und Quellnymphen, dem Schattenzelt,
Das um ein schlafend Mädchen Schweigen hält,
Und Verse, deren Einfluß seltsam wär,
Daß man stets neu sich fragt, wie und woher
Er kam. Auch werden Phantasien umschweben
Meinen Kamin und mir die Sicht beleben
Auf festlich schöne Weiten, wo ich wander
In heiterm Schweigen, klar wie der Mäander
Durchs stille Tal; und fand ich eine Stelle
Erhabnern Schattens, ob verwunschne Höhle,
Ob Hügel, zugedeckt vom bunten Kleid
Des Flors und bang ob solcher Lieblichkeit,
Schreib ich auf Tafeln alles, was erlaubt ist,
Was von des Menschen Sinnen noch geglaubt ist.
Dann griff' ich, was weltweit Geschehen heißt,
Stark wie ein Riese, reizte meinen Geist,
Bis seine Schultern stolz die Flügel spürten,
Die ihn in die Unsterblichkeit entführten.

Halt und denk nach! ein Tag ist's Leben nur;
Ein Tropfen Tau, der aus dem Wipfel fuhr
In die Gefahr; ein Schlummer im Kanu,
In dem auf Montmorencis Sturzwand zu
Arm ein Indianer treibt. Was sich so mühn?
Das Leben hofft wie Rosen bald zu blühn;
Ist's Lesen einer Mär, stets wechselnd reich;
Dem Lüften eines Mädchenschleiers gleich;
Die Taube, die durch Sommerbrisen jagt;
Der heitre Junge, den nichts sorgt und plagt,
Der lachend Ulmenäste reiten kann.

O nur zehn Jahre, und ich übermann
Mich selbst in Poesie; käm so dem nach,
Was meine eigne Seele sich versprach.
Dann werd ich all die Länder, die ich so
Lang schauend seh, durchquern und immer froh
Quellwasser schmecken. Floras Reich durchquer
Ich erst, und Pans: schlaf dort im Gras, ernähr
Von Erdbeern und von roten Äpfeln mich,
Und was erfreut mein Geist sieht, wähle ich;
Im kühlen Schatten blasse Nymphen fangen,
Um Küsse scheuer Lippen zu verlangen;
Mit Fingern spielen, weiße Schultern küssen,
Die's köstlich überläuft von meinen Bissen,
So fest wie Lippen beißen, bis, versöhnt,
Uns eine lebensbunte Mär verwöhnt.
Und einer zahmen Taube lehrt ein Kind,
Um meinen Schlaf zu fächeln kühlen Wind;
Und eins, zum flinken Fuß herabgeschraubt,
Läßt grüne Tücher fluten um sein Haupt,
Tanzt fort in stetig wechselnder Gestalt
Und lächelt auf die Blumen und den Wald.
Ein andres lockt mich fort, weit fort bestimmt
Durch Mandelblüten und duftreichen Zimt –
Bis wir in einem laubig tiefen Reich
Verschwiegen ruhn, zwei Perlenkugeln gleich,
Die Mulden einer Muschel eng umfassen.

Und kann ich diese Wonnen je verlassen?
Ja, für ein höhres Leben laß ich sie,
Wo ich den Kampf find und die Agonie
Menschlicher Herzen – schau! denn einen Wagen
Seh ich die blaue Schroffheit überjagen,
Den mähnenflatternd Rosse ziehn – mit Grausen
Sieht der erhabne Lenker Winde brausen,
Und leicht bebt eine Unzahl Trappelschläge
Nun einen Wolkenkamm entlang; und rege,

So rollt das Rad hinab in frischres Wehn,
Vom Sonnenaug ringsum mit Glanz versehn.
In weiten Wirbeln gleiten sie einher;
Auf grünem Berghang seh ich sie nunmehr
Unter geneigten Stengeln schnaubend ruhn.
Seltsame Zeichen gibt der Lenker nun
Wald und Gebirg; da tauchen bald darauf
Figurn voll Glück, Furcht und Geheimnis auf
Und ziehn dahin vor einem düstren Ort
Aus mächtgen Eichen – folgend scheinbar dort
Stets flüchtiger Musik, so hasten sie.
Sie murmeln, lächeln, weinen, schau nur wie! –
Der strengen Munds und hoch erhobner Hand,
Der das Gesicht bis zu den Ohrn verbannt
In seine Arme; der, ganz Kindlichkeit,
Geht froh und lächelnd durch die Dunkelheit;
Der schaut zurück, da der nach oben starrt –
Ja, tausende in tausenderlei Art
Huschen dahin – nun eine Mädchenschar,
Die wirr- und lockigtanzt ihr glattes Haar,
Nun breite Schwingen. Ehrfürchtigst gespannt
Neigt sich der Rosselenker wie gebannt
Und scheint zu lauschen: O könnt ich nur wissen,
Was er dort schreibt so fieberhaft beflissen.

Fort die Vision – der Wagen in die Helle
Des Himmelslichts fort, und an ihre Stelle
Tritt doppelt stark ein Sinn für Wirklichkeit
Und will die Seele, wie ein Schlammfluß, weit
Ins Nichts führn – aber alle Zweifel hier
Will ich bekämpfen, will lebendig mir
Den Lenker halten und wie sonderbar
Er fuhr.
Ist heut so wenig Raum denn da
Unter den Menschen, daß nicht mehr befreit
Die Phantasie dahinfliegt wie zur Zeit

Der Alten noch? Sich ihre Rosse zäumt,
Dem Licht entgegenscharrt und wie erträumt
Gewölk besucht? Was zeigte sie uns nicht?
Vom klaren Ätherraum zum Hauch, noch schlicht,
Des frisch geknospten Laubs? Bedeutsam schienen
Nicht Jovis breite Brauen noch das Grünen
Der Wiesen im April? Hier schien ihr Schrein,
Auf dieser Insel; was könnt ähnlich sein
Dem heißen Chor, der ein Geräusch anhob
Voll Wohlklang, daß er erst erwog darob,
Wie mächtig er war an geballtem Klang,
Groß wie ein Stern, den er zum Kreisen zwang,
Zum ewigen Umkreisen blinder Leeren?
Ja, damals warn die Musen aller Ehren
Fast satt, galt ihre Sorge keinen Dingen,
Als sanft ihr Haar zu glätten und zu singen.

Vergessen ist all dies? Ja, eine Spaltung,
Genährt durch Barbarei und Geckenhaltung,
Ließ Apollon sich schämen für dies Land.
Als weise galt ein Mann, der nichts verstand
Von seinem Glanz: mit kraftlosem Geplärr
Schwang man auf einem Schaukelpferd umher
Und hielt's für Pegasus. Ah, trübes Bild!
Der Wind des Himmels blies, die See hob wild
Die Wellen an – ihr fühltet's nicht. Das Blau
Entblößte seine ewge Brust, und Tau
Zusammensuchte noch die Sommernacht
Zur Zier des Morgens: Schönheit war erwacht!
Weshalb wart ihr nicht wach? Doch ihr wart tot
Für das euch Unbekannte – fein im Lot
Mit dem Gesetzstaub jämmerlicher Regeln
Und schnöder Rahmen, brachtet so dann Flegeln
Und Tölpeln Hobeln, Sägen, Stutzen bei,
Bis, wie die Stäbe Jakobs fehlerfrei,
Ihr Reimen paßte. Leicht ward es erfüllt:
Denn tausend Burschen werkten unterm Schild

Der Poesie. Unselge, dreiste Bande!
Dem hellen Leierspieler eine Schande
Und wußten es nicht! Nein, sie gingen um,
Schwenkten ein altes Bannerstück herum,
Versehn mit seichtsten Sprüchen und doch nur
Dem Namen Boileau!
O ihr, der'n Schwur
Dem Flug um unsre weichen Hügel gilt!
Der'n aufgehäufte Hoheit mich erfüllt
Mit grenzentbundner Ehrfurcht, daß mein Wort
Euch nur entweihte, an solch Lästerort,
Vor solchem Volk – erschreckte euch am Schluß
Ihr Schmähn? Erfreute euch der Themsefluß
Mit alten Klagen? Zogt ihr nie entlang
Am schönen Avon, mit betrübtem Klang,
Und weintet? Oder sagtet ihr dem Land
Schon ganz Adieu, wo nicht mehr Lorbeer stand?
Sagt, oder bliebt ihr und begrüßtet noch
Verlaßne Geister, die die Jugend doch
Versangen und stolz starben? So wird's sein.
Laßt mich vergessen diese Zeit der Pein:
Holder jetzt ist die Jahreszeit; ihr fandet
Reichere Segnungen für uns; ihr wandet
Frisch Kränze, denn man hörte süß Musik
An vielen Orten – eine davon stieg
Aus ihrem hellkristallnen Seeversteck
Durch einen Schwanenhals; aus einem Fleck,
Vom Dickicht eines linden Tals verhüllt,
Perlt ein Getriller – Klang umflutet wild
Die Erde: glücklich und vergnügt seid ihr.

Kein Zweifel – doch in Wahrheit hatten wir
Seltsame Donner an Gesangsgewalt;
Gebraut aus dem, was süß ist und geballt
An Hoheit – nur in Wahrheit warn die Themen
Häßliche Keulen, Dichter Polyphemen

Und störten bloß das Meer. Ein Sintflutregen
Aus Licht ist Dichtung; äußerstes Vermögen;
Ist Macht, halb schlummernd auf dem rechten Arm.
Der Bogen ihrer Lider schon schlägt warm
Eintausend Willige in ihren Bann,
Und stets mit mildstem Druck regiert sie dann;
Doch Kraft allein, auch die die Muse gab,
Gleicht dem gefallnen Engel: Bahrtuch, Grab,
Entrißne Bäume, Würmer, Finsternis
Erfreun sie; denn sie weidet sich am Riß,
Des Lebens Dornen; sie vergißt den Schluß
Der Poesie: daß sie ein Freund sein muß,
Der Sorgen lindert und den Geist belebt.

Doch jauchz ich: eine holdre Myrte hebt,
Als je in Paphos wuchs, aus bittrem Kraut
Das süße Haupt hoch in die Luft und baut
Aus immer frischem Grün ein stilles Reich.
Die zartsten Vögel bergen sich dort weich,
Flattern im Schatten munter mit den Schwingen,
Knabbern an vollgeschenktem Flor und singen.
So laßt uns Dornen, die im Wege stehen,
Rings von den Stengeln brechen; jungen Rehen,
Geborn zu einer Zeit, die ohne uns besteht,
Laßt satten Rasen wachsen, übersät
Mit schlichten Blumen: Rauhres sei dort nie
Als eines Liebenden gebeugtes Knie;
Nichts unsanfter als der, der ausgesöhnt
Auf ein geschloßnes Buch die Arme lehnt;
Nichts unruhiger als Gras den Hang besprießt
Zwischen zwei Hügeln. Hoffnung, sei gegrüßt!
Wie ehedem, so wird die Phantasie
In liebreizendste Labyrinthe ziehn,
Und die soll man zu Dichter-Fürsten wählen,
Die schlicht das Herzbeschwingendste erzählen.
O wär dies Glück, bevor ich sterbe, da.

Sagt dann nicht mancher bald, ich spräch fürwahr
Vermessen? besser sei, vor nahen Schrecken
Mein törichtes Gesicht gut zu verstecken?
Dies Kind fiel besser plärrend auf die Knie,
Eh es ein fürchterlicher Blitz trifft? Wie!
Versteck ich mich, so soll es ganz allein
Im Tempel selbst, dem Licht der Dichtung sein:
Stürz ich, wird man mich wenigstens bestatten
Im Schweigen unter einem Pappelschatten;
Und über mir wird glatter Rasen sein;
Und schmücken wird ihn ein Gedächtnisstein.
Doch fort, Verzagtheit! jämmerliche Pest!
Dich soll nicht sehn, wer, gierig auf das Fest
Des noblen Endes, jede Stunde giert.
Gut, meine Mitgift ist nicht reichverziert
Mit breitem Wissen; weiß ich nicht genug
Vom Wechsel mächtger Winde, der den Flug
Der menschlichen Gedanken hin und her
Wehn läßt; hilft auch kein großer Geist, um mehr
Vom finsteren Geheimnis zu verstehn
Um Menschenseelen – so sind doch Ideen
Weit vor mir ausgerollt und lese ich
Hier meine Freiheit; deutlich steht für mich
Dort Schluß und Ziel der Poesie. 's ist klar
Wie irgend Wahrstes; grad so wie das Jahr
Vier Jahreszeiten hat; fest wie mit Macht
Ein Kreuz, der alten Kathedrale Pracht,
In weiße Wolken ragt. Deshalb allein
Laßt mich der Ausbund von Entstelltheit sein,
Ein Feigling, zuckten meine Lider nur,
Wenn mir, was ich dreist dachte, auch entfuhr.
Ah! lieber laßt mich wahnsinnig vor Wonne
Auf einer Klippe rennen! laßt die Sonne
Mein Dädaluskleid schmelzen, mich auf Schwingen
Kopfüber taumeln! Nun! ein innres Ringen

Mahnt mich indes zu kühlerem Verstand.
Ein ödes Meer, besprenkelt mit manch' Strand,
Erstreckt sich riesig vor mir. Wieviel Plage!
Und Mühen voll Verzweiflung! wieviel Tage!
Eh seine Weite mir durchforscht erschien.
Ah, welch ein Unterfangen! auf den Knien
Es widerrufen, um – unmöglich! nein,
Unmöglich!
Ausruhnd, werd ich mich erfreun
An kleinern Dingen, und mein Sturm, so zart
Begonnen, legt sich auf gleich sanfte Art.
Da weicht der Lärm, der meine Brust bedrückt:
An die Gehilfen wend ich mich beglückt,
Die Ruhmespfade ebnen, Brüderschaft
Und Freundsein, Amme wechselseitger Kraft;
Der Herzensgriff, der ein Sonett versenkt
Ins Hirn, bevor man auch nur daran denkt;
Das Schweigen, wenn die Reime dann erschienen;
Und sind sie da, die hocherfreuten Mienen;
Die Nachricht, ganz gewiß erledigt morgen –
Genauso schön ist wohl, sich auszuborgen
Ein prächtig Buch aus einem Staubregal,
Um sich zu scharn darum beim nächsten Mal.
Mein Kritzeln stockt; denn Lüfte, lieblich warm,
Flattern durchs Zimmer wie ein Taubenschwarm,
Erneuern all das Glück, wie es mir heute
Mit zartem Fall die Sinne erstmals freute.
Und ihnen folgt ein eleganter Troß
Und krümmt die Schultern über einem Roß,
Sorglos und kühn – Finger, sanft und jung,
Die volle Locken teilen – und der Sprung
Des Bacchus aus dem Wagen, so voll Drang,
Daß er Ariadne zu erröten zwang.
So strömt in mir ein süßer Fluß herauf
Aus Worten, schlage ich Folianten auf.

Dinge wie diese sind stets erste Zeichen
Für Züge ruhiger Bilder: so das Streichen
Des Schwanenhalses, gut im Schilf versteckt;
Ein Hänfling, aus Gebüschen aufgeschreckt;
Ein Falter, breit geteilt die goldnen Schwingen,
Auf einer Rose, zuckend als durchgingen
Sie Wonneschauder – vieles, vieles mehr
Könnt ich gewähren lassen aus dem Heer
Der Hochgenüsse - doch vergäß ich ganz
Den Schlaf, schweigsam mit seinem Mohnlaubkranz,
Denn was dies Lied an Wert besitzen mag,
Dank ich auch ihm: so war der Glockenschlag
Freundlicher Stimmen einer süßen Stille
Eben gewichen, als ich all der Fülle
Des Tags auf einem Lager nochmals dachte.
Im Haus des Dichters, der den Schlüssel brachte
Zum Freudentempel, war ich. Um mich reihten
Sich Bilder großer Barden, die vor Zeiten
Gesungen hatten – kalter, heilger Stein,
Lächelten sie sich an. Wie froh muß sein,
Wer für den Liebling Ruhm die Zukunft sieht!
Dann waren Faune, Satyrn dort, bemüht,
Äpfel zu fischen mit hüpfendem Lauf
Und langen Fingern, tief im satten Hauf
Des Weinlaubs. Einen Tempel sah ich da,
Ganz Marmorstein, und zu ihm eine Schar
Von Nymphen lieblich auf dem Rasen gehn:
Die eine, schönste, bleibt geblendet stehn
Vom Morgenrot; zwei Schwestern hielten an
Und beugten sich herab, bis sie sich dann
Über dem Trippeln eines Kleinkinds trafen;
Noch andre lauschen, aufmerksam, dem scharfen
Getriller tauig sanfter Pfeiftiraden.
Sieh hier, ein andres Bild noch: Nymphen baden
Besorgt Dianas furchtsam scheue Glieder –
Ein Falz des Grasmantels schwappt auf und nieder

Am Rand des Bads und wiegt sanft hin und her
Das sinkende Kristall, ganz wie das Meer
Ruhig die geschwollne Glätte hebt entlang
Des Steilhangs und erneut geduldgen Tang
Aufnimmt, der jetzt, nicht mehr von Schaum beschmiert,
Sein welliges Zuhause gänzlich spürt.

Halb lächelten dort Sapphos edle Züge
Ein Nichts an; ganz, als ob die ernsten Kriege
Des Überdenkens von der Stirn nunmehr
Verschwunden und sie ganz alleine wär.

Alfreds des Großen gleichfalls, fast in Tränen,
Als hörte er nur immerfort das Stöhnen
Der geschundnen Welt, und Kosciuszkos erblaßt
Durch Schreckensgreuel – elend, ohne Rast.

Petrarca, tretend aus dem Schattengrün,
Erschrickt beim Anblick Lauras – doch hält ihn
Ihr süßes Antlitz fest. Glück, das hier waltet!
Denn über ihnen sah man frei entfaltet
Ein Flügelpaar und zwischen ihm auch schon
Das Haupt der Poesie: von ihrem Thron
Erblickte sie, was ich kaum sagen kann.
Schon die Erkenntnis, wo ich war, hielt dann
Den Schlaf fern – überdies nun aber kamen
Gedanken um Gedanken zu den Flammen
In meiner Brust, so daß des Morgens Pracht
Mich überraschte trotz durchwachter Nacht.
Und munter, frisch und froh erhob ich mich,
Entschlossen, heute noch beginne ich
Die Zeilen hier; und wie auch sei ihr Ton,
Ich laß sie wie ein Vater seinen Sohn.

Endymion

Eine poetische Romanze

Gespreiztes Metrum eines alten Lieds

Gewidmet dem Andenken
Thomas Chattertons

Buch I

Ein Ding von Schönheit ist ein Glück für immer:
Es nimmt noch zu an Liebreiz; es wird nimmer
Ins Nichts vergehn, doch hält's uns alle Zeit
Ein ruhiges Plätzchen süßen Schlafs bereit,
Voll Träumen und gesundem, ruhigem Atem.
Drum winden, jeden Morgen, wir aus Zartem
Ein Blumenband, das bindet an die Erde,
Trotz der Verzweiflung, unmenschlicher Bürde
Für edle Wesen, trotz der düstren Tage,
Der ganzen dunklen Wege voller Plage,
Die uns versuchen – ja, trotz allem Fluch,
Ist etwas schön, nimmt es das Leichentuch
Von unserm dunkeln Geist. So Mond und Sonne,
So Bäume, jung und alt, die Schattenwonne
Argloser Schafe; so die grüne Welt,
In der Narzissen leben, und das Zelt,
Das sich der Quell selbst baut und das ihn kalt
Bei Hitze hält; das Dickicht tief im Wald,
Prachtvoll besprenkelt von der Moschusrose,
Und ebenso die Herrlichkeit der Lose,
Die für die großen Toten wir begehrten;
Die Sagen, die wir lasen oder hörten –
Ein ewger Born, der endlos sich ergießt
Und uns vom Himmelsrand herab durchfließt.

Auch spüren wir dieser Essenzen Wirken
Nicht bloß für kurze Zeit; nein, wie die Birken,
Umwispernd einen Tempel, uns bald teuer
Wie jener Tempel selbst sind, folgen Feuer
Der Dichtung, Mond und Glorie ohne Grenzen
Uns nach, bis sie in unsern Seelen glänzen,
Voll Trost sind und so fest mit uns vereint,
Daß, ob es trüb ist, ob die Sonne scheint,
Wir sterben, bleiben sie nicht ewiglich.

Ein wahres Glück ist deshalb auch, daß ich
Endymions Geschichte schreiben kann.
Der Klang des Namens schon ging irgendwann
Ein in mein Wesen, und die Bilder blühn
Und wachsen frisch vor mir ganz wie das Grün
Unserer Täler – so beginn ich ungestört,
Jetzt, da man nicht der Stadt Getöse hört,
Jetzt, da die frühen Knospen grad neu sprießen
Und wild im jüngsten Farbton sich ergießen
Auf alten Wald; da köstlich Bernstein quillt
Aus Weiden und man Kannen reich gefüllt
Mit Milch nach Haus bringt. Und wenn's Jahr dann sich
In saftgen Halmen sattmacht, lenke ich
Mein kleines Boot, so manche stille Stunde,
Auf Flüsse über schattig-klarem Grunde.
Ich hoffe, daß ich manch, manch Verse fand,
Bevor das Tausendschön, weiß-rot am Rand,
Ins tiefe Gras taucht; und daß, eh die Bienen
An Erbsen und am Kleeball sich bedienen,
Ich die Geschichte nah der Mitte weiß.
O daß kein Winter, nackt und grau vor Eis,
Sie halb beendet seh; Herbst aber sollt,
In jeder Tönung sein gedämpftes Gold,
Wenn ich zum Ende komme, sein um mich.
Und nun sogleich, verwegen, schicke ich

Mein Herolddenken in ein ödes Tal –
Dort blas' sein Horn, deck' Grün mit einem Mal
Den ungewissen Pfad, damit ich dann,
Durch Flor und Kraut, leicht weitereilen kann.

Des Berges Latmos Felshänge umschloß
Ein mächtger Wald; aus feuchter Erde floß
Durch grasversteckte Wurzeln reichlich Saft
In schöne Früchte und Geäst voll Kraft.
Und es gab Schatten, abgeschieden tief,
Wo kein Mensch ging; und wenn ein Lamm entlief,
Weit in jene so engen Schluchten nieder,
Sah es die heitern Hürden nie mehr wieder,
In die die Brüder, blökend voller Dank,
Vom Hügel kamen, wenn die Sonne sank.
Schon immer aber glaubte hier ein Hirte,
Daß doch ein Lamm, das derart sich verirrte
Von seiner Herde, nie behelligt ward
Durch Wut und Gier von Wolf und Leopard,
Bis es auf unbetretne Ebnen hin
Und zu Pans Herden kam – ja, welch Gewinn,
Entfloh ein Lamm so. Pfade gab's dort viele,
Durch Fächerfarn, verschlammte Schilfrohrstiele
Und Efeubänke; alle liefen fein
In Wiesen aus, von wo aus man allein
Massige Stämme rings sich drängen sah
Um Gras und Unterholz – wem konnte da
Der klare Himmel nicht den Atem rauben,
Umrahmt von dunklen Wipfeln? wo oft Tauben
Die Flügel flattern ließen und nicht selten
Auch kleine Wolken durch die Bläue schnellten.

Inmitten diesem ganzen heitren Glanz
Stand marmorn ein Altar mit einem Kranz
Aus Blütenreisern; und im Reif der Nacht
Warn märchenhafte Phantasien erwacht,

Um Blumen aufs geweihte Gras zu streuen
Und so mit Pracht das Zwielicht zu erfreuen.
Denn Morgen war's: Apollos Himmelsglühen
Ließ östlich Wolken silbern Funken sprühen
Von solcher reinen Klarheit, daß durch sie
Ein dunkler Geist schnell die Melancholie
Vergäße und sein Innres in die Luft
Verströmte – regensatter Rosenduft
Süßte mit Milde dieses Sonnenschwellen,
Die Lerche träumte; kalt noch, wärmten Quellen
Die kühlsten Blasen auf im Gras der Flur;
Von Bergen rief der Mensch; und die Natur
Ließ Wunder und Lebendiges pulsieren,
Dies Morgenrot mit altem Glanz zu spüren.

[Angeführt von einem greisen Weihepriester, versammeln sich hier die Hirtenfamilien zum Pansfest. Ihr bunter Reigen hält um ein Gespann geschart Einzug.]

Von großem Ansehn bei den Scharen schien,
Wer in ihm stand. Die Jugend voll erblüht,
Glich er dem manngewordnen Ganymed.
Und für solch schlichte Zeiten war sein Kleid
Das eines Königs: von der Brust, befreit,
Hing ihm ein Horn aus Silber, auch hielt er
Zwischen durchsehnten Knien den Eberspeer.
Ein Lächeln trug sein Antlitz; er schien froh
Und, auf den ersten Blick, im Tagtraum so
Durch Haine im Elysium zu schlendern.
Einige aber spürten, es verändern
Verborgner Gram und Ärger seine Lippen,
Und sahn, oft glitten ihm die Zügelstrippen
Durch die vergeßne Hand – sie seufzten leis,
Gedachten gelben Laubs, des Eulenschreis,
Holz, feierlich gehäuft. Weh, was wir sehn –
Was ließ unsern Endymion so vergehn?

[Der Priester begrüßt die Latmier und bereitet den Schrein für ein Brandopfer vor. Der Chor stimmt seine Hymne an Pan an.]

»O du, des mächtiger Palastdachfries
An rauhen Stämmen hängt und schattig hält,
Was ewig wispert, trüb ist, wächst, lebt, fällt
An ungesehnem Flor in tiefer Ruh;
Der's liebt, kämmt eine Dryas sich im Nu
Ihr wirres Haar, wo dunkelnd Haseln rauschen;
Ernst stundenlang zu sitzen und zu lauschen
Der düstren Melodie des Rieds im Schlamm
Verlaßner Stellen, wo vor Nässe klamm
Durchblasner Schierling seltsam riesig sprießt;
Im Sinn, wie du dich traurig gehen ließt
Nach dem Verlust der Liebsten – sei nicht gram –
Bei Syrinx' Stirn aus Rahm! –
Bei all deinem durchbebten Liebeswahn –
Hör uns, o Pan!

O du, zu dessen Seelenruh durch Myrten
Tauben noch leidenschaft-erfüllter girrten,
Wann immer du im Sonnenuntergang
Durch Wiesen zogst, den äußern Saum entlang
Um dein bemoostes Reich. O du, für den
Die Feigen jetzt schon Früchte ausersehn
An breiten Blättern; Bienen, gelb gestreift,
Die goldnen Waben; unser Acker reift
Schönst-blühnde Bohnen und durchmohntes Korn;
Der Hänfling seine Brut, noch ungeborn,
Zu singen; Erdbeern, kriechend durch ihr Beet,
Die Sommerfrische; Puppen, fest umdreht,
Betupfte Flügel; ja, das junge Jahr
All sein erfülltes Keimen – sei rasch nah,
Bei jedem Wind, der durch die Kiefern schallt,
Gott, der du lebst im Wald!

Du, zu dem jeder Faun und Satyr flieht
Zu willgem Dienst – gilt's, daß er sich bemüht,
Geduckte Hasen aus dem Schlaf zu jagen,
Sich schroffe Abhänge hinaufzuwagen
Als Lämmerretter vor des Adlers Schlund,
Durch mysteriöse Lockungen am Grund
Verwirrten Hirten ihren Weg zu weisen –
Gilt's, atemlos ums wilde Meer zu reisen,
Um die bizarrsten Muscheln aufzuladen,
Zu zielen auf die Grotten der Najaden
Und, gut versteckt, ihr Staunen zu verhöhnen –
Oder mit irrstem Lauf dich zu versöhnen,
Wenn auf die Schädel sie sich treffen dürfen
Mit Galläpfel- und Tannenzapfenwürfen –
Bei jedem Echo, das du schallen hörst,
Hör uns, o Satyrfürst!

O Lauscher auf den scharfen Scherenton,
Wenn dann und wann ein Widder, blökend schon,
Zum Schurvieh drängt; du Bläser auf dem Horn,
Wenn Keiler, niederwalzend zartes Korn,
Jäger erbosen; unsres Anbaus Retter,
Der fortbläst Mehltau und verheernde Wetter;
Seltsamer Diener unbeschriebnen Klängen,
Die schwindend über hohle Böden drängen
Und dumpf verklingen über öden Mooren;
Du Wächter an den mysteriösen Toren
Zu allem Wissen – sieh, wie viele schon,
Dryopes großer Sohn,
Gekommen sind zu ihrem Treueeid,
Bekränzt hier aufgereiht!

Sei stets der unvorstellbar hohe Raum
Für tiefstes Denken; einer, der uns, kaum
Daß wir begreifend bis zum Himmel steigen,
Bloß nacktes Hirn läßt; du sei stets in Teigen,

Die treibend auf der klumpig-trägen Erde
Ätherisches verleihn – daß Neues werde;
Sei stets Symbol für Unermeßlichkeit;
Ein Sternenhimmel auf ein Meer gestreut;
Ein Element, das ein Dazwischen füllt,
Ein unbekanntes – doch nicht mehr! Verhüllt
Die Stirn, erhobner Hände, tief verneigt,
Mit einem Ruf, der noch den Himmel beugt,
Flehn wir, hör den bescheidenen Päan
Auf Lyziens Berg dir an!«

Kaum war ihr wechselnder Gesang vorbei,
Entstieg der Menge schon ein Jubelschrei,
Der in der Luft hing wie auf einer Düne
Das Donnern, stoßen ionische Delphine
In Schwärmen ihre Nasen durch das Meer.
Indes, auf kühlem Boden, moosig schwer,
Begann der flinke Tanz von jungen Leuten
Zu schrillen Pfeifen und summenden Saiten.
Ja, schönes Leben tanzte hier gemessen
Verschollne Tänze – damals unvergessen;
Schönheiten! zeugten deren Enkel doch
Thermopylaens Helden – leben noch,
In altem Marmor ewig voll Magie.
Nichtsahnend hohe Zeuger, pflückten sie
Der Zeit süßliche Erstlinge –

[Das Pansfest klingt aus mit Spiel und mit Gesprächen, die im Kreis der Ältesten den Äther-Heimen und Toten im Elysium gelten.]

So erfüllt
War jeder hier am Träumen – nur nicht er,
Die Augen hinter schweren Lidern leer,
Endymion: stets strebte er danach,
Den Giftbrand zu verbergen, der ihn stach
Und am Gedächtnis fraß. Nun allerdings
Schwand ihm der Sinn; er gab nicht acht auf rings

Entstandnes Schweigen, das gedämpfte Sprechen,
Die greisen Augen, trüb durch sein Gebrechen,
Die Rufe banger Mädchen, fest umarmt,
Ihr Stöhnen, das den Kummer selbst erbarmt. –
Nein, in erstarrter Trance blieb er befangen,
Als wäre er auf Erden nie gegangen.
Ja, tot fast wie ein Marmormensch schien er,
Erfroren in Arabiens alter Mär.

[Peona, seine Schwester, nimmt sich Endymions an und setzt mit ihm in einem Segelkahn auf ihre Lustinsel über. In einer Laube dort schläft der Hirtenfürst ein.]

O Zauber Schlaf! O trostspendender Vogel!
Schwebst überm Sturmmeer der Gedanken lang,
Bis es verstummt und glatt ist! O du Zwang
So zwanglos! Freiheitskerker! Schlüssel auch
Zu goldnen Schlössern, fremdem Liederbrauch,
Grotesken Brunnen, neuen Bäumen, Höhlen,
Beschmückt und hallend, in die Wogen spülen
Und Mondlicht; ja, zur ganzen irren Welt
Der silbernen Verzaubrung! Wer schon, hält
Dein Daunenflügel ihn drei Stunden fest,
Lebt nicht neu auf? – So fand, in seinem Nest,
Beruhigt ins Leben auch Endymion wieder.
Mit klarerem Verstand hob er die Lider
Und sprach: »So zärtlich liebst du, daß ich glaube
Mein Herz zu spürn – du bist wie eine Taube,
Die mich geschloßnen Augs und glatter Schwingen
Umflattert; und die Frühtauperlen bringen
Nicht solchen Morgenduft vom Feld im Mai
Gleich diesen hellren Tropfen, die so treu
Dies Aug durchstrahlen, wahrer Sitz und Ort
Der Schwesterliebe. Was will ich hinfort
Noch andres, Himmelnähres als solch Tränen?
Doch wisch sie ab – und fürchte nicht, mein Sehnen
Wär, weiterhin allein und schwermutsvoll
Zu leben. Nein, von Gipfeln schallen soll

Erneut mein Rufen; sprechen soll erneut
Mein Horn von ihren Stirnen, tief verschneit,
Die Meute meiner Hunde wieder treiben
Den atemlosen Eber; ranke Eiben
Kapp ich erneut für feinstes Jagdgerät;
Und wenn die schöne Sonne tiefer steht,
Werd ich erneut auf einer Böschung schlafen,
Lausch den betupften Drosseln und seh Schafen
Beim Grasen zu. Drum, Süße, freue dich
Und, ist hier deine Laute, bitt für mich
Die Seele, den entschloßnen Kurs zu halten.«

[Auf ihr besorgtes Drängen hin vertraut Endymion Peona den Grund für seine Verstörung an. Er erzählt, wie er eines Abends in einem zauberisch anmutenden Mohnbeet am Flußufer eingeschlafen war.]

»Ah, kann ich schildern,
Was ich nun sah an zauberhaften Bildern?
Zwar war es nur ein Traum – ein Traum jedoch,
Daß keine Zunge, und erschöpft sie noch
Den feinsten Ausdruck, gleich dem Quell im Schacht,
Je bildlich darstellt und begreiflich macht,
Was ich empfand und sah. Mir schien, ich sah
In den Zenit und lag den Sternen nah,
Die jungfräulich die Milchstraße durchglühn;
Und wie mein Auge schweift, bis offen schien
Nunmehr das Himmelstor für meine Flüge,
Bekam ich Angst, daß ich zu Boden schlüge
Aus solcher Höh durch einen Abwärtsblick –
Blieb steif so in dem luftigleichten Glück
Und schien erdachte Flügel auszubreiten.
Doch nun fing jeder Stern an zu entgleiten
Und schwand mir vorm begierigen Gesicht;
Ich seufzte tief, denn folgen konnt ich nicht,
Und ließ den Traum sich horizontwärts neigen –
Und sieh! aus offnen Wolken sah ich steigen

Den schönsten Mond, der silbern je umzog
Die Muscheln für Neptuns Gefäß; er flog
So fiebernd hell, daß meine blinde Seele,
Verströmt in seiner Silbersphären Helle,
Durch Dunst und Klarheit trieb noch als er schwand
Zuletzt in einem schwadendunklen Band –
Worüber, schien mir, auglidlose Scharen
Von Sternen wieder in der Bläue waren.
Ich hob, zu sprechen jene Körper dort,
Erneut den Blick, doch fiel auf ihn sofort
Ein helles Etwas, das herunterstieß
Und mich rasch Aug und Stirn verdecken ließ –
Ich schaute nochmals, und, o Göttermacht,
Die vom Olymp aus unser Los bewacht!
Woher solch reinste Form von aller Reinheit?
Woher kam solch Vollendung aller Feinheit?«
[...]
»Sie schwebte einen Kreis
Und kam dann auf mich zu, ganz eine Maid,
Errötend, zögernd, bang und doch bereit,
Und drückte meine Hand – da war's geschehn!
Mir schien, der Zauberdruck ließ mich vergehn,
Obwohl ich mir bewußt blieb, ganz wie der,
Der taucht, drei Faden tief, dort wo das Meer
Korallenriffs durchgurgelt. Nämlich schon
Fühlt ich mich hochgehievt in die Region,
Wo fallende Sterne ihre Schleudern schwingen
Und Adler mit den Böen des Nordwinds ringen,
Der leicht den Meteorfels balanciert –
Nicht Furcht noch Einsamkeit hab ich gespürt,
Fuhr nur, floß fast am finstren Himmel hin.
Bald, als die hohe Fahrt zu Ende schien
Und wir genau in ärgste Wirbel fielen,
Wie stets sich sammeln, wo die Vorzeit Höhlen
Und tiefe Krater grub in Berg und Tal –
Da weckte dumpfer Klang mich, und nochmal

So selig zu vergehen sehnt ich mich.
Ich war zerschmettert; taumelnd küßte ich
Den Arm, der mich umfing, und nie mehr heben
Die Lider wollte ich – doch galt's zu leben,
Zu schlucken Leben aus den goldnen Quellen
Des glühend zarten Blicks; zu zählen und zählen
Momente, gierig unterstützt dabei
Von einem Zweit-Ich, daß erhalten sei
Ein jeder und der Fracht an Glück bestohlen.
Verwegner Mensch! der ich selbst unverhohlen
Ihr Antlitz zur bekränzten Lippe führte
Und, kaum geschehn, den Körper tauchen spürte
In wärmre Luft – noch ein Moment, und weich
War Flor um unsre Füße.«

[Endymion erzählt nun, wie er, im Traum zurückgekehrt zur Erde, aus benommenem Schlaf aufgewacht war.]

»Ich ging – fort waren all die frohen Farben
Des Himmels und der Erde: tiefste Schatten
Warn tiefste Kerker; Lichtungen und Matten
Warn lichtverpestet; klare Bäche schienen
Rußig, bedeckt mit ausgestellten Kiemen
Sterbender Fische; Rosen blühten jetzt
Grell scharlach, hatten Dornen angesetzt
Wie Aloestachel. Flatterte ein Spatz
Vor meinen blinden Schritten Satz für Satz
Unschuldig auf und ab, war er mir hier
Maskiert ein Dämon, hergeschickt, um mir
Die Seele zu verdunkeln, der becircte,
Bis mich mein Stolpern in den Abgrund stürzte –
Drum packte ich mich und verfluchte Leid
Und Täuschung. Die betagte Amme Zeit
Gab mir Geduld. Dem Himmel danke ich!
Daß nun all dies, mit seinem Trost, um mich
Versunken ist und, Schwester, du so sehr

Mir anzusegeln hilfst das Ebbemeer
Des müden Lebens.«

[Lang ringt Peona um eine Antwort. Dann bricht sie ihr Schweigen:]

»Ist dies der Grund?
Nur dies? Wie sonderbar, ach! jammervoll,
Kann einer, der auf Erden schreiten soll,
Verweilen einem Halbgott gleich und streichen
Den Namen auf der Harfe, nichts erreichen,
Kein höhres Lied als simple Jungfraunglut,
Singend allein – und ängstlich – wie sein Blut
Die Wang verließ – und wie er ging, allein
Nicht wußte, wo – und wie er sagte nein,
Sprach wer von Liebe – wo doch Liebe war;
Was wär es sonst? – wie eine Taube gar
Ein Eibenzweiglein vor ihm fallen ließ –
Und wie er starb – daß Liebe es durchstieß,
Das sanfte Herz, wie Nordwind Rosen schändet –
Und die Ballade seiner Trübsal endet
Mit Stöhnen und mit ›Ach!‹ – Endymion!
Sei lieber in des Hornes Mund – bald schon
In jedem Wind, daß jeder lauschend munkelt!
Obgleich, eh sich die Luft kristalln verdunkelt,
Ich schwärmend auf die Silberseen schau,
Gemalt in westlichem Gewölk, genau
Goldfelsen nachgeformt, hellgoldnem Sand,
Inseln und Buchten, gelb zernagtem Strand,
Wo Pferde aufstolziern, Paläste liegen
Aus Amethyststein – würd mich mein Vergnügen
So quälen, bloß weil ich dies Reich der Helle
Wohl nicht erklimmen kann? Des Morpheus Quelle,
Aus deren Grundstoff Traum, Vision
Und Bilderflut des Schlafs sind, rauscht davon
In luftige Kanäle mit so dünnem,
So glattem Hauch, das Weberschiff der Spinnen,

Millionenfach umzirkelt in der Ritze
Zum Schwalbennest, entwürfe nicht die Skizze,
Den Grundriß ihrer Machart: wie leicht doch
Ein Traum erst selbst sein muß, ist er doch noch
Viel leichter als das Nichts, das ihn erweckt!
Was also hast du kranken Geists befleckt
Des hohen, edlen Lebens Gemmenbild?
Weshalb durchbohrt der Ehre festen Schild
Für nichts als einen Traum?«
[...]
»Peona! stets ersehnt ich, meinen Durst
Zu löschen auf das Lob der Welt: kein Dösen,
Kein niederes Phantom bloß, konnte lösen
Mein straffes Segeltuch, bereit zur Reise –
Zerfetzt ist's, nackt läßt's meine Barke Kreise
Der Trägheit ziehn. Mein höhres Hoffen jedoch
Zieht weitre, regenbogengroße noch,
Die nicht Myriaden Erdenwracks erschüttern.
Worin liegt Glück? Wo willigen Gemütern
Gemeinschaft winkt, ein göttliches Vereinen,
Gemeinschaft mit Essenz – bis daß wir scheinen,
Ganz aufgelöst und frei von Raum. Schau, sieh
Die klare Religion des Himmels! Zieh
Ein Rosenblatt ums schmalste Fingerglied
Und kos die Lippen; lausche, wenn ein Lied
Als leichter Kuß in freie Winde stößt
Und, einfühlsam berührt, sich darauf löst
Der Zauber Äols aus dem Schoß der Lüfte;
Weisen verlassen nun umwölkte Grüfte;
Ältere seufzen über ihren Ahnen;
Die Geister prophezeiender Klänge mahnen
An jeden Fleck, auf den Apollo trat;
Lärm bronzner Hörner tönt und sagt uns matt,
Wo einst sich eine Riesenschlacht entschied;
Und aus dem Gras durchzieht ein Wiegenlied

Die Plätze, wo der Knabe Orpheus schlief.
Fühlen wir dies? – in dem Moment durchlief
Man eine Art von Einssein, unser Zustand
Ist der schwebenden Geists. Es gibt jedoch
Reichres Umgarnen, Fesselungen noch
Ich-auslöschender, führnd, nach Rang bemessen,
Zum höchsten Stärkegrad: die Krone dessen
Besteht aus Liebe, Freundschaft und sitzt breit
Hoch oben auf der Stirn der Menschlichkeit.
Was Wert hat durch Gewicht und Umfang dort,
Heißt Freundschaft, so geht von ihr immerfort
Ein steter Glanz aus; doch am Scheitel oben,
An unsichtbarem Band, hängt lichtumwoben
Ein Tropfenball – die Liebe: ihr Erglühn,
Vom Aug erblickt, zeugt einen neuen Sinn,
Vor dem man stutzt und bebt, bis man am Schluß,
In ihren Glanz verströmt, verschmelzen muß
Mit ihr und als ein Teil von ihr verklingt –
Mit nichts kann sich die Seele so beschwingt
Verflechten. Ist die Bindung an sie stark,
Nährt sich das Leben selbst vom eignen Mark
Und wir uns wie der Pelikane Brut.
Ja, herrlich ist die satte Kost, so gut,
Daß Männer, tauglich, um ganz vorn zu ringen
Mit all der aufgehäuften Welt, zu schwingen
Und worfeln aus der Lauf der Zeit, zu fischen
Die Spreu des Brauchs, die Schleimspur fortzuwischen
Der Menschen-Schnecken, Schlangenmenschlichkeit,
Erfreut warn, schwand nur die Gelegenheit
Schlafend im Liebenden-Elysium.
Und wahrlich – lieber schlage man mich stumm,
Als diese heiße Mattheit anzuklagen;
Denn ich hab stets geglaubt, all unsren Tagen
Schenkt sie die Wohltaten und ahnt es kaum –
Wie es die Nachtigall tut, hoch im Baum

Und unterm buschig-kühlen Blätterdach:
Sie singt aus Liebe, doch denkt niemals nach,
Wie lang die Nacht den dunklen Schlapphut trägt.
Grad so mag Liebe, wenn sie unentwegt
Auch bloß als Mischen heißen Atems gilt,
Weit mehr bewirken als den Blick erfüllt.
Was, weiß ich nicht – doch wer, als Mensch, kann sagen,
Ob Blumen blühen, Bäume Früchte tragen,
Bis daß ihr Fleisch schmilzt, Fische helle Schuppen,
Die Erde Schmuck aus Flüssen, Wald und Kuppen,
Die Wiesen Bäche, Bäche Kieselhänge,
Die Saat die Reife, Lauten ihre Klänge,
Klang sein Entzücken und Entzücken Süßen,
Wenn Menschenseelen sich nicht küssend grüßen?

Ist's irdsche Liebe, die der Menschen Leben,
Das sterblich ist, unsterblich macht; ihr Streben
Aus dem Gedächtnis schüttelt und die Fülle
Ins Maß des Glücks gießt – welche bloße Grille
Scheint all dies Gieren nach dem Ruhm der Welt
Dem, der an seinem festen Ziel festhält,
Göttlicher Liebe, einer Göttin gar.
Schau du nicht so bestürzt – denn es ist wahr,
Ist niemals Winzigkeiten nur entstiegen,
Die unsern Schlaf umschwirrn, Gedanken-Fliegen,
Die hirnkrank machen. Nein, niemals, du weißt,
Ertrüge es mein ruheloser Geist,
So lang zu brüten über einer Lust,
Würd er nicht, wenn auch seiner Angst bewußt,
Ein Hoffen hinterm Dunst des Traums erspähn.

[Endymion berichtet, daß ihm sein Traumbild zweimal bereits auch tags erschienen war. In einer Höhle nahe Latonas Tempel hatte das fremde Antlitz kurz aus einem Quell gestrahlt; dann wieder war er ihm bis in die vermeintliche Grotte Echos gefolgt.]

Wo sind,
Ah! die Sekunden dort? wohin entflohn?
Peona, nie mehr lächeln, noch daß schon
Kummer mein Tod sei, will ich; nein, bereit
Die Stirn ihm bieten – drum leb wohl, mein Leid,
Und komme dafür ernstestes Versenken,
Mich gänzlich einzunehmen und zu lenken
Mein Pilgern an den finstern Rand der Welt.
Nicht länger messen will ich, Feld für Feld,
Den Stab des Grams; nicht trachten mehr zu finden
Die Halbvergessenheit in Bergeswinden,
Umbrausend meine Ohrn. Ja, ich zeig dir,
Mein Schwesterherz, welch Leben ich nun führ,
Welch stillen Stundenkreis mein Lebtag zieht.
Ein schwaches Hoffnungsschimmern gibt's, das glüht,
Wohin ich blick; doch jetzt mein ich, 's ist nichts –
Und hier sag ich, verglimm. Im Schein des Lichts,
Schau, seh ich nicht schon jetzt gesünder aus?
Die Sonne sinkt; mit dem Gespann zu Haus
Sind ein paar Nachbarn vielleicht gar nicht fern.«
Er schloß, stand auf, matt lächelnd wie ein Stern
Im Dunst des Herbsts, und nahm Peonas Hand. –
Ins Boot gestiegen, stießen sie von Land.

Buch II

O Allgewalt der Liebe! Gram! O Trost!
Was nicht von dir erzählt, kommt kühl, bemoost
Und schattig durch den Dunst vergangner Zeit;
Denn andres, Gut und Böse, Haß und Leid,
Wird schal alsbald, doch dich berührend klingt
Ein Seufzen her, sehnt sich ein Schluchzen, bringt
Ein Kuß den Honigtau begrabner Tage.
Qualm über Troja, Türme voller Klage,
Starr-steife Schilde, scharfe Speere, Hiebe,
Der Kampf, das Blut, Geschrei – all das wird trübe

In letzte Winkel des Gehirns verbracht;
Doch spüren in den Seelen wir mit Macht,
Was Troilus und Cressida verbindet.
Fort, Prunkgeschichte, güldner Trug! verschwindet!
Du schwärzlicher Planet im All der Taten!
Du Meer, an dem beständig Murmler waten
Entlang dem steinigen Erinnrungsstrand!
Manch altes morsches Boot liegt dort im Sand
Umschäumt an deiner Brust und ward erhoben
Zum prächtgen Schiff; manch Segel, stolz gewoben,
Und Goldkiel bleiben ungesetzt und trocken.
Weshalb jedoch? Was nützt's, daß Eulen umflogen
Den Mast von Hellas' großem Admiral?
Was nützt's, daß Alexanders Schritt einmal
Den Indus mit den Makedoniern querte?
Daß einst Odysseus den Zyklopen störte
Im satten Schlummer, was schon? – Julia, lehnend
In Fensterblumen, seufzend, zart entwöhnend
Ihr Denken seinem jungfräulichen Schnee,
Erreicht weit mehr. Die Silbertränen, Weh
Der Hero, Imogen, ihr Ohnmachtsjoch,
Und Pastorella im Banditenloch,
Sind Dinge, glühender mitanzuschauen
Als der Zerfall von Kaiserreichen. Grauen
Muß solche Überzeugung dem bereiten,
Der, mißvergnügt, bis hier gewagt zu schreiten,
Ohne ein Musenlächeln, ein Geheiß,
Den Pfad von Vers und Liebe. Rast, ich weiß,
Wenn man sich ruhlos wundreibt, peinigt eben
Mehr als zermalmt zu werden, will man heben
Der Liebe Banner auf die Dichtungszinnen.
Drum nochmals, Tage, Nächte! – meinem Sinnen
Helft wie ein Heer.
Hirnkranker Hirtenfürst,
Ob du treu dein Versprechen halten wirst
Vom Opfertag? Oder fand neues Sorgen
Das anhaltende Dämmern deiner Morgen?

Ach! 's ist sein alter Gram. Seit vielen Tagen
Streicht er umher auf ungewissen Pfaden –
Durch Wildnisse und Wald bemooster Eichen
Und mißt die schmerzzerschlißne Zeit an Streichen
Einsamer Holzfäller.

[Gelockt von einem goldenen Schmetterling, kommt Endymion in ein abgeschiedenes Tal, wo ihm eine Quellnymphe manche Prüfung, aber auch die letztliche Erfüllung ewiger Liebe verheißt.]

Dem Wandrer sanken,
Die Hand vorm Haupt, um schwelender Gedanken
Sich zu erwehrn, die schweren Knie ein;
Und während noch im müden Dämmerschein
Glühwürmer ansteckten den Sternenschimmer,
Hauchte er dies sich selbst zu: »Wer auch immer
Eine erträumte Stadt des Glücks belagert –
O wie versklavt ist er! und nach dem Schmerz,
Den Mühen, wenn sie sein ist, bar dem Herz
Der Hoffnungen zu sein – wie ärger noch.
Selbst in der Müh erholt er sich jedoch;
In einer andern Stadt sucht er sein Glück
Und zweifelt auch kein kieselkleinstes Stück,
Daß sie ihm reiche Honigwaben bietet –
Doch ach, sie sind vertrocknet; und er wütet
Und hastet weiter zu der nächsten Stadt.
Doch dies ist Menschenleben: Krieg, die Tat,
Enttäuschte Hoffnung, Streben, Ängstlichkeit,
Die ausgemalten Ziele, nah und weit,
Sind menschlich; tragen in sich die Erfahrung,
Daß sie die Luft sind, die subtile Nahrung,
Durch die man spürt, ich bin, und so ermißt,
Wie still der Tod ist. Wo auch Erdreich ist,
Gedeiht der Mensch, wird Kraut, wird Flor; nur ich
Kann nirgends Wurzeln schlagen, seh für mich
Nichts Irdsches, das mein Mitleid wert, steh stumm
Auf einem neblig-schroffen Kliff herum –

Allein? Nein, nein; und ich, bei Orpheus' Lied,
Wenn es den Wahn Eurydikes durchzieht,
Steh lieber auf dem Nebelgipfel hier,
Seufze um nichts und hab kein Ziel vor mir,
Nur der dreimal geschauten Liebsten Bilder,
Als – was weiß ich zu sein. O Taube, milder
Im Himmel! Cynthia, zehnfach strahlend schön!
Vom blauen Thron, nun überall zu sehn,
Send einen Strahl nur deiner linden Pracht
In meinen Busen, daß die Schreckensmacht
Der Liebestyrannei das Fürchten lernt!
Nein, süße Königin; die Qual entfernt,
Schon schmerzte mich das eifersüchtge Leid
Mehr als die Qual es selbst tat; lieber kleid
Mir Schwingen um die Schultern und erklär,
Wo meine Liebste wohnt. Mied dich das Heer
Verspielter Amors auch – du weißt zuviel,
Bist viel zu schön, um deinen Silberkiel
Nicht in der Liebe sanftsten Strom zu senken.
O sei mir gnädig, auch darfst du nicht denken,
Mein Wahn sei dreist; denn bei den Sternen droben,
Die dir gehorchen, glaube ich enthoben
All seiner Schranken meinen Geist – und gleite
Nun mit dir durch die schwindelnd hohe Weite!
Wie schön du bist! Wie dumpf die Welt dagegen!
Wie flackernd-blendend doch die Räder fegen
Um ihre Achse! Zügel dort, wie leicht,
Wie glitzernd! Hat dein Wagen erst erreicht
Sein luftig Ziel, verhüllt mir dann ein Dach
Den trüben Blick? Den Blick! – mein Geist wird schwach;
Hilf, Göttin! die weit-aufgesperrte Luft
Verschluckt mich sonst – hilf mir!«

[Aus einer nahen Grotte fordert eine Stimme Endymion auf, ins Erdinnere hinabzusteigen. Dort, wundersame Bilder, Bauten und einen Dianatempel passierend, gelangt er bis vor einen finsteren Durchlaß.]

Nun, vor sich keine neuen Wunder mehr
Und mit sich selbst allein, wie rauh und schwer
War da der Heimweg zum gewohnten Ich!
Verrücktes Jagen nach dem Nebelwicht
Und dessen Irrlicht, das durch Nesseln flieht,
Uns in ein Sumpfloch, in ein Feuer zieht,
Ins Innere von tiefverhaßten Dingen.

Welch Elend wird am schmerzlichsten erklingen
Im Ohr Endymions, kann er sich nun senken
Ins Zieltor des Bewußtseins? Ah, das Denken,
Das tödliche Gefühl, allein zu sein –
Denn schau! er sieht den Himmel nicht, nicht rein
Die Bäche, wilden Flor, der Hügel stürmt
Im Pink- und Purpurmuster, aufgetürmt
Gewölk, das langsam in den Westen rückt
Wie Elefantenherden; fühlt nicht, drückt
Nicht Gras, schmeckt nicht ermüdend frische Luft –
Nein, weit hinfort von solch Gesellschaft ruft,
Auf unbekannte Zeit, in Gram vergraben,
Sein Los ihn. Und Geduld soll er noch haben,
Fantastisches mit seinem Wurfspeer ritzen?
»Nein!« rief er, »weshalb sollte ich hier sitzen?«
»Nein!« schallte es unzählbar oft zurück.
Da stand er auf und lenkte Stück für Stück
Die Schritte wieder vor das Tempelbild,
Sich wärmend und vom Glauben heiß erfüllt,
Diana helfe ihm – so daß er dann,
Gewahrend die luftige Gestalt, begann,
Derweil er nähertrat: »O Herrin, reine,
Der Ufer, weiten Heiden und der Haine,
Wohin mit scharfem Pfeil und Silberbogen,
O Königin des Walds, bist du gezogen!
Welch sanfte Luft sucht deine sanftre Haut?
Wo lauschst du auf den hohen Hallo-Laut

Verirrter Nymphen, fällt dein Sichelschimmer
Durch einen dunklen Wipfel? Wo auch immer,
Es liegt im Hauch des Himmels: du erfährst
Die Freiheit, die nichts sonst erfährt, verheerst
Den Liebreiz nicht in trüben Elementen;
Nein, unsrer grünen Erde Glück in Händen,
Lebst du dort selig. Ah, ist sie für dich
Elysisch, wie reich erst klingt dann für mich
Verbannten Sterblichen ihr süßer Name!
Mein Herz erstickt an einer innren Flamme –
O laß mich's kühlen im Zephirwind-Geäst!
Ein Heimweh dörrt mir meine Zunge fest –
O löschen laß sie mich an frischen Quellen!
In meine Ohren will ein lautes Nichts mir gellen –
O wieder lauschen auf des Finks Tiraden!
Vor meinen Augen fluten Nebelschwaden –
O daß sie wieder Himmelslicht begieße!
Labst eben du die Fesseln und die Füße?
O denk, wie süß mir solch Erfrischung wäre!
Löschst eben du den Durst am Saft der Beere?
O denk, welch Glück er wär auf meinem Gaumen!
Und hörst du mich im sanften Schlummer raunen,
O denk, wie ich ein Blumenbett ersehn! –
Göttin! laß mich durchs Gras der Heimat gehn!
Führ mich aus dieser räuberischen Tiefe!«

[Gekräftigt betritt er den Gang – überall wachsen Blumen, Myrten. Endymion vernimmt ein weihevolles Summen und folgt dem Geräusch.]

O gab es je den Einsamen, der liebte –
Und den Musik nicht schlug? 's ist seine Pest,
Daß größtes Glück geringste Ruhe läßt;
Daß, was ihm kostbar war und zartster Wert,
Verschluckt wird, in versengte Not gekehrt
Durchs Zehren einer Flamme – wahren Segen
Kann sie ersticken und mit Fluch belegen.

Halb glücklich, könnte man doch selig sein,
Ist elend. So war's auch mit diesen fein
Tauleichten Klängen in des Kariers Ohren:
Erst Himmel, dann die Hölle, dann verloren,
Verweht im Urgrund aller Leidenschaft.

Und vor ihm hätt ein schwarzer Schlund geklafft,
Hätt ihn kein Himmelswink sanft fortgeführt
Und dichtes Myrtenzweigwerk nicht berührt
Am Haupt und aufgeweckt – nach kurzer Dauer
Erklang's leis neu, als ging ein Mittagsschauer
Über den Fleck hin, wo er wartend hielt;
Denn wie in Wald die Abendröte schielt,
So sah er flackernd Licht, folgte den Strahlen
Durch dichtes Laub, bis er – kaum auszumalen! –
Auf weichem Grün, hier einen, einen da,
Cupidos auf den Schwingen schlummern sah.

[Am Lager des Adonis wird Endymion Zeuge der allsommerlichen Erweckung des schönen Jünglings, der Venus' Liebe verschmäht hatte. Erfüllt vom eigenen Glück, lenkt die Göttin der Liebe das Augenmerk Amors auf das Schicksal des Hirtenfürsten.]

»Mein Kind,
Sei diesem Jüngling gnädig, ihm verrinnt
Der Tag vor Liebe – er – doch ach! ich seh,
Du kennst die Tiefe seines Elends eh.
Ah, lächle nicht, mein Sohn – ich will dir sagen,
Als ich durch schwerste Stunden mußte klagen
Hier um Adonis' endlos langen Schlummer,
Erbarmte dieser Fremde mich. Voll Kummer,
So floh ich eines trüben Morgens fort
Ins Sturmgewölk und weinte, flehte dort
Für meinen Liebsten, da mich längst Mars' Folter
Zu Tränen reizte. Dort dann, schon erholter,
Den Blick, leer, senkend durch verhangnen Wald,
Sah ich des Jünglings traurige Gestalt:

Die dunklen Locken wirr zerzaust im Wind,
Die wimpernreichen Lider nur mehr blind
Auf trüben Augen; sah, wie er sich schwer
Ins welke Laub warf, ganz als fände er
Den Tod nun; denn kein Jota hob er sich,
Raunte nur wild. Er liebe, hörte ich,
Ein Götterwesen und sein Arm hab schon
Es nachts umfangen. Keine Spur davon
Im Himmel: ich besah mir alle Wangen
Und denk, vergeblicher ist kein Verlangen;
Und nichts kann noch geheimer sein deswegen.
Endymion! es bleibt nicht aus dein Segen –
So folg der Hand nur, die dich ausgebreitet
Durch Wunder hier zu süßen Zielen leitet.
's ist höchst notwendig, dies Verborgensein,
Und glaubte ich's nicht auch, zum Sonnenschein
Aufsteigen solltest du mit mir. Adieu!
Hier scheiden wir nun.« – Unruhig in die Höh
Zog's schon die Tauben, stieg der Schwebewagen,
Hob sich das Himmelssummen. Fortgetragen,
Sah sie der Latmier ins Nichts vergehn –
Und warn auch alle fort, blieb doch zu sehn
Jenes erhabnen Bogens reges Gleißen.
Als wieder Nacht war, schloß mit Ätnas Kreißen
Sich auch die Erde – stöhnte im Gestein –
Und ließ erneut im Zwielicht ihn allein.

Er raste nicht, er starrte nicht entsetzt,
Daß all die Bilder fort, vergangen jetzt,
Und er verlassen war – denn heitrer Zeit
Versichert sah er sich, wenn all sein Leid
Dem großen Lohn nur eine Feder schiene.

[Weiter durcheilt Endymion die Erdmysterien. Er ruft Jupiter an, und ein Adler trägt ihn zu einem elysischen Wabengebilde.]

Es war ein Nest ganz aus Jasmin, durchsetzt
Mit goldnem Moos. Gereinigt war ihm jetzt
Ein jeder Sinn für Freude; ein Genuß
Flog über ihm, halb greifbar nur; sein Fuß
Trug ihn hesperisch; seine Ohren lauschten
Der Stille als ob heilge Sphären rauschten;
Taufeuchte Wohligkeit stand ihm im Blick;
Die Blumen spürten sein geseufztes Glück
Und regten es matt an. Durch grüne Zellen
Und Höhlen strich er, staunte oft solch Schwällen
Jäher Erregung nach – doch »Ach!« sprach er,
»Wird all dies strömende Gefühl nur mehr
In Einsamkeit vergehn? Und muß es schwinden,
Den Melodien gleich, die kein Echo finden
Auf kargen Ebnen? Dann soll ich allein
So schwermutsvoll, verwaist, so traurig sein!
Noch fühl ich mich unsterblich! O mein Herz,
Mein Lebenshauch, wo bist du? Himmelwärts,
Tanzt vor den Morgentoren seiner Fernen?
Hältst Wache unter jenen sieben Sternen,
Den Kindern Atlas'? Bist im Fluß zu finden,
Ein blondes Tritonskind beim Muschelwinden?
Dianas Nymphe etwa – ausgeschlossen –
Und bindest einen Kranz aus zarten Sprossen
Für wahren Müßiggang? Wo du auch bist,
Mir scheint, daß wohl an mir es nunmehr ist,
Dich zu umarmen: vor Auroras Heer
Dem Morgen dich zu rauben; übers Meer
Zu ziehn als wilder Vogel; dich zu greifen
Aus deiner Seeschaumwiege; abzustreifen
Dein Schäferkleid und dich im Laub zu küssen.
Nein, meine Seele will zu schnell vergessen,
Wie schwach sie ist. Ich weiß, dies kann nicht sein.
O laß mich denn durch süßes Träumen ein
In ihre Zauber. Schlaf! komm eine Weile!
Komm, mildster Schlaf, besänftigend zerteile
Die nahende Einsamkeit für ein paar Stunden.«

[Kaum eingeschlafen, findet Endymion das Traumbild in seinen Armen wieder. Dem Tod nah, bittet er die Liebste, sich zu erkennen zu geben und ihn zu entrücken.]

»Ich lieb dich, Jüngling, mehr als ich kann glauben;
Und solch Entfernung muß der Seele rauben
All ihre Ruhe – dennoch muß ich gehn.
Auch kann ich dich nicht in die Sternenhöhn
Erheben, noch mich dir, ob lauter Scham,
Ergeben. Ah, mein Liebster, sei nicht gram –
Zu lüften mein Geheimnis zwängst du mich,
Zu schämen mich im Himmel. O hätt ich
Es schon getan; wär das erhabne Lächeln
Über verlornen Glanz, mein Liebeshecheln
Gewichen von Olympus' Höh zurück
Und all den strengen Göttern – unser Glück
Schon ganz vergessen, außer von uns beiden!
Und weshalb Scham? Bloß um für ewge Freuden
Mit feiger Röte im Gesicht zu büßen:
Doch muß ich Feigling sein! – denn Grauen schießen
Zu greifbar auf vor mir – der Blick voll Gram
Des Zeus, Minervas Schreck – kein Busen warm
Vor keuscher Ehrfurcht, kein Cupidoflügel
Gesenkt in Demut, die kristallnen Hügel
Halb brach und all die Hymnen aufgegeben!
Doch was ist dies der Liebe? O zu schweben
Mit dir ins Sichtfeld dieser Himmelsmächte –
Wie würdst du so, für Stunden jener Nächte,
Mich so süß drücken.

[...]

Die Liebe wird die Schranken überwinden!
O laß mich in dich schmelzen, uns verbinden
Die dichten Stimmen beim Entstehen schon,
Laß schwebend uns verflechten – O der Hohn
Menschlichen Worts! rauh irdsche Sprachgewalt!
Erlernen soll dein Honigmund schon bald

Empyriums Lispeln – Lautenhauch, den ich
Dir keuche in dein Ohr, nun da ich dich
So halt und wein vor Liebe. – Wie sie quält,
Endymion. Leid! Leid! und Gram enthält
Die tiefste Wonne noch, mein ganzes Leben?«
Hier, oftmals schluchzend, ging ihr sanftes Streben
In Mattheit über. Weinend schwor er ihr
Im Traum die Treue.
Ihr, die schmachtet hier
Vor zuviel Leidenschaft, macht Halt und wißt
Bloß um der Wahrheit willen: Dies Lied ist
Keins unsrer Tage, einem alten Wald
Hat es ein Höhlenwind einst vorgeschallt;
Von jenem Wald erfuhr's sodann im Traum
Ein See, der schlief und dessen kühlen Saum
Ein Dichter sah auf seiner Wanderschaft
Zu Phöbus' Schrein; und der warf ohne Kraft
Die Glieder in ihn, schwamm ein Stündchen dort,
Bis er, noch an dem inspirierten Ort,
Dann in die Lüfte die Geschichte sang
Und ihr vollkommne Freiheit gab. Dort klang
Sie fort für jene Ohren, die noch heute
Heiß glühen von ihr. Die Legende freute
Solch Wächtersterne; auch muß, wer sie hört,
Sich selbst verdammen oder er erfährt:
Unlöschbar kommt ein Brennen übers Herz,
Verschärft durch Furcht, es könnte eine Terz
Verschlungen worden sein von Wirbelwinden.
Für immer wird ein Ruhelager finden
Soviel wie hier steht, dies bleibt klar und hell.
Doch nun verliert die fremde Stimme schnell –
Und nur ein weitentfernter Klang schallt her,
Daß jener schöne Gast zuletzt noch schwer
Die Glieder hob und von dem Schläfer schied. –
So singt die böige Tiefe dieses Lied.

[Erwacht und erneut allein, betritt Endymion gefestigt eine riesige Meeresgrotte und sinnt seinem Leben nach.]

»Jetzt, da ich ihre Seele ganz geschmeckt,
Sind alle andern Tiefen seicht – Essenzen,
Einst Geist, die schlammig nur am Boden glänzen,
Damit sie meine Erdenwurzel düngen
Und meine Äste goldne Früchte bringen
In den erblühten Himmel. Andres Licht,
Sei es auch schnell und scharf, daß es die Sicht
Dem Adler des Olympus raubt, ist dunkel,
Ganz wie des Chaos' Herkunft. Horch, Gemunkel!
Echoen die Muscheln lautlose Gedanken
Oder sind sie nur Geister, letztes Schwanken
Entfernter Töne? – lausch!«

[Zwei mächtige Wasserstrahlen jagen sich vor seinen Augen: Alpheus, der verliebte Fluß, in dem die Nymphe Arethusa badete, die nun, von Diana in einen Quell verwandelt, ewig vor seinem Werben fliehen muß.]

Er ging – da war ein dumpfer Ton – er schritt –
Da war ein kühlres Leuchten; und so glitt
Auf einem Sandweg er ihm zu und – seht!
Plötzlicher als ein Augenblick vergeht,
Verschwamm das Bild der Erde und entwich –
Riesig sah er den Ozean über sich.

Buch III

Manch einer spielt den Herrscher vor dem Rest,
Nur weil er reich an Flitter ist: er läßt
Die Eitelkeiten bähn, um weichen Rasen
Und saftiggrünes Heu ja abzugrasen
Von Menschenweiden; er – o quälend wahr! –
Der, nur irr blinzelnd, ungerührt sogar
Fuchsfackeln brennen und versengen sieht
Die Goldährn unsrer Hoffnungen. Umglüht

Von keinem heilgen Glanz, mit einem Blick,
Nicht den der Eule wert, putzt ihn noch dick
Das triefäugige Volk im Purpurkleid,
Krone und Turban. Seine Brust befreit,
Gebläht von Selbstlob nur, erklimmt er stolz
Die Stange seines Geists, sein Glück aus Holz,
Das Gipfelnichts, den Himmelsdunst, den Thron –
Im wilden, umsichgreifend trunknen Ton
Von Bläsern, durchgewalkten Trommeln, Jubel
Und Kanonaden. Ah! wie all der Trubel,
Im wachen Ohr, verschwand und wich als Krach –
Wie Donner, der zu Babylon einst sprach
Und die Chaldäer hintrieb auf ihr Ziel. –
Dann sind Regalien güldnes Maskenspiel?
Nein, Throne gibt's, wohin wir nur auf Schwingen,
Nur mit Geduld und stetem Zauber dringen
Oder Ätherischem, das, unbeschränkt,
Uns eine Leiter ewgen Windes schenkt
Und schweben läßt in düstren Donnerzelten,
Zu schaun die Schlund-Geburt der Urstoffwelten.
Ja, wo der Parze alte Lippen welk erkalten,
Sind heilge Staaten tausender Gewalten
Im Wasser, Feuer und im Reich der Luft
Und tagen, still wie die geweihte Gruft,
Zur festgesetzten Zeit im Sphärenraum.
Doch kaum, daß eine ferne Macht – ah, kaum! –
Ihr Wirken diesem Globus offenlegt –
Daß unsern Himmelsteil als Kleid sie trägt
Mit ganzer Pracht – in ihrer Güte mild
Wie unsre Ceres, die die Sinne füllt
Bis an den Rand mit geistger Süßigkeit
Gleich Bienen ihre Waben. Und beim Streit
Der Schöpfung mit dem Nichts: ich schwöre hier,
Apoll! daß deine holde Schwester mir
Die sanfter-mächtigste erscheint von allen.
Wenn deine goldnen Nebel westwärts wallen,

Stiehlt sie sich unbemerkt zu ihrem Thron
Und sitzt dort meist allein, meist wie zum Hohn;
Als könnte sie nicht über Pracht verfügen;
Als würd dein Aug, hoher Poet, nicht liegen
Auf ihr mit all den Musen tief im Herz;
Als brächten keine Sterne himmelwärts
Botschaften silberfüßig durch die Räume.
O Mondin! ältste Schatten ältster Bäume
Verspüren Zuckungen, willst du dich zeigen –
O Mondin! heilger lispelt's in den Zweigen,
Wenn sie nur fühlen, luftig naht dein Rund.
Du segnest alles, mit dem Silbermund
Küßt du ins Leben Totes. Vieh träumt reich
In deinem Licht von Feldern, himmlisch weich;
Unzählige Gebirge steigen, steigen,
Sich deinem heiligenden Blick zu zeigen;
Und doch verschmäht dein Segen kein Versteck,
Das noch so dunkel ist, dem kleinsten Fleck
Schickt er sein Glück. Der Zaunkönig im Nest
Hält dein Gesicht im ruhigen Sichtfeld fest
Und unterm Schutzdach seiner Efeuwohnung
Nach dir noch Ausschau; du bist die Belohnung
Für die Geduld der Auster, wenn sie schlief
In ihrem Perlenhaus. Das große Tief,
Das Meer, ist dein – das ungeheure Meer!
O Mondin! tief verneigt lenzt's vor dir her,
Und Tellus' Stirn spürt ihre schwere Last.

[Im durch die Fluten fallenden Mondschein wandelt Endymion auf dem Meeresgrund dahin, vorbei an versunkenen Dingen aller Zeiten.]

»Was, Mondin, ist in dir, daß du so heftig
Mein Herz bewegst? Schon als ein Kind schwand oft
Mein Weinen, lächeltest du unverhofft.
Du schienst die Schwester – uns zog's Hand in Hand
Von früh bis spät im Himmel übers Land.

Ich pflückte keine Äpfel mir vom Baum,
Bis du nicht köstlich kühltest ihren Flaum;
Kein Wasser sprach von taumelnden Romanzen,
Konnte mein Aug mit deinem nicht drauf tanzen;
Kein Laub war grün, war himmlisches Gefieder,
Bis du nicht öffnetest die feinen Lider;
Zur Säzeit hob ich keinen Pflanzstock auf,
Warf keine Saat, schienst du nicht wach darauf;
Und dann zur Sommerszeit, wenn alles blüht,
Da hörtest du nur mich mit frohem Lied
Taufeuchte Blumen über Nacht umschlingen.
Nie war wie ein vergehender Spuk mein Singen,
Galt's nicht der Feier deiner Herrlichkeit.
Ja, in der Kindheit waren Freud und Leid
Durch dich bestimmt zu gänzlich gleichem Ziel,
Und als ich älter ward, warst du im Spiel
Bei allem Eifer: warst die tiefen Schneisen –
Du warst der Gipfel – warst der Kiel des Weisen –
Des Dichters Harfe – Freundesstimme – Sonne.
Du warst der Fluß – du warst des Ruhmes Wonne.
Du warst mein Roß – warst meines Hornes Schallen –
Mein Becher Wein – die größte Tat von allen.
Du warst der Reiz der Frau, lieblicher Mond!
O welch ein wilder gleichgestimmter Ton
Durchzuckte meinen Geist aus all dem Schönen!
Auf einem glänzendhellen Wesen frönen
Der Ewigkeit war leicht: ich drückte nur
Im wachen Schlaf das Kissen der Natur.
Doch kam noch nähere Wonne, sanftes Rund!
Die fremde Liebste kam – der Glücksabgrund!
Sie kam, und du, du schwandest und verschwandst –
Jedoch nicht völlig. Nein, dein Sternenglanz
War dieser Stunde Neben-Leidenschaft.
Von neuem fühl ich deine Kugelkraft
Nun auf mich kommen – o sei gütig, Licht,
Laß deinen Einfluß ruhn und blende nicht

Mein höchstes Bild. – Liebstes, du mußt vergeben,
Kann ich mich von dir denken und doch leben! –
Verzeih mir, luftiger Planet, mein Weiden
Am Denken jenseits deiner Silberfreuden!
Wie weit doch jenseits!«

[Endymion trifft auf Glaukus. Von Circe verflucht, erkennt der einstige Fischer in dem Hirtenfürsten den ihm prophezeiten Erlöser und erzählt ihm seine Leidensgeschichte.]

»Was war ich's nicht zufrieden? Weshalb greifen
Nach Dingen, die, o Latmier! ohne dich
Mein trüber Tod wärn? Ich begann, Narr ich!
Verstört Sehnsüchte zu verspürn – wie's wäre,
Das höchste Vorrecht, das der Herr der Meere
Gewähren kann als Segen: frei zu sein
In seinem Reich. Lang streifte ich voll Pein
Dahin, eh ich in einem stärksten Beben
Auf Tod und Leben tauchte. Zu verweben
Die Sinne mit solch atmend-dichtem Stoff,
Mag schmerzvoll scheinen; kaum zu sagen hoff
Ich deshalb, wie kristallglatt ich's empfand,
Wie tragend um die Glieder. Erst durchwand
Ich reinstes Staunen, tage-, tagelang,
Vergaß mich völlig frei von Ziel und Zwang,
Glitt hin nur mit den mächtigen Gezeiten,
Dann, wie ein flügger Vogel, der im Gleiten
Erstmals die Schwingen zeigt der Morgenkühle,
Erprobte bang die Flügel auch mein Wille.
's war Freiheit! und sogleich besuchte ich
Die ganzen Wunder dieses Meers um mich.

[In einen Seegott verwandelt, hatte sich Glaukus in die Nereide Scylla verliebt und Circe um Rat aufgesucht. Auf Aiaia war er in den Bann der eifersüchtigen Zauberin geraten und, Zeuge ihrer Grausamkeiten, geschlagen worden mit zehntausendjährigem Siechtum im Meer. Scylla, von Circe getötet, hatte Glaukus in einem unterseeischen Kristallgebilde zurücklassen müssen.]

»Einst geschah's,
Daß ich umschäumt auf einem Felsen saß
Und wachsen auf des Horizontes Rand
Ein stolzes Schiff sah – bald schien mir, es schwand
Wieder dahin, als hätt es doch gehalten
Den alten Kurs, trotz hindernder Gewalten –
Verschwunden. Und nicht lang, schon hob sich dunkel
Gewölk und murrten Winde ihr Gemunkel.
Schlucken wollt Äolus seine blinde Wut,
Doch konnt er's nicht – so warf die grüne Flut
Den Gischtschaum silbern dem Gewölk entgegen.
Der Sturm kam: heikel sah ich Wanten fegen
Am Rumpf des Schiffs, an Deck indes ein Pack
Geschöpfe zittern. Vor mir war das Wrack;
Der letzte Sog; das Ringen armer Seelen;
Ich hörte sie im Donnerrollen gellen.
O alle wärn gerettet durch mehr Kraft
Als die gebrochnen Alters – doch erschlafft,
Gebeugt, bedenk, o Latmier, saß ich nur
Vor Mitgefühl krumm da und fluchte stur
Auf Circes Höllenreich. Die Schar indessen
War Mann für Mann verblichen ins Vergessen;
Und regungslos sah ich die Brandung dröhnen,
Mit mancher heißen Träne, manchem Stöhnen.
Da hob sich vor mir eines Greisen Hand,
Hielt diese Schrift, dies dürftige Gewand.
Ich kniete nieder – streckte mich – griff schon
Die Schätze – spürt die Hand – sie sank davon –
Mir blieb ein Finger – doch dem Sog hinab
Hielt ich nicht stand – er sank. Dann flaute ab
Der Sturm, und frostig kalten Dunst durchbrach
Die milde Sonne. Fiebernd sah ich nach,
Welch Buch dies war, trennte in wärmenden Weiten
Behutsam gierig die durchnäßten Seiten.
Absonderliches stand hier und zog fort
Die Seele Blatt für Blatt, nah an den Ort

Tiefsten Vergessens – als ich, taub nur mehr,
Die Worte las, und nochmals las, und schwer
Den Blick zum Himmel hob, und las, nochmal.
O welche Last an Elend und an Qual
Auf Atlas-Zeilen! – ein Strahl Hoffnung schien
Sein Gold um mich und forderte, sei kühn
Und trotz der Höllentyrannei. Hör zu!
Denn ihr Versprechen eingelöst hast du.

Im weiten Meer lebt ein vergeßner Knecht,
Geschlagen mit Entkräftung, um ihm recht
Sein Dasein zu verleiden tausend Jahre
Bis zum verlaßnen Tod. Wer fände wahre
Gewalt dagegen? Niemand. Darum müssen
Millionenfach des Ozeans Tiden fließen
Und er versklavt sein. Doch er wird nicht sterben,
Durchlebt dies alles. Kann er auch erwerben
Die Tiefen allen Zaubers und durchdränge
Den Sinn der Form, Bewegung und der Klänge;
Folgte er aller Größe und Substanz
Bis hin zu den Symbolessenzen ganz –
Er stirbt nicht. Nein, zuerst sei er bereit,
Sich frommstens in dies Werk voll Freud und Leid
Zu fügen – Liebende, vom Sturm vertrieben
Und übermannt im Tosenden geblieben,
Soll er zusammenbetten, bis erst dann
Kriechende Zeit die Öde füllen kann:
Nun wird, sind all die Mühen einst vollbracht,
Geleitet und geliebt durch Himmelsmacht
Ein Jüngling vor ihm stehn, dem er erzählt,
Wie alles sich vollende. Auserwählt,
Muß der es tun, sonst nämlich sterben beide.«

»Dann«, rief Endymion, überfroh vor Freude,
»Sind Zwillingsbrüder wir in diesem Los!
Sag, bitt ich dich, welch Tat, so hehr und groß,

Harrt meiner, hier in solch ruhloser Welt?
Was! – hätte mein Umherirrn dich verfehlt –
Wär unser Tod?« – Der Weise sprach: »Schau her!
Bemerkst du nicht ein Schimmern durch das Meer,
Von mannigfachem Glanz? Das ist der Ort,
Von dem ich sagte, Scylla liege dort;
Und frommstens hab ich gleichfalls dort begraben
Verliebte, die im Zorn der Stürme starben
Seit meinem Frondienst.«

[Im Kristall erwecken Glaukus und Endymion Scylla und alle versunkenen Liebenden zu neuem Leben. Glaukus erhält seine Jugend zurück und führt die Scharen zu Neptuns Meerespalast.]

Noch lauter tosten
Sie weiter in den sich erhellenden Osten.
Ein jeder Schritt voran hob stolze Dächer
Ins Blickfeld – Diamantglanz, goldne Fächer
Aus Bernstein auf ihre Gesichter richtend.
Freudig, wie Laub im Frühling sich verdichtend,
Wuchs weiter, wuchs die Pracht an bis zuletzt.
Opalne Kuppeln sah man, hoch gestützt
Von Jaspissäulen, schimmernd durch die Schäfte
Rot wie Korallen. Reiche Wunder-Säfte
Trank, wer dies sah; und reichre, trat er ein.
Denn was der Mensch zusammensucht als rein
Wie Marmor, gab's dort reichlich, war dort noch
Ein einziger Palast, weit größer doch
Als selbst gemeinsam die drei alten je,
Memphis und Babylon und Ninive.

[Bis in den Thronsaal dringt die Menge der Liebenden. Neben Neptun erwarten sie hier auch Venus und Amor.]

Weit wie der Seemann auf dem höchsten Mast
Die ruhige Weite ringsumher erfaßt,
War Neptuns Saal; und wie die Bläue schwer
Die Meere wölbt, zog ehrfürchtig das Meer

Die Kuppelvorhänge, hoch, reich besetzt,
Vom Thron empor. Und wenn es sturmzerfetzt
Sonst Donnerdunkel in Zeus' Luft erhellte
(Die nie so glatt war) – überall nun schnellte
Geräuschlos unterseeisch Gewölk und drang
Glitzernd als Tod ins Menschenaug: versank
Im Westen, Osten, Süden, Norden doch
Licht wie vier Sonnen, goldgrün flammend noch
Über des Meergotts Haupt als der Zenit.
Der Boden lichte Tiefe, ein Gebiet
Dem stillen See gleich, den das Kanu reich
Befiederter Indianer teilt, so weich,
Als wär er feinste Luft – Luft ganz und gar,
Nur daß man hier Gewölk und Himmel sah;
Der Boden Atemluft, nur daß man halt
Tief unten reglos Wunder und erstrahlt
Den Prachtdom sah, gespiegelt in der Gänze,
Kreisend ein goldnes Sphärenrund.

[Ein rauschendes Gelage beginnt, Venus verheißt auch Endymion die Erfüllung ewiger Liebe, und alle stimmen eine Hymne zu Ehren der drei Gottheiten an.]

»König des umstürmten Meers!
Bruder des Zeus und Mitbesitzer hier
Der Elemente! Ewig neigt vor dir
In Ehrfurcht sich die Brandung. Felsengrößen,
Schrumpfend vor deinem Dreizackhieb, entblößen
Ihr Fundament, verzischen als ihr Schaum.
Gebirgsbäche, verlorn im weiten Raum
In deiner Brust, sind ewiglich im Fluß.
Du grollst nur, schon sucht dein Feind Äolus
Den Schutz der Höhle, murrt noch barsch und geht
Mit allen Sturmrebelln. Gewölk verweht,
Senkt sich ein Silberstrahl, aus deinem Haar,
Auf blaue Reiche. Deine helle Schar
Verschlingt das Morgenlicht und lenzt's entlang,
Damit du näher seist dem goldnen Sang,

Den Apollon anstimmt, derweil sein Wagen
Vorm Tor des Himmels wartet. Dir behagen
Solch Szenen nicht: du hast ein finstres Reich,
Zerfurchend diese breite Stirn. Obgleich –
Wie frisch vom Himmel, harrst du nun zumindest
Der Dinge und verbindest
Das Herrschaftsjoch mit Stunden ohne Schwere.
O hehrer Fürst der Meere!
Du sollst auf ewig unser Herz durchdringen –
Wir preisen dich und singen!

Blast leise, Pfeifen;
Die Finger laßt, ihr Lauten, zarter greifen;
Und sei kein Horn zu hörn! Umsonst, vergebens –
Kein Flor, die Knospen eines Frühlingsregens,
Kein Hauch des Taubenschlafs, kein Quellbachwogen,
Nein, nicht das Äolssurrn von Amors Bogen
Erzeugt Musik, die gleich sanft würdig wäre
Der göttlichen Kythere!
Doch laß dir, Haupt der Schönheit, nicht verhehlen
Die Opfer unsrer Seelen.

Kind, hell beschwingt!
Wer weint noch, wenn dein Lächeln ihn durchdringt?
Auf Erden Glücklose, sehn wir, es reißt
Die Todesschemen, Dunkel, die den Geist
Verfinstern, schließlich fort kraft deiner Schwingen.
O süßeste Essenz! Ziel allem Ringen!
Gott heißem Pulsschlag, Locken, die sich lösten,
Keuchenden, nackten Brüsten!
Du unsichtbares Licht im Dunkel! Löscher
Des Lichts im Licht! erlesner Gifte Mischer!
Bis wir randvoll sind, trinken deinen Becher
Wir Zecher – Zecher!
Bei deiner Mutter Lippen – «

[Endymion glaubt sich weiteren Prüfungen nicht gewachsen und entschläft. Als Nereiden nunmehr ihn in den Kristall tragen, vernimmt er die Stimme der Geliebten, die verspricht, ihn in den Himmel zu entrücken.]

Sogleich erhob der Jüngling sich: ein See
Drang still in seinen Blick, Wald nahm kühlgrün
Wie keins der Wunder, die er nun gesehn,
Der Brust ihr Flattern durch sein schlichtes Lied.
Wie glücklich doch erneut im weichen Ried!

Buch IV

Du höchste Muse! Muse meines Lands!
O erste im Gebirg! gezeugt vom Glanz
Des Himmels in geistreiner Ätherluft!
Im Norden saßt du lang in einer Gruft,
Als Wölfe noch in England Lager bauten –
Eh unser Wald vernahm von Menschenlauten,
Eh Kind noch war der erste der Druiden,
Saßt du schon lang in wildesten Gebieten,
Versunken in die Einsamkeit der Seher.
Von Osten kam erhabnes Singen näher –
Doch harrtst du aus. Dann sangen fort die Neun,
Apollos Reigen – eignen Glorienschein
Sahst du jedoch, so weinten sie vergebens
»Komm, Insel-Schwester, Du!« Voll klaren Strebens
Sprach auch Ausonia, und erneut sprach sie,
Mahnte noch schärfer – du indes gabst nie
Das eigne Ziel preis. O du hast mit Macht
Dein Werk vollendet! Muse, 's ist vollbracht,
Was unvollbracht heut nichts wär als Bedrängnis
Auf wüsten Seelen. Du weißt, welch Gefängnis
Aus Fleisch und Blut die Flügel unserm Geist
Knickt, fesselt und verletzt. Verzweiflung heißt
Das Bett für uns, es scheint, der frische Morgen
Strahlt wie zum Hohn sein Licht auf unsre Sorgen

Und dumpfes, einfallsloses Schneckenleben.
Lang sagte ich, wie glücklich, wessen Streben
Dir gilt! – doch dacht an Dichter dann, längst stumm,
Und konnt nicht beten – wie auch jetzt. Darum
Schreit ich zum Ende fort in Herzensdemut.

[Im Wald belauscht Endymion das Klagen eines Indermädchens. Auf der Stelle verliebt er sich, hin und her gerissen nun zwischen göttlichem und irdischem Glücksversprechen. Mit einem Reigen will ihn das Mädchen trösten.]

»O Sorgen,
Warum borgen
Gesundes Rosigsein, von roten Lippen? –
Um Mädchenscham zu mischen
Mit weißen Rosenbüschen?
Taufeuchter Hand Maßliebchen anzutippen?

O Sorgen,
Warum borgen
Vom Falkenaug das strahlend helle Sehnen?
Den Glühwurm zu bestrahlen?
Bei Neumond anzumalen
Den Salzseeschaum, am Ufer der Sirenen?

O Sorgen,
Warum borgen
Die vollen Melodien von Klagechören? –
Sie fahlem Abendschein
Und Nachtigall zu leihn,
Um kalten Tau vielleicht hindurchzuhören?

O Sorgen,
Warum borgen
Des Herzens Leichtheit von der Maiennacht? –
Wer an die Liebe glaubt,
Tritt Primeln nicht aufs Haupt,

Tanzt er von spät auch bis der Tag erwacht –
Nicht einer matten Blume
In euerm Heiligtume,
Wo immer er auch spielen mag und lacht.

Den Sorgen
Sagt ich Guten Morgen
Und dachte, daß ich sie verlassen hätt.
Doch heiter, heiter
Liebten sie mich weiter;
Sie bleiben mir so treu und sind so nett:
Ich würde lügen,
Sie betrügen,
Doch ach! sie bleiben treu und sind so nett.

Am Ufer, unter meinem Palmenzelt,
Saß ich und weinte: auf der ganzen Welt
War niemand, der mich fragen kam, warum –
So goß ich stumm
In Wasserlilien Tränen meiner Wangen,
Kalt wie mein Bangen.

Am Ufer, unter meinem Palmenzelt,
Saß ich und weinte: welche Braut der Welt,
Getäuscht von einem düstren Wolkenfreier,
Verbirgt kein Schleier
Am Ufer unterm dunklen Palmenzelt?

Und wie ich saß, drang übers blaue Helle
Der Hügel Lärm von Schwärmern: aus der Quelle
Ward purpurrot gefärbt ein breiter Fluß –
's war Bacchus und sein Troß!
Das ernste Horn erklang, dann Silberschellen
Küssender Zimbeln, die man heiter schlug –
's war Bacchus und sein Zug!
Ganz wie ein Winzerschwarm kam er gerannt,

Bekränzt mit Laub, die Stirnen hell entbrannt –
Irr tanzend durch das linde Tal getragen,
  Dich, Schwermut, zu verjagen!
O da, o da warst du ja kaum benannt!
Und ich vergaß dich wie des Schafhirts Klagen
Die Ilexbeern vergißt, wenn, Juniwonne,
Hohe Kastanien stehn vor Mond und Sonne –
  Ich warf mich ins Behagen!

Der junge Bacchus stand im Wagen oben,
Voll Tanzlust, seinen Efeuspeer erhoben
  Und lachend winkend;
Und schmale Bäche roten Weins umwoben
Prallweiße Arme, Schultern, weiß gewiß
  Von Venus' Perlenbiß;
Und auf dem Esel bei ihm ritt Silen,
Bestreut mit Blumen und im Weitergehn
  Weinselig trinkend.

Wo, heitre Maiden ihr! wo kamt ihr her!
So viele, und so froh, und immer mehr?
Weshalb verließt ihr euren stillen Schoß,
  Lauten und sanftres Los? –
›Wir folgen Bacchus, Bacchus auf dem Flug,
  Auf Siegeszug!
Bacchus, jung Bacchus nach! – gut, schlecht, ganz gleich,
Kommt her, ihr schöne Frau, reiht euch nunmehr
  Ins wilde Sängerheer!‹

Wo, muntre Satyrn ihr! wo kamt ihr her!
So viele, und so froh, und immer mehr?
Weshalb verließt ihr das Versteck im Wald,
  Nüsse im Eichenspalt? –
›Für Wein, Wein ließen wir den Kernbaum leer;
Für Wein den gelben Ginster, Heidegras
  Und Pilzefraß;

Wir folgen Bacchus durch die Welt, wir Zecher,
Gott reiner Lust und atemloser Becher!
Kommt her, ihr schöne Frau, reiht euch nunmehr
   Ins tolle Sängerheer!‹

Wir zogen über Ströme, ins Gebirg hinauf
Und, schlug nicht Bacchus Efeuzelte auf,
Voran mit Tiger, Leopard und rannten
   Mit Asiens Elefanten:
Voran Myriaden hier – mit Tanz und Sang,
Gestreiften Zebras, Arabern, stolz schlank,
Schwimmfuß-Alligatoren, Krokodilen,
Auf ihren Rücken, breit geschuppt, zu vielen
Lachenden Kindern, nachahmend des Hafen
Matrosen und Galeeren derber Sklaven –
Ob gleitend seidner Segel, Ruder schlagend –
   Nach Wind und Flut nicht fragend.

Erklettert Löwenmähnen, Pantherfell,
Durcheilt die Ebnen noch der letzte schnell;
Drei Tage Fahrt ein Augenblick der Wonne:
Und immer, steigt am Horizont die Sonne,
Gehn sie mit Speer und Horn durch Wildnis jagen,
   Vom Einhorn murrend getragen.

Ich sah Ägypten, sah Osiris' Throne
   Knien vor der Weinlaubkrone!
Ich sah Äthiopien dürr, doch aufrecht singen
   Zum Silberzimbelklingen!
Ich sah die Feuerkraft des Weins durchfahren
   Die grausigen Tataren!
Juwelenzepter Indiens Fürsten schwenken
Und Perlen hagelnd ihren Schatz verschenken.
Gott Brahma stöhnt aus seinen Himmelreichen,
   Und alle Priester weichen,
Erbleichen, wenn sich Bacchus' Lider senken. –

Ihm folgend, kam ich bis in diese Stille,
Mit krankem Herzen, müde – eine Grille
Verschlug mich so in diesen düstren Hain,
    Fern meinem Volk, allein –
Soviel mag gut für dich zu hören sein.

    Du Fremder!
    Durch all die Länder
Trieb mich die Suche nach den Freuden –
    Doch ach, sie sind nicht mein!
    Verhext muß ich wohl sein,
Im Gram die Mädchenblüte zu vergeuden.

    Kommt denn, Sorgen!
    Holdeste Sorgen!
Daß ich wie meinem Kind die Brust euch reich:
    Ich wollte lügen,
    Euch betrügen,
Doch lieb nichts auf der Welt nun mehr als euch.

    Es gibt nicht einen,
    Nein, nein, nicht einen,
Der gleich euch tröstet eine arme Maid:
    Ihr seid ihr Mutter
    Wie auch Bruder,
Seid Freund und Freier in der Dunkelheit.«

[Verzaubert, verfällt Endymion der Liebe zu dem Indermädchen.]

»Ach, denken darf ich nicht – bei Phöbe, nein!
Laß mich nicht denken, Engel! – wird's so sein?
Sag, Schönste, werde ich niemals mehr denken?
O jenseits Grenzen der Erinnrung lenken
Könntst du mich! schließen mein besorgtes Lid,
Blutunterlaufen und Verzweiflung müd!
Die halbe Seele mord mir sanft, und ich
Spür so die andre Hälfte ganz durch dich! –

Mir schwindelt bei so schönen weichen Wangen;
O laß sie immer so erröten! fangen
Den Wahnsinn! laß sie rosig-heiß bestreichen
Der Liebe Rot, in sicherm Schrecken keuchen. –
Dies ist nicht deine Hand, und doch ist sie's;
Und sicher dies die andre zarte – dies
Sind deine Brüste und ich nah bei ihnen!
Du schläfst? O trinken laß mich diese Tränen!
Und wispere ein Wort, damit ich weiß,
Dies ist die Welt – tausüße Blüte!«

[Die Mondin, unsichtbar über den Hirtenfürsten wachend, läßt unterdessen Merkur zwei Flügelpferde herbeizaubern. Auf ihnen steigen Endymion und das Indermädchen schlafend in die Lüfte.]

Muse der Heimat, bin ich inspiriert?
Hier schwindelt mir, und halten muß ich mich
Auf breiten Flügeln; weder fürchte ich
Die Höhe, Tiefe, Weite noch mein Blicken
Hinab. Ich sehe unter mir die Rücken
Der Pferde und die kummervolle Fracht.
Könnt ich so segeln, sehn, wär vor der Macht
Des Denkens derart furchtlos, gäb's dich nicht?

Dort schläft ein Dämmern, duftet erstes Licht
Eines sich nahenden Wunders, und seht zittern
Die Flügelrosse, schwer die Nüstern wittern,
Matt Letztes schnaubend und wie müdgerannt,
Vom eignen Feuer aschig ausgebrannt!

[Im Traum auf dem Rücken des Pferdes sieht sich Endymion vertraut unter den Göttern des Himmels wandeln. Er erwacht und findet den Traum Wirklichkeit: Phöbe beugt sich zu ihm herab.]

O taumelndes Gefühl! Auf dem Gefieder,
Zu wach nur, spürt er die erglühte Hüfte
Des zarten Mädchens. Er, der durch Lüfte

Zur Sonne stieg und starb, zu kühn und stolz,
Der fühlte, als der Wachs ihm treulos schmolz,
Sich nicht so sprachlos wie Endymion.
Pulsend flog wie auf den verbrieften Thron
Zu jenem holden Schattenglück sein Herz –
Ah, welch ein Taumeln nur! Ah, welcher Schmerz!
So zart, so schön war seine Bettgenossin,
Er konnte sie nur küssen: dann umschloß ihn
Vergessen aller Schönheit außer der
Von Phöbes Haar; erneut bat er
Um Nachsicht, jedoch mußte nochmals blicken
Zur Schläfrin – seine Seele lag in Stücken:
Sie preßte schlummernd seine Hand; und wieder
Konnte er sie nur küssen und sank nieder.
Da weinte und zerschmolz der Schattenleib.
Der Latmier rief: »Helle Göttin, bleib!
Sieh dir mein Herz an! Bei der Wahrheit Zunge –
's ist nicht dädalisch. Was folgt seinem Schwunge
Stets die Verzweiflung? Nichts soll für mich sein
Am Ziel der Seligkeit, nichts als nur Pein?«

Da schrak die schwarzgelockte Fremde auf:
Endymion hüllt' ihr Liebesblick hierauf
In Sanftmut. Unten gähnte laut der Schlaf.
»Du Gangesschwan, nie wieder trennen darf
Dies düstre Traumbild uns! Du scheinst beglückt
Im Nest der Liebesmuße, nicht bedrückt
Vom Traum des Leids, das dich und mich bedroht.
Ah, brächt mein Herzverrat auch dir den Tod! –
Sie aber weint bloß – ihre Seele kennt
Die Rache nicht. Wenn ich, wie sie ganz brennt
Vor Zärtlichkeit, ganz in der Liebe wäre!
Kann ich dich ehrn, Kind, mehr als alle Ehre,
Wenn mein Gefühl rein wie die Unschuld wär?
Ich tu's. – Was ist die Seele denn? Woher

Kam sie? Mein Eigen scheint sie nicht, und mich
Treibt keine eigne Leidenschaft, kein Ich.
Bös enden wird es: wo, wo kann es sein?
Bei Nemesis, den Geist seh ich allein
Durchs Dunkel fliegen. Doch vergib mir, Süße –
Brechen wir auf?«

[Weiter empor tragen die Pferde beide, bis mit dem Aufleuchten des Monds das Mädchen zum Schrecken Endymions zerschmilzt.]

Es liegt eine Höhle
Jenseits des Raums, in dem in scheinbarn Grenzen
Die Seelen wandelnd ihre Existenzen
Erforschen, jenseits fernsten düstern Lüften.
Finstres Gebiet umgibt sie, wo in Grüften
Begrabnen Schmerz der Geist zwar sieht, doch nicht
Ein Stündchen weinend ausruht, denn schon sticht
Ein frischer Schmerz im Innern ihn nur mehr;
Und in dem Dunkel dort fliegt weit umher
Manch Giftpfeil; sie zum Heim sich auserkoren
Hat jedes Übel: der sei erst geboren,
Der nie durchreist hat diese Höllenglut.
Doch kaum wer spürte je, wie ruhig und gut
Der Schlaf in jener tiefen Höhle ist.
Dort bohrt die Angst nicht, kennt Glück keine Frist;
Stets schlagen Schmerz-Orkane an die Tür,
Doch hinter ihr ist alles still und leer.
Schmerzhafte Böen rings, ist in ihr kein Schlag
Lauter zu hörn als im verschloßnen Sarg
Die Totenuhr dumpf pickt. Niemand tritt ein,
Der danach strebt: urplötzlich ist sie dein.
Erst wenn des Dulders Leid auch Flammen schlug,
Steht sie ihm frei: aus einem Urnenkrug,
Den schmelzend Eis speist, nimmt er eine Kelle –
Semele schmeckte nie solch reine Fülle
In mütterlicher Sehnsucht! Selger Dämmer!

Nachtparadies! wo Blässe erster Schimmer
Von Wohl ist; die Verschwiegenheit der Leeren
Beredtste Sprache; Hoffnungen verheeren;
Wo das weit hellste Auge jenes ist,
Welches traumloser Schlaf am längsten schließt.
O selges Geist-Heim! O seltsame Seele!
Vergönnt, in eigne Tiefen durch solch Höhle
Dich ganz zu retten. Heil dir, Karier, dann!
Denn nie, seitdem dein Gram und Leid begann,
Sahst du dich so zufrieden: bittrer Streit
Trieb dich zur Höhle der Verschwiegenheit.

[Endymion träumt von einem rauschenden Himmelsfestzug: Hesperus, Zephir, Flora, Aquarius und andere Götter ziehen zur Hochzeitsfeierlichkeit Cynthias. Der Latmier aber stürzt auf seinem Roß zur Erde, findet das Indermädchen wieder und entsagt allem Überirdischen.]

»O nichts war ich ergeben,
Liebte ein Nichts, hab nichts gesehn, sogar
Gespürt, denn einen großen Traum! Ich war
Vermessen gegen Liebe, Himmel, Land
Und alle Elemente, gegen 's Band
Von Sterblichem zu Sterblichem, die Blüten
Der Blumen, Kraft der Quellen und die Mythen
Begrabner Helden! Gegen eignen Ruhm
Verschwor sich meine Seele: Zweiflertum,
Das Kindern ich erzähln will und bereu.
Nie hat ein Mensch gelebt, den frei
Der Hunger trieb fern angestammter Schranken,
Ohne zu sterben. Meine Indrin, danken
Auf Knien will ich, daß du errettet hast
Mich vor zu dünner Luft: fort und verblaßt
Trübe Phantasmen. Höhlen ihr, ade!
Luft der Vision, visionenreiche See
Monströser Fluten! Nein, nie wieder täuschen
Luftige Stimmen mich bis zu den Räuschen

Verworrner Wunder, sprachlos und entsetzt.
Adieu, mein schönster Traum! obschon noch jetzt
So heiß geliebt. Einst mag's die Stunde geben,
In der vereint wir im Elysium leben.
Hier kann ich dich nicht lieben; darum werde
Ich Tauben opfern, holdstes Gut der Erde
Durchs ganze Erntejahr – so wird dein Segen
Auf mich und meine Schöne hier sich legen
Ein schlichtes Leben lang!«

[Endymion schildert dem Indermädchen die Wonnen, die beide auf Erden nun erwarten, das Mädchen aber antwortet:]

»Glaub mir, glaub,
Endymion, flöchte ich aus dem Laub
Der Phantasien Girlanden süßen Lebens,
Wärst eine du. Ah, alle Müh vergebens!
Ich kann dein Herz nicht sein: ich bin verfemt –
Bin's wirklich – bin verflucht, verschmäht, gelähmt
Von furchtbarn Dingen und Gorgonenwut.
Zweimal fragtst du, wohin ich ging. Sei gut,
Frag mich nicht mehr! Ich kann es dir nicht sagen,
Noch deine Liebe sein. Wir wärn geschlagen
Mit Rache auf der Stelle; würden sterben;
Umschlungen sterben – Wollust, dies zu denken!
Vergrößre meinen Hunger nicht, sonst senken
Netze verderbter Wonne sich auf mich.
Nein, nein, nur das nicht – segnen will ich dich
Und lang Lebwohl dir sagen.«

[In Latmos' Wäldern begrüßt Peona die beiden und berichtet von den Vorbereitungen zu einem Freudenfest, welches Cynthia den Hirtenscharen verheißen habe. Endymion indes entsagt dem Thron und will fortan als Eremit dem Himmel dienen; das Indermädchen soll in den Kreis der Jungfrauen aufgenommen werden. Im Hain um Dianas Tempel wünscht er es ein letztes Mal zu sehen.]

»Ha! ich sagte
›Schmetterlingskönig‹ – nein, bei dieser Nacht,
Des alten Rhadamanthus Schicksalsmacht,
Dem Dämmerkult, dem Pomp der Einsamkeit,
Prometheus' Ton, dem sich ein Dieb geweiht,
Bei Greis Saturnus' Stirnhaar, seinem Haupte,
Vom Schlag ewig durchkrampft, verschrieben glaubte
Ich mich Dingen des Lichts seit Kindertagen –
Zu sterben so verstoßen, so geschlagen,
Unfehlbar läßt dies Sterbliche wie mich
Zu Zweiflern werden.«

[Zerrüttet und verklärt zugleich, erreicht Endymion den geweihten Ort. Gemeinsam mit Peona erlebt er die Verwandlung des Indermädchens.]

Ihr schwarzes Haar ward strahlender, am Rücken
Zu Gold; ein hellrer Tag in ihren Blicken
Brach blau, voll Liebe an. Ja, er gewahrte
Phöbe, sein Langen! Freudig offenbarte
Den lichten Bogen sie und sprach: »Trüb, trüb
War unser Zaudern; töricht ängstlich blieb
Ich dir erst fern; dann war es Schicksalswille;
Dann ward beschlossen, aus der Erdenhülle
Soll dich, Herz, Wandel nicht vorauszusehn
Vergeistigen. Peona, fortan gehn
Durch diesen Wald wir, der dir sicher sei
Wie deine Wiege; du flieh oft herbei,
Uns zu besuchen.« Cynthia gab entfacht
Peona einen Kuß zur Guten Nacht;
Dann küßte sie ihr Bruder und sank hin
Vor seine Göttin, selig auf den Knien.
Sie reichte ihm die holde Hand und da!
Eh dreimal ihn sie küssen man noch sah,
Entschwanden sie weit fort! – Peona ging
Verwundert heim durch Wald, den Nacht umfing.

Hyperion
Ein Fragment

Buch I

Tief in der finstren Schwermut eines Tals,
Fern von des Morgenhauches Wohl gesunken,
Fern feur'gem Tag und Abends einzgem Stern,
Saß grauen Haars Saturn, stumm wie ein Stein,
Still gleich dem Schweigen um sein Lager her;
Wald über Wald hing über seinem Haupt,
Wolke an Wolke gleich. Kein Lufthauch war,
Nicht soviel Leben als am Sommertag
Kein Samenkorn aus Federgräsern raubt;
Wohin ein totes Blatt fiel, blieb es ruhn.
Ein Bach lief stumm vorbei, gedämpfter noch
Vom Schatten, den gefallen seine Gottheit
Hier warf: im Röhricht preßte die Najade
Den kalten Finger fester auf die Lippen.

Den Ufersand lang liefen breite Fußspurn
Bis dort, wohin geirrt sein Fuß noch war
Und schlief seither. Auf dem durchtränkten Grund
Lag seine alte Rechte schwach, matt, tot,
Entzeptert; reichlos war sein Aug geschlossen,
Derweil gebeugt sein Kopf zu lauschen schien
Der alten Mutter Erde, ihn zu trösten.

Es schien, von hier könnt keine Macht ihn wecken;
Doch kam dort Eine, die verwandter Hand
Die breiten Schultern griff, voll Ehrfurcht tief
Verneigt, obschon er des nicht inneward.
Sie war eine Göttin der jungen Welt;
War von Gestalt, daß Amazonenwuchs
Vor ihr pygmäenhaft schien: sie hätt Achill

Beim Schopf gepackt, gebeugt den Nacken ihm,
Gehemmt, mit einem Finger, Ixions Rad.
Breit glich ihr Antlitz einer Sphinx zu Memphis,
Postiert vielleicht im Hof eines Palasts,
Als Weise betend gen Ägypten blickten.
Doch oh! wie war dies Antlitz Marmor ungleich,
Wie schön doch, hätt die Trauer nicht die Trauer
Noch schöner als die Schönheit selbst gemacht.
In ihrem Blick lag lauschend eine Furcht,
Als hätte nun das Unheil erst begonnen,
Als hätten Vorhutwolken böser Tage
Ihr Gift vergossen und die finstre Nachhut
Wälz' mit geballtem Donnern sich einher.
Mit einer Hand griff sie zum wehen Fleck,
Wo eines Menschen Herz schlägt, so als spürte,
Obschon unsterblich, sie dort furchtbarn Schmerz;
Die andre um Saturns gekrümmten Nacken
Gelegt und bis in Höhe seines Ohrs
Gebeugt mit offnen Lippen, sprach sie Worte
Ernsten Gehalts, in tiefem Orgelton –
Klagende Worte, die, mit schwacher Zunge
Wie unsrer, etwa klängen (o wie kraftlos
Gegen den reichen Ausdruck früher Götter!):
»Saturn, schau auf! Nur, alter, armer König –
Wozu? Ich bring dir keinen Trost, nein keinen:
Ich kann nicht sagen ›O weswegen schläfst du?‹
Denn dich verließ der Himmel, und die Erde
Erkennt dich, so geschlagen, nicht als Gott;
Der Ozean, all sein feierliches Tosen,
Ließ deinen Zepter sein; und alle Luft
Ist leer von deiner grauen Herrlichkeit.
Dein Donner, neuer Weisung nun gewahr,
Zürnt zage über uns gefallnes Haus;
Dein scharfer Blitz in ungeübten Händen
Versengt, verbrennt unser einst heitres Reich.
O Zeit voll Schmerz! Momente lang wie Jahre!

Verstreicht ihr, schwillt die Wahrheit an zum Monstrum
Und legt sich so auf unsern müden Gram,
Daß keiner Hoffnung Raum zum Atmen bleibt.
Schlaf fort, Saturn – O achtlos! was nur stör ich
Derart deine verträumte Einsamkeit?
Was öffnen deine schwermutsvollen Augen?
Schlaf fort, da ich zu deinen Füßen weine!«

So wie, in der verzückten Sommernacht,
Die grünberobten Senatorn der Wälder,
Eichen, von ernsten Sternen zweigverzaubert,
Nur träumen, reglos so die Nacht lang träumen,
Bis ein verlaßner zögerlicher Windstoß
Kaum in die Stille einfällt, und schon hinstirbt,
Als ebbte Luft nach einer Welle aus –
So kam ihr Wort und ging: derweil sie weinend
Mit schöner breiter Stirn den Grund berührte,
Wo ihr gefallnes Haar sich konnt verteilen,
Ein sanftes, seidnes Fußbett für Saturn.
Ein Mond, in stetem Wandellauf, goß vier
Der silbernen Gezeiten um die Nacht,
Und noch verharrten unbewegt die beiden
Wie ein Natursteinbild im Höhlendom:
Der starre Gott noch kauernd auf der Erde,
Die Göttin traurig weinend ihm zu Füßen –
Bis endlich die erloschnen alten Augen
Saturn hob und sein Königreich dahin sah,
Die Düsternis und Trübsal jenes Orts
Und kniend die holde Göttin – und nun sprach,
Die Zunge wie gelähmt, und ihm sein Bart
Von fürchterlichen Espenschaudern bebte:
»O zartes Weib des goldenen Hyperion,
Thea, ich fühl dich, eh ich dein Gesicht seh –
Sieh auf und zeig mir unser Los in ihm;
Sieh auf und sag mir, ob solch matter Leib
Saturns ist; sag mir, ob du noch die Stimme

Saturns hörst; sag, ob diese Stirn, sich furchend,
Nackt und beraubt des großen Diadems,
Der Stirn Saturns gleicht. Wer besaß die Macht,
Mich zu verelenden? Wo kam die Kraft her?
Wie nährte man solch berstende Gewalt,
Da mir im Würgegriff die Parze schien?
Doch ist es so, und selbst bin ich erstickt,
Verbannt von jedem göttlich hohen Amt
Des sanften Wirkens auf die fahlen Sphären,
Des Wachens über Winde, über Meere,
Des stillen Waltens ob der Menschen Ernte
Und allem Tun, an dem die höchste Gottheit
Ihr liebevolles Herz erwärmt. – Ich wandte
Vom eignen Inneren mich ab; verlassen
Hab ich mein festes Ich, mein wahres Selbst,
Wer weiß wo zwischen Thron und dem Fleck Erde,
Auf dem ich sitz hier. Such es, Thea, such es!
Öffne dein ewges Aug und laß es kreisen
In allem Raum – bestirnt und Licht verloren,
Besphärt mit Lebensluft, mit öder Leere,
In Feuerräumen und im Schlund der Hölle.
Such, Thea, such! und sag mir, ob du siehst,
Wie sich ein Leib, ein Schatten, einen Weg
Auf Flügeln bahnt, im Wagen, wild dem unlängst
Verlornen Himmel nach: es muß – es muß
Ein Fortgang reif sein: König sein Saturn.
Ja, kommen müssen goldener Triumph,
Der Sturz von Göttern und Trompetenschall
Gelaßnen Sieges, Hymnen eines Fests
Im goldenen Gewölk der Mutterstadt,
Sanfter Verkündung Ruf und silbern zitternd
Saiten in hohlen Muscheln; es soll Schönes
In neuem Glanz erstrahln zur Überraschung
Der Himmelskinder. Ich will es befehlen:
Thea! Thea! Thea! wo ist Saturn?«

Auf seine Füße hob ihn diese Leidenschaft,
Ließ ihn die Hände ringen in der Luft,
Zittern und schwitzen die Druidenlocken,
Herausfiebern sein Aug, vergehn die Stimme.
Er stand, vernahm nicht Theas tiefes Schluchzen;
Und kurz darauf ergriff er schon erneut
Das Wort und sprach: »Kann ich denn nicht erschaffen?
Kann ich nicht formen? Nicht gestalten weiter
Die andre Welt, ein andres Universum,
Zu stürzen dies, zu nichts es zu zermalmen?
Wo ist ein andres Chaos? Wo?« Dies Wort
Stieg zum Olymp und ließ erzittern
Die drei Rebellen. Thea war erstaunt,
Und eine Hoffnung schien durch ihr Gebaren,
Als sie hervorstieß, schnell, doch voller Ehrfurcht:

»Dies wird die Freunde stärken, o Saturn!
Komm fort, mach Mut unserm gefallnen Haus.
Ich kenne ihr Versteck, denn dorther kam ich.«
Nur dies; schon trat sie flehentlichen Blicks
Ein Stück weit rückwärtsschreitend durch das Dunkel.
Er folgte, und voran ging sie den Weg
Durch morsches Zweigwerk, das wie Nebel nachgab,
Den Adler teilen, steigen sie vom Horst.

Auch andernorts vergoß man viele Tränen,
Mehr Kummer, diesem gleich, und gleiches Leid,
Zu groß dem irdschen Wort und Stift des Schreibers.
In Fesseln oder selbst verborgen ächzten
Nach alter Lehnspflicht Rückkehr die Titanen,
Harrten in scharfem Schmerz dem Ruf Saturns.
Nur einer aus der ganzen Mammutsippe
Bewahrte Hoheit, Herrscherkraft und Größe –
Lodernd auf kugeligem Feuer saß
Hyperion, sog ein noch Weihrauch, dampfend
Von Mensch zu Sonnengott – doch sicher nicht:

Denn wie uns Sterbliche ein Omen
Schrickt und bestürzt, so schauderte auch ihn –
Kein Hundsgeheul, kein hassenswerter Schrei
Des Dämmervogels, nicht das Umgehn dessen,
Dem just die Totenglocke einmal schlug,
Noch mittnächtlicher Lampe Prophezeiung;
Nein, Grauen, einer Riesenkraft bemessen,
Peinigten oft Hyperion. Sein Palast,
Basteit mit glühend goldnen Pyramiden,
Wo bronzne Obeliske Schatten warfen,
Glomm ein Blutrot durch seine tausend Höfe,
Die Bögen, Kuppeln, feur'gen Galerien;
Und Vorhänge aurorischen Gewölks
Erglühten grimm, da oftmals Adlerschwingen,
Wie kein erstaunter Mensch, kein Gott je sah,
Den Ort verfinsterten und Wiehern laut ward,
Wie kein erstaunter Mensch, kein Gott je hörte.
Auch, wollt er kosten vom gewürzten Dampf
Des Weihrauchs, aufgeweht von heilgen Hügeln,
Schmeckte statt Süßigkeit sein weiter Gaumen
Giftiges Erz und ekliges Metall.
Und so, den müden Westen eingebracht
Nach gänzlicher Vollendung lichten Tags,
Statt Himmelsruhe auf erhabnem Lager
Und Schlummer in den Armen von Musik,
Schritt fort er auch durch heitre Mußestunden
Mit Riesensätzen, fort von Saal zu Saal;
Indessen tief in Seitengang und Winkel
Zu Trauben sich beschwingte Diener drängten,
Erschrocken und voll Furcht; den Bangen gleich,
Die keuchend sich auf weiten Ebnen sammeln,
Wenn Turm und Zinnen beben mit der Erde.
Grad da Saturn, erwacht aus eisger Starre,
Mit Thea Schritt für Schritt den Wald durchmaß,
Stieß auf des Westens Schwelle schräg herab
Hyperion, Zwielicht breitend hinter sich.

Nun, wie gewohnt, flog sein Palasttor leicht
Und lautlos auf, nur feierliche Tuben,
Die ernst die Zephyrn bliesen, gaben süß
Und schweifend Laut, gehauchte Melodien –
Und Rosen gleich in Scharlachrot und Form,
In zartem Duft und Kühle für das Auge,
Stand jener Einlaß zu erhabnem Glanz
Weit offen, auf daß eintrete der Gott.

Er trat ein, aber trat doch voller Zorn ein;
Sein Flammenkleid schlug ihm um seine Fersen
Mit einem Krachen wie von irdschem Feuer,
Daß die ätherisch sanften Horen, flatternd
Auf Taubenschwingen, flohn. Er flammte weiter
Von Schiff zu Schiff, Gewölbe zu Gewölbe,
Durch Lauben duftenden, umwirkten Lichts,
Arkaden, leuchtend, lang, demantbefliest,
Bis er die große Hauptkuppel erreichte.
Wild hielt er unter ihr, er stampfte auf
Und ließ vom Fundament bis zu den Türmen
Sein goldnes Reich erzittern; und bevor
Das Donnergrollen sich verlief darauf,
Brach seine Stimme, müd des Gottesmaßes,
Hervor und sprach: »O Träume Tag und Nacht!
O Mißgestalten! Bildnisse der Pein!
O Schemen, reg in kaltem, kaltem Dämmer!
Phantome, schmalbeohrt, krautschwarzer Tümpel!
Was kenn ich euch? hab euch gesehn? Weshalb
Ist so zerrüttet dies mein ewig Wesen,
Daß es erblickt und schaut solch neue Schrecken?
Gefallen ist Saturn, nun fall auch ich?
Muß ich die Freistatt meiner Rast verlassen,
Die Wiege meines Ruhms, die milden Breiten,
Den ruhigen Überfluß an selgem Licht,
Die Lauben von Kristall und reinen Tempel
In meinem ganzen lichten Reich? Es bleibt

Verödet, leer und mir nun keine Zuflucht.
Den Glanz, die Helle und das Ebenmaß,
Ich seh sie nicht – nur Dunkel, Tod und Dunkel.
Selbst hier, in meiner Ruhe Mittelpunkt,
Dringen die düstren Bilder, um zu herrschen,
Zu höhnen, blenden, würgen meine Pracht. –
Fall! – Nein, bei Tellus, ihren salzgen Kleidern!
Über die feur'gen Grenzen meiner Reiche
Will fürchterlich ich eine Rechte strecken,
Erschrecken Zeus, Rebell und Donnrersäugling,
Und auf den alten Thron Saturn erheben.« –
Er sprach, er schloß, indes nur härtre Drohung
Im Hals ihn würgte, aber nicht hervorbrach;
Denn so wie in Theatern voller Menschen
Der Lärm nur wächst, je mehr man ausruft »Leise!«,
Regten die fahlen Schemen sich aufs Wort
Hyperions dreimal grauenvoll und kalt;
Und von der Spiegelfläche, wo er stand,
Stieg Nebel auf wie von beschäumtem Sumpf.
Schon kroch durch seinen Leib die Todesangst
Heran, kroch von den Füßen bis zur Krone,
Wie eine Schlange, muskulös und riesig,
Sich vorschiebt langsam, Kopf und Hals gekrümmt
Vor überspannter Kraft. Befreit, floh er
Den Osttorn zu, und sechs taufeuchte Stunden,
Eh fristgemäß die Dämmrung sich würd röten,
Hieb wild sein Hauch an die verschlafnen Tore,
Wusch ihren schweren Dunst fort, sprengte sie
Weit auf jäh auf des Ozeans kalte Fluten.
Der Feuerballplanet, auf welchem täglich
Von Ost nach West den Himmel er durchritt,
Kreiste dahin in schwarzen Wolkendecken –
Nicht ganz verhüllt durch sie, blind und versteckt,
Glühten doch ab und an die lichten Sphären,
Breitgürtige Koluren, Bögen, Kreise,
Hindurch und wirkten aufs vermummte Dunkel

Formschöne Blitze vom Nadir empor
Bis zum Zenit – uralte Hieroglyphen,
Die Astrologen scharfsichtig und Weise,
Einst wandelnd auf der Erde, sinnend
Im Anblick durch Jahrhunderte gewannen –
Verlorn jetzt bis auf mächtige Verbleibsel
Aus Stein und schwarzem Marmor – ohne Sinn,
Ihr Wissen längst enteilt. Als Glorie trug
Zwei Schwingen dieser Ball, zwei Silberschwingen,
Allzeit erhoben bei des Gottes Nahn;
Und einzeln tauchten nun die mächtgen Federn
Im Dunkel auf, bis sämtlichst sie gespreizt warn,
Indes der Leuchtball Finsternis verblieb,
Erwartend den Befehl Hyperions.
Gern hätt befohln er, gern den Thron bestiegen
Und Tag es werden lassen – schon zum Wechsel.
Er durfte nicht. – Nein, war er auch ein Urgott:
Die heilgen Zeiten durfte niemand stören.
Daher verblieb das Werk der Dämmerung
In der Entstehung, ganz wie hier erzählt.
Die Silberschwingen spannten schwesterlich
Die Segel ihres Balls; weit öffneten
Die Tore sich aufs dunkle Reich der Nacht,
Und der Titan, gehetzt von neuer Qual,
Gewohnt zu strahln, nicht sich zu beugen, beugte
Den Geist in schwerem Zwang der Not der Zeit;
Und eine düstre Wolkenbank entlang,
Hin auf die Grenze zwischen Tag und Nacht,
Streckte er sich in Gram und mattem Glanz.
Wie er dort lag, sahn voller Mitleid auf ihn
Der Himmel und die Sterne, und die Stimme
Des Coelus, flüsternd aus dem Weltenraum,
Sprach ernst und leise solches in sein Ohr:
»O hellstes meiner Kinder, Erd-geborn
Und All-gezeugt, Sohn der Mysterien,
Verhüllt geblieben selbst dem Mächtepaar,

Das schaffend dich sich traf; bei dessen Freuden
Und süßen Zuckungen und sanften Wonnen
Ich, Coelus, staun, wie und woher sie kamen;
Bei dessen Früchten, welcher Form sie seien,
Deutlich und sichtbar – göttliche Symbole,
Verkörperungen jenes schönen Lebens,
Nicht sichtbar ausgestreut im ewgen Raum:
Von ihnen neugeformt wardst du, o Hellstes!
Von ihnen Brüder wie auch Göttinnen!
Ein böser Streit herrscht zwischen euch und Aufruhr
Von Sohn zu Stammherrn. Fallen sah ich ihn,
Vom Thron gestürzt sah ich den Erstgebornen!
Nach mir die Arme reckte er, nach mir
Schrie aus den Donnern um sein Haupt sein Ruf!
Bleich ward ich und verbarg im Dunst mein Antlitz.
Auch du bist solch Verhängnis nah? Fast fürcht ich's:
Ich sah auch meine Söhne Göttern ungleich.
Göttlich geschaffen wurdet ihr, und göttlich
In ernster Haltung, sorglos, feierlich,
Ruhig gleich hehrn Göttern lebtet ihr und herrschtet:
Nun seh ich Furcht in euch, Hoffnung und Zorn;
Taten der Wut und Leidenschaft – grad so
Wie bei den Menschen der vergehnden Welt,
Die sterben müssen. Dies ist Leid, o Sohn!
Vorzeichen von Zerfall, jäh'm Schrecken, Sturz!
Doch kämpfe du, soweit du es vermagst,
Dich rühren kannst, ein offenbarer Gott,
Und jeder bösen Stunde kannst entgegnen
Ätherische Gestalt. Ich bin nur Stimme;
Ich leb das Leben von Gezeit und Wind,
Mehr als Gezeit und Wind richt ich nicht aus –
Du aber kannst's. Du sei im Vortrab der
Ereignisse; ja, greif des Pfeiles Haken,
Bevor die straffe Sehne surrt. – Zur Erde!
Denn dort findst du Saturn und seine Qualen!
Derweil will ich bewachen deine Sonne

Und sorgsam Hüter deiner Zeiten sein.« –
Halb war dies Sphärenwispern hergedrungen,
Schon stand Hyperion und hob zu Sternen
Seine gewölbten Lider, hielt sie offen,
Bis es verklang; und noch hielt er sie offen;
Und noch warn sie die duldsam hellen Sterne.
Dann, seine breite Brust geruhsam beugend,
Dem Taucher gleich in perlenreichen Meern,
Bog übers luftge Ufer er sich vor
Und sprang ganz lautlos in die tiefe Nacht.

Buch II

Beim gleichen Schlag der großen Zeitenflügel,
Als in durchrauschte Luft Hyperion glitt,
Kam Thea mit Saturn zum traur'gen Ort,
Wo Kybele und die Titanen klagten.
's war eine Höhle, wo kein Lichtstrahl spöttisch
Auf Tränen konnte schimmern; wo ihr Stöhnen
Sie fühlten, doch nicht hörten im Gebrüll
Donnernden Wasserfalls und heisern Sturzbachs,
Guß eines steten Schwalls, wer weiß, wohin.
Grat vorspringend vor Grat und Felsen, scheinbar
Ewig wie eben sich vom Schlaf erhebend,
Hielten die Riesenhörner Stirn an Stirn
Und schufen so in tausend reichsten Launen
Ein rechtes Dach für dieses Nest der Qual.
Anstatt auf Thronen saßen hart auf Flint sie,
Lager aus rauhem Stein und Schiefergrat,
Starrend vor Erz. Versammelt warn nicht alle:
In Folterketten die, umherirrnd andre.
Koeus und Gyges und Briareus,
Typhon und Dolor und Porphyrion
Und andre waren, Stämmigste im Angriff,
Gepfercht in Schichten mühevollen Atmens,

Gekerkert in opakes Element, damit
Verbissen blieben Zähne, ihre Glieder,
Metallnen Adern gleich, verkrampft umschlungen;
Bewegungslos bis auf die großen Herzen,
Wogend im Schmerz und schauderhaft durchzuckt
Vom roten Tiegel fieberheißen Pulsschlags.
Es irrte Mnemosyne durch die Welt;
Weit fort von ihrem Mond geschweift war Phöbe;
Frei, streiften viele andre noch umher,
Ihr Großteil aber fand hier triste Zuflucht.
Kaum Bild voll Leben, lagen sie verstreut,
Riesig und seitlings, wie in trübem Kreis
Druidensteine im verlaßnen Moor,
Wenn kalter Regen anhebt abends im
Finstern November und ihr Chorgewölbe,
Der Himmel selbst, die Nacht hindurch verhängt ist.
Jeder hielt sich bedeckt, gab seinem Nachbarn
Nicht Wort noch Blick noch Regung der Verzweiflung.
So Kreus; seine schwere Eisenkeule
Lag bei ihm, und zerschlagne Felsenrippen
Zeugten von Wut, eh so erschlafft er hinsank.
Auch Iapetus; gepackt den fleckigen
Hals einer Schlange, ihre Hakenzunge
Dem Schlund entquetscht, entrollt in ganzer Länge,
Tot – weil die Kreatur nicht konnte speien
Ihr Gift ins Aug des triumphiernden Zeus.
Dann Kottus; rücklings lag er, Kinn zu oberst,
Ganz wie gepeinigt, denn noch immer hielt
Am Flint er seinen Schädel, offnen Munds,
Die Augen furchtbar rollend. Ihm zunächst
Asia, entstammt der ungeheuren Kaf,
Die, obgleich weiblich, ihrer Mutter Tellus
Zufügte ärgre Qual als irgend Sohn:
Gedanken mehr als Schmerz verriet ihr Antlitz,
Denn düster träumte sie von ihrem Ruhm,
Und in dem weiten Phantasiereich standen

Wetteifernd hohe Tempel palmbeschattet
Am Oxus und auf heilgen Gangesinseln.
Wie sich an ihren Anker lehnt die Hoffnung,
So lehnte, wen'ger hold, an einem Zahn sie,
Verlorn vom größten ihrer Elefanten.
Auf einem rauhen Felssims über ihr,
Gestützt auf einen Arm, sonst hingestreckt,
Enkeladus, der finstre – zahm und sanft einst
Gleich einem Ochsen, weidend in den Auen;
Nun tigerwild, löwengesinnt, erzürnt,
Sann, plante er und schleuderte schon jetzt
Gebirge im nicht lange mehr verschobnen,
Im zweiten Krieg, der schreck die jüngern Götter,
Bis sie in Vogel-, Viehgestalt sich flöhn.
Ihm unweit Atlas; neben ihm am Boden
Phorkus, Herr der Gorgonen. Dicht benachbart
Okeanus, dann Thetis, ihr im Schoß
Klymene, schluchzend unter wirrem Haar.
Inmitten aller Themis, Ops zu Füßen,
Die Königin verhüllt vor jedem Blick,
Verschwommner die Gestalt, als wenn die Wipfel
Von Kiefern dichte Nacht mit Wolken mengt –
Und andre mehr, mit Namen nicht zu nennen.
Denn spreizen sich der Muse Schwingen luftwärts –
Wer hemmte ihren Flug? So sing sie von
Saturn und Führerin, entstiegen nun
Auf schlüpfrigfeuchten Pfaden einem Abgrund
Noch größrer Grauen. Über finstrer Klippe
Erschienen ihre Köpfe, wuchsen an,
Bis beider Schritt auf gleicher Höhe trat,
Da streckte Thea zitternd ihre Arme
Über die Grenzen jenes Nests der Qual aus
Und blickte seitwärts in Saturns Gesicht.
Dort sah sie ärgsten Streit – den hehren Gott
Im Kampf mit all der Schwäche von Betrübtheit,
Von Wut, von Furcht, von Angst, von Rache, Reue,

Wahn, Hoffnung, doch vor allem von Verzweiflung.
Umsonst focht er solch Plagen an; die Parze
Hatte ein Sterbeöl auf ihm vergossen,
Ein Gift, ihn zu entweihen, so daß Thea,
Erschrocken, an sich hielt und ihn vorbei,
Als ersten einließ zur gefallnen Sippe.

Wie das beladne Herz uns Sterblichen
Nur mehr gequält, nur mehr durchfiebert wird,
Wenn es dem trauervollen Haus sich nähert,
Wo andre Herzen siech von selben Wunden –
So fühlte kraftlos, als er in den Kreis trat,
Saturn sich und wär in ihn hingesunken,
Wär nicht Enkeladus' Blick er begegnet,
Bei dessen Größe, dessen Ehrfurcht vor ihm
Er jäh wie inspiriert ward und er rief
»Titanen, seht euren Gott!« Da stöhnte mancher;
Sprang mancher auf; rief mancher ebenfalls;
Schrien manche, weinten, alle tief verneigt;
Und Ops, die schwarzen Schleierfalten lüftend,
Zeigte die bleiche Stirn und blassen Wangen,
Die Brauen, dünn und schwarz, und hohlen Augen.
Ein Brausen ist in ödgewachsnen Kiefern,
Hebt Winter seine Stimme; ein Geräusch
Fährt durch Unsterbliche, bestimmt ein Gott
Durch Fingerzeig, wie er die Zung beladen
Mit unaussprechlicher Gedanken Wucht will,
Mit Donner, mit Musik und mit Gepränge:
Es gleicht dem Brausen ödgewachsner Kiefern,
Dem, wenn in solch bebergter Welt es ausklingt,
Kein Laut mehr folgt; hier, unter den Gefallnen,
Verklingend aber, wuchs daraus die Stimme
Saturns wie eine Orgel neu beginnt
Ihr Tönen, wenn, verstummt kurz, andrer Wohlklang
Noch silbrig zittern läßt die klirrnde Luft.
So schwoll sie an: »Nicht meine traur'ge Brust,

Die selbst sich Richter und Erforscher ist,
Nennt mir den Grund, weshalb ihr so zu sein habt.
Nicht die Legenden aus der Tage ersten,
Studiert in jenem geist-erfüllten Urbuch,
Das Uranus, gestirnt, mit lichtem Finger
Vom Strand des Dunkels hob, als es die Wellen
Flach ebbend noch im seichten Dämmer bargen –
Und Buch, das, wie ihr wißt, ich stets erhielt
Als mir grundsichern Schemel – Ah, unsichern!
Nicht dies noch Zeichen, nicht Symbol noch Omen
Im Element, ob Erd, Luft, Wasser, Feuer –
Im Kampf, im Frieden oder Streit des einen
Gegen das andre, zwei, drei oder alle
Für sich gegen die andern drei, wie Feuer
Laut mit der Luft kämpft, Regenfluten beide
Ersäufen, beide pressen auf die Erde,
Wo, Schwefel findend, vierfach Wut die Welt
Aus öden Angeln hebt – nicht jener Kampf,
Aus dem ich seltsam tiefe Lehren zieh,
Nennt mir den Grund, weshalb ihr so zu sein habt –
Nein, nichts enträtselt mir, obgleich ich such
Und mich versenk ins Allbuch der Natur
Bis hin zur Ohnmacht, was ihr, Gottheiten,
Die Ersten der gestalthaft tastbarn Götter,
Euch ducken solltet unter, im Vergleich,
Machtlose Stärke. Dennoch seid ihr hier!
Titanen, soll ich sagen ›Auf!‹? – Ihr stöhnt;
Soll sagen ›Kriecht!‹? – Ihr stöhnt. Was kann ich tun?
O weiter Himmel! Unsichtbarer Vater!
Was tu ich? Sagt mir, all ihr Brudergötter,
Wie kämpfen wir und lenken unsern Zorn!
O sprecht jetzt euren Rat, das Ohr Saturns
Ist ausgehungert. Du, Okeanus,
Wägst Höhn und Tiefen, und in deinem Antlitz
Seh ich erstaunt die würdevolle Ruhe,
Mit der man sinnt und nachdenkt. Hilf uns weiter!«

So endete Saturn; der Gott des Meers,
Sophist und Weiser keines Hains Athens,
Doch der Versenkung in sein Schattenwasser,
Stand auf, sein Haar nicht triefend, und hub an –
Ein Murmeln, das die Zunge, erstmals willig,
Kindgleich vom schwer umschäumten Sandstrand lernte.
»O ihr, die Wut verzehrt! die, zorndurchbohrt,
Besiegt euch krümmt und eure Qual noch nährt!
Schließt eure Sinne und verstopft die Ohren,
Kein Blasebalg dem Zorn ist meine Stimme.
Doch, wer da will, hör zu, wie ich beweise,
Daß, notgedrungen, euch zu beugen frommt;
Und im Beweis will viel an Trost ich geben,
Wollt ihr den Trost in seiner Wahrheit nehmen.
Wir fallen durch Naturgesetz, nicht kraft
Des Donners oder Zeus. Großer Saturn,
Wohl hast durchsiebt du der Atome All;
Doch eben aus dem Grund, weil du als König
Geblendet schon aus bloßer Vormacht bist,
Blieb deinem Aug verschattet eine Straße,
Auf welcher ich zur ewgen Wahrheit schritt.
Zuerst: wie du nicht warst der Mächte erste,
Bist du die letzte nicht – es kann nicht sein:
Weder der Anfang bist du noch das Ende.
Aus Chaos kam und mütterlichem Dunkel
Licht, erste Frucht des inneren Tumults,
Der trägen Gärung, die zu Wundersamem
Reif ward in sich. Die reife Stunde kam,
Und mit ihr Licht, und Licht, vereinend sich
Mit seinem eignen Schöpfer, stieß alsbald
Den ganzen ungeheuren Stoff ins Leben.
Zu dieser Stunde waren, die uns zeugten,
Der Himmel und die Erde, offenbar;
Dann, Erstgeborner, fandst du mit uns Riesen
Regiernd dich über neue, schöne Reiche.
Nun kommt der Wahrheit Schmerz, wem Schmerz sie ist –

O Torheit! denn ertragen nackte Wahrheit,
Ins Auge sehn den Dingen, ganz gefaßt,
Das ist die höchste Macht. Merket es wohl!
Wie Erde, Himmel schöner sind, weit schöner
Als Chaos, leeres Dunkel, zwar einst Höchste,
Und wie wir Erde, Himmel übertreffen
In Form und schöner, kräftiger Gestalt,
Im Willen, freien Tun, Gemeinsamkeit
Und tausend andern Zeichen reinern Lebens,
So folgt uns frisch Vollkommnes auf den Fersen,
Macht stärkrer Schönheit noch, aus uns geborn,
Bestimmt, zu überragen uns wie wir
An Glanz das alte Dunkel. Auch sind dadurch
Wir nicht besiegter als durch uns die Herrschaft
Des ungestalten Chaos. Sagt mir, zürnt
Der dumpfe Grund dem stolzen Wald, den er
Nährte und noch nährt, schöner als er selbst?
Kann er die Herrschaft grüner Haine leugnen?
Soll neidisch auf die Taube sein der Baum,
Weil jene gurrt und schneeige Flügel hat,
Weithin zu schweifen und ihr Glück zu finden?
Wir sind solch Wald, und unser lichtes Zweigwerk
Erzeugte nicht verlaßne, bleiche Tauben,
Nein, Adler, goldgefiedert, deren Schönheit
Sie über uns hebt und die daher rechtens
Auch herrschen. Denn 's ist ewiges Gesetz,
Daß größte Schönheit größte Macht verleih'.
Ja, bring durch dies Gesetz ein neu Geschlecht
Unsern Bezwingern Leiden wie jetzt uns.
Erblicktet ihr den jungen Gott der Meere,
Der mich vom Thron stieß? Saht ihr sein Gesicht?
Erblicktet seinen Wagen, hingeschäumt
Von stolz beschwingten Wesen, die er schuf?
Ich sah ihn hineiln auf gestillten Wassern
Mit solchem Glühn von Schönheit in den Augen,
Daß mich's bezwang, ein trüb Lebwohl zu sagen

All meinem Reich: trüb sagte ich Lebwohl
Und kam hierher, zu sehn, welch schmerzvoll Los
Gewirkt auf euch und wie am besten ich
Euch brächte Trost in diesem größten Elend.
Empfangt die Wahrheit und sei sie euch Balsam.«

Ob spielend überzeugt oder verächtlich
Sie Schweigen wahrten, als Okeanus
Sein Raunen ließ, welch tiefstes Sinnen weiß es?
Doch war's so; eine Zeit gab niemand Antwort
Bis auf die eine, unbemerkt, Klymene;
Doch nein, sie gab nicht Antwort, klagte bloß
Sanft aufblickenden Augs, die Lippen fiebernd,
Sprach zaghaft solches unter den Ergrimmten:
»O Vater, als hier einfältigste Stimme
Weiß ich nur, daß die Freude uns verließ
Und dies Ding Leid sich schlich in unsre Herzen,
Um ewig dortzubleiben, wie ich fürcht.
Ich kündete kein Unheil, glaubte ich,
Solch schwach Geschöpf könnt abwenden die Hilfe,
Die rechtens kommen sollt von mächtgen Göttern.
Doch laßt mein Leid mich sagen, laßt mich sagen,
Was ich vernahm, wie es mich weinen machte
Und wissen, daß uns alle Hoffnung floh.
Ich stand am Strand, an einem heitern Strand,
Umweht vom süßen Lufthauch eines Lands
Des Dufts, der Ruhe, Bäume und der Blumen.
Voll stiller Freude war's, wie ich voll Gram;
Zu voll der Freude, herrlich sanfter Wärme,
So daß im Herzen ich die Regung spürte,
Zu tadeln und zu schmähn solch Einsamkeit
Mit Schmerzgesängen, Klängen unsrer Qualen,
Mich setzte, einer Muschel Mund nahm
Und in ihn summte und ihm Melodie gab –
O Melodie dahin! denn da ich sang
Und arm an Kunst verwehn ließ in die Brisen

Der dumpfen Muschel Hall, drang aus dem Schatten
Des Nachbarstrands, ein Eiland in der See,
Mit wechselvollem Wind ein Zauber her,
Der mich vergehn ließ und zugleich belebte.
Ich schleuderte die Muschel in den Sand,
Wo sie die Gischt durchfloß wie meinen Sinn
Durchfloß dies neue seliggoldne Lied.
Ein Tod voll Leben war in jedem Klangschwall,
Den Gruppen hingerißner rascher Töne,
Die, nach und nach und alle doch zugleich,
Wie Perlen, jäh vom Faden tropfend, fielen.
Und dann ein andrer, dann ein andrer Klang,
Jeder gleich einer Taube, die vom Ölzweig
Musikbeschwingt, nicht stillen Fittichs auffliegt,
Zu kreisen um mein Haupt, mich krank zu machen
Vor Glück und Schmerz zugleich. Der Schmerz blieb siegreich,
Und ich hielt die berauschten Ohrn mir zu,
Als, auch durchs Zittern meiner Hände dringend,
Süßer als alle Töne eine Stimme
Nun immer rief: ›Apoll! junger Apoll!
Des Morgens Glanz Apoll! junger Apoll!‹
Ich floh, sie folgte mir und rief ›Apoll!‹
O Vater, Brüder, hättet ihr solch Schmerz
Empfunden – o Saturn, hättst du's empfunden,
Ihr hießt nicht diese zu willfährge Zunge
Vermessen, wagt sie so, gehört zu werden.«

Bis hier floß ihre Stimme, scheu dem Bach gleich,
Der, einen Kieselstrand entlang sich schlängelnd,
Aufs Meer zu stoßen bangt – doch stieß aufs Meer sie
Und schauderte: denn sie verschlang der Zorn
Enkeladus', des Riesen mächtge Stimme –
Die schweren Silben, ähnlich trägen Wogen
In den halbvollen Höhln der Felsenriffe,
Dröhnten heran, da auf den Arm gestützt

Er blieb, nicht aufstand aus reinster Verachtung:
»Sollen wir hören nun auf Allzu-Kluge
Oder auf Allzu-Törichte, Giganten?
Nicht Donnerkeil auf Donnerkeil, bis all
Das Rüstzeug des Empörers Zeus verbraucht wär,
Nicht Welt um Welt, getürmt auf diese Schultern,
Zermarterten mich mehr als Kinderplappern
Inmitten dieser quälenden Entthronung.
Sprecht! Brüllt! Schreit! Heult! ihr schläfrigen Titanen.
Vergeßt die Schläge ihr, die schnöden Stöße?
Fällte euch nicht ein jugendlicher Arm?
Vergißt du denn, du Scheinmonarch der Wogen,
Dein Kochen in den Meern? Was, ich entfachte
Mit den paar simplen Worten euren Zorn?
O Glück, nun seh ich, ihr seid nicht verloren.
O Glück, nun sehe ich wohl tausend Augen
Auf Rache offen glühn!« – Als dies er sagte,
Erhob er seinen mächtgen Leib und stand,
Nun sprechend ohne Unterbrechung solches:
»Jetzt da ihr Flammen, lehr ich euch zu brennen,
Zu fegen aus dem Äther unsre Feinde;
Wild anzufachen krumme Feuerdengel
Und wegzusengen Zeus' geschwollne Wolken,
In seinem Zelt ersticktes Schwächlingswesen.
O laßt ihn spürn das Übel, das er tat;
Denn spott ich auch der Lehr Okeanus',
Mich schmerzt weit mehr als der Verlust von Reichen:
Frieden und schlummerhafte Ruhe flohn;
Die Zeit, ganz unberührt von bittrem Krieg,
Als all die schönen Himmelsexistenzen
Aug-offen ratend, was wir sprächen, kamen –
Das war, eh unsre Stirn das Runzeln lernte,
Die Lippe mehr als feierliche Laute;
War, eh wir wußten, das beschwingte Ding,
Sieg, kann gewinnen man, kann man verlieren.

Und denkt daran, daß unser lichtster Bruder,
Daß unentehrt noch immer ist Hyperion! –
Hyperion, seht! sein Strahlen, es ist hier!«

Ein jeder Blick lag auf Enkeladus
Und sah, indes Hyperions Name noch
Von seinen Lippen aufflog ins Gewölbe,
Ein blasses Schimmern auf den finstern Zügen –
Wild nicht mehr, denn so manchen Gott sah er
Grimm wie er selbst. Er blickte auf sie alle
Und sah in jedem Antlitz einen Lichtglanz,
Nur strahlnder in Saturns, wo weiße Locken
Wie Gischtschaum leuchteten um einen Kiel,
Taucht in die mittnächtliche Bucht der Bug.
In bleich-silberner Stille blieben sie,
Bis plötzlich Helligkeit, dem Morgen gleich,
Durch all die vorstehnd dunklen Schroffen drang,
All die betrübten Orte des Vergessens
Und jeden Schlund, durch jede alte Kluft
Und jede Höhe, jede düstre Tiefe,
Ob stumm, ob brüllnd vor laut gequälten Bächen.
Und all die immerwährnden Katarakte
Und ungestümen Ströme fern und nah,
Gehüllt zuvor in Nacht und Riesenschatten,
Sahn nun das Licht und machten es entsetzlich.
Es war Hyperion: granitnen Gipfel
Berührnd mit lichtem Fuß, stand er zu schauen
Das Elend, ausgeliefert durch sein Strahlen
Dem hassenswertsten Anblick seiner selbst.
Golden sein Haar numidisch kurzer Locken,
Ein König von Gestalt, ein weiter Schatten
Inmitten seiner Helle wie die Masse
Des Memnonbilds bei Sonnenuntergang,
Reist man vom dämmerigen Osten an.
Seufzer, auch sie gleich Memnons Harfe klagend,

Entfuhrn ihm, da gedankenvoll die Hände
Er aneinanderrieb und schweigend dastand.
Neu griff Verzweiflung die gefallnen Götter
Beim Anblick des betrübten Herrn des Tags,
Und mancher barg sein Antlitz vor dem Licht.
Wild aber warf Enkeladus den Blick
Auf seine Brüder – und, bei dessen Funkeln,
Erhoben sich nach Iapetus auch Kreus
Und Phorkus, meergeborn, und schritten einig
Zum Platz, wo er auf seinem Gipfel ragte.
Dort riefen jene vier Saturnus' Namen;
Vom Gipfel rief Hyperion: »Saturn!« –
Saturn saß nahe bei der Göttermutter,
Die freudlos blieb, obwohl die Götter riefen
Aus dumpfen Kehlen alle nun »Saturn!«

Buch III

So zwischen Aufruhr und betrübtem Frieden,
Waren zutiefst zerrüttet die Titanen.
O laß sie, Muse! laß sie ihrem Schmerz;
Du bist zu schwach, solch grausen Kampf zu singen:
Ein einzeln Elend, das steht deinen Lippen
Am besten, Hymnen auf einsamen Gram.
Laß sie, o Muse! fortan findest du
So manche alte und gefallne Gottheit
Vergeblich irrn um aufgegebne Küsten.
Indessen rühr du fromm die Delph'sche Harfe
Und wird nur Himmelswind mit seinem Hauch
Sanft trillern helfen auf der Dor'schen Flöte,
Denn sieh! es gilt dem Vater aller Dichtung.
Gib Röte allem, was zu Scharlach neigt,
Laß Rosen glühn, daß sie die Luft erwärmen,
Und das Gewölk des Abends und der Früh
In Vliesen üppig über Hügel fahrn;

In Bechern wallen laß den roten Wein,
Kalt sprudelnd Quelln gleich; zartbelippte Muscheln,
Am Strand, in großen Tiefen, purpurn werden
Im letzten Labyrinth; und laß das Mädchen
Rot brennen, wie nach heißem Kuß verwirrt.
Belaubte Mutterinsel der Kykladen,
Frohlock, o Delos, grünen Ölbaums voll,
Voll Pappeln, Palmen, schattigkühl, und Buchen,
In denen lautste Lieder bläst der Zephyr,
Und Haselbüschen, dunklen Stamms im Schatten:
Apoll ist wiederum das goldne Thema!
Wo weilte er, als der Gigant der Sonne
Hell dastand, ringsumher das Leid der Seinen?
Vereint verlassen hatte schöne Mutter
Und Zwillingsschwester er im Schlaf der Laube
Und war im Morgenzwielicht hingewandert
Entlang den Uferweiden eines Bachs,
Bis zu den Knöcheln tief in Maienlilien.
Die Nachtigall war still, und wenig Sterne
Säumten im Himmel, während schon die Drossel
Sanftkehlig anhub. Auf der ganzen Insel
War kein Versteck, keine verlaßne Höhle
Nicht heimgesucht vom Murmellaut der Wellen,
Obgleich kaum hörbar in manch grünem Winkel.
Er lauschte, weinte, und die Tränen rannen
Am goldnen Bogen, den er hielt, hell nieder.
So stand er halbgeschloßnen, trüben Augs,
Indes aus schweren Zweigen nahebei
Gemessen eine hehre Göttin trat
Und Nachricht für ihn lag in ihren Mienen,
Die eifrig rätselnd er verwirrt begann
Zu lesen, während er voll Wohllaut sprach:
»Wie kamst du übers unbegangne Meer?
Strich denn solch hehre Stirn und Leib in Tüchern
Durch diese Täler unsichtbar bisher?
Sicher vernahm ich dies Gewand schon streifen

Über gefallnes Laub, wenn ich allein
Im kühlen Wald saß. Sicher spürte ich
Dem Rascheln dieser breiten Säume nach
Auf grasgen Einsamkeiten und sah Blumen
Die Köpfe heben, da noch schwand das Wispern.
Göttin! schon früher sah ich diese Augen
Und ihre ewge Ruh, dies ganze Antlitz,
Oder ich träumte.« – »Ja«, sprach die Erhabne,
»Du hast von mir geträumt und fandst erwachend
Ganz golden eine Leier neben dir,
Der, schlugst du ihre Saiten, all das weite,
Nie müde Ohr des Universums
Lauschte in Pein und Lust bei der Geburt
Solch klingend neuen Wunders. Ist's nicht seltsam,
Daß, so beschenkt, du weinst? Erzähl mir, Jüngling,
Welch Schmerz du spüren kannst; denn ich bin traurig,
Vergießt du Tränen. Deinen Gram erklär
Einer, die hier auf dieser öden Insel
Die Hütrin deines Schlafs und Wachseins war
Vom Tag, da erstmals deine Kinderhand
Blind schwache Blumen pflückte, bis dein Arm
Den Heldenbogen ewig konnte spannen.
Zeig, was dein Herz birgt, einer greisen Macht,
Die Throne, heilig und uralt, verließ,
Dich zu verkündigen und Schönheit, die
Geboren ist.« – Darauf erwiderte,
Nun plötzlich prüfend und erhellten Blicks,
Apoll, indes die tönendweiße Kehle
Erbebte von den Silben: »Mnemosyne!
Dein Name fliegt mir zu, ich weiß nicht, wie;
Warum dir sagen, was so ganz du siehst?
Warum mich mühn zu zeigen, was dein Mund
Nicht als geheim kennt? Mir schließt dunkel, dunkel
Und schmerzvoll schnöd die Augen das Vergessen:
Ich such zu sehn, was ich so traurig bin,
Bis eine Schwermut meine Glieder lähmt;

Dann setz ich mich ins Gras und klag wie einer,
Der Flügel hatte früher. O was muß ich
Betrogen und verdammt mich fühln, wenn herrnlos
Die Luft weicht meinem Schritt, der aufstrebt? Was
Nach Rasen treten, so dem Fuß verhaßt?
Weis, holde Göttin, mir ein Unbekanntes:
Gibt es nicht andres Land als diese Insel?
Was sind die Sterne? Dort die Sonne, Sonne!
Und der so gleichmäßige Glanz des Monds!
Und Tausende von Sternen! Weis den Weg mir
Zu einem ganz besonders schönen Stern,
Und ich will in ihn fliegen mit der Leier
Und selig beben sehn sein silbern Scheinen.
Ich hörte Wolken donnern. Wo ist Macht?
Wes Hand, wes Wesenskraft, welch eine Gottheit
Bewirkt solch Aufruhr in den Elementen,
Da ich hier müßig lausche an den Ufern
In furchtlosem doch schmerzendem Nichtwissen?
O Göttin, einsame, sag bei der Harfe,
Die wehklagt jeden Morgen, jeden Abend,
Sag, was so irr ich red, in diesen Hainen!
Stumm bleibst du – stumm! doch wundersame Lehre
Kann ich auf deinem stillen Antlitz lesen:
Ein ungeheures Wissen macht mich Gott.
Und Namen, Taten, graue Sagen, Aufstand,
Blut, Herrscher, hehre Stimmen, Todesqual,
Erschaffung und Zerstörung, all dies strömt
Jäh in die weiten Höhlen meines Hirns,
Vergöttlicht mich, als hätt ich frohen Wein,
Ein einsam helles Elixier getrunken
Und wär so jetzt unsterblich.« So der Gott,
Da sein entflammtes Aug, mit stetem Blick
Unter den weißen sanften Schläfen, zitternd
Vom Lichtglanz fest auf Mnemosyne lag.
Bald griff ihn wilde Regung und ließ aufglühn
All seiner Glieder ewig helle Schönheit –

Ganz ähnlich wie im Kampf am Tor des Tods
Und ähnlicher noch dem, der Abschied nehmen
Vom bleichen, ewgen Tod soll und mit Stichen,
Heiß wie des Todes kalt, mit wilden Krämpfen
Ins Leben sterben: so wand sich Apoll.
Sein Haar noch, die berühmten goldnen Locken,
Hielt Wellenform um den gereckten Hals.
Während der Qual hob Mnemosyne weit
Wie weissagend die Arme. – Da schrie auf
Apoll – und sieh! von allen seinen Gliedern,
Himmlisch …

Der St.-Agnes-Abend

I

St. Agnes' Abend – bitter eisig war's!
Dem Kauz, trotz all der Federn, wurde kühl;
Der Hase lahmte durchs gefrorne Gras,
Und kein Schaf schrie im wolligen Gewühl –
Steif des Fürbitters Finger, da er still
Den Rosenkranz sprach, und sein Atem schien,
Wie durch ein altes Rauchfaß Weihrauch fiel,
Auch ohne Tod gen Himmel zu entfliehn,
Am süßen Jungfraunbild hin, betend auf den Knien.

II

Er betet, der geduldig fromme Greis;
Nimmt dann die Lampe, steht vom Knien auf
Und schleppt sich hager, barfuß und blaßweiß
Am Seitenschiff entlang zurück darauf. –
Tote aus Stein, scheint's, frieren hier zuhauf,
Von Fegefeuergittern schwarz umragt;
Ritter und Damen beten sieht sein Lauf,
In dumpfen Zellen, und sein Geist versagt,
Sinnt er, wie sie in Hauben, Panzern Schmerz wohl plagt.

III

Nordwärts kehrt er durch eine kleine Tür,
Und kaum drei Schritt, schon rührt mit goldnen Zungen
Musik den armen Greis zu Tränen hier;
Doch nein – sein Totenläuten war erklungen:
Sein ganzes Lebensglück gesagt, gesungen –
Sein war am Agnesabend harte Buße.
Er drehte um und saß schon bald, gezwungen
Von seinem Seelenheil, in herbem Ruße
Und litt die Nacht hindurch, wach um der Sünder Muße.

IV

Der Fürbitter hörte das Vorspiel klingen;
Und das, weil vielfach Türn weit offen waren
Von regem Hin und Her. Bald, droben, fingen
Die Silberhörner an, scharf aufzufahren;
Die ebnen Säle, nicht mit Prunk zu sparen,
Glühten, wohl tausend Gäste zu empfangen;
Schnitzengel, mit stets scharfen Augenpaaren,
Sahn auf zu Kränzen, die ihr Haupt umschlangen,
Das Haar im Wind, von Flügeln überkreuz umfangen.

V

Nun brach herein des Festtags silbern Flirrn
Mit Federbusch, Tiara, reichem Kragen,
Zahlreich wie Schemen feenhaft das Hirn
Durchziehn, das, jung, erfüllt von alter Sagen
Triumphe, glüht. Nach denen laßt nur fragen,
Bis, einen Sinns, zu einer Maid wir kamen,
Die tief im Herz an diesen Wintertagen
Der Liebe nachsann und St. Agnes' Amen,
Wie sie es kundtun hörn oft hatte alte Damen.

VI

Am Agnesabend, sagten ihr die Alten,
Wär mancher Jungfrau Glücksvision erwacht
Und kann sie huldigend ihr Liebster halten
Zur honigsüßen Mitte dieser Nacht,
Hat sie nur auf die rechten Bräuche acht –
So ohne Abendbrot zu Bett zu gehn,
Die Schönheit ausgestreckt, ganz Lilienpracht;
Nicht rings umherzuschaun, nur abzuflehn
Dem Himmel frommen Blicks, was ihre Träume sehn.

VII

Dies schwirrte wirr im Kopf umher Madeleine –
Die Klänge, jammernd wie ein Gott im Schmerz,
Vernahm sie kaum: sie blickte keusch und schön
Zu Boden, sah manch Schleppe festsaalwärts
Vorbeiziehn – ihr war's gleich. Umsonst voll Herz,
Kam manch ein Kavalier kaum trippelnd nah,
Schon ging er – nicht vergrault durch Schmach,
durch Scherz –
Sie sah's nicht – weil ihr Herz woanders war:
Ihr war nach Agnes' Traum, dem süßesten im Jahr.

VIII

Sie tanzte mit verschwommnem, leerem Blick,
Die Lippen bang, ihr Atem schnell und flach.
Die hohe Stunde kam: sie sinkt zurück
Inmitten Tamburinen, all dem Krach
Von zornigem Geflüster und Gelach,
In Blicken voller Herz, Trotz, Hohn und Strafe
Beseelt von Märchenzaubern – für nichts wach
Als für St. Agnes' ungeschorne Schafe
Und all die Seligkeit vorm morgendlichen Schlafe.

IX

So, jeden Augenblick zu gehn gespannt,
Hielt sie noch aus. Inzwischen war, durchs Moor,
Jung Porphyro genaht, das Herz entbrannt
Nur für Madeleine. Neben dem Eingangstor,
Geschützt vorm Mondlicht, steht und fleht hervor
Er alle Heiligen, zu sehn Madeleine,
Einmal in den so langen Stunden nur
Sie anzuschaun, voll Huld, selbst ungesehn,
Gar sprechen, küssen, knien – ja, derlei war geschehn.

X

Er wagt es – daß kein Schwatzen es beschriebe!
Blind alle Augen! – hundert Schwerter fahren
Sonst in sein Herz, die Fieberburg der Liebe.
Ihm waren jene Räume voll Barbaren,
Heißblütgen Herren und Hyänenscharen –
Noch deren Hunde heulten ihr Gegröle
Auf sein Geschlecht: bar jeden Mitleids waren
Die Herzen hier, in dieser falschen Höhle,
Bis auf ein Mütterchen, schon schwach in Leib und Seele.

XI

Ah, Glück! – das greise Wesen kam gebückt,
Schlurfend am elfenbeinbeknauften Stab,
Dorthin, wo er, vorm Fackelschein verdeckt
Durch einen breiten Pfeiler, stand – weitab
Von Rundgesang und fröhlichem Geklapp.
Er schreckte sie; doch bald, sehend, wer er war,
Als sie ihm zitternd ihre Gichthand gab,
Sprach sie: »Gott, Porphyro! flieh die Gefahr –
Alle sind hier heut nacht, der Blutrunst ganze Schar!

XII

Nur fort! nur fort! da ist Zwerg Hildebrand –
Er fluchte jüngst in einem Fieberstich
Auf dich, die Deinen, euer Haus und Land;
Da ist Lord Maurice – alt, doch kein Stück wich
Sein Zorn mit grauem Haar – Flieh! tu's für mich!
Flieh wie ein Geist.« – »Ach Muhme, glaube mir,
Hier droht uns nichts. In diesen Stuhl setz dich
Und sag mir, wie –« – »Bei Gott! nicht hier, nicht hier;
Kind, folg mir, dieser Grund wird sonst zur Bahre dir.«

XIII

Er ging ihr unter niedren Bögen nach,
Spinnweben streifend mit dem Helmbuschflaum,
Und als sie murmelte »Ach, Elend, ach!«
Stand er in einem kleinen Mondlichtraum,
Fahl, kühl, vergittert, still wie Gräber kaum.
»Verrat mir nun«, sprach er, »wo ist Madeleine,
O Angela – beim heilgen Webstuhl, Traum,
Den nur geheime Schwesternschaften sehn,
Wenn sie voll Frömmigkeit St. Agnes' Wolle drehn.«

XIV

»St. Agnes? Ah! St. Agnes' Abend schlug –
Doch kann ein Mord auch feiertags geschehn.
Ein Hexensieb hast du als Wasserkrug
Und scheinst der Lehnsherr aller Elfen, Feen,
Das Glück so zu versuchen: dich zu sehn,
Erstaunt mich, Porphyro! – St. Agnes schlug!
Gott hilf! – grad heut nacht muß beschwören gehn
Die junge Herrin. Täusch sie Engelstrug!
Lachen laß mich derweil, für Gram bleibt Zeit genug.«

XV

Matt kichert sie im schwachen Mondenschein,
Da Porphyro in ihre Miene blickt
Wie ein verdutztes Balg dem Mütterlein,
Das nicht das Rätselbuch voll Wundern zückt,
Ist es bebrillt an den Kamin gerückt.
Doch funkelte sein Aug, als sie behende
Von seiner Liebsten Plan sprach: unterdrückt
Kaum Tränen, sann er kalten Spuk zu Ende
Und nach Madeleine, die schlief im Schoß alter Legende.

XVI

Wie Rosen blühn, kam ihm plötzlich ein Plan,
Warf heiße Stirn und Herz, von Qualen leck,
Purpurn in Aufruhr; ihr erzählt' er dann
Von einer List, die sie erfüllt' mit Schreck:
»Wie bist du grausam und doch gottlos keck!
Die Süße, bet sie, schlaf und träum allein
Mit ihren guten Engeln, weit weit weg
Von Männern schlecht wie du. Geh, geh! – Nein, nein,
Der, der du einmal schienst, kannst du gewiß nicht sein.«

XVII

»Bei allen Heiligen – ich tu ihr nichts!«
Rief Porphyro. »O finde nimmer Gnade
Mein letztes Flehn am Tage des Gerichts,
Falls einem ihrer Löcklein ich nur schade,
Ihr Antlitz roh in gier'gen Blicken bade.
Ach Angela, glaub mir bei diesen Zähren –
Oder ich brüll mit schrecklicher Tirade,
Gleich jetzt, den Feind wach, reize ihn, und wären
Noch schärfer seine Klauen als die des Wolfs und Bären.«

XVIII

»Ah! was der matten Seele Angst einjagen,
Daheim im Kirchhof, arm, schwach, schlagflußlahm –
Der diese Nacht die Stunde noch mag schlagen,
Der noch kein Tag, kein Abend unterkam
Ohne Gebet für dich?« – Dies hörend, nahm
Ein sanftres Wort der glühnde Porphyro,
Ergreifend und so voller tiefem Gram,
Daß Angela verspricht zu folgen, so
Wie immer er es wünscht, ob furchtsam oder froh.

XIX

Dies hieß, in strenger Heimlichkeit ihn führen
Bis in Madeleines Gemach, daß er, versteckt
Im Beigelaß, von niemand aufzuspüren,
Sehn könne ihre Schönheit, unentdeckt,
Und nachts vielleicht die reinste Braut erweckt,
Derweil ein Feenheer um die Decke strich,
Ihr Lid von fahlem Spuk schlafschwer gestreckt.
Nie traf zu solcher Nacht solch Liebe sich,
Seit Merlin seinem Dämon all die Schuld beglich.

XX

»Wie du es wünschst«, sprach sie, »soll es geschehn:
Naschwerk und Schmaus rasch aufgehäuft vor dir
Sei diese Festnacht; ihre Laute sehn
Wirst du am Stickrahmen. Doch eilen wir,
Ich trau all die Besorgungen vor mir
Kaum zu solch wirrem Kopf und trägem Leib.
Du wart, mein Kind; knie du und bete hier
Derweil. Ah! nimm sie nur gewiß zum Weib,
Daß ich am Jüngsten Tag nicht gar im Grab verbleib.«

XXI

Verstummt, hinkte sie emsig-ängstlich fort.
Endlos des Liebenden Minuten jetzt;
Sie kam zurück und wisperte ein Wort,
Daß er ihr folg – ihr greises Aug entsetzt,
Im Finstern Späher fürchtend. Doch geschützt,
Nach manchem Flur, umgab sie leis,
Seidig und keusch Madeleines Gemach zuletzt,
Wo Porphyro sich barg, beseligt heiß.
Rasch glitt die Helfrin fort, die Stirn voll Fieberschweiß.

XXII

Auf dem Geländer zitternd ihre Hand,
Stieg Angela treppab durch Dunkelheit,
Als unversehens, geistgleich hergesandt,
Madeleine erschien, St. Agnes' Zaubermaid:
Mit Silberleuchter und ganz Sorgsamkeit
Kehrte sie um, führte die Greisin so
Auf sichern, ebnen Grund. Nun sei bereit
Auf jenes Bett zu starren, Porphyro –
Sie kommt, sie kommt zurück, ein Täubchen, das erst floh.

XXIII

Der Docht erlosch, als sie den Raum betrat;
Sein Qualm verstrich im blassen Mondenlicht.
Sie schloß die Tür, sie keuchte, ganz verwahrt
In Luftgeistern und weitem Traumgesicht.
Kein Laut jetzt, oder weh dir – reg dich nicht!
Nur daß ihr Herz, ihr Herz nicht innehält
Und ihre Balsambrust geschwätzig sticht –
Wie zungenlos umsonst die Kehle schwellt
Und stirbt, das Herz erstickt, die Nachtigall im Feld.

XXIV

Da war ein dreigeteilter Fensterbogen,
Umkränzt mit ausgeschnitzten Bilderein,
Von Früchten, Flor und Knöterich durchzogen,
Das Glas in Rauten wunderlich und fein,
Unendlich bunt in seinem Farbenschein
Wie der Damast der Bärenspinnerflügel;
Und mitten unter tausend Wappenreihn,
Düsteren Heiligen und Waffenspiegel
Ein Schild, tiefrot das Blut von Königen im Siegel.

XXV

Der Wintermond, der auf dies Fenster schien,
Warf warmes Rot auf Madeleines holde Brüste,
Als sie des Himmels Huld erbat auf Knien;
Rosig die Hände, die sie faltend preßte,
Ihr silbern Kreuz ganz milde Amethyste,
Gleich Heiligen den Glorienschein im Haar:
Sie schien, nur flügellos, ein Engel, küßte
Den Himmel – schwach nahm's Porphyro noch wahr:
Dort kniete sie, so rein, so allen Makels bar.

XXVI

Neu lebt sein Herz auf: ihr Gebet durchgangen,
Trennt sie ihr Haar von jedem Perlenstrick;
Löst nach und nach die warmen Schmuckstückspangen;
Öffnet ihr duftend Mieder; Stück für Stück
Kriecht raschelnd auf die Knie ihr Kleid zurück.
Der Meerjungfrau im Tang gleich, halb bedeckt,
Sinnt sie im Wachtraum nach derweil, im Blick
Des Geists St. Agnes, auf ihr Bett gestreckt,
Doch fürchtet hinzusehn, den Zauber schon verschreckt.

XXVII

Bald, zitternd in dem weichen, kühlen Nest,
Schwand sie, wie ohnmachtswach, benommen hin,
Bis den gelösten Leib mohnwarm und fest
Der Schlaf hielt und entdämmern ließ den Sinn –
Wie ein Gedanke fort bis Tagbeginn;
Selig beschützt vor Wonne wie vor Pein;
Ein Meßbuch schwarzen Kultes, stumm darin;
Beschirmt vor Regen wie vor Sonnenschein,
Als schlöß die Rose sich und würd neu Knospe sein.

XXVIII

Ein Dieb im Paradies, und so gebannt,
Sah Porphyro starr auf ihr leeres Kleid
Und lauschte ihrem Atem jetzt, gespannt,
Wann er erwach zu müder Zärtlichkeit.
Als er ihn hörte, dankte er der Zeit
Und holte selbst Luft. Dann, aus dem Verschlag,
Stumm wie die Furcht in weiter Ödigkeit,
Glitt er den leisen Teppich lang, still, zag,
Und lugte durch den Stoff, wo schau! – sie schlummernd lag.

XXIX

Dann, im schon schwächer silbermatten Glühn
Des Mondlichts, schob er einen Tisch ans Bett
Und warf, noch immer ängstlich, über ihn
Ein Tuch, durchwirkt von Gold, Karmin und Jett –
O einschläfernd jetzt Morpheus' Amulett!
Der gellend mittnächtliche Zinkenton,
Die Kesselpauke und das Klarinett
Schrecken sein Ohr, verklingen sie auch schon –
Als sich die Saaltür schließt, ist aller Lärm entflohn.

XXX

Und noch schloß Schlaf azurlidrig sie ein
Im Linnen, weich, lavendelfrisch und warm,
Als er in Mengen aus dem Kämmerlein
Kandierte Äpfel, Quitten, Pflaumen nahm,
Mit lindern Säften noch als Sahnerahm,
Und Sirup, in dem leuchtend Zimt zerronn;
Datteln und Manna, das im Prachtschiff kam
Aus Fez; und Spezerein, jede davon
Vom Seidensamarkand bis Zedernlibanon.

XXXI

Dies Naschwerk häufte er mit glühnder Hand
In goldne Schalen und die Körbepracht
Getriebnen Silbers; sie stehn hell entbrannt
Im abgeschiednen Schweigen dieser Nacht,
Haben dem kühlen Raum sacht Duft gebracht.
»Nun sei, Geliebte, Seraph, zu erfüllen
Dich Himmel als dein Eremit, erwacht!
Öffne die Augen um St. Agnes' willen,
Sonst sink ich neben dich, so leide ich im stillen.«

XXXII

Dies wispernd, sank sein heißer Arm erschlafft
Ins Kissen. Schattig hielt ihr Traumgesicht
Der Vorhang – mitternächtlich war die Kraft,
Dem Eis gleich, das der Strom nicht länger bricht.
Die Teller funkeln blank im Mondenlicht;
Ein breiter Goldsaum liegt am Teppich an –
Erlösen, schien's, würd er im Leben nicht
Der Liebsten Aug von derart festem Bann;
So woben Phantasien ihn ein, derweil er sann.

XXXIII

Erwacht, ergriff er ihre dumpfe Laute,
Und wild, in Klängen zartster Harmonie,
Sang er das lang verstummte und ergraute
Lied der Provence »La Belle Dame sans Mercy«,
Zupfend nah ihrem Ohr die Melodie –
Von ihr im Schlaf gestört, stöhnte sie weich:
Er schwieg – sie keuchte schnell – da öffnet sie
Die blauen Augen und erschrickt sogleich.
Er sank auf seine Knie, wie glatter Marmor bleich.

XXXIV

Ihr Aug war offen, doch noch immer sah,
Auch wach, ihr Traum sie fest in seinem Bann –
Verwandelt, schmerzte er, vertrieb beinah
Die doch so reinen, tiefen Wonnen dann.
Als nun zu weinen gar Madeleine begann,
Zu seufzen wirre Worte und Gestöhn,
Sah sie noch immer Porphyro starr an,
Der betend, flehentlichen Blicks auf Knien,
Nicht wagte, sich zu rührn, da so verträumt sie schien.

XXXV

»Ah, Porphyro!« rief sie, »noch eben jetzt
Durchzog dein Klang mein Ohr in süßem Glück,
Ein jeder Schwur in Melodie gesetzt,
Und klar, ätherisch war dein trüber Blick –
Wie anders bist du! – bleich, kühl und bedrückt!
Laß jenen Götterblick mich wiedersehn,
Die Stimme hören, Klagen so verzückt!
O laß mich nicht in diesen ewgen Wehn,
Denn, Liebster, wenn du stirbst, weiß ich nicht, wohin gehn.«

XXXVI

Weitmehr als je ein Mensch erregt vor Wonne
Durch solche Wollust, hat er sich erhoben,
Verzückt, erglüht und bebend wie die Sonne
Im tiefen Schweigen des Saphirblaus droben.
In ihren Traum schmolz er hinein, verwoben
Wie Rosen- sich mit Veilchenduft verbindet –
Süß aufgelöst. Schon gellt des Schneesturms Toben
Gleich Amors Warnsignal, und Hagel findet
Prasselnd ans Fensterglas; St. Agnes' Mond verschwindet.

XXXVII

’s ist Nacht: scharf prasselt sturmgepeitschter Regen.
»Dies ist kein Traum, du meine Braut, Madeleine!«
’s ist Nacht: die eisgen Böen hämmern und fegen.
»Kein Traum! Elend, Elend und mein die Wehn!
Porphyro läßt mich hier schwinden und vergehn. –
Verrat! Welch Rohling konnt dich zu mir bringen?
Ich fluch nicht, ist’s doch um mein Herz geschehn,
Kannst du auch mir Betrognen dich entringen –
Mir Taube so verlorn, zerzaust und lahmer Schwingen.«

XXXVIII

»Madeleine! mein süßer Träumer! holde Braut!
Sag, darf ich stets dein selger Sklave sein?
Der Schönheit Schild, rot, wie ein Herz gebaut?
Ah, hier will ich mich ausruhn, Silberschrein,
Nach all der Zeit der Irrfahrt und der Pein,
Schmachtender Pilger – den nun Wunder tränken.
Entdeckt auch, raub ich deinem Nest allein
Dein süßes Selbst – sollltst du es recht bedenken
Und dein Vertraun, Madeleine, nicht rohen Heiden schenken.

XXXIX

Horch! Elfenwind des Märchenlands weht da –
So wild er scheint, er hat uns Glück gebracht.
Steh auf – steh auf! der Morgen ist schon nah.
Keiner der aufgeblähten Säufer wacht. –
Fort laß uns jetzt, mein Herz, mit aller Macht –
Kein Ohr hört her, kein Auge wundert sich,
Alle verschluckt vom Met- und Rheinweinschacht.
Wach auf, mein Herz! komm, halt dich nur an mich –
Südwärts, jenseits des Moors, hab ich ein Heim für dich.«

XL

Dem lauschend, eilte sie – von Furcht bedrückt,
Schliefen Dragonerdrachen doch ringsher,
Wachten voll Zorn vielleicht, den Speer gezückt:
Die Treppe fanden sie im Dunkeln leer;
Nichts Menschliches im Haus vernahm man mehr.
An Ketten schwankten Leuchter auf dem Gang;
Gobelins, verziert mit Habicht, Hund und Heer,
Flatterten in des Winds Erstürmungsdrang,
Der Teppich hob sich schwer den kalten Flur entlang.

XLI

Sie gleiten, wie Phantome, in den Saal;
Phantomgleich gleiten sie zum Haupttor hin;
Dort liegt der Wächter, krumm an einem Pfahl,
Den riesenhaften Krug leer auf den Knien.
Der Bluthund schüttelt sich, die Augen glühn,
Bis sie die Herrin zu erkennen meinen.
Riegel nach Riegel löst sich ohne Mühn –
Die Ketten ruhn auf ausgetretnen Steinen –
Das Schloß des Tors gibt nach, und seine Angeln greinen.

XLII

Und fort sind beide – ja, vor langer Zeit
Ist in den Sturm dies Liebespaar entflohn.
Dem Freiherrn träumte jene Nacht manch Leid,
Und lang vom Alp gedrückt durch Spuk und Hohn
Von Hexen, Sarggewürm und manch' Dämon
Ward all sein Gästeheer. Angela starb alt,
Vom Schlag gelähmt, ihr Antlitz Knochen schon;
Der Fürbitter, nach tausend Aves bald,
Entschlief, nie mehr vermißt, wie seine Asche kalt.

Der St.-Markus-Abend

Er fiel auf einen Sabbattag;
Zweimal so fromm der Glockenschlag,
Als es zur Abendandacht scholl.
Die Straßen glänzten wundervoll
Von satten Regen des April,
Und auf die Westfenster fiel kühl
Ein Abendrot, das leise sprach
Von kalten Tälern, grün und brach,
Von grünen Hecken, nicht erblüht,
Von Flüssen, frisch im Frühlingsried,
Geschützten Quelln von Tausendschön
Und Primeln auf bereiften Höhn.
Zweimal so fromm der Glockenschlag:
Auf den sonst stillen Straßen lag
Zuhauf der Laut von ernsten Frommen,
Warm vom Kaminbetplatz gekommen,
Die nun, mit sittsamstem Gebaren,
Auf ihrem Weg zur Vesper waren.
In jeden Bogen, jedes Tor
Schob Volk sich still, bedächtig vor,
Leis raunend und mit schurrnden Füßen,
Da laut und süß die Orgeln bliesen.

Es schwieg vom Turm, Gebet ward laut,
Und Bertha war nicht halb vertraut
Ein seltsam Buch, befleckt, zerschunden,
Daß heute, seit den Morgenstunden,
Mit seinen goldverzierten Spalten
Ihr Auge hatte festgehalten;
Verwirrt war sie von tausend Dingen –
Den Himmelssternen, Engelsschwingen,
Märtyrern am Flammenpfahl,
Heilgen, blau im Silberstrahl,

Aarons Brustschild, Leuchtern, sieben,
Wie Johannes sie beschrieben,
Sankt Markus' Löwen, seinem Flügel,
Und der Bundeslade, Siegel
Voll Mysterien am Gehäuse,
Cherubim und goldne Mäuse.

Keusch und schön sah Bertha aus
Und war am Münsterplatz zuhaus;
Seitlich all die Pracht um ihn
Sah sie vom Winkel am Kamin
Bis an den Wall vom Bischofsgarten,
Wo Sykomorn und Ulmenarten
Laubüppig Wälder überragten,
Da scharfe Norde sie nie plagten,
So schützte sie der Prachtbau dort.
Bertha stand auf und las noch fort,
Die Stirn gedrückt ans Fensterglas.
Sie las von neuem, las und las,
Bis sie im Dunkeln blieb am Ende
Vor Markus' düsterer Legende.
Vom krausen Halsstreif, fein und dünn,
Hob sie ihr weiches, warmes Kinn,
Der Nacken steif, der Blick verschwommen,
Von frommem Bildwerk ganz benommen.

Alles schwieg, Nacht überall,
Nur dann und wann von Schritten Hall,
Die jemand spät erst stadtwärts zogen,
Vorbei am hallenden Münsterbogen.

Der Dohlenschwarm, der seit es tagte
Krächzend um Turm und Wipfel jagte,
Schlief nun Paar für Paar längst fest,
Ein jedes im Gestühl ein Nest,
Wo sie früh in Schlummer fallen,
Da einlullend die Glocken schallen.

Nacht war, alles schwieg, kein Schimmer
Vorm Fenster und im trauten Zimmer:
Da setzt' sie sich, getäuschte Seele!
Und schürt' die Glut, damit sie schwele,
Beugt' sich, ihr Haar hell vorm Gesicht
Und schräg das Buch, dicht an das Licht.
Ihr Schatten streifte ruhelos
Im Raum umher, glitt riesengroß
Von Balken, Eichenstuhl und Mauer
Auf ihren Papageienbauer
Und Ofenschirm, warm und geknickt,
Auf dem man manch Getier erblickt,
So Lima-Mäuse, Siam-Tauben,
Avadavat, fußlose Trauben
Von Vögeln aus dem Paradies,
Angorakatzen, Kolibris.
Sie las und las, nie stand ihr Schatten,
Als ob den Raum er auszustatten
Mit wildstem Spuk und Schemen plane,
Als würd der Geist einer Pik-Dame
Voll Hohn sie hinterrücks umbrausen
Und ihr das schwarze Kleid zerzausen.
Sie las und las in der Legende
Vom heilgen Markus, Anfang, Ende,
An Land, auf See, versklavt von Heiden,
Frohlockend ob all seiner Leiden.
Der weise Eremit wies gern
Mit reichem Kreuz, mit goldnem Stern
Auf fromme Verse hin, ein jeder
Getuscht mit feinster Rabenfeder
Unter den Text; durchbrochen ward
Sein Fluß von Zeit zu Zeit derart:
»– Also von träumen schreibet Er /
Vor man wacht auff in seeligkeit /
Wan freunde meynen / umb uns her
Sey tieff im grunt das lailachklaid:

Vnd wie ein heyliger seyn kan /
Ein kindelein / das nicht geborn /
Wan bloß die mutter (Amen dan!)
Selbs einsamkeit sich außerkorn
Vnd fromm das heylig kreutz geküßt.
Von Herrgots lieb vnd Satans macht
Schreibt Er: was sunst geschriben ist /
Das sey drumb ich muß breyten nacht.
Warlich jedoch muß ich Euch sagen
Von Sankt Ciciliens jrdisch streben /
Fürnehmlich aber / wie sein klagen
Umb Sankte Marci todt vnd leben.«

Nun tat ihr stetes Lid sich um
Im glühenden Martyrium,
Sah endlich seinen Heilgenschrein,
Erhöht inmitten Kerzenschein
Einst zu Venedig. …

Lamia

Teil I

Zu einer Zeit, eh noch die Schar der Feen
Satyr und Nymphe trieb von Wald und Seen,
Eh König Oberons Juwelenkranz,
Zepter und Rock, verschnallt in hellem Glanz,
Verjagten die Dryade und den Faun
Von grünem Schilf, Gestrüpp und Primelauen,
Ging Hermes, stets in Flammen und genug
Des goldnen Throns, auf Liebesbeutezug:
Hoch vom Olympus stahl er sich gewandt
Diesseits Zeus' Wolken, blieb auch unerkannt
Von seinem hohen Herrn und barg sich bald
An Kretas Inselstrand in einem Wald:
Lebte doch hier, in heiligen Gebieten,
Die Nymphe, vor der alle Satyrn knieten,
Zu deren weißen Füßen Perlen gossen
Tritonen, die an Land vor Huld zerflossen.
Nah bei den Quelln, wo sie zu baden pflegte,
Und in der Au, in die sie sich oft legte,
Warn Gaben reich verstreut, den Musen fremd,
Als flöß der Phantasieborn ungehemmt.
Ah, ihr zu Füßen welche Welt der Liebe!
So dachte Hermes, himmlisch Hitzeschübe
Von den beschwingten Fersen bis ans Ohr,
Aus dessen Weiße, rein wie Lilienflor,
Rot eine Rose ward in goldnem Haar,
Erregt gelockt ums nackte Schulternpaar.
Von Tal zu Tal flog er, von Hain zu Hain,
Sprach Blumen von der neuen Liebespein
Und mußte mit manch' Bach sich quellwärts winden,
Um jener Nymphe süß und stilles Bett zu finden.
Umsonst; er fand die süße Nymphe nicht
Und ruhte deshalb aus, in trübem Licht,

Gramvoll, erfüllt von Eifersucht die Träume
Auf Wäldergötter, ja selbst auf die Bäume.
Da hörte er ein Klagen voller Schmerz,
Eins, das, einmal gehört, dem edlen Herz
Voll Pein bloß Mitleid läßt; die Stimme sprach:
»Wann nur entsteig ich der verschlungnen Schmach!
Reg mich im süßen Leib, der taugt zum Leben,
Zu Liebe, Wonne und dem roten Beben
Des Munds und Herzens! Ah, ich Unglückswaise!«
Der Gott, auf Taubenfüßen nun, glitt leise
Um Busch und Stamm, schob weich, in diesem Tanzen,
Beiseite höhres Gras und blühende Pflanzen,
Bis er die wild durchpulste Schlange fand,
In finstrem Busch umrollt und hell entbrannt.

Gordisch geformt war sie und blendend bunt,
Tiefrot gescheckt, Gold, Grün und Blau ihr Grund;
Gestreift dem Zebra, fleckig Pardern gleich,
Beäugt wie Pfaue, an Karminrot reich;
War voller Silbermonde, die, im Atemholen,
Zerschmolzen, heller strahlten, dann verstohlen
Ihr Leuchten in die dunklern Gründe schlangen. –
So regenbogenhäutig, leidbehangen,
Schien sie wie eine Büßerelfe jetzt,
Braut eines Dämons, Dämon selbst zuletzt.
Als Krone trug sie einen matten Glanz
Aus Sternen, ähnlich Ariadnes Kranz;
Ihr Haupt war Schlange, doch ah, bitter-süß!
Ganz Frau jedoch der Mund, der alle Perln aufwies;
Ihr Auge nun – was tun, als dort vereint
Zu weinen, weinen, weil es so schön scheint,
Wie um Siziliens Luft Proserpina noch weint.
Ihr Hals war Schlange, doch ein jedes Wort
Entstieg, wie Honig schäumend, Liebe dort,
Da 's sprach – und Hermes auf den Schwingen lag
Wie der gebückte Falke stößt zum Schlag –

»Hermes, bekränzt mit Federn, flatternd sacht,
Herrlich geträumt hab ich von dir die Nacht:
Auf einem Thron aus Gold sah ich dich sitzen,
Unter den Göttern, auf Olympus' Spitzen,
Du einzig gram; an dir vorüber gingen
Der Musen Lautenspiel und helles Singen
Und selbst Apollos, als allein er sang,
Taub für der Stimme schwingend langen Klageklang.
Ich träumte, du, gehüllt in Purpurlicht,
Brachst heiß durch Wolken, wie der Tag anbricht,
Und stießt, geschwind gleich Phöbus' hellem Speer,
Gen Kretas Insel – und schon kamst du her!
Zu edler Hermes, fandst du nun die Maid?«
Da schob die rosige Beredsamkeit
Nicht auf mehr Lethes Stern und mußte fragen:
»Du, lippensanfte Schlange, kannst es sagen!
Du, schöner Kranz, mit schwermütigen Augen,
Nimm, was auch immer mag zum Glück dir taugen,
Nur sag, wo meine Nymphe ist – den Ort,
An dem sie lebt!« – »Heller Planet, dem Wort,
Dem«, sprach die Schlange, »gib nun Schwur und Siegel!«
»Ich schwör«, sprach er, »bei deiner Augen Spiegel,
Dem Schlangenstab hier, deinem Sternenkranz!«
Leicht wog sein ernstes Wort, umringt von Blütenglanz.
Da gab zurück das weiblich-helle Licht:
»Zu schwaches Herz! verloren ist sie nicht,
Frei wie die Luft, nur unsichtbar, streift sie
Durch dornenlose Wildnis ohne Müh,
Froh und nicht sichtbar; unsichtbare Spuren
Drückt zart ihr Fuß in Flor und Gras der Fluren;
Sie pflückt von matten Ranken, sattem Grün
Obst ungesehen, badet ungesehn;
Und meine Macht hüllt ihre Schönheit ein,
Läßt unbestürmt und unversehrt sie sein
Von Liebesblicken unliebsamer Freier,
Von Satyr, Faun, Silenus' falscher Leier.

Verblassend die Unsterblichkeit vorm Leid
All der Verliebten, voller Traurigkeit,
Nahm ich mich ihrer an, riet ihr, das Haar
In Zaubersaft zu baden, unsichtbar
Würd ihre Schönheit sein, doch frei von andern
Könnt sie, wohin sie's zög, in Freiheit wandern.
Du sollst sie schauen, Hermes, du allein,
Willst du, wie du es schworst, mir dankbar sein!«
Verzaubert, stieß der Gott erneut hervor
Den Eid, bis er sich in der Schlange Ohr
Warm, zitternd, innig, psaltergleich verlor.
Ihr circehaftes Haupt hob sie berückt,
Damastrot glühend, und lispelte beglückt:
»Ich war ein Weib, gib du wie einst mir wieder
Die weibliche Gestalt, den Reiz der Glieder.
Ein Jüngling aus Korinth – er ist mein Glück!
Laß wieder Frau mich sein, laß mich zu ihm zurück.
Knie, Hermes, hauchen laß auf deine Brauen,
Und gleich sollst du die süße Nymphe schauen.«
Halboffner Schwingen sank er wonnig hin,
Sie hauchte auf sein Aug, und schon erschien
Die Nymphe wohlbewahrt und lächelnd auf dem Grün.
Es war kein Traum; doch mag man Traum es nennen:
Träume sind Göttern wirklich, Götter kennen
Das Glück als sanften, endlos langen Traum.
Ein warmer Strom, ein Nu des Schwebens, kaum
Ertrug er ihre Schönheit, so war er entbrannt;
Trat leicht aufs spurenlose Grün, gewandt
Zur starren Schlange, um mit matten Händen,
Sanft, seines schlanken Stabs Gewalt nun anzuwenden.
Geschehn dies, sah er auf die Nymphe wieder,
Voll heißer Tränen und berückt die Lider,
Trat er zu ihr – sie, wie der Mond verblaßt,
Sank hin vor ihm und brach, nicht mehr gefaßt,
In Schluchzen aus, wie Blumen sich selbst falten
Und in sich schließen, will die Nacht erkalten;

Doch als der Gott die kühlen Hände nahm,
Hob sanft die Lider sie, ihr wurde warm,
Und blühend, wie der Flor beim Morgentanz
Der Bienen, gab sie ihren Honig ganz.
Sie flohen in den grünverschlungnen Wald,
Nicht blaß, wie sterbliche Verliebte bald.

Allein, so wechselte die Schlange jetzt
Den Leib; ihr Elfenblut floß wild gehetzt,
Ihr Mund spie Schaum, und Gras, mit ihm besprengt,
Verwelkte so von süßem Gift versengt;
Ihr Auge, qualerstarrt und schmerzgebannt,
Heiß, glasig, weit, die Lider ausgebrannt,
Schlug Phosphor, Funkenflug, den keine Träne fand.
In allen Farben stand ihr Schwanz in Flammen,
Sie wand sich, sank vor Scharlachschmerz zusammen –
Ein tiefes Schwefelgelb trat an die Stelle
Der vorher milder mondnen Körperhelle
Und, wie die Lava eine Au verdorrt,
Wusch Silberschild und goldne Borte fort;
Trieb Dunkel auf die Streifen, Balken, Flecken
Und Monde, um noch Sterne aufzulecken.
So war sie, kurz darauf, entkleidet ganz
Saphiren, Amethysten, grünem Glanz,
Rubinem Silber; und beraubt dem Kleid,
Blieb nichts zurück als Schmerz und Häßlichkeit.
Noch schien ihr Kranz; doch schwand auch er, und fahl
Zerschmolz sie ganz, verschwand mit einem Mal;
Und ihre neue Stimme, säuselnd droben,
Rief »Lycius! sanfter Lycius!« – Aufgehoben
Mit hellen Schwaden über Bergschneefeldern
Verklang ihr Ruf: unhörbar Kretas Wäldern.

Wohin floh Lamia, nun ein stolzes Weib
Mit neugebornem, herrlich schönem Leib?
Sie floh in jenes Tal, das die durchstreichen,
Die von Kenchreä aus Korinth erreichen,

Und saß am Fuß von jenen schroffen Höhen,
Wo laut Peräas Bäche niedergehen,
Und an dem Bergkamm, dessen karger Nacken
Südwestlich allen Dunst und düstre Zacken
Bis nach Kleonä streckt. Dort stand sie bald,
Ein junger Vogel, flatternd aus dem Wald,
Schön, auf ergrünten Hängen voller Moos,
An einem Teich, in dem sie es genoß,
Sich anzusehn, so schwerer Qual entrissen,
Während ihr Kleid sich bauschte mit Narzissen.

Ah, froher Lycius! – denn so schön wie sie
Flocht eine Maid ihr Haar zu Zöpfen nie
Und seufzte, breitete aufs Lenzgras bang
Vor Scham ein grünes Kleid zum Minnesang:
Ja, Jungfrau reinster Lippen, jedoch kund
Der Liebe bis zum roten Herzensgrund –
Nicht eine Stunde alt, verstand sie blind,
Wie Glück und Nachbar Leid zu trennen sind,
Zu ziehen schmale Grenzen, festzustellen
Gemeinsames und Austausch zu erhellen;
Mit sichrer Kunst ihr Scheinchaos zu meiden
Und dunkelste Atome hier zu scheiden –
Als hätt in Amors Schule sie gesessen,
Ein lieblicher Student, und keusch indessen
Dort müßig sehnsuchtsvoll den Rosenkurs durchmessen.

Weshalb dieses Geschöpf so feenhaft schön
Am Wegrand harrte, werden wir noch sehn;
Erst aber sei erzählt, wie sie doch sann
Und träumen konnte, auch im Schlangenbann,
Und allem lauschte, seltsam oder prächtig:
Wohin sie wollte, schwang ihr Geist sich mächtig;
Ob zu Elysiumsschimmern, zu den Wogen,
Wo Nereiden, feucht ihr Haar durchsogen,
In Thetis' Reich hinab auf Perlenstufen zogen;

Zu Bacchus, seinen Götterwein getrunken,
Zur Rast ans Harz des Pinienstamms gesunken;
Oder zu Plutos Schlössergartendunkel,
Wo im Piazza-Rund Vulkanus' Säulen funkeln.
Und manchmal mochte sie in Städte senden
Den Traum, an Festen und Betrieb sich blenden;
Und einmal, träumend unter Menschen hier,
Sah so sie Lycius von Korinth vor ihr,
Ganz vorn in einem mißgünstigen Jagen
Dem jungen Zeus gleich ruhig und stolz im Wagen,
Und fand sich ohnmächtig verliebt in ihn.
Wenn abends dann die Mottenaugen glühn,
Würd er zurückgehn, denn sie wußte dies,
Vom Strand heim nach Korinth; denn frischer blies
Der weiche Ost, seine Galeere schlug
Ans Mauerwerk des Kais den bronznen Bug,
Dort in Kenchreä, wo aus Ägina
Sie kürzlich einlief; hatte er doch da
Jüngst Zeus geopfert, dessen Tempelgarten
Und Marmortore dort auf Blut und Weihrauch warten.
Zeus hörte ihn, erhörte sein Begehren;
Denn eine Laune ließ ihn heimwärtskehren
Getrennt von den Gefährten, und er schied,
Vielleicht des Schwatzens von Korinth nun müd.
Gedankenlos an stummen Hügeln hin
Zog er, doch eh der Abendstern erschien,
Verlor er sich, wo die Vernunft zerfällt,
In Platos Schatten sanfter Dämmerwelt.
Und Lamia sah ihn näher-, näherkommen –
Sah ihn von tristem Gleichmut eingenommen
Still in Sandaln durchs Moosgras weitergehn.
So nah bei ihm und doch so ungesehn
War sie: er ging, versenkt in sein Geschick,
Sein Denken wie ummantelt, da ihr Blick
Ihm folgte und, nun fürstlichweiß gedreht
Den Hals, sie silbelnd sprach: »Ah, Lycius, steht!

Ihr laßt mich auf den Hügeln hier allein?
Schaut um! und laßt das Herz voll Mitleid sein.«
Er tat's – nicht kühl erstaunt, nicht schreckhaft wähnend,
Nein, Orpheus-gleich Eurydike ersehnend –
So herrlich warn die Worte, die sie sang,
Ihm schien, er liebte sie schon einen Sommer lang.
Und ihre Schönheit leer trank bald sein Blick,
Ließ nichts in diesem Taumelkelch zurück,
Und noch war der Kelch voll – indes er, bang,
Sie schwände, eh von seinen Lippen drang
Ein rechtes Wort des Lobs, ein Lob begann
(Und scheuren Blicks sah sie, schon hielt sie ihn im Bann):
»Zurücksehn! Lassen dich! Ah, Göttin, hier –
Schau, ob mein Blick sich abwendet von dir!
Täusch nicht aus Mitleid dies zerquälte Herz –
So wie du schwindest, sterbe ich vor Schmerz.
Bleib! bist du auch Najade aus den Wellen!
Dein Wunsch ist auch von fern Befehl den Quellen.
Bleib! und sind auch die grünsten Wälder dein,
Den Morgenregen trinken sie allein.
Stiegst du herab als eine der Plejaden,
Wird keine Schwester singen die Tiraden
Der Sphärn und stellvertretend silbern scheinen?
So süß klang dein so süßer Gruß in meinen
Verzückten Ohrn, daß ich, von dir verlassen,
Mit deinem Bild zu einem Schatten würd verblassen –
Aus Mitleid schmilz nicht fort!« – »Blieb ich bei dir«,
Sprach Lamia, »auf dem harten Lehmgrund hier,
Würd durch zu rauhen Flor die Schritte plagen,
Was könntst du tun an Zaubern oder sagen,
Damit ich mein mir teures Heim vergesse?
Du bittest mich, daß ich mit dir durchmesse
Hügel und Täler, wo es Glück nicht gibt –
Wo nichts unsterblich selig immer liebt!
Du bist gebildet, Lycius, und du weißt,
Es kann nicht atmen ein viel feinrer Geist

In eurer Welt und leben. Welcher Hauch
Von reinrer Luft hier, Jüngling, koste auch
Meine Essenz? Welch Schlösser, lärmerfüllte,
Wo jeder Sinn sich in Gefallen hüllte
Und ich geheimnisvoll mir hundert Dürste stillte?
Es kann nicht sein – Adieu!« Flink aufgerichtet,
Hob sie die weißen Arme. Er, vernichtet
Den holden Ausblick ihrer Klagen meinend,
Sank hin, erbleicht vor Pein, von Liebe weinend.
Da hob das harte Weib, ohne ein Herz
Zu zeigen für des zarten Lieblings Schmerz,
Vielmehr als könnt ihr Blick nun heller strahlen,
Mit hellerm Blick und schleichendem Gefallen,
Den neuen Mund zum Kuß und gab den Wangen
Das Leben wieder, das ihr Netz gefangen;
Und wie er aus der einen Trance erwachte
In eine andere, sang sie und lachte
Von Schönheit, Liebe, Glück und allen Dingen, brachte
Ein Lied hervor, zu süß für Erdenleier:
Den Sternen stockte, Atem gleich, ihr keuchend Feuer.
Schon flüsterte sie voller Ängstlichkeit
Wie jene, die, allein in Sicherheit
Zum ersten Mal seit furchterfüllten Tagen,
Nicht nur durch Blicke sprechen; aufrecht tragen
Sollt er sein Haupt, nicht mehr in Zweifeln wandern,
Daß eine Frau sie sei, mit keinem andern,
Subtilern Körperfluidum im Herzen
Als pulsend Blut, mit ganz denselben Schmerzen
In der zerbrechlich-schwachen Brust wie er.
Dann staunte sie, weshalb sie ihm bisher
Nicht auffiel in Korinth, wo, sagte sie,
Sie zwar im stillen lebte, es ihr nie
An Freuden mangelte, von Gold beschieden
Auch ohne Liebe; jedoch ganz zufrieden,
Bis ihn einst sie, dahinschreitend in Eile,
Versunken lehnen sah an einer Säule

Des Venustempelhofs, wo aufgehäuft
In Körben Liebeskraut und Blumen, erst gereift
An jenem Abend, standen, war doch nah
Adonis' Fest – von welchem sie nichts sah,
Weinend allein daheim, denn was verehren da?
Vom Tod erwachte Lycius ins Erstaunen,
Sie noch zu sehn und so süß Weisen raunen;
Und vom Erstaunen fiel er ins Betören,
So frei von Frauendingen hier zu hören;
Und jede Silbe lockte ihn zurück
Zu unverstelltem, einst gekanntem Glück.
Laßt die verrückten Dichter noch so schön
Von Peris singen, Göttinnen und Feen,
Nicht eine unter ihnen schenkt Genuß,
Bewohnt sie Grotte, Wasserfall und Fluß,
Wie eine echte Frau, ob ihre Ahnen kamen
Von Pyrrhas Kieseln oder Adams Samen.
Derart sann Lamia, und sie sann zu Recht,
Halbfürchtend liebe Lycius sie nicht echt,
Warf so die Göttin ab und nahm ihn ein
Mit Sanftheit, als sie vorgab, Frau zu sein,
Mit Scheu, wie ihre Schönheit sie erteilte,
Die, wenn sie Wunden schlug, zugleich doch heilte.
Beredte Antwort gab ihr Lycius jetzt,
In Zwillingsseufzer jedes Wort gesetzt,
Und fragte, weisend nach Korinth, voll Süße,
Ob dorthin sie noch trügen ihre Füße.
Der Weg war kurz, denn Lamias glühende Eile
Verkürzte durch ein Zauberwort die Meile
Zu ein paar Schritten, unbemerkt vollkommen
Von Lycius, blind nun von ihr eingenommen.
Sie kamen durch das Tor, er sah nicht wie,
So leise, und er fragte es sich nie.

Wie man im Traum spricht, so klang ganz Korinth
Mit mächtigen Palastbauten im Wind,
Und Straßen, voller Leben, Tempel, lüstern,
Erhoben, wie ein ferner Sturm, ein Flüstern
Ins weite Dunkel über dem Gewühle.
Frauen, Männer, Arm und Reich, sie trieb die Kühle
Aufs weiße Pflaster, schurrend die Sandalen,
Begleitet und allein, da manch ein Strahlen
Berauschter Feste hier und da erglühte
Und Schatten wandernd auf die Mauern sprühte
Oder gedrängt fand in die dunkle Enge
Der Wölbung eines Tors und Tempelsäulengänge.

Verborgen sein Gesicht vorm Gruß Verwandter,
Hielt fest er ihre Hand, als ein Bekannter
Graubärtig, scharfen Blicks, die Stirn kahlglatt,
Im Rock der Philosophen nähertrat:
Lycius sank tiefer, als sie ihn umgingen,
In seinen Mantel und lief hin auf Schwingen,
Da Lamia hastend bebte. »Ah«, sprach er,
»Weshalb, mein Liebes, schaudert dich so sehr?
Was löst die zarte Hand sich auf in Schweiß?« –
»Ich bin erschöpft«, sprach Lamia; »sag, der Greis,
Wer ist er? Ich erinnere mich nicht
An ihn – sag, weshalb bargst du dein Gesicht
Vor seinen raschen Blicken?« Er sprach leise:
»'s ist Apollonius, der treue Weise
Und gute Lehrer; nur scheint er heut nacht
Der Narrheit Geist, der meinen Traum verlacht.«

Da er noch sprach, erreichten sie ein Tor
Mit einem hohen Säulenhof davor,
Wo einer Silberlampe Phosphorglühn
Den glatten Stufengang hinunterschien,
Weich wie ein Stern in Wasser; denn so rein,
So unbefleckt war noch der Marmorstein,

Durchrannen die Kristallglanzpolitur
Die dunklen Adern – Göttersohlen nur
Warn hier hinabgestiegen. Äolsklänge
Hauchten die Angeln, als in voller Länge
Das Tor aufschwang auf einen Platz, bekannt
Lang niemandem als ihnen Hand in Hand
Und ein paar stummen Persern, die dies Jahr
Am Markt erschienen: wo ihr Wohnort war,
Das wußte keiner; Neugierigste noch,
Die ihnen folgten, narrten sie stets doch.
Das flügelflatternde Gedicht allein
Muß spätres Leid erzähln, wahrhaftig sein,
Gefiel's manch' Herz auch, sie hier zu verlassen,
Aus regerm Treiben so, mehr Argwohn noch entlassen.

Teil II

Liebe in Hütten, nur bei Wasser, Brot,
Ist – Amor, o vergib! – Staub, Asche, Tod;
Doch Liebe im Palast erst birgt wohl Leid
Wie keines Eremiten Fastenzeit.
Dies ist ein Stück rein aus dem Märchenland,
Schwer für nicht auserkorenen Verstand.
Hätt Lycius nur gelebt, es zu berichten,
Ein Feuer flammte wohl in den Geschichten,
Sie stünden fest: doch war zu kurz ihr Segen,
Um Zischen voller Haß, um Zwietracht zu erregen.
Auch ließ dort, nachts, mit fürchterlichem Blick,
Amor, ganz Neid auf so vollkommnes Glück,
Die Flügel surren, stieß Gegroll hervor
Vorm Quersturz über ihrem Kammertor
Und warf ein glühendes Licht entlang den Korridor.

Trotz alldem kam das Ende: Seit an Seit,
So ruhten sie vereint zur Abendzeit
Auf einem Lager, einem Vorhang nah,
Der, leicht gewebt, an goldner Kordel da
Ins Zimmer flutete und unverstellt
Den Himmel sehen ließ, blau aufgehellt
Zwischen zwei Marmorschäften. Sie genossen,
Wie oft schon, hier zu ruhn, die Lider fast geschlossen,
Nur einen Spalt noch offenstehend aus Liebe –
Damit, fast eingenickt, der andre sichtbar bliebe –
Als jetzt von einem äußren Hügelhang
Das Schwalbenzwitschern dämpfend Hörnerklang
Erscholl – Lycius erschrak – der Lärm verstummte,
Doch ein Gedanke in ihm weitersummte.
Zum ersten Mal seit seinen ersten Schritten
Im purpurnen Palastsaal süßer Sitten,
Betrat sein Geist, vorbei an goldnen Schranken,
Die Lärmwelt fast entsunkener Gedanken.
Die Frau, stets wach, mit Blicken, die durchdrangen,
Sah dies mit Schmerz, schloß so auf ein Verlangen
Nach Höherm, Höherm als ihr Herrscherreich
Der Lüste; und so seufzte sie sogleich,
Sann anderem er nach, wohl überlegt,
Daß Leidenschaft, die denkt, die letzte Stunde schlägt.
»Was seufzst du, holdes Wesen?« raunte er;
»Was denkst du?« fragte zärtlich sie nur mehr;
»Verlassen hast du mich – wo bin ich jetzt?
In deinem Herzen nicht, das Gram verletzt:
Nein, es verstieß mich; und ich bin allein
Ohne ein Haus nun – ja, es muß so sein.«
Er aber sprach, da er sich zu ihr bückte
Und klein sich selbst im Paradies erblickte:
»Mein Silberstern am Abend wie am Morgen!
Was nennst du dich verlassen voller Sorgen,
Indes zu füllen ringe ich mein Herz
Mit tieferm Rot und doppelt großem Schmerz?

Zu fangen, zu umgarnen deine Seele
In meiner, Labyrinth, das sie verhehle
Wie Rosenknospen den verborgnen Duft?
Ach, küß mich – schau, dein Weh ist nur mehr Luft.
Mein Denken! – soll ich's offentun? Hör her!
Welch Mann macht einen Fang, der andre mehr
Als nur beschämt, sie demütigt damit,
Doch ihn nicht zeigt auf einem stolzen Ritt
Und triumphiert, wie ich mich deiner freute
Im heisern Lärm all der Korinther Leute?
Laß Feinde fluchen, Freunde Trommeln schlagen,
Da durch die volle Stadt dein Brauttagswagen
Die blanken Speichen dreht.« Die Herrin sprach
Kein Wort; sie bebte, wankte bleich und schwach,
Sank hin vor ihn und weinte einen Schauer
Des Kummers, als er schloß; zuletzt nur Trauer,
Bat sie ihn, fest umschlungen seine Hand,
Sein Vorhaben zu ändern. Er, entbrannt,
War nur gewillt, mit schlauen Winkelzügen
Ihr wild und scheues Wesen zu besiegen;
Auch fand, trotz Liebe und sein beßres Ich
Verachtend, er Gefallen nun für sich
An ihrem Kummer, derart neu und zart.
Und seine Leidenschaft verfärbte sich, ward hart,
Sanguinisch, wie's nur möglich ist bei jenen,
Die Stirnen haben ohne dunkle Venen.
Schön war dies sanftstimmende Zürnen gleich
Apolls, als der erschien und schon sein Streich
Die Schlange traf. – Ha, Schlange! Wahrlich, sie
War keine. Heiß, so liebte sie die Despotie,
Und willigte, ganz unterwürfig, ein,
Daß, wann er es gebot, sie seine Braut würd sein.
Flüsternd um Mitternacht sprach Lycius dann:
»Welch Namen hast du, den ich nie ersann
Und nicht erfragte, glaubte ich dich doch
Nicht sterblich – nein, vom Himmel kommend noch

Glaub ich dich. Hast du einen Erdennamen,
Benennend diesen blendend schönen Rahmen?
Verwandte, Freunde, die auf Erden weilen
Und Hochzeitsfest und -freuden mit uns teilen?«
»Ich habe keine Freunde«, sprach sie, »nein;
Von ganz Korinth kennst mich wohl du allein:
Staub meiner Eltern füllt in düstrer Gruft
Zwei Urnen, doch wallt dort kein Weihrauchduft,
Denn glücklos starb ihr Stamm aus bis auf mich,
Und ich versäum den heilgen Brauch für dich.
Drum lad die Gäste ein, wie du es willst;
Doch wenn du, wie es scheint, noch Freude fühlst,
Siehst du mich an, bitt Apollonius nicht
Dazu – vor ihm verbirg mein Angesicht.«
Verwirrt von solch verdecktem dunklem Wort,
Drang Lycius tiefer in sie; sie glitt fort,
Stellte sich schlafend, bis die trägen Schatten
Des Schlafs auch ihn umfangen hatten.

Damals war Sitte, wenn auf roten Schwingen
Der Tag schwand, aus dem Haus die Braut zu bringen,
Verhüllt, in einem Wagen, sie entlang
An Blumenjungfern, Fackeln, Brautgesang
Und anderm Prunk zu führn – sie aber kannt
Nicht einen Freund. Als sie sich einsam fand
(Lycius war fort, zu laden seine Schar)
Und wissend, daß nicht abzubringen war
Sein Narrenherz von seiner Prahlerei,
Sann ernst sie nach, wie einzukleiden sei
Mit ihr gebührnder Pracht ihre Beschwer.
Sie fand sie, fraglich nur, wie und woher
Sie kam, wer ihre flüchtgen Diener waren.
Durch Flur und Türen hörte man in Scharen
Jetzt Flügel schwirren, und nach kurzer Zeit
Schon schien der dumpfe Saal vor Anmut hoch und weit.

Geistermusik, wohl einzig und allein
Die Trägerin des Märchendachs, fiel ein,
Klagte wie bang, der ganze Zauber schwände.
Nachahmend Schneisen, zeigten Zedernwände
Palmen und Feigen, die, von allen Seiten,
Zu Ehrn der Braut sich an die Decke reihten;
Zwei Palmen, dann zwei Feigen und so fort
Rankten von allen Seiten Zweige dort
In Nischen ab; darunter lief ein Band
Von Leuchtern gradewegs entlang von Wand zu Wand.
So überwölbt, stand ungeschmeckt bereit
Ein duftend Mahl. Lamia, in königlichem Kleid,
Schritt stumm umher und hieß, in blassen Zügen
Genugtuung auf ihrem Mißvergnügen,
Die unsichtbaren Diener aufzufrischen
Den Glanz des Schnitzwerks noch der letzten Nischen.
Zwischen die Stämme, erst nur Marmorstein,
Kamen nun Jaspisplatten; ihre Reihn
Durchflocht schon bald das Bildwerk schmalrer Bäume
Und ließ den größeren noch kleinre Zwischenräume.
Besehn ein jedes, so verschwand sie nun,
Schloß ab und ließ verstummt das Zimmer ruhn,
Bereit und fertig für die rohen Feste,
Wenn ihre Einsamkeit zerstörten Lärm und Gäste.

Der Tag kam, mit ihm schwatzend all die Rotten.
O stumpfer Lycius! Irrer! was verspotten
Das segnend-stille Los, den Stundenreigen,
Und jedem Blick geheimste Winkel zeigen?
Die Menge nahte; Gäste kamen raunend
Ans Tor, verstummten und, verwundert staunend,
Gingen hinein – die Straße kannte sie,
Und Lücken warn seit ihrer Kindheit nie
In ihr gewesen, und doch sah zuvor
Niemand dies fürstlich-schöne hohe Tor.
So drängten sie hinein, verwirrt, gebannt und stumm –

Nur einer sah sich finstren Blickes um,
Ging kühl-gesetzter Schritte ernst herum.
's war Apollonius: lachend bald auch er,
Als wäre ein Problem, das lang schon schwer
Seine Geduld gekostet, nun getaut,
Zerschmolzen, fort – ganz wie vorausgeschaut.

Im Vestibülgemurmel traf er auch
Den jungen Zögling. »Zwar ist es nicht Brauch,
Lycius«, sprach er, »als ungeladner Gast
Sich dir so aufzudrängen und zur Last
Zu fallen unerwünscht inmitten Scharen
Von jüngern Freunden. Dennoch – mein Gebaren
Wirst du verzeihn.« Lycius ward rot, ging vor
Und zog den Greis durchs offne innre Tor,
Beschwichtigenden Worts und demutsvoll
Wandelnd zu süßer Milch so des Sophisten Groll.

Prächtig erleuchtet war das Festtagszimmer,
Erfüllt von Duft und durchdringendem Schimmer:
Vor jeder lichten Wand, in Rauch gehüllt,
Ein Faß, mit Myrrhn und Würzholz aufgefüllt
Und vom geweihten Dreifuß hochgehalten,
Die Füße schlankgeschweift in wollne Falten
Des Teppichs; fünfzig Rauchsäuln stiegen auf
Aus fünfzig Fässern, schwerelos hinauf
Zur Decke und noch nachgeahmt im Steigen
Die Spiegelwände lang von Zwillingswolkenreigen.
Zwölf runde Tische, seidne Sitze rings,
Brusthoch und auf die Tatzen einer Sphinx
Gestellt, bedeckten Becher und Pokal
Aus schwerem Gold, Obst wie geleert dreimal
Der Ceres' Horn und, in Karaffen, Wein,
Der dunklem Faß entquoll mit heitrem Schein.
So warn die Tische für das Mahl gefüllt,
Ein jeder wie ein Schrein mit einem Götterbild.

Nachdem in einem Vorraum allen Gästen
Emsige Sklaven kühle Schwämme preßten
Auf die erfreuten Handrücken und Füße
Und feierlich mit Ölen voller Süße
Ihr Haar beträufelten, traten sie ein
In weißem Kleid und legten sich in Reihn
Auf seidne Lager hier, erstaunt noch immer,
Woher der Prunk wohl kam, der Reichtum, all der Schimmer.

Weich glitt Musik die weiche Luft entlang,
Während das Griechisch fließend noch erklang
Unter den Gästen, die still diskutierten,
Da wenig Tropfen Weins erst zirkulierten;
Doch kaum traf auf ihr Hirn der frohe Saft,
Wurden sie laut, und laut mit aller Kraft
Die Instrumente. Farbenfrohes Blühn,
Der Raum, die helle Pracht der Draperien,
Die reich verzierte Decke, Rausch von Weinen,
Die schönen Sklaven, Lamia – sie erscheinen,
Jetzt, da der Wein sich rosig ihnen weiht
Und ihre Seelen hemmungslos befreit,
Nicht länger fremd; dem Wein, dem frohen Wein
Wird das Elysium nicht zu schön, zu himmlisch sein.
Bald stand nur mehr Gott Bacchus im Zenit;
Heller das helle Aug, die Wang durchglüht;
Kränze von jedem Grün, von jedem Duft,
Geraubt aus Tälern, oder Hochwaldluft,
Trug man in weiden-goldnen Körben her,
Bis an die Henkel voll, ganz nach Begehr
Jedweden Gasts – daß alle, wie sie mochten,
Auf Seide hingestreckt, sich ihre Stirn umflochten.

Und Lamia? Was krönt sie? Was Lycius?
Was krönt den Weisen, Apollonius?
Sei ihre schmerzzerquälte Stirn umschlungen
Vom Laub der Weiden und der Natterzungen;

Und für den Jüngling, schnell, laßt uns entwinden
Den Thyrsus, laßt sein waches Auge schwinden
In die Vergessenheit; doch für den Weisen
Laßt Speergras und das Distelschwert sich beißen
Um seine Stirn. Flieht nicht alle Magie
Vorm bloßen Hauch kalter Philosophie?
Stolz stand am Himmel einst ein Regenbogen:
Bekannt sind Bau, Textur; sind einbezogen
In einen Katalog der Alltagsdinge.
Philosophie stutzt eine Engelsschwinge,
Ficht Wunder an durch Regeln und Axiome,
Leert die beseelte Luft, den Schacht der Gnome –
Entwirrt den Regenbogen wie zuvor
Die Lamia, zart gebaut, als Schemen sich verlor.

Lycius, froh neben ihr am Ehrenmahl,
Sah kaum ein anderes Gesicht im Saal,
Bis er, zurückgedrängt sein Liebesglück,
Sich randvoll eingoß und quer einen Blick
Über den Tisch warf, um dort von des Alten
Durchfurchtem Haupt ein Nicken zu erhalten,
Ihm zuzutrinken. Kahlen Kopfs jedoch
Blickte der Philosoph, nun starrer noch,
Nur die erschrockne Schönheit Lamias an,
Verstörte ihren Stolz, sog sie in seinen Bann.
Da preßte Lycius innig ihre Hand,
Die fahl er auf dem Rosenlager fand:
Doch es durchfuhr ihn kalt, sie war wie Eis;
Dann glühte sie jäh, unnatürlich heiß,
Und Angst schoß ebenso heiß in sein Herz.
»Lamia, was ist? Was zitterst du vor Schmerz?
Kennst du den Mann?« Lamia gab nichts zurück.
In ihre Augen starrte er, kein Blick
Traf sein verliebtes, mitleidiges Bitten;
Er starrte mehr, mehr; seine Sinne stritten;

Ein Zauber schien die Schönheit aufzusaugen;
Nichts von Erkennen lag in diesen Augen.
»Lamia!« rief er – kein sanfter Ton darauf.
Die Menge lauschte, und der laute Hauf
Ward stumm; die herrliche Musik entschwirrte;
In tausend Kränzen welkte alle Myrte.
Die Stimmen, Lauten und die Wonnen schwanden,
Totenstille war nach und nach entstanden,
Die bald schon furchtbar gegenwärtig war,
Daß keiner mehr als Schreck empfand in seinem Haar.
»Lamia!« schrie er – doch nichts als nur sein Schall
Durchbrach die Stille mit betrübtem Hall.
»Fort, fauler Traum!« rief er, starrend einmal mehr
In ihr Gesicht, wo alle Adern leer
Um schöne Schläfen strichen; nichts besprühte
Die Wangen; keine Leidenschaft durchglühte
Das eingefallne Antlitz. Alles fahl;
Lamia, nicht länger schön, saß totenbleich im Saal.
»Die Hexeraugen zu, herzloser Mann!
Sieh fort, Schuft! oder der gerechte Bann
All jener Götter, deren hehres Bild
Statt ihrer Schatten hier den Raum erfüllt,
Durchbohr sie auf der Stelle mit dem Dorn
Qualvoller Blindheit; gebe dich verlorn,
Zitternd und dein Gewissen eine Nacht
Voll Angst, ob ihrer lang gereizten Macht,
Ob gottlos hochmütger Sophisterein,
Der Lügen, Lockungen, dem falschen Schein.
Korinther! auf den greisen Schuft seht nieder!
Seht, wie besessen wimpernlose Lider
Sein Dämonauge wölbt! Korinther, seht!
Wie meine Braut vor seiner Macht vergeht.«
»Narr!« sagte der Sophist, in einem Ton
Barsch vor Verachtung; todestrunken schon,
Stöhnte da Lycius nur – das Herz in Stücken,
Sank an den schmerzerfüllten Geist sein Rücken.

»Narr! Narr!« sprach er erneut, während sein Blick
Reglos nicht abließ: »Jedes Mißgeschick
Im Leben hielt ich fern von dir bis heute,
Um dich zu sehn als einer Schlange Beute?«
Da keuchte Lamia tödlich; wie ein Speer
Durchdrang sie des Sophisten Blick nunmehr,
Scharf, grausam, bohrend, stechend: ihre Hand,
So gut sie schwach noch irgend Ausdruck fand,
Bat ihn vergeblich nur, doch still zu sein.
Gleichbleibend starrte er und starrte – *Nein!*
»Ja, Schlange!« rief er; kaum gesagt dies Wort,
War sie mit fürchterlichem Schrei schon fort –
Und Lycius' Arm umfing sein Glück nie wieder,
Ganz wie seit dieser Nacht das Leben seine Glieder:
Hoch droben lag er da! – und Freunde standen
Um ihn, die weder Puls noch Atem fanden
Und in sein Hochzeitskleid den schweren Körper wanden.

Der Fall des Hyperion

Ein Traum

Canto I

Fanatikern sind ihre Träume Webstoff
Für einer Sekte Paradies, der Wilde
Auch ahnt in den erhabensten Gestalten
Des Schlafs den Himmel – schade, daß sie nicht
Auf Pergament, auf wild-indianisch Blatt
Die Schatten wohlklingenden Ausspruchs pausten.
Doch Lorbeers bar sind, träumen, sterben sie;
Denn Poesie allein kann ihre Träume
Verkünden, mit der Worte heller Formel
Befrein die Phantasie aus düsterm Bann
Und stummem Zauber. Wer, der lebt, kann sagen
»Du bist kein Dichter – künd nicht deine Träume«?
Da jeder, ist kein Holzklotz seine Seele,
Visionen hat und spricht, wenn er geliebt hat
Und wohlgenährt ward von der Muttersprache.
Ob folgender Traum nun der eines Dichters
Oder Fanatikers ist, wird man wissen,
Liegt dieses warmen Schreibers Hand im Grab.

Mir schien, ich stand, wo Bäume aller Breiten,
Palme und Myrte, Eiche, Ahorn, Buche
Mit Wegerich und Blattgewürz ein Schirm warn –
In Nachbarschaft von Quellen, da ihr Klang
Sanftrieselnd in mein Ohr drang, und, berührt
Von Duft, nicht fern von Rosen. Drehte ich mich,
So sah ich schweren Daches eine Laube
Aus Rebengittern, Glocken, größern Blüten,
Blumigen Weihrauchfässern gleich frei schwingend.
Vor der umrankten Tür, auf einer Bank
Aus Moos, lag bunt ein Mahl von Sommerfrüchten,

Das, trat man näher, übrig schien von Speisen,
Die Engel aßen oder Mutter Eva;
Denn leere Schalen warn verstreut im Gras,
Halb nackt erst Traubenstengel und auch Reste,
Süßduftend, deren bloße Art mir fremd war.
Noch war mehr Fülle, als der Fabel Horn,
Dreifach geleert, vergösse zum Gelage
Proserpinas, zurück auf ihren Feldern,
Wo weiße Färsen brülln. Und Appetit,
Verlangend wie ich nie auf Erden fühlte,
Im Innern wachsend, aß ich köstlich
Und, kaum geschehn, auch durstig, stand nahbei
Doch ein Gefäß kühl durchsichtigen Safts,
Geschlürft von Wanderbienen, den ich nahm
Und, feiernd alle Sterblichen der Welt
Und all die Toten, Namen unsern Lippen,
Trank. Dieser Trunk ist Quelle meines Themas.
Kein Asisch-Mohn, kein feines Elixier
Des bald vergehenden neidvollen Kalifats,
Kein Gift, erzeugt im engen Mönchsgelaß,
Verringernd scharlachne Konklavengreise,
Rafft derart unbequemes Leben hin.
Im Duft der Hülsen und der Beern, zerdrückt
Am Boden, stemmte ich mich schwer entgegen
Dem herrischen Gebräu; allein vergebens –
Der Rausch drang an, und ich sank hin,
Wie ein Silenus auf antiken Vasen.
Wie lang ich schlummerte – 's ist schwer zu sagen.
Zurück die Lebenssinne, fuhr ich auf,
Als hätt ich Flügel; doch die schönen Bäume,
Die Moosbank und die Laube waren fort.
Rings sah ich auf die reichbehaunen Seiten
Eines uralten Tempels mit erhabnem,
So hohem Dach – mir schien, daß Schleierwolken
Hier hinziehn könnten wie hoch droben Sterne.
So alt der Ort war, ich entsann mich keines

Auf Erden ähnlichen: was ich gesehn
An Domen, Wällen, Türmen, schief und rissig,
Den Ruheständlern von versunknen Reichen,
Naturfels, schwer geplagt in Wind und Wellen,
Schien bloß Verfehl von hinfälligen Dingen
Vor solch allzeit gewölbtem Monument.
Zu meinen Füßen auf dem Marmor lagen
Manch sonderbar Gefäß und langes Tuch,
Gewoben wohl aus farbigem Asbest
Oder von Motten war's hier nicht zu fressen,
So weiß das Leinen; andre dann, ganz deutlich,
Durchliefen Bilder eines dunklen Garns.
In wirren Haufen durcheinander lagen
Gewänder, goldne Zangen, Schalen, Pfannen,
Auch Gürtel, Ketten, heilige Juwelen. –

Mich abwendend voll Ehrfurcht, hob ich nochmals
Den Raum allseits durchmessend meine Augen –
Das bossierte Dach, die massigstumme Reihe
Der Säuln von Nord nach Süd, endend im Nebel
Des Nichts; nach Osten dann, wo schwarze Tore
Verschlossen warn allzeit gen Sonnenaufgang.
Dann blickte ich nach Westen und sah fern
Ein Bildnis dort vom Ausmaß einer Wolke,
Zu dessen Füßen eben ein Altar schlief,
Erreichbar beidseitig durch Treppen,
Marmorne Balustraden und Geduld,
Mühsam zu zählen unzählge Stufen.
Gesetzten Schrittes zum Altar trat ich,
Hast unterdrückend als zu ruchlos hier
Und, näherkommend, sah zunebst des Schreins
Jemanden walten; und ein Feuer ging dort.
Wenn Mitte Mai der drückendschwere Ostwind
Jäh südwärts dreht, der dünne warme Regen
Aus allem Flor gefrornen Weihrauch schmilzt
Und mit so viel an heiterm Wohl die Luft füllt,

Daß selbst der Sterbende sein Grab vergißt –
Grad so warf jenes hehre Opferfeuer,
Verströmend Majas Weihrauch, ringsumher
Auf alles – außer Seligkeit – Vergessen
Und hüllte den Altar in weichen Rauch,
Aus dessen duftig weißen Schleiern ich
Die Worte hörte: »Kannst du nicht ersteigen
Die Stufen hier, stirb, wo du stehst auf Marmor.
Dein Fleisch, naher Verwandter nackten Staubs,
Wird ausdörrn mangels Nährstoff – dein Gebein
Zerfalln in ein, zwei Jahrn und so verwehn,
Daß nicht das schärfste Aug ein Gran wird finden
Von dem, was du nun bist auf kalten Fliesen.
Dein Lebenssand verrinnt mit dieser Stunde,
Und keine Hand im Universum dreht
Dein Stundenglas, verbrennt dies Laub voll Harz,
Eh diese ewgen Stufen du erklommen.«
Ich hörte, sah: zwei Sinne auf einmal,
So fein, so scharf, spürten die Tyrannei
Solch wilden Drohns und hart verfügten Loses.
Gewaltig schien die Anstrengung; noch brannte
Das Laub – als plötzlich von den Fliesen aufwärts
Ein Schauder lähmend meine Glieder schlug
Und rasch, um kalten Griffs zu fassen
Die Ströme, pulsend an der Kehle, stieg.
Ich schrie; und meines Aufschreis helle Angst
Drang mir ins Ohr – der Taubheit zu entgehn,
Rang ich, die tiefste Stufe zu erreichen.
Schwer, langsam, todgleich war mein Schritt; die Kälte
Wuchs würgend, es erstickend, in mein Herz;
Und faltend meine Hände, fühlt ich sie nicht.
Dem Tode nah, erklomm mein Fuß durcheist
Die tiefste Stufe; sie berührt, schien Leben
Zu strömen in die Zehen: ich stieg aufwärts
Wie holde Engel einst an einer Leiter
Vom Gras gen Himmel flogen. »Heilge Macht«,

Rief ich, mich nähernd dem behörnten Schrein,
»Was bin ich, das erlöst so soll vom Tod sein?
Was bin ich, daß ein andrer Tod nicht kommt,
Mein schänderisches Wort hier zu ersticken?«
Da sprach verhüllt der Schatten: »Du verspürtst,
Was sterben heißt und dann erneut zu leben,
Eh deine Stunde schlug. Daß dessen mächtig
Du bist, erlöst dich; aufgeschoben hast du
Dein Los.« – »Hohe Prophetin«, sprach ich, »fortwisch,
Gütge, gefällt's dir, meines Geistes Schleier.«
»Keinem frommt diese Höhe«, sprach der Schatten,
»Als jenen, denen alles Leid der Welt
Ihr Leid ist und nicht ruhn sie lassen wird.
All die, die Zuflucht finden in der Welt,
Wo sorglos man verschlafen kann sein Leben,
Die, bringt der Zufall sie in diesen Tempel,
Verwesen in ihm, wo du halb verwestest.«
»Sind Tausende nicht auf der Welt«, sprach ich,
Ermutigt durch des Schattens reine Stimme,
»Die bis zum Tod noch ihre Brüder lieben;
Das ungeheure Leid der Welt verspüren;
Die noch, gleich Knechten einer armen Menschheit,
Sich mühn um sterblich Wohl? Sehn müßt ich sicher
Noch andre hier – doch ich bin ganz allein.«
»Jene, die du erwähnst, sind keine Seher«,
Sprach nun die Stimme, »keine schwachen Träumer,
Suchen kein Wunder als des Menschen Antlitz,
Keine Musik als heiterklingende Stimmen –
Sie kommen nicht, sie denken nicht ans Kommen –
Und du bist hier, weil weniger du bist. –
Was kannst du Gutes tun, was all dein Stamm,
Der großen Welt? Du bist ein träumend Ding,
Ein Fieber deiner selbst. Denk an die Erde;
Selbst Hoffnung – welches Glück birgt sie für dich,
Welch Zuflucht? Ein Geschöpf hat seine Heimat;
Ein jeder Tage voller Freud und Leid,

Gleich ob sein Werk erhaben oder niedrig –
Das Leid; die Freude; deutlich unterschieden.
Der Träumer nur vergällt sich alle Tage,
Erduldet Schmerz, den keine Schuld verdient.
Deshalb, auf daß gerecht das Glück verteilt sei,
Wird eingelassen dann ein Ding wie du
In solche Gärten, wie du jüngst durchwandert,
Und in den Tempeln dort geduldet; darum
Droht nichts dir unter dieser Statue Knie.«
»Daß ich, nichtswürdig, doch bevorzugt bin,
Durch so geneigte Rede Heilung findet
Nicht unedles Gebrechen, das beglückt mich –
Ja, und ich könnte weinen vor solch Gunst.«
So sprach ich und fuhr fort: »Wenn dir's gefällt,
Erhabner Schatten, sage mir: gewiß ist
Nicht jedes Lied, ins Ohr der Welt gesungen,
Nutzlos. Ein Dichter ist gewiß ein Weiser,
Ein Humanist, ein Arzt für alle Menschen.
Ich bin's nicht, spür ich wie der Geier spürt,
Er ist kein Vogel, wenn ein Adler kreist.
Was bin ich dann? Du sprachst von meinem Stamm –
Welch Stamm?« – Gehüllt in niederhängendes Weiß,
Sprach da so ernst der Schatten, daß sein Atem
Das dünne Leintuch auftrieb, niederhängend
Aufs goldne Rauchfaß, welches an der Hand
Ihm schwang. – »Gehörst du nicht zum Stamm der Träumer?
Der Dichter und der Träumer sind verschieden,
Anders, schier gegensätzlich, Antipoden.
Der eine schüttet Balsam auf die Welt,
Der andre peinigt sie.« Da rief ich aus,
Mir selbst verhaßt, in einem Anfall Pythias:
»Apoll! entschwundner, ferner Apollon!
Wo dampft dein Pesthauch nun, um unterm Türritz
Hineinzukriechen in die Wohnungen
Der Spottlyristen, großen Selbstanbeter

Und saubern Laffen hoher mieser Dichtkunst.
Saug ich wie sie den Tod ein – Leben sein wird's,
Sie vor mir hingestreckt ins Grab zu sehn.
Erhabner Schatten, sag mir, wo ich bin,
Wessen Altar dies ist; wem Weihrauch aufsteigt;
Welch Bildnis dies, des Antlitz ich nicht seh
Vor breiten Marmorknien, und wer du bist,
Du mit dem Stimmklang einer Frau, so gütig.«

Da sprach, gehüllt in niederhängendes Leintuch,
So ernst der große Schatten, daß sein Atem
Die dünne Gaze rührte, niederhängend
Aufs goldne Rauchfaß, welches an der Hand
Ihm schwang; und ich hört langverwahrte Tränen
Ihn weinen. »Dieser Tempel, grau und einsam,
Ist, was verschont vom Tosen eines Kriegs ward,
Gekämpft einst von der Hierarchie der Riesen
Wider den Aufruhr; hier dies alte Bildnis,
Züge im Stein, die, als es fiel, sich furchten,
Ist das Saturnus'; ich, Moneta, blieb
Höchste, einzige Priestrin seiner Ödnis.«
Ich sprach kein Wort darauf, denn meine Zunge,
Nutzlos, fand unterm Runddach ihres Heims
Nicht einen Laut einer gebührnden Hoheit,
Um zu erwidern auf Monetas Klage.
Es herrschte Stille, da die Glut des Schreins
Auf süße Nahrung brannte: ich sah hin,
Sah auf den Fliesengrund, wo dicht geschichtet
Reiser des Zimtbaums warn nebst manchem Stoß
Von anderm mürben Würzholz – sah erneut
Auf den Altar dann und auf seine Hörner,
Weiß von der Asche, seine schwache Flamme
Und nochmals auf die Opfergaben dann,
So hin und her – bis schwer Moneta ausrief:
»Das Opfer ist vollbracht, gleichwohl jedoch
Will gut ich zu dir sein ob deines Wohlwollens.

Die mir noch immer Fluch ist, meine Macht,
Sie sei für dich ein Wunder; denn die Szenen,
Noch lebhaft schwindelnd im gewölbten Hirn
Vor aufgeladen wechselvollem Elend,
Sollst du mit sterblichstumpfen Augen schaun,
Von Schmerzen frei, wenn Wunder dich nicht schmerzen.«
Wenn einer Göttlichen gerundet Wort
Sanft muttergleich sein könnte, dann dies letzte;
Und doch verspürt ich Furcht vor ihren Kleidern,
Am meisten vor dem Schleier, der ihr bleich
Vom Haupt hing und sie hüllte in Mysterien,
Daß mir mein Herz zu klein ward für sein Blut.
Die Göttin sah's und teilte heilger Hand
Den Schleier – da sah ich ein fahles Antlitz,
Welk nicht von irdschem Leid, doch hell gebleicht
Durch Krankheit, die, nicht sterblich, auch nicht tötet;
Die steten Wandel bringt, dem selger Tod
Kein Ende setzt; todwärts schritt fort dies Antlitz
Zu keinem Tod; schon hatt' es überholt
Die Lilie und den Schnee; und weiter jetzt
Darf ich nicht denken, sah ich auch dies Antlitz –
Nur um der Augen willen floh ich nicht.
Sie hielten mich zurück, mit gütgem Leuchten,
Besänftigt-mild durch göttlichholdste Lider,
Die, halb geschlossen, gänzlich blind doch schienen
Für alles Äußere – sie sahn mich nicht,
Ihr Glanz war stumpf gleich dem des milden Monds,
Der dem Trost gibt, den er nicht sieht, nicht weiß,
Welch Auge aufwärtsblickt. Als hätte ich
Ein Körnchen Gold auf einem Hang entdeckt,
Gepackt von Gier geweitet meine Augen,
Das finstre Innre, reich an Gold, zu suchen,
So brannte ich beim Blick zur Stirn Monetas,
Zu sehn, welch Dinge das durchhöhlte Hirn
Im Schoß trug hinter ihr; welch reich Tragödie
In den verborgnen dunklen Schädelkammern

Gespielt ward, die solch furchtbarn Nachdruck legte
Auf kalte Lippen, mit solch' Glanz erfüllte
Planetengleiche Augen und der Stimme
Solch Schwermut beigab. – »Schatten der Erinnrung!«
Rief ich im Fußfall der Verehr vor ihr,
»Bei all der Nacht um dein gefallnes Haus,
Bei diesem letzten Tempel, goldner Zeit,
Bei Gott Apollo, deinem Pflegekind,
Sowie bei deiner selbst, verlaßne Gottheit,
Dem blassen Omega versunkner Sippen,
Laß mich erblicken wie du es versprachst,
Was so im Hirn dir hin und wider gärt.«
Kaum daß passierte meine frommen Lippen
Dies Anflehn, standen wir schon Seit an Seit
(Verholztem Busch gleich an erhabnen Kiefern)
Tief in der finstren Schwermut eines Tals,
Fern von des Morgenhauches Wohl versunken,
Fern feur'gem Tag und Abends einzgem Stern.
Ich blickte tiefer in das düstre Zweigwerk
Und sah, was erst ein mächtig Bildnis schien,
Ganz ähnlich ersterem, postiert so hoch
Im Tempelbau Saturns. Da traf die Stimme
Monetas kurz mein Ohr: »So saß Saturn,
Als seine Reiche er verlorn.« Schon wuchs
Die Kraft der ungeheuren Sicht in mir,
Zu sehen wie ein Gott sieht, leicht die Tiefe
Der Dinge zu durchdringen wie von außen
Ausmaß und Form das Aug. Das hehre Thema
Des knappen Worts hing riesig mir vorm Geist,
Mit halbentwirrtem Netz. Ich setzte mich
Auf eines Adlers Ausguck, um zu sehen
Und sehend nie zu vergessen. Kein Hauch Leben
Traf dies verhüllte Tal, nicht so viel Luft
Als im Umkreisen eines Sommertags
Kein Samenkorn aus Federgräsern raubt;
Wohin ein totes Blatt fiel, blieb es ruhn.

Ein Bach lief stumm vorbei, gedämpfter noch
Von Schatten, die die abgefallne Gottheit
Hier warf; im Röhricht preßte die Najade
Den kalten Finger fester auf die Lippen.
Den Ufersand lang liefen breite Fußspurn
Bis da, wo ausgeruht der greise Fuß
Saturns und schlief nun – welch ein langer Schlaf!
Entwürdigt, kalt auf dem durchtränkten Grund,
Lag seine alte Rechte schwach, matt, tot,
Entzeptert; reichlos war sein Aug geschlossen,
Indes gebeugt sein Haupt zu lauschen schien
Der alten Mutter Erde, ihn zu trösten.

Es schien, von hier könnt keine Macht ihn wecken;
Doch Eine kam, die, mit verwandter Hand,
Die breiten Schultern griff, voll Ehrfurcht tief
Verneigt, obschon er des nicht inneward.
Da tönte traurig Mnemosynes Stimme,
Und traurig lauschte ich. »Die Gottheit, welche
Du kommen sahst aus jenem ödsten Wald,
Sich langsam nähernd dem gefallnen König,
Ist Thea, sanftmütigste unsres Stamms.«
In holder Ausbildung sah ich die Göttin
Monetas Blässe haupthoch überragen,
In ihrer Trübsal Frauentränen näher.
In ihrem Blick lag lauschend eine Furcht,
Als hätte nun das Unheil erst begonnen;
Als hätten Vorhutwolken böser Tage
Ihr Gift vergossen und die finstre Nachhut
Wälz' mit geballtem Donnern sich einher.
Mit einer Hand griff sie zum wehen Fleck,
Wo eines Menschen Herz schlägt, so als spürte,
Obschon unsterblich, sie dort furchtbarn Schmerz;
Die andre um Saturns gekrümmten Nacken
Gelegt und bis in Höhe seines hohlen Ohrs
Geneigt mit offnen Lippen, sprach sie Worte

Ernsten Gehalts, in tiefem Orgelklang,
Klagende Worte, die, mit schwacher Zunge
Wie unsrer, solchen Klanges wärn – wie kraftlos
Gegen den reichen Ausdruck früher Götter! –
»Saturn, schau auf! – nur, arm verlorner König –
Zu was? Ich bring dir keinen Trost, nein – keinen;
Ich kann nicht rufen *Weshalb schläfst du so?*
Denn dich verließ der Himmel, und die Erde
Erkennt dich, so geschlagen, nicht als Gott;
Und auch der Ozean, all sein ernstes Tosen,
Ließ deinen Zepter sein, und alle Luft
Ist leer von deiner greisen Herrlichkeit.
Dein Donner, nicht gewogen neuer Weisung,
Zürnt zage über uns gefallnes Haus;
Dein scharfer Blitz, in ungeübten Händen,
Versengt, verbrennt unser einst heitres Reich.
So reuelos schnell kommt stets neuer Schmerz,
Daß keine Hoffnung Raum zum Atmen hat.
Schlaf fort, Saturn. Ich Achtlose, was stör ich
Derart deine verträumte Einsamkeit?
Was öffnen deine schwermutsvollen Augen?
Schlaf fort, da ich zu deinen Füßen weine.«

So wie, in der verzückten Sommernacht,
Wälder, von ernsten Sternen zweigverzaubert,
Träumen, lautlos so die Nacht lang träumen,
Bis ein verlaßner zögerlicher Windstoß
Kaum anschwillt in der Stille; schon verklingt;
Als ebbte Luft nach einer Welle aus –
So kam ihr Wort, so gings; derweil sie weinend
Die schöne breite Stirn aufs Erdreich preßte,
Wo ihr gefallnes Haar sich locken konnte,
Ein sanftes, seidnes Fußbett für Saturn.
Lang, lang verharrten unbewegt die beiden,
Wie Standbilder, errichtet auf dem Grab
Der eignen Stärke. Furchtbar lange Zeit

Sah ich sie an: sie lagen noch genauso –
Der starre Gott noch zugeneigt der Erde,
Die Göttin traurig weinend ihm zu Füßen.
Moneta stumm. Mit nichts als Halt und Stütze
Als meiner eignen schwachen Sterblichkeit
Ertrug ich dieses ewgen Schweigens Last,
Die stete Trübsal und die drei Erstarrten
Beschwerend die Sinne einen ganzen Mond.
Denn brennenden Gehirns ermaß ich sicher
Zur Nacht vergoßne silberne Gezeiten,
Und jedes Tagfürtag schien mir, ich würde
Hagrer und geisterhafter. Oft wünscht ich
Zutiefst, der Tod führ mich aus diesem Tal fort,
All seinem Drücken. Keuchend aus Verzweiflung
Am Wandel, verfluchte ich mich Stund um Stund –
Bis aufschlug sein erloschnes Aug Saturn
Und rings um ihn sein Königreich dahin sah,
Die Düsternis und Trübsal jenes Orts
Und kniend die schöne Göttin ihm zu Füßen.
Wie feuchter Duft von Blumen, Gras und Blättern
Waldtäler mit durchdringender Luft erfüllt,
Vertraut des Forstes Nüstern, so erfüllte
Das Wort Saturns das moosge Dunkel rings
Bis in die Höhlen zeitzerfreßner Eichen
Und tiefen Windungen im Bau des Fuchses
Mit leiser Trauer, als er sprach und preisgab
Befremdliches dem abgeschiednen Pan:
»Stöhnt, Brüder, stöhnt; sind wir geschluckt doch,
Verbannt von jedem göttlich hohen Amt
Des sanften Wirkens auf die fahlen Sphären,
Des stillen Waltens ob der Menschen Ernte
Und allem Tun, an dem die höchste Gottheit
Ihr liebevolles Herz wärmt. Stöhnt und klagt.
Stöhnt, Brüder, stöhnt; denn seht! die Aufruhrsphären
Drehn sich, die Sterne sind auf altem Kurs,
Gewölk folgt schattigfeucht der Erde noch,

Saugt sich noch satt am Licht von Mond und Sonne,
Noch knospt der Baum, noch murmeln die Gestade.
Es ist kein Tod im ganzen Universum,
Kein Hauch von Tod. – Nun sei Tod da. – Stöhnt, stöhnt,
Stöhn, Kybele – durch deine bösen Kinder
Wurde ein Gott zu einer Schüttellähmung.
Stöhnt, Brüder, stöhnt, denn mir bleibt keine Kraft,
Schwach wie das Schilf – schwach – matt wie meine Stimme –
Oh, oh, die Pein, die Pein der Mattigkeit.
Stöhnt, stöhnt, denn noch erwärmt's mich – oder helft mir:
Stürzt jene Sprosse und schenkt mir den Sieg.
Laßt andern Groll hörn und Trompetenschall
Gelaßnen Sieges, Hymnen eines Fests,
Auf goldnen Gipfeln hochgetürmter Wolken,
Sanft künden Stimmen und erzittern silbern
Saiten in hohlen Muscheln; und laßt Schönes
In neuem Glanz erstrahln zur Überraschung
Der Himmelskinder. –« Hier nun schloß er matt,
Senkte so jämmerlich und dünn die Stimme –
Mir schien, ich hört' beklagen einen Erdgreis
Den Erdverlust; auch konnten meine Augen
Und Ohrn nicht jenen schönen Sinneneinklang herstelln,
Der süßen Ton mit Anmut von Gestalt eint
Und Schmerzensklänge einer Trauerharfe
Mit langgliedrigen Formen. Mehr erforscht ich:
Noch saß er starr unter den düstern Bäumen,
Die schlangenförmig breiteten die Arme,
Ihr Laub verstummt; sein Bild des Jammers dort
(Da alles still war) strafte tödlich Lügen,
Was ich zuvor gehört – nur seine Lippen
Bebten in weißen Ringeln seines Barts.
Sie sprachen wahr, wenn, rund, die schneeigen Locken
Auch edel hingen wie am Himmelsantlitz
Ein Mittagsvlies Gewölk. Thea erhob sich
Und streckte weiß den Arm durchs hohle Dunkel,
Wohin auch weisend; darauf stand auch er auf

Wie ein Gigant, gesehn von Seefahrern,
Bald fahl vom Gischtschaum trüber Mitternacht.
Sie schwanden meinen Blicken in den Wald;
Ich sah's kaum, als Moneta rief: »Die beiden
Eilen zu ihren Leidgenossen, schmachtend
Von schwarzen Felsen zugedeckt, in Schmerz
Und Dunkel, hoffnungslos.« Und sie sprach weiter,
Wie lesen mag, wer nimmermüd voran
Kann schreiten aus dem Vorraum dieses Traums,
In dessen offnen Türen noch ich selbst
Kurz säumen muß und sammeln mein Erinnern
An ihr hoch Wort – vielleicht kein weitres wage.

Canto II

»Damit du, Sterblicher, auch recht verstehst,
Vermenschlich ich mein Sprechen für dein Ohr
Und stell Vergleiche an mit Irdischem;
Ansonsten lauschtest besser du dem Wind,
Der dir ein tauber Lärm ist, keine Sprache,
Bläst er vor Sagen schwer auch durch die Bäume. –
Viel fließen Tränen an betrübtem Ort,
Mehr Kummer, diesem gleich, und selbes Leid,
Zu groß dem irdschen Wort, dem Stift des Schreibers.
In Fesseln oder selbst verborgen, ächzen
Nach alter Lehnspflicht Rückkehr die Titanen,
Harrend in ihrem Los dem Ruf Saturns.
Nur einer unsrer ganzen Adlersippe
Bewahrt die Hoheit, Herrscherkraft und Größe:
Lodernd auf kugeligem Feuer sitzt
Hyperion, saugt ein noch Weihrauch, wirbelnd
Von Mensch zu Sonnengott – doch sicher nicht.
Denn wie ein schlechtes Zeichen auf der Erde
Schrickt und bestürzt, so schaudert hier auch ihn:
Kein Hundsgeheul, kein abendlicher Schrei

Des Dämmervogels, nicht das Umgehn dessen,
Dem just die Totenglocke einmal schlug –
Doch Grauen, einer Riesenkraft bemessen,
Peinigen Gott Hyperion. Sein Palast,
Basteit mit glühend goldnen Pyramiden,
Wo bronzne Obeliske Schatten werfen,
Glimmt ein Blutrot durch all die tausend Höfe,
Die Bögen, Kuppeln, feur'gen Galerien;
Und Vorhänge aurorischen Gewölks
Erglühen zornig: kostet er vom Dampf
Des Weihrauchs, aufgeweht von heilgen Hügeln,
So schmeckt statt Süßigkeit sein weiter Gaumen
Giftiges Erz und eklige Metalle.
Deshalb, den müden Westen eingebracht,
Nach gänzlicher Vollendung lichten Tags,
Statt Himmelsruhe auf erhabnem Lager
Und Schlummer in den Armen von Musik,
Durchmißt er auch die heitern Mußestunden
Mit Riesenschritten, fort von Saal zu Saal;
Indessen tief in Seitengang und Winkel
Zu Trauben sich beschwingte Diener drängen,
Erschrocken und voll Furcht; den Bangen gleich,
Die sich auf weiter Ebne traurig sammeln,
Wenn Turm und Zinnen beben mit der Erde.
Grad da Saturn, erwacht aus eisger Starre,
Mit Thea, Schritt für Schritt, aus jenem Wald kommt,
Senkt schräg hinab sich zu des Westens Schwelle
Hyperion, Zwielicht breitend hinter sich –
Dorthin ziehn wir.« – In hellem Licht stand ich,
Dem düstern Tal entkommen. Mnemosyne
Saß nun auf einem glatten Vierkantstein,
Der unverzerrt aus lichtem Tief zurückwarf
Ihr Priestertuch. Mein rascher Blick lief hin
Von Schiff zu Schiff, Gewölbe zu Gewölbe,
Durch Lauben duftenden, umrankten Lichts,
Arkaden, leuchtend, lang, demantbefliest.

Da rauschte hell Hyperion heran;
Sein Flammenkleid schlug ihm um seine Fersen
Mit einem Krachen wie von irdschem Feuer,
Daß die ätherisch sanften Horen, flatternd
Auf Taubenschwingen, flohn. Er flammte weiter …

Drama

König Stephen

Ein Fragment einer Tragödie

Erster Aufzug

Erste Szene

Schlachtfeld. Kriegsgeschrei. Es treten auf König Stephen, Ritter und Soldaten.

STEPHEN.
Kann Schmach auf wilddurchpulsten Kriegerstirnen
In tieferm Rot stehn als die Mühn der Schlacht,
So glüht, vom Helm verhüllt! – denn seht doch, seht!
Dort meine Ritterschaft, Stolz meines Feldzugs,
Gesprengt von Eisenhand aus Reih und Glied,
Schlägt es, bar aller Ehre, in die Flucht
Auf Schlammgrund. Oh, daß meine Stimme gellte
In eure Memmenohrn, sie mehr euch schreckte!
Flieht, Feiglinge, flieht! Gloucester naht im Rücken!
Den schlaffen Zaum werft um zerzauste Mähnen,
Schlagt zu mit Sporn an zittrig-schwachen Fersen,
Zu Tode schließlich lauft davon!

ERSTER RITTER. Der Feind
Bläht die Standarte dicht an ihrer Nachhut.

ZWEITER RITTER.
Blutigen Streichs gewiß, sieht er sie doch
Gurttief vom Sumpf verschluckt.

STEPHEN. Sei's ganz und gar,
Ganz einerlei! Ein ritterlicher Feind ist's –
Wie er einem Kometen ähnlich hinstreicht.
Doch in die Flanke ihm gebohrt! – He, Freunde:
Wir holen kräftig Luft – kommt!
(Graf Baldwin und Soldaten treten auf, wie vernichtet.)

STEPHEN. De Redvers!
Welch gräßliches Gespenst gibt's, vor dem Baldwin
Sich fürchtet?
BALDWIN. Popanz keinen, doch den Glücksstern
Des wilden Chester, dessen Lanze grausig
In Richtung auf das Siegestor nun weist.
Hier führt sein Weg entlang, und bliebt Ihr gern
Auch weiterhin verschont von bittrer Übermacht,
Sitzt auf, Mylord.
STEPHEN. Und wohin fliehn ums Leben?
Dem Himmel dankend steh ich im Getümmel
Bei Kriegern, die bezeugen, wie mein Arm
Die Fesseln sprengt. Kein Adler liebt es mehr,
Sich ins tyrannische Gestürm zu schwingen,
Als ich den Andrang meines Feinds zu treffen.
Ich tu mich groß – so sei's. Doch falle ich,
Schreibt es mir auf mein schildbeschmücktes Grab.
Kommt, Schlachtgefährten! Graf de Redvers, weicht!
Nicht zwanzig Grafen Chester drohen finster
Der Krone.
(Ab. Schlachtenlärm.)

Zweite Szene

Ein anderer Teil des Schlachtfelds. Trompeten blasen zum Sieg. Gloucester, Ritter und Soldaten treten auf.

GLOUCESTER.
Nun lüftet das zerstoßene Visier
Und atmet die umschmeichelnd frische Luft,
Indes der Lärm des Schlachtgedröhns in die
Vergangenheit verklingt, doch sicher nachhallt
Auf stillen Blättern unserer Chronisten.
ERSTER RITTER.
Wird Stephens Tod notiert sein dort, Mylord,
Oder daß wir im Turm ihn einquartiern?

GLOUCESTER.
Gern wüßt ich um des großen Throndiebs Schicksal.
(Von verschiedenen Seiten zwei Feldherrn.)
ERSTER FELDHERR. Mylord!
ZWEITER FELDHERR. Edelster Graf!
ERSTER FELDHERR. Der König –
ZWEITER FELDHERR. Die Kaisrin grüßt –
GLOUCESTER. Der König was?
ERSTER FELDHERR. Allein noch er entfacht
Sinnlos die Wut der ausschwärmenden Trupps
Und greift mit flinker Bissigkeit sie an,
Flieht, bläst zu wilderm Ansturm, weicht erneut
Dem Tod aus und schlägt tot den, der es wagt,
Den Umkreis seines Schwerts nur zu betreten!
Gefallen wird er sein. Baldwin sitzt fest;
Der Herzog der Bretagne nun – dem Hirsch gleich
Flieht er, um doch Wales' Beaglen zu erliegen.
Gott schütz die Kaiserin!
GLOUCESTER. – nun unsre Herrschrin:
Was bringt Ihr von der Hoheit?
ZWEITER FELDHERR. Kaisrin Maud
Sah hoch von den bedrängten Türmen Lincolns
Wie Pallas von den Mauern Ilions
Den Feind zugrundegehn zu ihren Füßen.
Von Herzen grüßt sie ihren edlen Gloucester,
Ihn, Feldherrn und die tapfern Krieger bittend,
Zu zieren ein Bankett. Gespannt erwartet
Die Stadt, durch welches hohe Tor Ihr einzieht;
Die Straßen füllt Musik.
(Ein zweiter Ritter tritt auf.)
GLOUCESTER. Woher kommt Ihr?
ZWEITER RITTER.
Von Stephen, hoher Fürst – Stephen! Stephen!
GLOUCESTER.
Was läßt Euch seinen Namen derart nachhalln?

ZWEITER RITTER.
Daß ich der Ansicht bin, Mylord, er ist kein Mensch,
Vielmehr ein Dämon, heilgesalbt von Wunden
Und fälschlich wohl getauft in Christi Namen.
GLOUCESTER.
Ein mächtiger Soldat! – Er hält *noch* aus?
ZWEITER RITTER.
Beschämt so unsern Sieg. Noch hält sein Mut
Den Ellenbogenraum im Klingenandrang
Und unsre Sichelschwerter sämtlich ab. –
Die Streitaxt, glühend und vom Schlachten schwindlig
Geschlagen auf die Haube eines Flamenritters,
Zerbarst in seiner Hand, worauf den Stiel
Mit derart zorngespeister Macht er fortwarf,
Daß er das Roß Graf Chesters hieb, der dann,
Vom Groll gepeitscht, in vollem Lauf ihn antrat.
GLOUCESTER.
Ließ niemand denn die Überzahl ihn spüren?
ZWEITER RITTER.
Drei warfen sich im Tigersprung nun auf ihn,
Die, rasch gezückt sein Schwert und aufgestellt,
Er wegstach wieder, Luft zu holen und –
Zu lächeln. Schon warf sich erneut ein Heer
Von Feinden auf ihn, und in jenem Ansturm
Traf mein Schwert seins und sprang am Heft entzwei.
GLOUCESTER.
Kommt, zeigt mir diesen Mars – und gehn wir lautlos
Zu ihm, verhöhnen nicht sein trübes Los
Mit lärmendem Trompetenschall. Der Kaisrin
Sagt meinen Gruß, wenn es die Zeit erlaubt.
(Ab Gloucester und Soldaten.)

Dritte Szene

Das Schlachtfeld. Stephen tritt auf, unbewaffnet.

STEPHEN.
Ein andres Schwert! Und was, könnt eines ich
Mir greifen aus Bellonas lichten Kammern,
Den schönsten Speer aus ihren Garben wählen!
Wo sind die Feinde? Hier, zum Greifen nah,
Hier grollt die Brut heran. Oh, jetzt ein Schwert!
Gebt Zaunpfahl – oder schweren Stein zum Wurf
Erfüllter Rache wie dem Landmann Kain.
Heran! Lebwohl, mein Königreich, und Heil dir,
Befiederter, behelmter, großer Ruhm,
Heil dir! Nicht tauscht ich diesen Tag voll Glanz,
Um Pylos zu regiern mit Nestors Bart –
Heran!
(De Kaims, Ritter usw. treten auf.)

DE KAIMS.
Ist's Wahnsinn oder Hunger nach dem Tod,
Was waffenlos Euch unser spotten läßt?
Ergebt Euch, Stephen, soll mein Schwert nicht tauchen
Im dunklen Strom eines Verräterherzens.

STEPHEN.
Nur zu, De Kaims, ich weich nicht einen Zoll.

DE KAIMS.
Gut, so bezieht den Lohn für Euren Wahn.

STEPHEN.
Ihr wagt's?

DE KAIMS. Wie, gegen einen Unbewaffneten?

STEPHEN.
Welch Waffe hat der Löwe als sich selbst?
Kommt mir nicht nah, De Kaims, denn bei der Fülle
An Ruhm, die ich am heutgen Tag errang:
Als König, der ich bin, weich ich lebendig
Niemandem als dem zweiten Mann des Reichs,
Robert von Gloucester.

DE KAIMS. *Mir* ergebt Euch besser.

STEPHEN.

Dies tun, da ich dem abgeschworen, Sire?
Kühn scheint Euch, fangt Ihr den lebendgen König,
Daß, dienernd vor Gericht und stolzer Maud,
Der ehrfürchtge Audienzsaal unerschrocken
Dann flüster: Dort den Mann seht, der lebendig
Stephen fing – mich – Gefangnen. Doch, De Kaims,
Die Absicht ist schon edel.

DE KAIMS. Ganz richtig,
Und, Stephen, ich vollführ sie auch.

STEPHEN. Nein, nein,
Verlockt mich nicht, Euch an den Hals zu gehn und
Den Brustkorb einzudrücken mit dem Handschuh,
Da Eure Ritterschaft just reif ist doch
Zur Lordschaft.

EIN SOLDAT. Eines treuen Bauern Speer
Wär unnütz in der Not? Nehmt dies!

STEPHEN. Ah, Feigling!

DE KAIMS.

Was, Ihr verwundbar? – mein Gefangner!

STEPHEN.

Noch nicht. Dem widersprech ich und klag ein
Den Tod als höchstes Recht für einen König,
Der keinem sich ergibt als seinesgleichen,
Wenn nicht durch Titel so durch edle Taten –
Dem Grafen Gloucester. Stoßt nur zu, De Kaims,
Gemeine Hände führen mich niemals
Von solch ruhmreichen Feld. Hört Ihr! So eilt!
(Trompeten. Auftreten Graf Chester und Ritter.)

Vierte Szene

Ein Audienzsaal. Königin Maud auf einem Thron, die Grafen Gloucester und Chester, Lords und Gefolgschaft.

MAUD.
Gloucester, genug. Sehn will ich jenen Boulogne:
Bringt ihn mir her. Doch nicht, um jämmerlich
Ein Stündlein mit des Königs Prunk zu prahlen,
Wie Ihr bedachtsam, jedoch durchaus deutlich,
Es nahelegt.

GLOUCESTER. Mein Rat war gutgemeint;
Bedacht war ich um Euer Hoheit Wohl.

MAUD.
Verbiet der Himmel mir, nicht so zu denken,
Verdank ich Euerm Mut doch dieses Reich
Und führ's für immer nun dank Eurer Klugheit.
Zu weisen Ratgebern laßt stets mich neigen
Ein freundlich-offnes Ohr, daß sie Gesetz
Und Macht des weiten Königreichs behandeln,
Nicht tastend in allein uns Vorbehaltnes.
Beraten, nicht belehrt sein will ich; fortan
Bedacht mit klaren, steten, offnen Worten –
Seitwärts bepredigt nicht.

GLOUCESTER. So sag ich offen:
Der König, nun gestürzt –

MAUD. Vergebt, mein Bruder,
Doch davon nichts mehr; denn, ich sagte es,
Um selbst zu glänzen, will ich den Rebellen
Nicht sehn, doch um als Richterin zu fällen
Den Urteilsspruch, den seine Schuld verdient.

GLOUCESTER.
Wenn es so sein muß, führe ich ihn vor Euch.
(Gloucester ab.)

MAUD.
Ein einfacherer Bote tät es auch –
Ist's wahr, guter Lord Chester, was ich höre

Von Stephen von Boulogne, unserm Häftling –
Daß er, zur rechten Buße seiner Taten,
Bekömmlich, süß und reich beköstigt wird
Von Gloucesters goldnen Tellern – reinen Wein trinkt,
Fein wohnt?

CHESTER. Mehr, meine gnädgste Königin,
Erbost mich noch. Der edle Graf, scheint mir,
Ganz Krieger, der er ist und ohnegleichen
Im Ratschluß, träumt zuviel vor seinen Büchern.
Liest sich's auch gut, es ist nicht an der Zeit,
Darius Alexander spieln zu lassen.

MAUD.
Wie wahr! So ist's und, Himmel, darf's nicht bleiben!

CHESTER.
Erstaunen, Hoheit, wird Euch zu erfahren,
Wie Gloucester mehr als höflich sich erweist
Dem frevelliebenden Rebelln Boulogne –

MAUD.
Dem Undankbarn!

CHESTER. Zu dessen ganzem Undank
Vor dem verschiednen König, edlen Sire,
Der großmütige Graf noch kondoliert
Und mit lakaienhafter Freundlichkeit fast
Die Stirne ihm von tiefen Falten freispricht,
Ja wirbt um ihn, zu lächeln im Duett
Und, falls genehm, ein Stündlein Schach zu spielen –

MAUD.
Ein meineidiger Knecht!

CHESTER. Und für den Meineid
Winkt Gloucester tüchtig Lohn – nein, wie mir scheint,
Nutzt er geschäftig seinen Dienersinn
Zur Schmeichelei, daß Stephens Los sich mildre
Und Himmel werd aus seinem Purgatorium;
Schmückt Knechtschaft mit dem angenehmen Glanz
Von Fest, Musik und all der Pracht und Muße
Häuslichen Prunks; indes Sirenenwispern,

Bestimmt für Stephens Ohrn, halbstockend flieht
Von den rubingleich rotsten, weichsten Lippen
Des Reichs, bestaunend seine Heldentaten.

MAUD.
Frost seinem Sommer!

CHESTER. *Ein* Wink der Kön'gin –
Dezember wird sein Juni sein. Hier kommt er. …

Briefe

An John Hamilton Reynolds

Carisbrooke, 17. April [1817]

[...] Wollen Sie die Güte haben, Folgendes zu tun? Leihen Sie sich ein botanisches Wörterbuch. Schlagen Sie nach unter »Lorbeer« und »Pflaume«, und zeigen Sie die Erläuterungen Ihren Schwestern und Mrs. Dilk[e], und dann machen Sie ihnen ohne viel Federlesens Beine, damit sie mir den Geschirrkorb und die Bücher schicken, was sie nämlich verbummelt und ein ums andere Mal aufgeschoben haben, solange ich in der Stadt war. Fragen Sie Mrs. Dilk[e], warum sie mich so betrüben muß. Lassen Sie mich wissen, wie es um Janes Gesundheit bestellt ist. Das Wetter ist nicht gut für sie. Sagen Sie George und Tom, sie sollen schreiben. Ich werde Ihnen auch sagen, was – am 23. ist Shakespeares Geburtstag –, wenn ich nun an diesem Tag einen Brief von Ihnen und einen von meinen Brüdern bekäme, wär's ein trefflich Ding. Sooft Sie mir schreiben, sagen Sie doch ein paar Worte über irgendeine Stelle bei Shakespeare, die sich Ihnen vielleicht ganz neu erschlossen hat; das geschieht ja fortwährend, auch, wenn wir ein und dasselbe Stück vierzigmal gelesen haben – zum Beispiel hat mich folgende Passage aus dem »Sturm« nie so stark berührt wie gerade jetzt:

»Igel sollen
Die Nachtzeit durch, wo sie sich rühren dürfen,
An dir sich üben;«

Ich muß Sie noch an folgende Zeile erinnern –

»Im dunklen Hintergrund und Schoß der Zeit.«

Ich fühle, daß ich ohne Dichtung nicht leben kann, ohne ewige Dichtung. Die Hälfte des Tages genügt nicht, der ganze Tag. Ich habe mit kleinen Dosen angefangen, aber die Gewöhnung hat einen Leviathan aus mir gemacht. Mich hatte schon das große Zittern gepackt, weil ich in der letzten Zeit nichts geschrieben habe – das umseitige Sonett hat meinen Zustand etwas gelindert. Ich schlief dadurch besser vergangene Nacht, aber heute morgen geht es mir wieder beinahe genauso schlecht. Gerade schlug ich Spenser auf, und folgende Verse fielen mir zuerst ins Auge:

»Ein edles Herz, das reine Tugend birgt
Und schwanger geht mit ruhmvoll großem Ziel,
Kommt erst zur Ruhe, wenn es hat bewirkt
Das endlos Gute, das es schaffen will.«

[...]

An Leigh Hunt

Margate, 10. Mai [1817]

[...] Ich sage Dir, noch vor kurzem habe ich wegen dieser Arbeit den Kopf hängen lassen. In den letzten beiden Tagen allerdings war mir schon zuversichtlicher zumute. Ich habe mich so oft gefragt, warum gerade ich eher als andere Menschen ein Dichter sein sollte – wo ich doch sehe, was für eine großartige Sache es ist, wie großartig das, was man dadurch erlangen kann, was es bedeutet, in aller Munde zu sein – daß meine Vorstellung davon schließlich so riesenhaft über meine anscheinende Schaffenskraft hinauswuchs, daß ich anderntags beinah selbst überzeugt war, nichts als ein Phaeton zu sein. Doch selbst in einem gewaltigen Versuch zu versagen, ist eine Schande, und augenblicklich vertreibe ich den Gedanken. Ich fing mein Gedicht vor rund zwei Wochen an und habe täglich einiges getan, die Reisezeit ausgenommen. Vielleicht habe ich für diese Zeit auch ein gutes Stück geschafft, aber es kommt mir so nadelspitzenklein vor, daß ich nichts davon abschreiben mag. Wenn ich bedenke, wie viele solcher Nadelspitzen erst die Spitze eines Dolchs bilden (Gott verhüte, daß ich mein Leben mit einem gewöhnlichen Dolch, einer Schusterahle, beende) und daß tausend Dolche nötig sind für einen

Speer, glänzend genug, um ein Licht auf die Nachwelt zu werfen – sehe ich dann anderes als stetes Bergaufpilgern vor mir? Und gibt es wohl etwas Leidigeres [...] als so zu pilgern und zuletzt sein Ziel doch zu verfehlen? – Aber ich habe vor, all diese Überlegungen ins Meer zu pfeifen, wo sie hoffentlich Stürme erzeugen, die heftig genug sind, um jegliche Ausfahrt aus Rußland zu blockieren. Erzählt Shelley noch immer seltsame Geschichten über den Tod von Königen? Sag ihm, es gibt seltsame Geschichten über den Tod von Dichtern – [...].

An Benjamin Robert Haydon

Margate, Samstag abend [10.–11. Mai 1817]

Mein lieber Haydon,

»Mag Ruhm, den jeder sucht, solang er lebt,
Leben in Schrift auf unserm erznen Grabe,
Und dann uns zieren in des Todes Unzier;
Wenn, trotz der räuberisch gefräßgen Zeit,
Das Streben dieser Gegenwart uns kauft
Die Ehre, die der Sichel Schärf' ihr stumpft,
Und uns zu Erben macht der ganzen Zukunft.«

Zu denken, ich hätte kein Recht, mich mit Ihnen in diesem Spruch vereint zu sehen, wär mein Tod, so hab ich ihn gar hergeschrieben, und ich bete zu Gott, daß unsere erznen Gräber nahe beieinander liegen mögen. Es kann schließlich nicht lange währen, das Streben dieser Gegenwart wird bald ein Ende haben, und doch, wie gut ist es, für die Dauer unseres Erdendaseins frei atmen zu können. Wie gut ist es, daß diese Geldangelegenheit Ihnen keine Pein bereitet hat, diese Rechnungspestilenz. Dennoch muß ich denken, daß Schwierigkeiten den Geist eines Mannes anspornen; sie machen das, was uns das Höchste ist, uns zum Refugium wie zur Passion. Die

Fanfare des Ruhms gleicht einem starken Hort, der Strebende bläst sie und ist gerettet. Da Sie mir rieten, Ahnungen nicht nachzugeben, nehme ich an, daß George Ihnen gesagt hat, was ich ihm in meinen letzten Briefen schrieb. Die Wahrheit ist, ich war in einer solchen Geistesverfassung, daß ich meine Verse durchlas und sie haßte. Ich bin »einer, Fenchel sammelnd – schrecklich Handwerk«, über mir den Gipfel mit den Festen der Poesie – doch wenn mir Tom, der in Plutarchs Lebensbeschreibungen zufällig auf ein paar von Popes Homer-Übersetzungen stieß, ein paar Verse daraus vorliest, so scheinen sie mir »Mäusen gleich«, verglichen mit den meinen. Ich lese und schreibe acht Stunden. Es gibt ein altes Sprichwort: »Frisch gewagt, ist halb gewonnen!« Das ist schlecht. Ich würde statt dessen sagen: »Was nicht halb gewonnen, ist noch nicht begonnen.« Und demnach habe ich mein Gedicht noch nicht einmal begonnen und kann folglich (a priori) nichts darüber sagen. Gott sei Dank! Ich fange in der Tat mit Feuereifer immer da an, wo ich aufgehört habe, ungeachtet gelegentlicher Anfälle von Schwermut, und ich hoffe auf die Hilfe einer höheren Macht, wenn ich zum Gipfel dieses Berges hinaufklimme, und das besonders in meinen besten Arbeitsjahren. Ich erinnere mich daran, wie Sie einmal sagten, Sie hätten eine Ahnung, als ob ein guter Genius Sie beherrsche. Ich habe in letzter Zeit denselben Gedanken gehabt. Dinge, die ich halbwegs aufs Geratewohl mache, bestätigen sich im Nachhinein in meinem Urteil in dutzendfacher Hinsicht als richtig. Ist es zu gewagt, wenn ich annehme, Shakespeare sei dieser Genius? [...]

Im Augenblick bin ich in keiner beneidenswerten Lage, ich spüre, daß ich nicht in der Stimmung bin, heute überhaupt etwas zu schreiben; und ich fürchte allemal, wenn mir diese Stimmung abhanden kommt, könnte es den Anfang aller möglichen Unregelmäßigkeiten bedeuten. Ich bin unsagbar froh, daß all das eines Tages spurlos verschwunden sein wird. Sie sagen, ich soll nie die Hoffnung aufgeben. Ich wollte, ich könnte diese Worte so einfach befolgen. Die Wahrheit ist, ich leide unter schrecklichen, krankhaften Gemütszuständen, die in Abständen auftreten – das ist, daran hege ich keinen Zweifel, der ärgste Feind und Hemmschuh, den ich zu fürchten habe. Ich kann sogar sagen, daß das wahrscheinlich die Ursache meines Scheiterns ist. Doch jedes Übel hat auch sein Gutes – gerade dieses Verderben setzt mich instand, jederzeit mit festem Blick dem Teufel selbst ins Aug zu schauen – ja, so stolz darauf zu sein, daß man der Geringste unter den Menschen ist, wie Alfred stolz darauf sein konnte, daß er zu den Höchsten gehörte. Ich glaube ganz gewiß, daß ich ein rebellischer Engel geworden wäre, wenn sich die Gelegenheit ergeben hätte. Ich bin ganz sicher, daß Sie mich wie Ihren eigenen Bruder lieben. Ich habe das an Ihrer fortwährenden Sorge um mich gesehen, und ich versichere Ihnen, daß Ihr Wohlergehen und Ihr Ruhm mir Anlaß zu größter Freude sind und mein Leben lang bleiben werden. Ich weiß keinen außer Ihnen, der die Unruhe und Beängstigung so völlig mitempfinden kann, jenes Hinopfern all dessen, was man Genuß nennt, die Bereitschaft, die Zeit zu messen an dem, was man vollbracht hat, und in sechs Stunden zu sterben, wenn man Geplantes zu einem Ende geführt hat. Die Betrachtung der Sonne, des Mondes, der Sterne, der Erde und dessen, was auf ihr ist, als Stoffe, aus denen Größeres sich erschaffen läßt – will sagen Ätherisches – doch nun rede ich wie ein Geisteskranker von Dingen, die gar gewaltiger sind als unser Schöpfer selbst sie schuf! [...]

Vielleicht ist es Selbsttäuschung, das zu sagen, aber ich glaube, ich könnte mich nie so betrügen wie Hunt es tut, wenn doch, so will ich morgen tot umfallen. Es gibt nach den sieben Todsünden keine ärgere Sünde, als sich selbst zu schmeicheln, indem man sich einbildet, man sei ein großer Dichter oder eines jener Geschöpfe, die das Privileg besitzen, ihr Leben damit zuzubringen, daß sie nach Ehre streben. Wie tröstlich ist doch die Ahnung, daß solch ein Verbrechen schwere Strafe nach sich ziehen muß! Daß einem, wenn man sich selbst betrügt, die Rechnung dafür präsentiert werden wird! [...] Ich verzweifle niemals ganz, und ich lese Shakespeare. Ich glaube wahrhaftig, ich werde nie ein anderes Buch so gründlich lesen. Dies könnte mich nun zu weitschweifigem Geplauder verleiten, doch ich lasse es sein. Ich bin sehr nahe daran, Hazlitt zuzustimmen, daß wir an Shakespeare genug haben. [...]

An Benjamin Bailey

Hampstead, Oktober, Mittwoch [8. Oktober 1817]

[...] Die Literaten widern mich so an, und ich will außer Wordsworth keinem von ihnen begegnen. Nein, nicht einmal Byron. Hier ein Beispiel, was solche Leute Freundschaft nennen. Haydon und Hunt kennen einander seit vielen Jahren – nun leben sie, pour ainsi dire als eifersüchtige Nachbarn. Haydon sagt mir: Keats, zeigen Sie Hunt um keinen Preis Ihre Verse, sonst wird er behaupten, die Hälfte sei von ihm. Hunt will anscheinend, daß man das denkt. Als er Reynolds im Theater traf, erzählte ihm John, daß ich bald 4000 Verse fertig hätte. Ach, sagt Hunt, wenn ich nicht gewesen wäre, wären's 7000! Wenn er so etwas schon zu Reynolds sagt, was wohl dann erst zu anderen Leuten? Haydon bekam vor einer Weile in dieser Angelegenheit einen Brief von einer Dame, in dem ich in dieser Angelegenheit gewarnt werde. Sagen Sie selbst, ist all dies nicht eines der erbärmlichsten Dinge, die man sich vorstellen kann? Sie können die ganze Sache aus dem folgenden Auszug aus einem Brief ersehen, den ich im Frühjahr an George schrieb. »Auf das, was Du über mich als Dichter sagst, kann ich Dir nicht anders antworten, als indem ich sage, daß die hohe Auffassung, die ich vom Dichterruhm habe, mich glauben läßt, ich sehe ihn sich zu hoch über mir erheben. Jedenfalls habe ich kein Recht, davon zu reden, ehe nicht der ›Endymion‹ abgeschlossen ist. Er wird eine Prüfung sein, er wird die Kraft meiner Imagination auf die Probe stellen und vor allem meine Erfindungsgabe, die wahrlich ein seltsam Ding ist – mit der ich 4000 Zeilen aus einem nackten Sachverhalt machen und sie mit Poesie erfüllen muß; und wenn ich bedenke, daß dies eine große Aufgabe ist und daß, wenn ich sie erfüllt habe, mich das dem Tempel des Ruhms doch nur eben ein Dutzend Schritte näherbringt, dann muß ich sagen: Gott behüte, daß ich ohne eine solche Aufgabe wäre! Ich hörte Hunt sagen – und man könnte mich fragen –, warum soll man danach streben, ein langes Gedicht zu schreiben? Worauf ich antworten würde: Verlangt es die Liebhaber der Dichtkunst nicht nach einem kleinen Reich, in dem sie umherstreifen, wo sie etwas herausgreifen und auswählen können und wo es der Bilder so viele gibt, daß nicht wenige in Vergessenheit geraten und beim zweiten Lesen aufs neue entdeckt werden: Proviant genug, um eine Sommerwoche lang davon zu zehren? Ist das nicht mehr nach ihrem Geschmack als etwas, das sie durchlesen können, bevor Mrs. Williams die Treppe hinunterkommt? Woran sie höchstens einen Vormittag zu tun haben? Übrigens ist ein langes Gedicht eine Probe auf die Erfindungsgabe, die ich für den Polarstern der Dichtung ansehe, so, wie die Phantasie das Segel ist und die Imagination das Ruder. Haben unsere großen Dichter etwa kurze Stücke geschrieben? Ich meine Geschichten – man scheint wirklich in den letzten Jahren vergessen zu haben, daß eben diese Erfindungsgabe ein Vorzug des Dichters ist. Doch genug davon, ich werde mir keinen Lorbeerkranz aufs Haupt setzen, ehe ich nicht den ›Endymion‹ vollendet habe, und ich hoffe, Apollo zürnt mir nicht, weil ich seiner bei Hunt gespottet habe.«

Sie sehen, Bailey, wie unabhängig ich in meinem Schreiben bin. Hunts Abraten war nutzlos. Ich habe mich geweigert, Shelley zu besuchen, um mir meinen eigenen, uneingeschränkten Spielraum bewahren zu können, und trotz alledem stehe ich in dem Ruf, Hunts Schüler zu sein. Die Eingeweihten werden seine Korrekturen und Streichungen in dem Gedicht ausfindig machen. Das mag mich wohl einen Tag lang verdrießen, doch verliere ich zu keinem darüber viel Worte; nur zu denjenigen, denen, wie ich weiß, mein Wohl und mein Ansehen am Herzen liegen. [...]

An Benjamin Bailey

Montag – Hampstead [3. November 1817]

[...] Die in der Welt Rang und Würde besitzen, haben die fixe Idee, daß sie sich vor jemandem, der unter ihnen steht, keine Blöße geben dürfen, doch ist nicht die Unverschämtheit eines Höherstehenden gegen einen Untergeordneten gemeiner und widerwärtiger als die des Niederen gegen den Höheren? Selbstherrliche, himmelschreiende Unverschämtheit, die sich als Gewissen tarnt, hat etwas so Widerliches. Das würdigt den Bischof von Lincoln zu einem zertretenen, stinkenden Frosch herab: Daß einer, der sich so wider die allgemeine Sittlichkeit vergeht, dem Schandpfahl entkommen soll! Daß eine Mitra einen Mann decken soll, der sich der geckenhaftesten, tyrannischsten und gefühllosesten Unverschämtheit schuldig gemacht hat! Ich wiederhole dieses Wort, denn die Beleidigung erscheint mir als ganz besonders unverschämt, und die Rute wäre eine sehr treffende Entgegnung. Er aber sitzt in seinem Palast. So ist nun einmal die Welt, und wir leben – Sie jedenfalls ganz gewiß – in einem fortwährenden Kampf gegen den Druck der Geschehnisse. Wir müssen – (und mir läuft davon schier die Galle über) »des Stolzen Mißhandlungen« ertragen. Ach, gäbe es doch eine einigermaßen menschliche Zuflucht dagegen, außerhalb des erhabenen Trostes der Religion und unverdorbener Gefühle für das Schöne, das Poetische in allen Dingen. Ach, gäbe es doch ein Heilmittel gegen solche Übel in der weltlichen Gerichtsbarkeit! Sollten solche Dinge nicht reines Ergötzen sein, darf man sie der Gefahr aussetzen, gegen Bischöfe ins Spiel gebracht und dadurch in den Schmutz gezogen zu werden? Reichen nicht die irdischen Dinge? Beim

Himmel, mein lieber Bailey, ich weiß, Sie haben eine Ahnung von dem, was ich meine. Sie können mich verstehen und begreifen mich in den schwierigen Situationen, in die ich geraten mag. Ich weiß, Sie haben einen Stolz, der dem Teufel so in die Kinnlade treten möchte, daß er Sterne sähe. Nichts kann einer Seele, die so verbittert ist, wie die Ihre es sein muß, bessere Linderung bringen als Stolz. Wenn wir zum Himmel schaun, können wir nicht stolz sein, doch sollen Stock und Stein die Unverschämtheit haben dürfen zu sagen, es stünde uns nicht an, sie zu treten? Jetzt nehme ich Sie bei der Hand. Lassen Sie uns den Gipfel des gesunden Menschenverstandes erklimmen, und wenn unser Stolz hoffärtig wäre, so würde diese Stütze wohl versagen, doch Sie spüren festen Halt – und nun schauen Sie hinab auf dieses Pack von Spitzbuben und Narren. Manch eine Mitra ist darunter. Ich kann es nicht in Worte fassen, wie sehr ich den Mann verachte, der Ihnen übelwill oder unverschämt gegen Sie ist – der Gedanke, daß wir sterblich sind, macht uns stöhnen –. [...]

An Benjamin Bailey

[22. November 1817]

[...] Ein Mensch von Ihrer Wesensart muß einen Brief wie den von Haydon als überaus kränkend empfinden. Was verursacht den größten Teil allen Haders in der Welt? Ganz einfach dies: Zwei Gesinnungen begegnen sich und lernen einander nicht gründlich genug kennen, um zu vermeiden, daß des einen Betragen den anderen erschreckt oder überrascht. Kaum, daß ich Haydon drei Tage kannte, wußte ich auch schon genug über seinen Charakter und hätte mich über einen Brief wie den, mit dem er Sie gekränkt hat, nicht mehr wundern können. Ich brauchte, nachdem mir klar war, wie sein Charakter beschaffen ist, nicht so grundsätzlich zu sein, daß ich den Umgang mit ihm abgebrochen hätte; Sie hingegen müssen das dringende Bedürfnis verspüren, just dies zu tun. Wüßten Sie nur alles, was ich über Genie und Herz denke, doch ich glaube wohl, daß Ihnen ganz und gar vertraut ist, was ich im Innersten dazu meine, sonst könnten Sie mich nicht selbst nach so langer Bekanntschaft noch immer für würdig halten, Ihr guter Freund zu sein. Nebenbei muß ich jedoch von einer Sache sprechen, mit der ich mich jüngst arg herumgeplagt habe, wodurch nicht nur meine Demut gewachsen ist, sondern auch meine Fähigkeit, mich unterzuordnen. Und das ist die eine Wahrheit – geniale Menschen gleichen in ihrer Bedeutung gewissen ätherischen Chemikalien; sie wirken auf die Masse des neutralen Verstandes, besitzen indes keinerlei Individualität, keinen bestimmten Charakter – die wenigen ganz Auserlesenen von ihnen, die ein eigenes Selbst haben, würde ich als starke Menschen bezeichnen.

Doch ich verrenne mich bei einem Thema, dem ich gewiß nicht ohne fünfjähriges Studieren und in weniger als drei vollgeschriebenen Oktavbänden gerecht werden kann, und außerdem drängt es mich ja eigentlich, von Imagination zu sprechen. Mein lieber Bailey, denken Sie doch nach Möglichkeit nicht an diese unerfreuliche Angelegenheit. Tun Sie's nicht. Ich bin dagegen, daß hieraus Böses entsteht – ich bin dagegen. Ich werde diese Woche an Crips schreiben und ihn bitten, mir von Zeit zu Zeit in einem Brief zu erzählen, was er so treibt, mir zu schreiben, ganz gleich, wo ich mich gerade aufhalte. Es wird alles gut werden, drum seien Sie nicht verdrießlich, nur, weil Sie plötzlich eine Kälte an Haydon wahrgenommen haben. Bitte nicht, mein lieber Freund. Ach, könnte ich nur ebenso sicher glauben, daß all Ihre Sorgen recht bald ein Ende haben werden, wie ich glaube, daß Ihr augenblickliches Zweifeln an der Echtheit der Imagination bald vorüber sein wird. Sicher bin ich mir nur der Heiligkeit der Neigungen des Herzens und der Wahrheit der Imagination. Was die Imagination als Schönheit erfaßt, das muß Wahrheit sein, ob es zuvor existiert hat oder nicht, denn ich habe von all unseren Leidenschaften dieselbe Auffassung wie von der Liebe; durch ihre

Sublimierung bringen Sie das ganze Wesen der Schönheit hervor. Mit einem Wort, Sie können meine Lieblingsideen aus meinem ersten Buch erfahren und aus dem kleinen Lied, das ich Ihnen mit letztem schickte, welches eine phantasievolle Darstellung des möglichen Vorgehens in diesen Dingen ist. Die Imagination kann man mit Adams Traum vergleichen, er erwachte und erkannte ihn als Wahrheit. Ich lasse mich um so weniger von dieser Sache abbringen, als ich noch nie begreifen konnte, wie man irgend etwas durch folgerndes Denken als Wahrheit erkennen kann, und doch muß es das geben. Hätte wohl selbst der größte Philosoph jemals sein Ziel erreichen können, ohne sich über mannigfache Einwände hinwegzusetzen? Wie auch immer – oh, alles für ein Leben der Empfindungen statt der Gedanken! Es ist eine »Vision von Jugend«, ein Schatten der künftigen Wirklichkeit – und diese Betrachtung hat mich in meinen Ansichten noch bestärkt, kam sie doch einer anderen Lieblingsidee von mir zu Hilfe, daß wir im Künftigen deshalb Freude haben werden, weil wir das, was wir auf Erden Glück heißen, in verfeinertem Ton wiederholen und es uns so wiederholen. Indes kann solch Geschick nur jenen widerfahren, die sich an Empfindungen ergötzen, anstatt so wie Sie nach Wahrheit zu dürsten. Adams Traum genügt hierbei und beweist augenscheinlich, daß die Imagination und ihre himmlische Widerspiegelung dasselbe ist wie das menschliche Leben und seine Wiederholung im Geiste. Aber wie ich eben sagte – die einfache Imagination kann in der Wiederholung ihres eigenen stillen Wirkens Befriedigung finden, das den Geist fortwährend mit schöner Plötzlichkeit überkommt, um das Große mit dem Kleinen zu vergleichen. Haben Sie nie, wenn Sie von einer alten Melodie überrascht wurden – an einem lieblichen Ort von einer lieblichen Stimme vorgetragen – aufs neue genau dieselben Gedanken und Ahnungen empfunden, die Sie hatten, als sie zum erstenmal an Ihre Seele rührte? Erinnern Sie sich nicht, wie Sie sich das Antlitz der Sängerin unwirklich schön vorstellten und sich dessen doch im Hochgefühl des Augenblicks gar nicht bewußt waren? Da trugen Sie die Schwingen der Imagination so hoch hinaus, daß das Urbild danach existieren muß – jenes liebliche Gesicht ist es, das Sie sehen. Du liebe Zeit! Ich schweife immer wieder vom Thema ab – sicherlich kann das bei einem komplexen Gemüt nicht genauso sein – einem Gemüt, das Imagination besitzt und zugleich sorgsam mit seinen Früchten umgeht, das zu einem Teil durch die Empfindung existiert und zu einem Teil durch das Denken, das sich unvermeidlich mit den Jahren zum philosophischen Geiste bilden muß – als solches erachte ich das Ihre, und deshalb ist es zu Ihrem dauernden Glück wichtig, daß Sie nicht nur den alten Wein des Himmels trinken – womit ich das Wiederkäuen unserer ätherischen Betrachtungen auf Erden meine –, sondern auch Ihr Wissen mehren und alles kennenlernen. Es freut mich zu hören, daß Sie glauben, bis Ostern fertig zu sein. Bald werden Sie Ihre unerfreuliche Lektüre geschafft haben, und dann! Doch die Welt ist voll von Verdruß, und ich habe eigentlich kaum Grund zu der Annahme, ich sei besonders übel dran. Ich glaube, Janes oder Mariannes Meinung über mich ist besser als ich verdiene, denn ich glaube ganz und gar nicht, daß zwischen der Krankheit meines Bruders und meiner eigenen ein Zusammenhang besteht. Sie kennen die wahre Ursache besser als die beiden, ich muß auch nicht fürchten, so wie Sie gequält zu werden. Sie dachten vielleicht früher einmal, es gäbe so etwas wie irdisches Glück, das man nach einem bestimmten Zeitplan erlangen könne. Ihre Veranlagung mußte Sie zwangsläufig auf diesen Irrweg leiten. Ich erinnere mich kaum, jemals auf irgendein Glück gebaut zu haben. Ich suche es nur in der gegenwärtigen Stunde – nur der Augenblick bewegt mich. Der Sonnenuntergang bringt mich allemal wieder ins rechte Lot – oder wenn ein Sperling an mein Fenster kommt, dann schlüpfe ich in seine Existenz und picke im Kies herum. Das erste, was mir einfällt, wenn ich vom Unglück eines anderen höre, ist dies: »Nun, nichts zu machen – dafür hat er jetzt Gelegenheit, die Kräfte seines Geistes zu erproben.« Und ich bitte Sie, mein lieber Bailey, sollten Sie hernach so etwas wie Kälte an mir beobachten, es nicht für Herzlosigkeit, sondern für ein Absondern zu halten. Glauben Sie mir, manchmal fühle ich eine ganze Woche lang nicht die Spur einer Leidenschaft oder Gemütsbewegung, und manchmal hält das so lange an, daß ich an mir selbst und an der Echtheit der Gefühle, die ich zu anderen Zeiten habe, zu zweifeln beginne, und dann halte ich sie für nicht mehr als ein paar armselige Theatertränen. [...]

An George und Thomas Keats

[21.–27. (?) Dezember 1817]

[...] Den Freitagabend verbrachte ich mit Wells und ging am nächsten Morgen, mir den »Tod auf dem bleichen Pferd« anzusehen. Es ist ein wunderbares Bild, wenn man Wests Alter bedenkt. Aber es hat nichts, was einen tief berührt, keine Frauen, die zu küssen man fast vergeht, kein Gesicht, das sich mit Wirklichkeit erfüllt. Die Vortrefflichkeit jeder Kunst besteht in ihrer Intensität, die in enger Beziehung zu Schönheit und Wahrheit steht und die Gabe besitzt, alles Unangenehme dahinschwinden zu lassen. Seht Euch den »König Lear« an, und Ihr werdet dies ganz und gar bestätigt finden; in diesem Bild aber haben wir das Unerquickliche, ohne daß durch die Betrachtung irgendeine tiefere Ergriffenheit geweckt wird, die einen das Abstoßende daran vergessen ließe. Das Bild ist größer als »Christus wird von den Juden verleugnet«. Den Sonntag nach Eurer Abreise speiste ich mit Haydon und hatte einen sehr angenehmen Tag, ich speiste auch (denn ich bin in letzter Zeit zu oft ausgegangen) mit Horace Smith und traf seine beiden Brüder samt Hill, Kingston und einen gewissen du Bois. Die haben mir bloß bestätigt, wieviel vergnüglicher als der Witz doch der Humor ist. Diese Männer sagen Dinge, die einen zwar überraschen, aber nicht berühren, sie sind alle gleich. Ihr Gehabe ist dasselbe, sie kennen alle, die man »kennen muß«, noch beim Essen und Trinken sind sie manieriert, schon die Art, wie sie eine Weinkaraffe anfassen. Sie sprachen über Kean und seine unfeine Gesellschaft. Wäre ich doch bei dieser Gesellschaft anstatt bei Euch, sagte ich mir! Ich weiß, solche Bekanntschaften werden mir nie genügen, und trotzdem werde ich am Mittwoch Reynolds besuchen – Brown und Dilke gingen mit mir von der Weihnachtspantomime heim. Ich hatte zwar keinen Disput, aber doch eine eingehende Auseinandersetzung mit Dilke über verschiedene Dinge; manches leuchtete mir ein, und plötzlich verstand ich, welche Eigenschaft es ist, die einen Mann bedeutend macht, besonders in der Literatur, und die Shakespeare in so überaus reichem Maße besaß – ich meine die *Negative Befähigung,* d.h. wenn jemand fähig ist, das Ungewisse, die Mysterien, die Zweifel zu ertragen, ohne alles aufgeregte Greifen nach Fakten und Verstandesgründen. Coleridge zum Beispiel würde sich eine schöne isolierte Wahrscheinlichkeit, erhascht aus der Tiefe des Mysteriums, entgehen lassen, weil er unfähig ist, sich mit halbem Wissen zu begnügen. Und wenn wir diesen Gedanken auch durch Bände hindurch verfolgten, so wären wir doch noch immer nicht weitergekommen als zu der Feststellung, daß bei einem großen Dichter der Sinn für das Schöne jede andere Erwägung überwältigt oder besser, jegliche Erwägung auslöscht. [...]

An Benjamin Robert Haydon

Freitag, den 23. [Januar 1818]

[...] Ich möchte meinen, daß Sie im »Endymion« viele tiefe und gefühlvolle Sachen finden können – der Charakter des »Hyperion« wird mich nötigen, ihn nackter und mehr nach griechischer Manier anzugehen. Und Verlangen und Streben werden unaufhaltsam vorwärtsschreiten, und der gewaltige Unterschied zwischen den beiden wird sein, daß der Held des fertigen Epos, eben weil er sterblich ist, wie Bonaparte durch die Umstände vorangetrieben wird; wohingegen der Apollo im »Hyperion«, der ein vorausschauender Gott ist, als ein solcher frei handeln kann. Doch ich schwätze etc. [...]

An Benjamin Bailey

Freitag, 23. Januar [1818]

Mein lieber Bailey,

Zwölf Tage sind vergangen, seit Dein letzter [Brief] mich erreichte – was ist seit dem 12. nicht alles durch die Myriaden von menschlichen Köpfen gegangen. Da sprechen wir von der immensen Anzahl von Büchern, den Tausenden und Abertausenden aufgereihter Bände – dabei geht vielleicht in 12 Tagen mehr durch den menschlichen Geist als je geschrieben wurde. Wie hat jene unglückliche Familie die zwölf überstanden? Einen Ausspruch von Dir werde ich nie vergessen – du wirst dich kaum an ihn erinnern, tatest ihn seinerzeit vielleicht in einem Moment rein oberflächlicher Betrachtung der menschlichen Natur, ohne dabei an Vergangenheit und Zukunft oder auch die Abgründe von Gut und Böse zu denken – eine Theorie lag Dir fern in dem Moment, und ich glaube, Du hättest auch genug Argumente gegen den in der Hand, der ihn vor Dir geäußert hätte – das ist mir eine formidable Einleitung für eine so einfache Sache – Du sagtest bloß: »Warum sollten Frauen leiden müssen?« Ja. Warum sollten sie? [...] Diese Dinge sind, und wer begreift, wie wenig noch das himmlischste Fahrende Rittertum solch geschundene Schönheit zu heilen vermag, der liegt wie ein zartes Blatt auf der heißen Hand des Gedankens. [...] Die Menschen sollten miteinander auskommen – der Mensch lebt nicht, den man nicht runtermachen kann, ja in Stücke hacken dort, wo er am schwächsten ist. Auch die besten Menschen haben nur einen Funken Gutes in sich – eine Art geistiger Hefe in ihren Wesen, der den Gärstoff der Existenz bildet – wodurch sie zum Handeln, zum Streben und zum Kampf mit den Verhältnissen angetrieben werden. Der sicherste Weg, Bailey, ist, erst eines Menschen Fehler kennenzulernen und dann passiv zu sein. Wenn er dich dennoch unmerklich anzieht, dann steht es nicht in deiner Macht, das Band zu zerreißen. […]

An John Hamilton Reynolds

Hampstead, Dienstag [3.2. 1818]

Mein lieber Reynolds,

ich danke Ihnen für Ihre Mahlzeit Haselnüsse. Ach, könnte ich doch davon nur jeden Tag einen Korb für zwei Pence zum Nachtisch kriegen. Ach, wären wir doch nur so eine Art ätherische Schweine, und man hätte uns losgelassen, damit wir uns mit geistigem Mastfutter und Eicheln vollfressen, was bloß hieße, daß man ein Eichhörnchen wäre und sich an Haselnüssen vollfräße, denn was ist ein Eichhörnchen anderes als ein Luftschwein, was eine Haselnuß als eine Art erzengelhafte Eichel. Dazu, ob die Nüsse das Knacken verlohnen, kann ich nur sagen, daß da, wo sich die wunderbaren Bilder nur so drängeln, vollkommene Einfachheit das einzig Wahre ist. […] Es ist wohl wahr, wir sollten unsere Zeitgenossen lesen – wir sollten Wordsworth und den andern allen unseren Tribut zollen. Aber müssen wir uns um ein paar guter, phantasievoller oder schlichter Passagen willen eine bestimmte Philosophie aufzwingen lassen, die irgendein selbstgefälliger Kerl sich aus einer verrückten Laune heraus ausgedacht hat? Jeder hat seine Anschauungen, aber nicht jeder brütet darüber und spreizt sich damit wie ein Pfau, bis er zum Falschmünzer wird und sich selbst betrügt. Manch einer kann bis in den Äther hinauf gelangen, und doch fehlt ihm der Mut, das niederzuschreiben, was er halb erschaut hat. Sancho kann sich so gut wie jeder andere eine Reise zum Himmel ausdenken. Wir hassen Dichtung, die uns handgreiflich zu beeinflussen sucht und uns, wenn wir nicht zustimmen wollen, gewissermaßen mit der Hand in die Hosentasche fährt. Dichtung sollte groß und unaufdringlich sein, ein Ding, das in die Seele dringt und nicht an sich, sondern durch seinen Gegenstand frappiert oder in höchstes Erstaunen versetzt. Wie schön sind die Blumen, die im verborgenen blühen! Wie würden sie ihre Schönheit verlieren, müßten sie sich auf die Landstraße drängen und ausrufen: »Bewundert mich, ich bin ein Veilchen! – Verliebt euch in mich, ich bin eine Primel!« Die modernen Dichter unterscheiden sich von den Elisabethanern in folgendem: Jeder einzelne von den Modernen regiert wie ein hannoveranischer Kurfürst in seinem Kleinstaat und weiß ganz genau, wie viele Strohhalme jeden Tag von den Bürgersteigen all seiner Territorien gefegt werden, und es juckt ihn immerzu zu hören, ob die Hausfrauen auch alle ihr Kupferzeug fein scheuern. Die Alten waren Kaiser über unermeßlich weite Provinzen; von den abgelegenen hatten sie nur gehört und waren kaum begierig, sie zu besuchen. Ich will mit alldem nichts mehr zu tun haben – Von Wordsworth und vor allem von Hunt will ich nichts mehr wissen. Was sollen wir in Manasses Stamm verharren, wenn wir mit Esau ziehen können? Was sollen wir über die Dornen daherstolpern, wenn wir auf Rosen wandeln können? Warum uns über »schönäugige Bachstelzen« ärgern, wenn wir den »Cherub Kontemplation« vor Augen haben? Warum über »Matthew mit einem Zweig vom Wildapfelbaum in der Hand« von Wordsworth, wenn wir auch Jacques, »hingestreckt an einer Eiche etc.« haben können. Das Geheimnis des Zweiges vom Wildapfelbaum werden Sie geschwinder kapieren, als ich's hinschreiben kann. Der alte Matthew sprach vor ein paar Jahren mit ihm über irgendwelche Nichtigkeiten, und weil er sich zufällig bei einem Abendspaziergang einbildete, die Gestalt des alten Mannes gesehen zu haben, muß er's schwarz auf weiß festhalten, und fortan ist es geheiligt. Ich will Wordsworths Größe und Hunts Verdienste nicht leugnen, aber ich meine sehr wohl, daß wir uns nicht mit Größe und Verdiensten dieser Art herumplagen müssen, wenn wir beides auch rein und unaufdringlich haben können. Halten wir uns besser an die alten Dichter und an Robin Hood. Ihr Brief und die Sonette darin haben mir mehr Freude gemacht als das vierte Buch von »Childe Harold« es könnte. [...]

An John Hamilton Reynolds

[19. Februar 1818]

Mein lieber Reynolds,

ich kann mir vorstellen, daß ein Mensch auf folgende Weise sein Leben sehr angenehm verbringen könnte – wenn er zum Beispiel an einem Tag eine Seite vollkommene Poesie oder verdichtete Prosa liest und darüber nachsinnt und sich in seinen Gedanken damit beschäftigt und darüber nachdenkt und sich alles eindringlich ausmalt und sich in Ahnungen darüber ergeht und davon träumt, bis es ihm fad wird. Aber wird es das je? Niemals! Wenn der Mensch eine gewisse Reife des Verstandes erlangt hat, so dient ihm jede großartige und geistvolle Stelle als Ausgangspunkt seiner Fahrt zu »allen zweiunddreißig Palästen«. Welch ein Glück ist doch so eine »Reise in der Phantasie«, welch köstliche, emsige Lässigkeit. Ein Dämmerstündchen auf dem Sofa tut ihm keinen Abbruch, und ein Schläfchen im Klee zeugt himmlische Fingerzeige. Das Geplapper eines Kindes verleiht ihm Flügel, und das Gespräch derer, die in der Mitte des Lebens stehen, schenkt ihm die Kraft, sie zu entfalten. Eine Melodie trägt uns in »einen öden Winkel« jener Insel, und wenn die Blätter raunen, »zieht's rund um die Erde einen Gürtel«. Doch soll die Zurückhaltung im Umgang mit kostbaren Büchern keineswegs bedeuten, daß wir ihre Schöpfer geringschätzen, denn vielleicht sind ja die Ehren, die der Mensch dem Menschen erweist, nur hohler Plunder, verglichen mit dem Heil, das große Werke »am Geist und Puls des Guten« tun durch ihr bloßes, passives Vorhandensein. Erinnerung sollte man nicht Wissen nennen. Viele haben eine originellen Geist und glauben es gar nicht – sie sind nur Opfer der Gewohnheit. Nun, ich möchte meinen, daß jeder Mensch wie die Spinne aus seinem Inneren heraus sich seine eigene luftige Zuflucht weben kann. An wenigen Blattspitzen und Zweigenden nur beginnt die Spinne ihr Werk, und sie erfüllt die Luft mit schönen Kreislinien. Der Mensch sollte sich mit ebenso wenigen Punkten begnügen, daran das feine Gewebe seiner Seele zu heften und eine himmlische Tapisserie weben, voll von Symbolen für sein geistiges Auge, ganz weich, wenn er sie im Geiste berührt, und weit, daß er im Geiste drin umherschweifen kann, und mit klaren Linien für seine Lust. Doch die Gemüter der Sterblichen sind so verschieden und zu so mannigfaltigen Zielen hingezogen, daß es auf den ersten Blick aussehen mag, als könne es unter diesen Voraussetzungen unmöglich eine Gemeinsamkeit des Urteils und Verbundenheit bei nur zweien oder dreien geben. Dennoch ist das ganze Gegenteil der Fall. Die Gemüter gehen in verschiedene Richtungen auseinander, kreuzen sich an unzähligen Punkten und treffen sich schließlich am Ende der Reise wieder. Ein alter Mann und ein Kind reden miteinander, und dem alten Mann wird sein Weg gewiesen, und das Kind bleibt nachdenklich zurück. Der Mensch sollte nicht streiten oder auf seiner Meinung beharren, sondern seinem Nachbarn nur leise von seinen Einsichten berichten; und wenn jede Faser der Seele so aus dem übersinnlichen Nährboden Kraft saugt, dann können alle Menschen großartig werden; die Menschheit wäre nicht mehr länger ein weites Heideland mit Stechginster und Dornengestrüpp und einem einsamen Eichenbaum oder einer vereinzelten Kiefer hier und da, sondern sie würde zu einer gigantischen Demokratie von Waldbäumen! Es gibt einen altbekannten Vergleich für unser Vorwärtsdrängen: der Bienenstock; doch scheint mir, wir sollten eher die Blume sein als die Biene – denn es ist eine falsche Vorstellung, daß Empfangen einem mehr Gewinn einträgt als Geben. Nein, der Empfangende und der Gebende haben gleichen Nutzen. Die Blume, daran hege ich keinen Zweifel, empfängt einen gerechten Lohn von der Biene – ihre Blätter leuchten im nächsten Frühling noch strahlender. Und wer kann sagen, wer wohl – ob Mann oder Frau – die größere Wonne empfindet? Nun ist es vornehmer, stillzusitzen wie Jupiter, als umherzufliegen wie Merkur – drum laßt uns nicht hastig ausfliegen, Honig zu sammeln, bienengleich hier und da herumschwirren, voll Ungeduld im Wissen um einen Zweck; laßt uns vielmehr wie eine Blume unsere Blütenblätter öffnen und passiv und empfänglich sein – geduldig erblühen unter Apollos Auge und dem Rate eines jeden prächtigen Insekts folgen, das uns mit seinem Besuch beehrt. Nektar wird unsere Speise sein und Tau unser Trank. Zu diesen Gedanken, mein lieber Reynolds, regte mich die Schönheit des Morgens an, die auf einen müßigen Geist wirkte –. Ich habe noch kein Buch angeschaut. Der Morgen sagte: »Recht so.« Ich dachte an nichts als an den Morgen, und die Drossel sagte: »Recht so!« – schien zu sagen:

O du, des Antlitz Winterwind gespürt,
Des Aug durch Nebel Schneegewölk gesehn
Und Ulmenwipfel, schwarz im Sternenfrost,
Dir wird der Frühling eine Erntezeit.
O du, der Licht von größter Finsternis
Als einzig Buch besaß, das dich erhielt
Von Nacht zu Nacht, wenn Phöbus ferne war,
Dir soll der Frühling dreimal Morgen sein.
O plag dich nicht nach Wissen – ich hab keins,
Doch mit der Wärme kommt mein Lied von selbst.
O plag dich nicht nach Wissen – ich hab keins,
Und doch lauscht mir der Abend. Wen sein Denken
An Trägheit traurig stimmt, der kann nicht träg sein,
Und wach ist jener, der sich schlafend wähnt.

Nun, ich weiß schon, all das ist bloße Sophisterei (wie nah es auch der Wahrheit kommen mag), um meine eigene Lässigkeit zu entschuldigen. So will ich mir nicht einreden, der Mensch gliche Jupiter, vielmehr sollte ich meinen, er kann zufrieden sein, wenn er so eine Art Aushilfsmerkur ist oder auch nur eine bescheidene Biene. Es spielt keine Rolle, ob ich recht hab oder nicht, ob's so ist oder so, wenn es nur dazu dient, Ihnen ein wenig die Zeit zu vertreiben.

Von ganzem Herzen Ihr Freund
John Kents

An John Taylor

Hampstead, den 27. Februar [1818]

[...] Es ist eine traurige Angelegenheit für mich, daß jemand, der meine Verse liest, Vorurteile zu überwinden haben sollte – das kränkt mich mehr als irgendwelches Herumkritteln an einzelnen Stellen. Im »Endymion« habe ich höchstwahrscheinlich nur das Gängelband mit dem Laufwagen vertauscht. In der Dichtung habe ich einige Axiome, und Sie werden gleich sehen, wie weit ich noch davon entfernt bin, bis zum Kern desselben vorgedrungen zu sein. Erstens glaube ich, Dichtung sollte durch wunderbare Übersteigerung, nicht durch Einzigartigkeit in Erstaunen versetzen. Sie sollte den Leser anmuten, als seien seine eigenen besten Gedanken in Worte gefaßt worden, so daß sie ihm beinahe wie eine Erinnerung vorkommt. Zweitens sollten ihre Schönheiten niemals halb vollendet sein und den Leser dadurch atemlos machen, statt ihn zu befriedigen: das Aufsteigen, das Wandern, das Untergehen der Bilder sollte ihm so natürlich erscheinen wie der Gang der Sonne – sollte ihn bescheinen und dann gemächlich und dennoch prachtvoll versinken und ihn zurücklassen im üppigen Zwielicht. Doch es ist leichter, darüber nachzudenken, was Dichtung sein sollte, als Gedichte zu schreiben, und das bringt mich auf ein weiteres Axiom. Nämlich: Wenn Dichtung nicht so natürlich wächst wie die Blätter an einem Baum, soll man besser überhaupt nicht dichten. Wie es bei mir nun auch immer sein mag, ich muß beständig nach neuen Ländern Ausschau halten und seufzen: »Oh! Eine Feuermuse, die hinan (den hellsten Himmel der Erfindung) stiege!« Wenn »Endymion« mir den Weg dorthin ebnet, so sollt ich wohl zufrieden sein. Ich habe allen Grund zufrieden zu sein, denn Gott sei Dank kann ich Shakespeare lesen und ihn vielleicht bis in seine tiefsten Tiefen begreifen, und ich habe, das weiß ich wohl, viele Freunde, die, sollte ich versagen, jede Veränderung in meinem Lebenswandel und meiner Stimmung eher als Bescheidenheit, denn als Stolz auslegen; eher als ein Kauern unter den Schwingen großer Dichter, denn als Verbitterung darüber, daß man mich nicht genug schätzt. Ich möchte gern, daß der »Endymion« recht bald gedruckt ist, damit ich ihn vergessen und etwas Neues beginnen kann. [...]

An Benjamin Bailey

Teignmouth, Freitag [13. März 1818]

[...] Sie kennen ja meine Ansichten über Religion. Ich glaube nicht, daß ich mehr als andere Menschen im Recht bin und daß irgend etwas auf dieser Welt beweisbar ist. Könnte ich doch nur für kurze zehn Minuten auf all Ihre Gefühle zu diesem Thema eingehen und ein oder zwei Seiten nach Ihrem Gusto darüber schreiben. Ich bin manches Mal so skeptisch, daß ich selbst die Dichtung für ein bloßes Irrlicht halte, das den erfreut, den sein Schein eben zufällig trifft. Wie die Kaufleute sagen: ein jedes Ding ist so viel wert, wie es einbringt, so wird wahrscheinlich jedes geistige Streben erst wirklich und erhält seinen Wert aus dem Eifer des Strebenden und ist an sich gar nichts. Übersinnliche Dinge können zumindest insoweit wirklich sein, als man sie in drei Kategorien einteilen kann: Wirkliche Dinge – halbwirkliche Dinge – und Nicht-Dinge. Wirkliche Dinge: die Existenz der Sonne, des Mondes und der Sterne, Stellen bei Shakespeare. Halbwirkliche Dinge: Liebe, die Wolken etc., welche der Geist nur einmal streifen muß, damit sie ganz existieren, und Nicht-Dinge, die allein durch glühendes Streben groß und erhaben werden, was, nebenbei, die Flaschen unseres Geistes mit der Burgundermarke prägt, insofern er fähig wird, »zu heiligen, was immer er betrachtet«. [...]

Es war schon seit jeher mein Grundsatz und wird sicherlich wohlbekannt sein, daß jeder Gedanke Mittelpunkt einer geistigen Welt ist. Die beiden Hauptgedanken im Kopfe eines Menschen sind die zwei Pole seiner Welt, er kreist um sie, und mit ihrer Hilfe ist jedes Ding für ihn nördlich oder südlich. Für uns sind's nur drei Schritt von Federn bis Eisen. Ich muß Ihnen nun ein für allemal sagen, mein lieber Freund, ich habe nicht die mindeste Ahnung, ob meine Überlegungen richtig sind. – Ich werde nie ein Räsoneur werden, weil mir nichts dran liegt, recht zu haben, wenn ich aus den Streitereien heraus und in wirklich philosophischer Stimmung bin. [...]

An Benjamin Robert Haydon

Mittwoch [8. April 1818]

[...] Ich bin mir schon immer viel zu deutlich des labyrinthischen Pfades zur Größe in der Kunst bewußt gewesen (ausgehend von der Dichtung), als daß ich je hätte glauben können, ich verstünde das Wesen der Malerei. Die unzähligen Verknotungen und Wiederauflösungen, die zwischen dem Verstand und seinen tausenderlei Baustoffen vonstatten gehen, ehe er dahin gelangt, die Schönheit wahrzunehmen – zitternd und empfindsam wie mit der Schnecke Fühlhorn. Ich kenne nicht die vielen Refugien Ihrer Intensität und werde sie auch niemals kennenlernen, aber dennoch hoffe ich, daß mir nichts von dem, was Sie vollbringen, entgeht: Schon als Schulbub hatte ich eine abstrakte Vorstellung von einem heroischen Gemälde, die ich nicht beschreiben kann. Ich sah es in meiner Phantasie groß, plastisch, geschlossen und in prächtigen Farben – etwa so wie das Gefühl, das ich bei »Antonius und Kleopatra« habe. Oder bei Alkibiades, wie er auf seinem karmesinroten Ruhebette ausgestreckt liegt in seiner Galeere, und seine breiten Schultern heben sich kaum merklich mit dem Wogen der See. Gibt es eine Stelle bei Shakespeare, die herrlicher wäre als diese:

»Seht auf der Mauer den finstern Warwick hausen!«

[...]

An John Hamilton Reynolds

Donnerstag morgen [9. April 1818]

Mein lieber Reynolds,

da Ihr Euch alle einig seid, daß das Ding schlecht ist, muß es wohl so sein, wenngleich ich mir nicht bewußt bin, daß irgendwas daran nach Hunt klingen soll (und wenn doch, so ist es mein natürliches Wesen, und ich habe etwas mit Hunt gemein). Schauen Sie's sich noch einmal an, und prüfen Sie die Motive, den Samen, aus dem jeder einzelne Satz gewachsen ist. Ich empfinde nicht im mindesten ein Gefühl der Demut vor dem Publikum oder vor irgend etwas Existierendem, außer vor einem ewigen Sein, dem Prinzip der Schönheit und dem Andenken großer Männer. Wenn ich für mich allein schreibe, um der bloßen Freude des Augenblicks willen, treibt die Natur vielleicht ihr Spiel mit mir – ein Vorwort aber wird fürs Publikum geschrieben, für ein Wesen, das ich nur als meinen Feind ansehen und an das ich mich nicht ohne feindselige Gefühle wenden kann. Wenn ich ein Vorwort in eleganter oder unterwürfiger Manier schriebe, so stimmte es nicht mit meiner Rolle als öffentlicher Sprecher überein. Meinen Freunden unterwerfe ich mich wohl und bin ihnen dankbar, wenn sie mich zur Unterwerfung bringen, aber vor der Menge habe ich nicht das Gefühl, mich verbeugen zu müssen; der Gedanke, mich vor ihr zu demütigen, widert mich an. –

Niemals schrieb ich eine einzige Zeile, bei der ich auch nur im Traum an das Publikum gedacht hätte.

Verzeihen Sie, daß ich Sie belästige und aus solch einer Mücke – was die Sache selbst und auch mich betrifft – einen Elefanten mache; aber es hilft mir, Ihnen davon zu erzählen. Ich könnte ohne die Liebe meiner Freunde nicht leben. Ich würde für ein hohes Gemeinwohl vom Ätna herunterspringen, aber ich hasse abgeschmackte Popularität. Ich kann mich ihnen nicht unterwerfen. Mein Ruhm sollte es sein, die tausend Schwätzer einzuschüchtern und zu entmutigen, die über Bilder und Bücher plappern. Ich sehe Scharen von Stachelschweinen mit emporgereckten Federkielen, »Leimruten gleich fängt's meiner Seele Flügel«, und ich will sie mit einer Fackel fortscheuchen. Sie mögen einwenden, mein Vorwort habe nicht sehr viel Ähnlichkeit mit einer Fackel. Es wäre zu beleidigend gewesen, beim Zeus anzufangen, und ich konnte einem Ding von Lehm keinen Kopf aus Gold aufsetzen. Wenn an diesem Vorwort etwas falsch ist – geheuchelt ist es nicht: Doch ein Unterton von Respektlosigkeit dem Publikum gegenüber schwingt darin mit. Wenn ich ein anderes Vorwort schreibe, dann muß es ohne einen Gedanken an diese Leute geschehen. Ich werde es mir überlegen. Wenn Sie in vier bis fünf Tagen kein neues bekommen haben, sagen Sie Taylor, er möge es ohne Vorwort veröffentlichen und einfach die Zueignung »Dem Andenken Thomas Chattertons gewidmet« stehenlassen. [...]

An John Hamilton Reynolds

Teignmouth, den 3. Mai [1818]

[...] Müßte ich noch einmal Heilkunst oder vielmehr Medizin studieren, so würde dies, das spüre ich, meine Dichtung nicht im mindesten verändern: Wenn sich der Verstand noch im Stadium der Kindheit befindet, ist ein Vorurteil tatsächlich ein Vorurteil, doch wenn wir zu größerer Festigkeit gelangt sind, wird das Vorurteil kein Vorurteil mehr sein. Dann erscheint uns jedes Wissensgebiet als ein besonderes, auf ein großes Ganzes hin berechnetes. Davon bin ich so fest überzeugt, daß ich froh bin, meine medizinischen Bücher nicht fortgegeben zu haben, die ich mir wieder ansehen will, um das Wenige wachzuhalten, was ich auf diesem Felde weiß. Überdies habe ich vor, mit Ihrer und Rices Hilfe so eine Art Juristenküken zu werden. Denkende Menschen brauchen ein breites Wissen – es vertreibt die Hitze und das Fieber und hilft, indem es die Denkfähigkeit erweitert, die Last des Mysteriums zu verringern, was ich langsam zu begreifen beginne und was auch Sie in dem düstersten und wahrhaftigsten Satz Ihres Briefes bedrückt hat. Der Unterschied zwischen starken Empfindungen mit und solchen ohne Wissen scheint mir der zu sein: Im letzteren Falle stürzen wir fortwährend 10000 Klafter tief und werden wieder hochgewirbelt ohne Flügel und mit allem Grauen eines flügellosen Geschöpfes. Im ersteren Falle sind unsere Schultern mit Flügeln versehen, und wir schweben ohne Furcht durch dieselbe Luft, denselben Raum. Doch das heißt, mit einem nur gedachten Vorteil Schabernack zu treiben. Wenn wir uns nämlich das menschliche Leben und die Stimmungen vornehmen, so können wir unmöglich wissen, wie man Kopf und Herz miteinander in Einklang bringen soll. Sie werden mir verzeihen, daß ich so treuherzig aus meinen Tiefen hervortrete, wie wenn ein Schulbub Wasser tritt – Wir können unmöglich wissen, inwieweit Wissen uns über den Verlust eines Freundes und die Übel, »die unsres Fleisches Erbteil« sind hinwegzutrösten vermag. [...]

Sie sagen: »Ich fürchte, es ist wenig Hoffnung auf etwas anderes in diesem Leben.« Demnach müssen Sie wohl mit noch schmerzhafterem und heftigerem Eifer durch das gleiche Labyrinth wie ich gegangen sein. Ich bin soweit zu den gleichen Schlüssen gelangt. So manches hab ich daraus abgeleitet, hab zum Beispiel Wordsworths Genius betrachtet und mich – gleichsam als Hilfsgröße, wie das Gold die Meridianlinie allen weltlichen Reichtums ist – gefragt, worin er sich von Milton unterscheidet. Und hier habe ich nur Vermutungen, weil ich mir nicht sicher bin, ob Miltons scheinbar geringere Sorge um die Menschheit daraus herrührt, daß er weiter sieht als Wordsworth, oder nicht: Und ob Wordsworth wahrhaft epische Leidenschaft besitzt und sich martert um das menschliche Herz, den wichtigsten Bezirk seiner Dichtung. Nehmen wir nur seinen Genius. Wir empfinden als wahr, was er sagt, soweit wir es selbst erfahren haben, und wir können nur durch größere Erfahrung weiter urteilen, denn Axiome der Philosophie sind keine Axiome, solange sie nicht an unserem Puls erprobt sind: Wir lesen etwas Gutes, doch können wir's nie ganz nachempfinden, solange wir nicht dieselben Schritte gegangen sind wie der Schreiber. – Ich weiß, ich drükke mich unklar aus; Sie werden ganz genau verstehen können, was ich meine, wenn ich Ihnen sage, daß ich Hamlet jetzt mehr denn je genießen werde. Besser gesagt, Sie wissen sehr wohl, daß kein Mensch die körperliche Liebe als tierische oder freudlose Sache empfinden kann, ehe er ihrer nicht überdrüssig ist, und deshalb wäre alles Philosophieren darüber bloßes Gerede. Ehe wir etwas nicht satt haben, begreifen wir's nicht; genauer also, wie Byron sagt: »Wissen ist Leid.« Ich gehe indessen noch weiter und sage: »Leid ist Weisheit« und weiter, soviel wir überhaupt etwas sicher wissen können: »Weisheit ist Narrheit!« Da sehen Sie, wie ich Wordsworth und Milton hinter mir lasse und auch noch weiter über alles, was in meinem Kopfe ist, hinausgehen will, damit ich am Ende erkenne, daß manche Briefe schön quadratisch sind, manche hübsch oval und manche rund, manche sphäroidisch, und warum sollte es nicht auch noch welche geben mit zwei scharfen Zacken wie eine Rattenfalle? Ich hoffe, Sie rechnen meine langen Briefe alle dieser Spezies zu, dann ist alles gut, denn durch die bloße zarte und ätherische Berührung der Feder wird das gezackte Ding sogleich zu einem geschlossenen Gebilde einrasten; und so können Sie aus meinen Bruchstükken einen schönen runden Laib mit Ihrem eigenen Sauerteig darin machen. Wenn Ihnen die besagte Rattenfalle nicht handlich genug ist, um so schlimmer für mich, weil es meiner Tinte von Natur aus unmöglich ist, sich auf andere Weise zu verklecksen: Wenn ich lange Briefe hinkritzele, müssen meine Launen sich dabei austoben können. Ich muß seitenlang ganz tiefschürfend oder aber ganz oberflächlich sein, ich muß lokker sein und frei von Metaphern und Formen, ich muß meine Züge ausspielen können, wie es mir paßt, und um meines Vorteils und Ihrer Gelehrsamkeit willen einen weißen Stein zu einer schwarzen Dame machen oder einen schwarzen zu einer weißen und nach Schwarz oder nach Weiß ziehen können, weit oder kurz, wie es mir paßt. Ich muß von Hazlitt zu Patmore springen und Wordsworth und Coleman ein Bockspringen veranstalten lassen oder einen von beiden einen ganzen Sonntagnachmittag beim Strumpfbandhissen niederhalten, »von Gray zu Gay, von Little zu Shakespeare«. Und wie ein langer Prozeß zwei oder mehr Sitzungen auf dem Gericht braucht, so braucht ein langer Brief zwei oder mehr Sitzungen auf dem Hosenboden, weshalb ich nach dem Essen fortfahre.

Haben Sie nicht eine Möwe, einen Schwertwal, eine Seeschwalbe oder irgendwas gesehen, womit man diese Zeile auf die passende Länge bringen und zudem diese Lücke schließen kann; daß ich, gleich einer Möwe, eintauchen kann – ich hoffe, nicht auf Nimmerwiedersehen. Auch hoffe ich, gleich einer Möwe mit etwas Glück einen ansehnlichen Fisch zu erwischen. Diese Art, einen Brief kreuzweise zu schreiben, ruft Gedankenverbindungen hervor, denn Kariertes bringt uns natürlich auf ein Milchmädchen, ein Milchmädchen auf Hogarth, Hogarth auf Shakespeare, Shakespeare auf Hazlitt –

Hazlitt auf Shakespeare, und so setzen wir, nur dadurch, daß wir an einem Schürzenbande ziehen, ein ganz schönes Glokkenläuten in Gang. Lassen wir's nur ruhig weiterläuten, derweil ich mit Ihrer gütigen Erlaubnis auf Wordsworth zurückkommen will, ob er Weitblick hat oder von beschränkter Größe ist, ob er ein Adler in seinem Horst ist oder im Flug. Und, um deutlicher zu werden und Ihnen zu zeigen, wie gut ich neben dem Giganten bestehe, will ich Ihnen ein Gleichnis vom menschlichen Leben geben, soweit ich es jetzt begreife, das heißt, bis zu jenem Punkt, an dem wir beide jetzt, wie ich meine, angelangt sind. Alsdann – ich vergleiche das menschliche Leben mit einem großen Haus mit vielen Gemächern, von denen ich nur zwei beschreiben kann, weil die Türen der anderen mir noch verschlossen sind. Das erste, in das wir eintreten, nennen wir die Stube der Kindheit oder der Gedankenlosigkeit, in der wir bleiben, solange wir nicht denken. Wir bleiben dort eine lange Weile, und wiewohl die Türen der zweiten Stube all die Zeit über geöffnet sind und leuchtende Helle offenbaren, beeilen wir uns dennoch nicht, dorthinein zu gelangen, sondern werden endlich unmerklich dadurch, daß das denkende Prinzip in uns erwacht, hineingedrängt. Kaum haben wir indes die zweite Stube, die ich die Stube der Jungfräulichkeit des Denkens nennen will, betreten, so machen das Licht und die Luft uns ganz benommen, wir sehen nichts als herrliche Wunder und möchten gern für immer und in Freuden dort verweilen. Doch eine der Wirkungen, die dieses Atemschöpfen zeitigt, ist jene gewaltige, daß wir lernen, den Menschen tiefer in ihr Herz und in ihr Wesen hineinzuschauen und mit jeder Faser zu begreifen, daß die Welt voll ist von Elend und Herzeleid, Schmerz, Krankheit und Bedrängnis, wodurch die Stube der Jungfräulichkeit des Denkens sich allmählich verdüstert, und gleichzeitig öffnen sich zu allen Seiten viele Türen, doch alle sind dunkel, alle führen in dunkle Gänge. Wir sehen nicht, wie das Gute und das Böse einander die Waage halten, um uns ist Dunst. Diese Stufe haben wir jetzt erreicht – wir spüren die »Last des Mysteriums«. An dem Punkt war Wordsworth wohl angekommen, als er »Tintern Abbey« schrieb, und mir scheint, sein Genius ist dabei, jene dunklen Gänge zu erforschen – wenn wir leben und weiterdenken, werden auch wir sie erforschen. Er ist ein Genie und uns darin überlegen, daß er besser als wir Entdeckungen machen und sie ins Licht rücken kann. Hierin scheint mir Wordsworth tiefer zu gehen als Milton, obwohl ich glaube, daß das mehr mit dem allgemeinen gesellschaftlichen Fortschreiten des Verstandes als mit seiner individuellen Geistesgröße zu tun hat. Ich hoffe nur, es ist, selbst unter uns, nicht zu vermessen, aus dem »Verlorenen Paradies« und anderen Werken Miltons den Schluß zu ziehen, daß seine Philosophie, die menschliche wie die göttliche, recht wohl von jemandem verstanden werden kann, der noch nicht sehr reich an Jahren ist. Zu seiner Zeit hatten sich die Engländer eben von einem großen Aberglauben emanzipiert, und die Menschen waren zu gewissen festen Angelpunkten und Ruheplätzen gelangt, die noch zu jung waren, um schon angezweifelt zu werden und die vom übergroßen Teil Europas zu heftig angefochten wurden, um nicht für erhaben und wahrhaft göttlich gehalten zu werden. Wer hätte wohl zu einer Zeit, da man eben den Hosenlatz und Hunderte anderer Schändlichkeiten abgeschafft hatte, den Auffassungen von Tugend, Laster und Keuschheit widersprechen sollen, die Milton im »Comus« dargelegt hat? Wer hätte sich, als man der Scheiterhaufen in Smithfield eben ledig war, nicht mit den Ansichten über Gut und Böse zufriedengeben sollen, die er im »Verlorenen Paradies« geäußert hat? Die Reformation brachte so unmittelbare und große Wohltaten hervor, daß man glaubte, der Protestantismus sei unmittelbar vom Auge des Himmels erleuchtet, und dessen eigene überkommene Dogmen und Wunderlehren bildeten, als sie dann wieder auferstanden, jene Ruheplätze und scheinbar sicheren Angelpunkte für das Denken. Wie schon erwähnt, scheint Milton, betrachtet man seine Werke, ganz gleich, was er auch in der Folgezeit gedacht haben mag, mit diesen einverstanden gewesen zu sein. Er versenkte sich nicht ins menschliche Herz wie Wordsworth, aber dennoch war Milton als Philosoph gewiß ebenso groß wie Wordsworth. Was läßt sich dann also schlußfolgern? Oh, vieles – es beweist, daß es wirklich einen gewaltigen Vormarsch der Denkfähigkeit gibt. Es beweist, daß eine mächtige Vorsehung die mächtigsten Geister in den Dienst der herrschenden Zeit – für das menschliche Wissen, oder für die Religion – zwingt. Oft habe ich die Lehrer bedauert, die sich fortwährend »Nominativ: Musa« ins Ohr blasen lassen müssen. Ich hoffe, mein Geschreibsel bereitet Ihnen nicht dieselbe Pein. Mag sein, daß ich das alles früher schon einmal gelesen habe, doch hatte ich mir nie zuvor auch nur ganz vage einen Begriff davon gemacht, und überdies sage ich meine Lektion gern einem auf, der meine Langatmigkeit mir zuliebe aushält. Schließlich gibt es gewiß auch etwas Wirkliches in der Welt. Moores Geschenk für Hazlitt ist etwas Wirkliches. Ich mag diesen Moore, und ich bin froh, daß ich ihn unmittelbar, bevor ich die Stadt verließ, im Theater traf. Tom hat heute nachmittag ein ganz klein wenig Blut gespuckt, und das ist ein ziemlicher Dämpfer, doch ich weiß, die Wahrheit ist, es gibt etwas Wirkliches in der Welt. Die dritte Stube des Lebens soll heiter und freundlich sein und wohl versehen mit dem Wein der Liebe und dem Brot der Freundschaft. […]

An Benjamin Bailey

[21.–25. Mai 1818]

[…] Ich fühle mich heute vormittag wie gelähmt, so daß ich nicht schreiben kann. Oft ist dieses Gefühl der Grund dafür, daß ich einen Brief aufschiebe. Ich warte auf eine bessere Gemütsverfassung. Da Sie mich nun aber um sofortige Antwort bitten, möchte ich nicht einmal bis morgen warten. Ich bin freilich so niedergeschlagen, daß mir gar nichts einfällt. Meine Hand ist wie aus Blei, und obgleich es eine unangenehme

Taubheit ist, nimmt sie den Schmerz der Existenz nicht fort. Ich weiß nicht, was ich schreiben soll. – Montag, den 25. Mai. – Sie sehen, wie lange ich es aufgeschoben habe, und selbst jetzt habe ich nur eine verschwommene Vorstellung davon, was ich mir vornehmen soll. Mein Geist scheint sich im Zustand der Auflösung zu befinden. Es muß wohl so sein, denn während ich über Gott weiß was schreiben sollte, langweile ich Sie mit den Stimmungen meines Geistes beziehungsweise meines Körpers, denn Geist ist keiner da. Meine Stimmung ist so, daß ich, wenn ich unter Wasser wäre, kaum strampeln würde, um wieder nach oben zu kommen. Ich weiß wohl, das ist alles Unfug. Binnen kurzem hoffe ich, in der Stimmung zu sein, mich mit dem, was Sie über mein Buch schreiben, befassen zu können. Ganz umsonst habe ich bis Montag gewartet, um Interesse daran oder an etwas anderem zu bekommen. Der Gedanke, daß mein Bruder nach Amerika geht, erregt mich nicht, und mein Herz ist angesichts seiner Heirat beinahe wie versteinert. All das wird vorübergehen. Ich bedaure einzig und allein, daß ich Ihnen in so einer Zeit schreiben muß, doch ich kann meine Briefe nicht in ein Mistbeet stecken. Ich würde mich unbehaglich fühlen, wenn ich bei Ihnen Sprüche klopfen müßte. Ich bin in Ihrer Schuld. Ich muß es immer bleiben. Ich möchte nicht einmal über meine wirkliche Schuld im Bilde sein. Es ist tröstlich, sich dem Mitgefühl seiner Freunde zu überlassen – wie der Albatros, der im Fluge schläft. Ich will Wein im Keller für Sie sein, und je bescheidener beziehungsweise träger ich mich in das hinterste Faß zurückziehe, desto falernischer werde ich beim Genusse sein. [...]

An Benjamin Bailey

London [10. Juni 1818]

Mein lieber Bailey,

über Ihre Briefe in der Oxforder Zeitung habe ich mich sehr gefreut und war zugleich sehr verärgert: weil Enthusiasmus, wenn man von dem ungerechtfertigten und vergänglichen Gefühl der Freude über Lobpreisung absieht, etwas Glorreiches hat; und weil die Welt boshaft genug ist, über die ehrbarste Einfalt zu kichern. Ja, bei meiner Seele, mein lieber Bailey. Sie sind zu einfältig für die Welt, und der Gedanke daran macht mir dieselbe widerwärtig. Wie kommt es bloß, daß wir, obwohl wir so grundverschieden sind, doch beide so tief enttäuscht wurden. Sie haben Ihr Leben lang (glaube ich) allen vertraut – ich habe allen mißtraut. Und obwohl Sie so getäuscht worden sind, erlassen Sie solch einen arglosen Appell. Die Welt hat anderes zu tun, und ich bin froh darüber. Wenn ich die Wahl hätte, ich würde eine petrarkische Krönung ablehnen – im Hinblick auf meine Todesstunde und weil Frauen Krebs bekommen. Ich sollte eigentlich nicht so zu Ihnen reden, denn es ist ein aufwieglerischer Geist, der aus mir spricht. Doch ich bin weder alt noch edelmütig genug, mich selbst zu verleugnen – und das hieße vielleicht auch, Ihnen ein falsches Kompliment zu machen. Noch vor kurzem hoffte ich, ich könnte Ihren Trübsinn durch meine gute Laune vertreiben, Ihnen Dinge zeigen in der Welt, die es wert sind, daß Sie sich ihrer erfreuen. Jetzt aber macht es mich immer, wenn ich allein bin, froh, zu wissen, daß es etwas wie den Tod gibt, und ich will mein Äußerstes tun für den Ruhm, für einen großen menschlichen Zweck zu sterben. Vielleicht hätte ich das Obige nicht geschrieben, wenn es anders um meine Angelegenheiten stünde. Sehen Sie selbst: Ich habe zwei Brüder, den einen treibt die »Last der Gesellschaft« nach Amerika, der andere, der das Leben über alles liebt, siecht dahin. Meine Liebe zu meinen Brüdern hat sich durch den frühzeitigen Verlust unserer Eltern und durch gar noch frühere Schicksalsschläge zu einer Zuneigung ausgewachsen, die »sonderlicher als Frauenliebe« ist. Ich habe meine schlechte Laune an ihnen ausgelassen, ich habe sie geärgert, doch der Gedanke an sie hat allemal die Empfindungen zunichte gemacht, die sonst wohl eine Frau in mir wachgerufen hätte. Ich habe auch eine Schwester und kann ihnen nicht folgen, weder nach Amerika noch ins Grab. Man muß durch das Leben hindurch, und der Gedanke, daß ich wohl noch ein, zwei Gedichte schreiben mag, bevor es endet, ist mir wahrlich ein Trost. [...]

An Thomas Keats

Auchencairn, den 3. Juli [– 9. Juli 1818]

[...] Der Dialekt an den benachbarten Küstenstreifen von Schottland und Irland ist fast gleich, und doch kann ich zwischen den beiden Nationen einen gewaltigen Unterschied feststellen, und zwar an dem Zimmermädchen dieses Landgasthofes, der einem Herrn Kelly gehört. Es ist blond, freundlich und zum Lachen aufgelegt, weil es nicht der Schreckensherrschaft der schottischen Kirche untersteht. Ein schottisches Mädchen hat furchtbare Angst vor den Kirchenältesten – die armen kleinen Susannas. Sie trauen sich kaum einmal zu lachen, man kann sie nur bedauern, und die Kirche kann man nur verdammen. Diese Kirchenmänner haben Schottland genützt (oder?). Sie haben alle, ob Männer oder Frauen, ob Greise oder Jugendliche, ob alte Frauen oder junge Frauen, ob Knaben, ob Mädchen oder Säuglinge, so sehr zur Sparsamkeit erzogen, so daß sie zu regelrechten Schlachtreihen von Sparern und Verdienern formiert sind. Solch eine haushälterische Armee muß ihr Land natürlich reich machen, so daß es den Anschein hat, als herrsche hier größerer Wohlstand als bei dem armen irischen Nachbarn. Diese Kirchenmänner haben Schottland geschadet – sie haben die Späße und das Lachen und das Küssen verbannt (außer in Fällen, wo die bloße Gefahr und der Frevel es gewiß erst richtig süß und verlockend machen. Ich setze lieber einen Punkt hinter das Küssen, denn danach wäre wohl besser eine Parenthese angebracht, und fahre fort, indem ich Dir das Schicksal von Burns in Erinnerung rufe. Der arme, unglückliche Kerl – er hatte ein durch und durch südliches Naturell – wie traurig ist es, wenn eine reiche Imagination zu ihrem eigenen Schutz gezwungen ist, ihr Feingefühl im Vulgären und in greifbaren Dingen abzutöten, daß sie nicht die Muße findet, sich nach den Dingen zu verzehren, die es nicht sind. Kein Mann kann sich in diesen Dingen mit den Erfahrungen anderer begnügen. Freilich, aus dem Leiden erwächst keine Größe, keine Würde; selbst im geistigsten Genusse ist kein bleibendes Glück; doch wer würde sich nicht gern einmal selbst davon überzeugen, daß Kleopatra falsch war, Helena gemein und Ruth verschlagen? Meine Verstandeskräfte reichen nicht aus, um mit der Erwerbsdoktrin zu Rande zu kommen, wenn sie mit der Würde der menschlichen Gesellschaft, mit dem Glück der Häusler in Einklang stehen soll. Ich kann nur grob eines gegen das andere halten. Wurden die Finger geschaffen, eine Guinee zu halten oder eine weiße Hand? Wurden die Lippen geschaffen, einen Federkiel zu pressen oder einen Kuß? Und doch wird der Mensch in den Städten von seinesgleichen gemieden, wenn er arm ist; die Häuslerin muß in Schmutz und großem Elend leben, wenn sie nicht auf Erwerb aus ist. Der gegenwärtige Zustand der Gesellschaft gebietet es so, und dies bringt mich zu der Überzeugung, daß die Welt sehr jung und noch im Stande ziemlicher Unwissenheit ist. Wir leben in einem barbarischen Zeitalter. Ich möchte lieber ein Stück Wild sein als ein Mädchen unter der Fuchtel der schottischen Kirche, und lieber wär ich ein Wildschwein, als daß ich der Anlaß sein möchte, wenn so ein armes Geschöpf vor diesen abscheulichen Ältesten Buße tun muß. [...]

9. – Wir sind nur ganz kurz in Irland geblieben, und damit Du gar nicht dazu kommst, Dich über unsere schnelle Rück-

kehr nach Port Patrick zu wundern, will ich Dir sagen, daß das Leben in Irland so teuer ist wie im Hummums-Hotel – alles kostet dreimal soviel wie in Schottland. Wir hätten 15 Pfund bezahlen müssen für die kurze Zeit. Überdies stellten wir fest, daß die 48 Meilen irische sind und an die 70 englische ausmachen. Nachdem wir also an einem Tag bis nach Belfast gewandert waren und am nächsten zurück nach Donoghadee, verließen wir Irland bei frischer Brise. Letzte Nacht schliefen wir in Port Patrick, wo mich ein Brief von Dir erfreute. Auf unserer Tour durch Irland hatten wir nur allzu reichlich Gelegenheit, die unvorstellbarste, nackteste Armut zu sehen, die Lumpen, den Dreck und das Elend der armen einfachen Iren. Ein schottischer Katen ist, obwohl der Rauch aus ihm zuweilen nur durch die Tür entweichen kann, ein Palast, verglichen mit einem irischen. Dieses auffahrende Wesen konnten wir bei allen, ob Mann, Knabe oder Frau, feststellen. Wir hatten das Vergnügen, uns durch ein Torfmoor von mindestens drei Meilen Länge zu schlagen – öde, schwarz, feucht, trist und sumpfig: Hier und da waren arme, schmutzige Kreaturen und ein paar kräftige Männer dabei, Torf zu stechen oder abzufahren. Als wir auf dem Weg nach Belfast einen überaus erbärmlichen Vorort durchquerten, hörten wir das widerlichste aller Geräusche – schlimmer als die Sackpfeife, als Affengelächter, als Weibergeschnatter, vergleichbar solus dem Schrei eines Papageien – ich meine den Lärm des Weberschiffchens. Wie ungeheuer schwierig ist es doch, die Lebensbedingungen dieser Leute zu verbessern! Ich wüßte nicht, wie ein Geist, der »schwanger geht« mit Menschenliebe, das anpacken sollte – ich empfinde nichts als Verzweiflung. In einer elenden Schenke auf halbem Wege zwischen Donoghadee und Belfast saßen zwei Männer beim Whisky – der eine ein Landarbeiter, und der andere schien mir ein betrunkener Weber zu sein. Der Landarbeiter hielt mich für einen Franzosen, und der andere fragte nach Handgeld und sagte, er würde es gern annehmen. Als wir uns in Port Patrick nach Post erkundigten, fuhr der Mann uns an: »Welches Regiment?« Als wir aus Belfast zurückkamen, begegneten wir einer Sänfte – drin saß die Duchess vom Misthaufen, aber das ist ganz und gar nicht zum Lachen – Du mußt Dir das so vorstellen: die miserabelste Hundehütte, die Du je gesehen hast, das Ganze auf zwei Pfählen von einem verschimmelten Gitterzaun. In diesem elenden Ding saß eine erbärmliche Alte, zusammengekauert wie ein Affe, der auf der Überfahrt von Madagaskar zum Kap schon beinahe verhungert ist, weil es an Schiffszwieback mangelt. Sie hatte eine Pfeife im Mund und schaute mit starrem, leerem Blick unter faltigen Lidern hervor, und wackelte dabei mit dem Kopf wie eine Geisteskranke. Zusammengekauert und dürr saß sie da und paffte den Rauch vor sich hin, während zwei zerlumpte, abgerissene Mädchen sie durch die Gegend trugen. [...]

An John Hamilton Reynolds

Maybole, den 11. [–13.] Juli [1818]

[...] Mein lieber Reynolds, ich kann Ihnen nichts über die Landschaften und die Sehenswürdigkeiten hier schreiben. Die Phantasie ist in der Tat kleiner als die greifbar vorhandene Wirklichkeit, aber sie ist größer als die Erinnerung. Sie würden wohl auch vom Homer aufblicken, wenn Sie die wirkliche Insel Tenedos nahe vor sich sähen. Und danach würden Sie lieber weiter in Homer lesen, als Ihren Erinnerungen nachzuhängen. Ein Lied von Burns ist für Sie wertvoller als alles, was ich mir denken könnte, wenn ich ein ganzes Jahr in seiner Heimat bin. Sein Elend legt sich wie ein Bleigewicht auf die Behendigkeit der eigenen Feder. Ich versuchte, es zu vergessen, ganz unbekümmert meinen Punsch zu trinken, ein lustiges Sonett zu schreiben – es ging nicht. Er redete mit Huren, er trank mit Schurken, er war erbärmlich. Wir können sehen, wie sich in den Werken eines solchen Mannes sein ganzes Leben mit erschreckender Deutlichkeit widerspiegelt. [...]

An Benjamin Bailey

Inverary, den 18. Juli [1818]

[...] Ihr letzter Brief ließ mich vor Scham erröten wegen des Leids, das ich Ihnen zugefügt habe. Ich kenne mein Wesen gut genug, um zu wissen, daß ich Ihnen bestimmt hernach noch viele Male in der gleichen Weise schreiben werde – nun wissen Sie, wie ernst Sie mich darin zu nehmen haben. Sie müssen es der Imagination nachsehen. Ich weiß, ich werde das nicht ändern können. Es tut mir leid, daß Sie bekümmert sind, weil ich meine Besuche in Little Britain nicht fortgesetzt habe, doch ich denke, ich bin so lange hingegangen, wie jemand, der Bücher lesen und über Dinge nachdenken muß, tun kann. Aus diesem Grunde bin ich nirgendwo gewesen außer in Wentworth Place, was gleich nebenan ist. Überdies war ich nur allzuoft in einer gesundheitlichen Verfassung, die mich glauben ließ, es sei klüger, sich nicht der Nachtluft auszusetzen. Doch darüber hinaus will ich gestehen, daß ich mich in Gesellschaft nicht wohl fühle, ganz gleich, ob in einer kleinen oder in einer größeren. Ich weiß genau, daß unsere schönen Freundinnen sich freuen würden, wenn ich käme und einfach nur da wäre; aber ich weiß genau, daß ich eine Verdrießlichkeit mitbringe, ohne die sie besser dran sind. Wenn ich, ganz gleich wann, merke, daß meine Launen mich überkommen, nehme ich sogar von versprochenen Besuchen Abstand. Ich weiß genau, ich habe Frauen gegenüber nicht die richtige Haltung – in diesem Augenblick versuche ich gerecht gegen sie zu sein, aber ich kann nicht. Ob es wohl daran liegt, daß sie so gänzlich hinter den Vorstellungen meiner Knabenzeit zurückblieben? Als ich ein Schulbub war, glaubte ich, eine schöne Frau sei eine reine Göttin, mein Gemüt war ein weiches Nest, in dem eine schlummerte, wenn sie es auch nicht wußte. Ich habe kein Recht, mehr von ihnen zu erwarten als das, was sie wirklich sind. Ich glaubte, sie seien ätherische Wesen, die über den Männern stehen. Jetzt finde ich, sie sind ihnen etwa gleich. Großes wird durchs Vergleichen ganz klein. – Man kann jemanden nicht nur mit Worten oder Taten kränken, jemand, der selbst empfindlich gegen Kränkungen ist, mag nichts denken, was einen anderen kränken könnte. Ich mag in Gesellschaft einer Dame nichts Kränkendes denken. Ich begehe ein Verbrechen an ihr, was in ihrer Abwesenheit nicht geschehen wäre. Ist das nicht absonderlich? Wenn ich unter Männern bin, habe ich keine schlechten Gedanken, keine Boshaftigkeit, keinen Groll. Ich habe das Gefühl, reden oder schweigen zu können, wie es mir beliebt, ich kann zuhören und kann von jedem etwas lernen, ich habe die Hände in den Taschen, ich bin gänzlich ohne Argwohn und fühle mich wohl. Wenn ich unter Frauen bin, habe ich schlechte Gedanken, Boshaftigkeit, ich kann weder reden noch schweigen, ich bin voller Argwohn und höre deshalb gar nicht richtig zu, ich habe nur das Verlangen, schnell wegzukommen. Sie müssen nachsichtig sein und all diese Widernatürlichkeiten dem Umstand zugute halten, daß ich seit meiner Knabenzeit immer wieder enttäuscht worden bin. Doch mit solchen Gefühlen bin ich lieber allein unter einer Masse von Männern, ganz für mich oder mit ein, zwei Freunden. Bei alldem, glauben Sie mir, Bailey, bin ich ganz und gar nicht der Meinung, daß Männer mit anderen Gefühlen und Neigungen kurzsichtiger wären als ich. Nichts hat mich mehr gefreut als die Heirat meines Bruders, und ebenso wird mich die eines jeden meiner Freunde freuen. Ich muß unbedingt damit fertig werden – bloß wie? Der einzige Weg ist, die Wurzel des Übels zu finden und es zu kurieren »mit rückwärts gemurmelten Sprüchen, die den Zauber bannen«. Das ist eine schwierige Sache; denn solch ein abscheuliches Vorurteil kann schwerlich anders entstehen als durch eine gordische Verknotung von Gefühlen, die zu entwirren man viel Zeit braucht und viel Vorsicht, damit sie sich nicht von neuem verheddern. Ich könnte noch so allerlei dazu sagen, aber ich will es bleibenlassen und auf bessere und passendere Gelegenheiten hoffen. Auch bin ich überzeugt, daß ich keiner Unrecht tue, denn schließlich denke ich nicht so schlecht von den Frauen, als daß ich annähme, sie könnten sich was draus machen, ob ein Mr. John Keats, fünf Fuß hoch, sie mag oder nicht. [...]

An Mrs. James Wylie

Inverness, den 6. August 1818

[...] Tom sagt mir, daß Sie Mr. Haslam mit einer Zeitung aufgesucht haben, in der über einen Herrn mit einer Pelzkappe berichtet wird, der in Kirkcudbrightshire einen Abhang hinuntergestürzt ist. Wenn ich das gewesen bin, dann tat ich's entweder im Traum oder in einem verwunschenen Augenblick zwischen der ersten und der zweiten Tasse Tee, was gar nichts besonderes ist, wenn wir hören, daß Mohammed, als er aus dem Bett aufstand, eine Wasserkanne umstieß, und während sie fiel, einen zweiwöchigen Ausflug machte – wie man annimmt in den Himmel –, und doch war er rechtzeitig zurück, um zu verhindern, daß ein einziger Wassertropfen verschüttet wurde. Was Pelzkappen angeht, so kann ich mich nicht erinnern, eine außer meiner eigenen gesehen zu haben, nur eine in Carlisle – das war eine sehr schöne Pelzkappe, ich begegnete ihr in der High Street, und ich wage zu behaupten, daß dies die Unglückskappe war. Ich wage weiter zu behaupten, daß die Parzen, als sie nur zwei Pelzkappen im ganzen Norden sahen, dies für so außergewöhnlich hielten, daß sie darum würfelten, welche von beiden ertrinken sollte. Das Los fiel auf Jonas. Ich wage zu behaupten, daß er Jonas hieß. Ich hoffe nur, daß die hehren Damen nicht vom Hängen sprachen, und wenn doch, so wird es mir eines Tages leid tun, daß ich nicht in Kirkcudbright beinahe ertrunken bin. Halt! Lassen Sie mich nachdenken! – beinahe ertrunken zu sein, weil man in einen Abgrund fiel, das ist doch eine sehr romantische Angelegenheit. Warum soll ich das eigentlich nicht auf meine Kappe nehmen? Wahren Sie mein Geheimnis, und ich tu's auch. Wie ehrenvoll, wenn man in einem Salon einer Dame, die gern Romane liest, vorgestellt wird mit den Worten: »Mr. Soundso, der einen Abgrund hinunterfiel und beinahe ertrunken wäre.« [...]

An John Hamilton Reynolds

[22. (?) September 1818]

[...] Ich war noch nie verliebt. Aber seit zwei Tagen haben mich die Stimme und Gestalt einer Frau nicht mehr losgelassen – und das zu einer Zeit, in der das Versinken, das fieberhafte Versinken ins Dichten ein viel geringeres Verbrechen scheint. Heute früh hat das Dichten gesiegt – ich bin wieder in jene Abstraktionen verfallen, die allein mein Leben sind. Mir ist, als sei ich einem neuen, fremden und drohenden Leiden entronnen. Und ich bin dankbar dafür. Eine wundervolle Wärme liegt um mein Herz, es ist wie mit Unsterblichkeit befrachtet. [...]

An James Augustus Hessey

[8. Oktober 1818]

[...] Ich kann diesen Herren, die meine Partei ergriffen haben, nur dankbar sein. Ansonsten fange ich an, mir allmählich etwas mehr über meine Stärken und Schwächen klarzuwerden – Lob und Tadel haben nur eine momentane Wirkung auf einen Mann, dessen Liebe der Schönheit im Geistigen gehört, was ihn zum gestrengen Kritiker seiner eigenen Werke macht. Meine eigene, private Kritik hat mir unvergleichlich mehr Pein bereitet als mir Blackwood oder das »Quarterly« je zufügen könnten, und auch wenn ich glaube, auf dem rechten Wege zu sein, kann kein Lob von außen mir ein solches

Glücksgefühl geben wie die eigene, einsame Nachempfindung und Bestätigung von etwas Schönem. J. S. hat ganz recht, der »Endymion« kommt auf wackligen Beinen daher. Das ist indes nicht meine Schuld. Nein, auch wenn es vielleicht ein bißchen paradox klingen mag. Ich hab ihn so gut gemacht, wie ich es aus eigener Kraft tun konnte. Hätte ich mich damit unter Druck gesetzt, daß er unter allen Umständen etwas Vollkommenes werden muß, und unter diesem Blickwinkel alle möglichen Leute um Rat gebeten und um jede Seite gezittert, dann hätte ich ihn nicht schreiben können; denn diese Fummelei liegt mir nicht. Ich will unabhängig schreiben. Ich habe unabhängig geschrieben, *ohne Urteilskraft.* Hiernach werde ich vielleicht unabhängig und *mit Urteilskraft* schreiben können. Der Genius der Poesie muß im Menschen sein eigenes Heil entfalten: Er kann nicht durch Gesetz und Vorschrift zur Reife gebracht werden, sondern nur durch Empfindung und Wachsamkeit sich selbst gegenüber. Was schöpferisch ist, muß sich selbst erschaffen. Im »Endymion« habe ich einen Kopfsprung ins Meer getan, und dadurch bin ich mit den Tiefen, dem Treibsand und den Felsen besser vertraut geworden, als wenn ich an den grünen Ufern geblieben wäre und albern geflötet und Tee getrunken und bequeme Ratschläge angenommen hätte. Ich habe nie Angst vor dem Scheitern gehabt, denn lieber will ich scheitern, als nicht unter den Größten sein. Aber es fehlt nicht mehr viel, und ich gerate ins Schwärmen. [...]

An Richard Woodhouse

[27. Oktober 1818]

Mein lieber Woodhouse,

Ihr Brief erfüllte mich mit großer Befriedigung, und zwar mehr noch wegen seiner Freundlichkeit, als etwa weil mir jene Sache gefällt, die dem »genus irritabile« so sehr willkommen ist. Die beste Antwort, die ich Ihnen geben kann, ist, nach Beamtenmanier ein paar Bemerkungen zu zwei grundsätzlichen Dingen zu machen, die mir wie zwei Zeigefinger genau ins Zentrum der ganzen Debatten über Genie und Ansichten und Verdienste und Ehrgeiz und so weiter zu deuten scheinen. Erstens: Was den poetischen Charakter selbst angeht (ich meine diejenige seiner Abarten, die ich, sofern ich überhaupt etwas bin, vertrete, jene Abart, die sich unterscheidet von der wordsworthischen oder selbstgefälligen Erhabenheit, die ist eine Sache für sich und steht allein) so ist er nicht er selbst – er hat kein Selbst – er ist alles und nichts. Er hat keinen Charakter, er erfreut sich an Licht und Schatten gleichermaßen: Er lebt seinen Neigungen, sei er schlecht oder gut, hoch oder niedrig, reich oder armselig, gemein oder erhaben. Er ersinnt einen Jago mit ebensoviel Vergnügen wie eine Imogen. Was den tugendhaften Philosophen schreckt, entzückt den chamäleonhaften Dichter. Sein Gefallen an der düsteren Seite der Dinge richtet sowenig Schaden an wie seine Lust an ihrer lichten Seite, weil ja beide im Spekulativen enden. Von allem, was existiert, ist der Dichter am unpoetischsten, weil er keine Identität hat. Er ist fortwährend darauf aus, nach einem anderen Körper zu suchen und ihn auszufüllen. Die Sonne, der Mond, das Meer und Mann und Frau, beides Geschöpfe mit impulsivem Wesen, sind poetisch und haben ein unabänderliches Attribut an sich. Der Dichter hat keins, keine Identität – er ist bestimmt das unpoetischste von allen Geschöpfen Gottes. Wenn er also kein Selbst hat und wenn ich ein Dichter bin, was Wunder, wenn ich sage, daß ich nie mehr schreiben werde? Könnte es nicht sein, daß ich gerade im selben Moment über die Eigenheiten von Saturn und Ops nachgedacht habe? Es ist ein trauriges Eingeständnis, aber es ist einfach eine Tatsache, daß man mir kein Wort von dem, was ich sage, als aus meinem ureigenen Wesen erwachsene Ansicht abnehmen kann – wie denn auch, wo ich doch gar kein Wesen habe? Wenn ich mit anderen in einem Zimmer bin und einmal nicht über die Schöpfungen meines eigenen Hirns nachsinne, dann kehrt sich mein Ich nicht in sich selbst, sondern die Identität eines jeden, der mit im Zimmer ist, fängt an, sich mir so stark aufzuprägen, daß ich in kürzester Zeit ausgelöscht bin, und das nicht nur unter Erwachsenen, in einer Stube voller Kinder wäre es genau das gleiche. Ich weiß nicht, ob ich mich ganz verständlich machen kann: Ich hoffe doch, gut genug, damit Sie sehen, daß dem, was ich damals sagte, kein Gewicht beizumessen ist.

An zweiter Stelle will ich von meinen Ansichten sprechen und von dem Leben, das ich zu führen gedenke. Ich habe den Ehrgeiz, der Welt Gutes zu tun. Sollte ich es erleben, so mag dies das Werk meiner reiferen Jahre sein – in der Zwischenzeit will ich versuchen, in der Dichtung einen so hohen Gipfel zu erreichen, wie die mir verliehenen Kräfte es erlauben. Die vage Vorstellung, die ich von zukünftigen Gedichten habe, läßt mir oft das Blut zu Kopfe steigen. Ich hoffe nur, daß ich nicht ganz die Anteilnahme an den menschlichen Angelegenheiten der anderen verliere, daß die einsiedlerische Gleichgültigkeit, die ich selbst gegenüber dem Beifall der erlesensten Geister empfinde, nicht das Bißchen Scharfblick abstumpft, was ich vielleicht habe. Ich glaube nicht, daß es so weit kommt. Ich fühle mich darin bestätigt, daß ich schreiben muß, aus der bloßen Sehnsucht, der Begeisterung heraus, die ich für das Schöne habe, selbst wenn ich jeden Morgen verbrennen müßte, was ich des Nachts geschrieben habe, und kein Auge es je erblicken sollte. Doch sogar jetzt spreche ich vielleicht nicht ganz aus mir selbst, sondern aus irgendeinem Wesen, in dem ich gerade lebe. [...]

An George und Georgiana Keats

[14.–31. Oktober 1818]

[...] Stadttratsch habe ich nicht für Euch, weil ich nicht viel unter Leuten gewesen bin. Was die Politik angeht, so sind da meiner Meinung nach nur deshalb alle jetzt so schläfrig, weil sie allzubald wieder hellwach sein werden. – Aber vielleicht auch nicht, denn der lang anhaltende innere Friede in England hat uns ein Gefühl persönlicher Sicherheit gegeben, das sehr wohl dazu angetan ist, die Wiederherstellung unserer nationalen Ehrenhaftigkeit zu verhindern. Es gibt ja wirklich nirgends in der Regierung noch Mannhaftigkeit und Wahrhaftigkeit. Es gibt viele Verrückte im Lande, ich zweifle nicht daran, die sich mit Freuden auf dem Tower Hill köpfen lassen würden, bloß um einen Skandal herbeizuführen. Es gibt viele Männer vom Schlage eines Hunt, die es aus Gründen des guten Geschmacks gern sähen, wenn die Dinge besser stünden; es gibt viele vom Schlage eines Sir F. Burdett, die gern obenan sitzen wollen bei politischen Banketten, aber es gibt keinen, der bereit wäre, im verborgenen für sein Land zu leiden. Unsere Schlechtesten treibt die Geldgier, unsere Besten die Eitelkeit zum Handeln. Wir haben keinen Milton, keinen Algernon Sidney. Heutzutage tauschen die Regierenden den Titel Mensch gegen den Titel Diplomat oder Minister ein. Wir atmen gewissermaßen Kanzleimief. In allen Bereichen der Regierung hat man sich meilenweit entfernt vom Einfachen, welches doch die größte Stärke ist. In dieser Beziehung besteht zwischen der gegenwärtigen Regierung und der von Oliver Cromwell ein genauso großer Unterschied wie zwischen den zwölf römischen Gesetzestafeln und den von Justitian zusammengetragenen Bänden bürgerlichen Rechts. Wenn heute einer einen Kanzlertitel trägt, erweist man ihm in jedem Fall dieselbe Ehre, gleichgültig, ob er ein Hog ist oder ein Lord Bacon. Nicht die Größe erregt Aufsehen, sondern die Anzahl der Orden, die einer in den Knopflöchern hat. Ganz gleich, welche Stellung die Liberalen zu Bonaparte beziehen, ich finde ganz entschieden, er hat der Sache der Freiheit mehr geschadet als sonst irgendwer: Nicht daß etwa diese Herren von Gottes Gnaden etwas Gutes getan hätten oder zu tun gedächten. Nein, sie haben von ihm gelernt und werden, ohne daß sie auch nur eine einzige seiner guten Seiten haben, all den Schaden stiften, den auch er weiter angerichtet hätte. Das Schlimmste, was er getan hat, ist, daß er sie gelehrt hat, wie man die ungeheuren Armeen aufstellt. Man sagt, daß Zar Alexander sein Reich, wie einstmals Diokletian, aufzuteilen gedenkt, zwei Nebenzaren einsetzen will und beabsichtigt, selbst weiterhin der höchste Herrscher über das Ganze zu bleiben. Wenn er das täte und sie über eine Reihe von Jahren hinweg untereinander Frieden hielten, so könnte Rußland seine Eroberungen bis nach China ausdehnen. Ich halte es für sehr wahrscheinlich, daß China fallen wird, die Türkei fällt mit Sicherheit. In der Zwischenzeit wird das europäische Nordrußland seine Hörner gegen das restliche Europa gesenkt halten und nicht aufhören, mit Frankreich zu intrigieren. Dilke, den Ihr als Vertreter des Godwinschen Perfektibilitätsprinzips kennt, liebäugelt mit dem Gedanken, daß Amerika das Land sein wird, das den menschlichen Geist da fortsetzen kann, wo England ihn aufgibt. In diesem Punkt denke ich entschieden anders – ein Land wie die Vereinigten Staaten, dessen größte Männer Franklin und Washington sind, wird das niemals tun. Das sind zweifellos große Männer, aber wie könnte man sie mit unseren Landsleuten wie Milton und den beiden Sidneys vergleichen! Der eine ist ein philosophischer Quäker mit geizigen und gewinnsüchtigen Maximen, der andere hat gerade das Streitroß verkauft, das ihn durch all seine Schlachten getragen hat. Diese Amerikaner sind groß, aber sie sind nicht der erhabene Mensch – das menschliche Wesen kann in den Vereinigten Staaten niemals Erhabenheit erlangen. Birbecks Geist bewegt sich zu sehr im amerikanischen Stil. Ihr müßt versuchen, in die Kolonie einen etwas anderen Geist hineinzutragen, aber immer schön vorsichtig, denn dadurch könnt Ihr Euren Nachfahren mehr dienen als Ihr Euch vorstellen mögt. [...]

Ungeachtet Eures Glücks und Eurer Empfehlungen hoffe ich, daß ich niemals heiraten werde. Und wenn auch am Ziel einer Reise oder eines Spazierganges das allerschönste Geschöpf meiner harrte, wenn auch der Teppich von Seide wäre und aus Morgenwolken die Vorhänge, die Sessel und das Sofa gestopft mit Schwanendaunen, die Speise Manna, der Wein vortrefflicher als Claret, das Fenster hinausginge auf den Winandermere, würde ich mich doch nicht so wohl fühlen – oder vielmehr mein Wohlbefinden wäre nicht so groß, wie meine Einsamkeit erhaben ist. Denn an Stelle all dessen, was ich beschrieben habe, ist da etwas Erhabenes, das mich daheim willkommen heißt. Das Tosen des Windes ist mein Weib, und die Sterne, die durchs Fenster hereinschauen, sind meine Kinder. Die mächtige allumfassende Vorstellung, die ich von der Schönheit in allen Dingen habe, erstickt das zerstreutere und unbedeutendere häusliche Glück – eine liebenswerte Frau und süße Kinder sehe ich als Bestandteile jener Schönheit an, doch ich brauche tausend solcher Schönheitspartikel, damit mein Herz erfüllt ist. Ich spüre mit jedem Tag mehr, wie meine Imagination erstarkt. Ich lebe nicht allein in dieser Welt, sondern in tausend Welten. Kaum bin ich allein, schon nehmen rings um mich her Gestalten von epischer Größe Aufstellung und dienen meinem Geist geradeso wie einem König die Leibgarde – dann »rauscht die Tragödie mit Szepter und Purpur herein«. Je nachdem, in welcher Gemütsverfassung ich bin, brülle ich mit Achilles in den Festungsgräben oder ich bin mit Theokrit in den Tälern Siziliens. Oder ich werfe mein ganzes Sein in Troilus und spreche jene Verse nach: »Verlorne Seele, wandre ich an den Ufern des Styx und harre der Überfahrt.« Ich verschmelze in der Luft und empfinde dabei so köstliche Wollust, daß ich zufrieden bin, allein zu sein. All dies und dazu noch die Meinung, die ich im allgemeinen von den Frauen habe, die mir wie Kinder vorkommen, denen ich viel lieber eine kandierte Pflaume schenken möchte als meine

Zeit – das erzeugt in mir eine Abwehr gegen die Ehe, über die ich sehr froh bin. Ich habe dies geschrieben, damit Ihr seht, daß ich meinen Teil habe an den höchsten Freuden und daß ich, auch wenn ich mich dafür entscheiden mag, meine Tage allein zuzubringen, nicht einsam sein werde. Ihr seht, das alles ist durchaus nicht verstiegen. Das einzige, was mich länger als einen Tag lang bedrücken kann, ist jeglicher Zweifel an meinem dichterischen Vermögen – ich zweifle selten daran, und ich sehe voller Hoffnung einer näherrückenden Zeit entgegen, da ich gar nicht mehr daran zweifeln werde. Ich bin so glücklich, wie ein Mensch nur sein kann, das heißt, in meinem Innern wäre ich glücklich, wenn Tom gesund wäre und wenn ich wüßte, daß Ihr frohe Tage habt. – Dann wär ich auf das höchste zu beneiden – wenn die sehnsüchtige Leidenschaft, die ich für das Schöne hege, eins geworden wäre mit dem Ehrgeiz meines Verstandes. Und vergleicht doch nur einmal die Freuden, die die Einsamkeit mir gewährt, mit meinem Treiben in der Welt. Dort bin ich ein Kind – dort kennt mich keiner – nicht einmal meine vertrautesten Bekannten. Ich gehe auf ihre Ansichten ein, als ob ich vermeiden will, ein kleines Kind zu verwirren. Manche finden mich mittelmäßig, andere albern, wieder andere närrisch – jeder denkt, daß er gegen meinen Willen meine Schwächen sieht, und in Wirklichkeit sieht er sie, weil ich es will. Ich hab nichts dagegen, daß sie mich so oder so finden, weil ich in meiner eigenen Brust eine so reiche Quelle habe. Das ist ein wichtiger Grund, weshalb man mich so gerne mag; weil alle sich im Salon von ihrer vorteilhaften Seite zeigen können und aus einem gewissen Taktgefühl heraus, einen, der allenthalben als guter Dichter gilt, im Schatten lassen. Ich hoffe, ich spiele nicht »solchen Wahnsinn, daß Engel weinen«; aber ich glaube nicht, denn ich hege nicht die leiseste Verachtung gegen meine Spezies; und wenn es auch paradox klingen mag: die erhabensten Momente meiner Seele machen mich jedesmal bescheidener. [...]

An Benjamin Robert Haydon

Wentworth Place, Dienstag [22. Dezember 1818]

Mein lieber Haydon,

bei meiner Seele, ich habe überhaupt nicht bemerkt, daß Sie aus dem Zimmer gegangen sind, und glauben Sie mir, ich bramarbasiere nur dann, wenn Sie dabei sind, im allgemeinen pflege ich in Gesellschaft zu schweigen. Ich sehe mich mit allen Lastern eines Dichters behaftet: Reizbarkeit, Effekthascherei und Gefallsucht, und von diesen Teufeleien besessen, mag ich wohl zuweilen mehr Unsinn reden, als mir gewahr wird, aber ich werde dem ein Ende bereiten, und zwar auf eine Weise, die ich mir seit langem ausgedacht habe. Ich werde einen goldenen Ring kaufen und ihn mir anstecken, und von dem Augenblick an soll kein gescheiter Kopf mehr Gelegenheit haben, mich zu bedauern, und kein blöder Nonnenschädel, über mich zu lachen. Freilich halte ich mehr von Größe im Schatten als im hellen Tageslicht. Ich rede als Sterblicher. Ich möchte meinen, daß mir der Vorzug, Großes in Einsamkeit zu sehen, mehr gilt als der Ruhm, ein Prophet zu sein. Doch jetzt versündige ich mich, drum will ich mich lieber einem Thema zuwenden, über das ich mehr nachgedacht habe: Ich meine Ihre Finanzen bis zur Fertigstellung Ihres Bildes. Darüber denke ich nicht erst jetzt nach, sondern schon seit anderthalb Jahren. Glauben Sie mir, Haydon, in meinem Herzen brennt ein solches Feuer, daß ich alles, was ich habe, für Sie opfern würde – ich sage das ganz rückhaltlos – ich weiß, Sie würden dasselbe für mich tun. Ich will Sie mit wenigen Worten in mein Herz blicken lassen, eh man Sie pfändet, werde ich es tun, doch lassen Sie mich Ihr letzter Ausweg sein, fragen Sie zuerst die reichen Kunstliebhaber. Ich sage Ihnen auch, warum: Ich habe etwas Geld, das es mir ermöglicht, drei, vier Jahre lang Studien zu treiben und zu reisen. Ich rechne nicht damit, daß ich jemals an meinen Büchern verdienen werde, und überdies möchte ich gar nichts mehr veröffentlichen. Ich bewundere die menschliche Natur, aber die *Menschen* mag ich nicht. Ich möchte Dinge schaffen, die dem Menschen zur Ehre gereichen, aber nicht zu befingern sind von *Menschen.* Deshalb gebe ich mir Mühe, daß ich auskomme, ohne den Laufburschen der Druckerei Arbeit zu machen oder Männern und Frauen Bewunderung entlocken zu müssen – und ich hoffe, Gott gibt mir die Kraft, mich dieser erhabenen Einsamkeit zu erfreuen. Versuchen Sie's mal bei den Geldsäcken, aber verkaufen Sie nicht Ihre Zeichnungen, das würde ich als einen Bruch unserer Freundschaft ansehen. [...]

An George und Georgiana Keats

[16. Dezember 1818 – 4. Januar 1819]

[...] Wie geht es Euch jetzt? Der Lauf der Welt macht mich schwindlig – dort seid Ihr bei Birbeck – hier bin ich bei Brown – manchmal scheint es mir, als wäret ihr ungeheuer weit weg, und manchmal, wie gerade jetzt, habe ich das Gefühl, in Gedanken bei Euch zu sein. Das mag zum Herrlichsten an der Unsterblichkeit zählen, daß da kein Raum sein wird und folglich der Verkehr zwischen den Seelen einzig über ihr Wissen voneinander vollzogen werden wird, wenn sie einander vollkommen verstehen, wohingegen wir einander auf Erden stets nur in unterschiedlichen Graden begreifen können, und je höher der Grad der Güte, um so größer sind unsere Liebe und Freundschaft. Ich bin in letzter Zeit des Schreibens beinahe entwöhnt, so daß ich befürchte, Ihr könntet nicht ahnen, was ich meine. Deshalb laßt mich Euch ein Beispiel geben. Stellt Euch vor, Brown oder Haslam oder sonstwer, den ich – verglichen mit Euch – in geringerem Maße verstehe, wäre in Amerika – sie wären mir um soviel ferner, wie ihre Identität sich mir weniger aufgeprägt hat. Daß ich mich Euch im Augenblick nicht so fern fühle, liegt also daran, daß ich an Eure Art, Euer Benehmen und Treiben denke: Ich kenne Eure

Denkweise, Eure Art zu fühlen: ich weiß, wie Ihr Eure Freude und Euern Kummer äußert. Ich kenne Eure Art zu gehen, zu stehen, zu schlendern, Euch hinzusetzen, zu lachen, zu scherzen und alles, was Ihr tut, so gut, daß Ihr mir nahe seid. Ihr werdet Euch meiner in derselben Weise erinnern – und dies um so mehr, wenn ich Euch sage, daß ich jeden Sonntag um zehn Uhr eine Stelle von Shakespeare lesen werde – lest Ihr eine zur gleichen Zeit, und wir werden einander so nahe sein, wie Blinde sich sein können in ein und demselben Zimmer. [...]

Ich werde mit Sicherheit einem ganz neuen Menschenschlag begegnen. Mit noch größerer Sicherheit werde ich keine Zeit für diese Menschen haben. Hunt bat mich, irgendwann einmal Tom Moore zu treffen, also werdet Ihr von ihm hören. An dem Abend, als wir zu Novello gingen, schwätzte die ganze Bande nur über Mozart und witzelte herum. Ich hatte so gründlich genug davon, daß ich, wenn es nach mir ginge, nie wieder einen von dieser Bande sehen möchte, nicht mal Hunt – der bestimmt ein angenehmer Bursche ist, wenn man mit ihm zusammen ist. In Wirklichkeit aber ist er eitel, selbstgefällig und in Fragen des guten Geschmacks und der Moral einfach widerlich. Er versteht eine ganze Menge von schönen Sachen; anstatt aber nun den anderen den gleichen Grad an Erkenntnisfähigkeit zuzutrauen, den er selber hat, fängt er an, alles so genau zu erklären, daß es den Geschmack und das Selbstbewußtsein der anderen fortwährend beleidigt. Hunt schadet einem, indem er einem die guten Dinge verächtlich und die schönen Dinge verhaßt macht. Er ist schuld daran, daß mich Mozart kaltläßt, ich mache mir nichts aus Alabasterbüsten, und so manche herrliche Sache wird zunichte, wenn sie ihm in die Hände gerät. Das verdreht einem den Kopf – bringt einen auf sonderbare Ideen – läßt einen unsicher werden am Richtmaß des Schönen. [...] – Ich verbringe einen ruhigen Tag, was ich lange nicht mehr getan habe, und wenn ich so weitermache, dann muß ich, das spüre ich, wieder anfangen zu schreiben, denn wenn ich nicht tätig bin, sei es geistig oder körperlich, empfinde ich Schmerz, und deshalb leide ich sehr, wenn ich an Geselligkeiten teilnehme, auf denen ich mit Rücksicht auf die gesellschaftlichen Spielregeln oder aus einem natürlichen Stolz heraus gezwungen bin, meinen Geist zu ersticken und wie ein Idiot auszusehen, weil ich spüre, es würde sie zu sehr befremden, wenn ich meinen Impulsen nachgäbe. Ich lebe in immerwährender Selbstbeschränkung, die nie aufgehoben wird, außer, wenn ich dichte, also will ich weiterschreiben. [...]

Soll ich Dir Miss Brawne schildern? Sie ist ungefähr so groß wie ich – hat ein ebenmäßiges, eher längliches Gesicht – es fehlt ihren Zügen gänzlich an Empfindsamkeit. Sie weiß ihr Haar gut zu tragen, ihre Nase ist fein, wenngleich ein wenig spitz. Ihr Mund ist schlecht und gut – im Profil sieht sie besser aus, als wenn man ihr ins volle Gesicht schaut, das in Wirklichkeit gar nicht voll ist, sondern blaß und schmal, ohne die Knochen hervortreten zu lassen. Ihre Gestalt ist sehr graziös, ebenso ihre Bewegungen. Ihre Arme sind schön, ihre Hände mäßig, ihre Füße annehmbar, sie ist noch keine siebzehn. Aber sie ist ungebildet, ungeheuerlich in ihrem Benehmen, sie wird nach allen Richtungen ausfallend und beschimpft die Leute derart, daß ich neulich nicht umhinkonnte, sie als *Biest* zu bezeichnen. Das kommt aber, glaube ich, nicht von irgendeinem angeborenen Laster her, sondern von ihrer Neigung, sich stilvoll zu geben. Ich bin dieses Stils jedoch überdrüssig und weigere mich, fürderhin mit derlei behelligt zu werden. Sie hatte kürzlich eine Freundin zu Besuch – wie Du sie zur Genüge kennst – ihr Gesicht ist so rauh, als ob sie im Frost gestanden hätte – ihre Lippen sind rauh und anscheinend jederzeit bereit, ein Hühnchen zu verspeisen. Sie spielt Klavier, ohne etwas anderes dabei zu spüren als das Elfenbein unter ihren Fingern. Sie ist ein richtig reizloses Fräulein – wir mochten sie nicht leiden und hänselten und ärgerten sie und haben sie, glaube ich, vertrieben. Miss B. hält sie für ein Muster an Eleganz und sagt, sie sei die einzige Frau, mit der sie gern tauschen würde. (Was für eine Närrin sie doch ist. Sie ist der anderen so überlegen wie eine Rose dem Löwenzahn.) Als wir schlafen gingen, bemerkte Brown beim Auslöschen der Kerze, was für eine häßliche alte Frau diese Miss Robinson doch einmal werden würde – worauf ich bestimmt volle zehn Minuten lang laut stöhnte. Diesen Kingston-Irgendwas habe ich nicht wieder gesehen. George wird ihn Dir beschreiben. Ich werde ein paar von diesen Geschöpfen irgendwann einmal in einer Komödie unterbringen, und vielleicht nehme ich Hunt gleich mit dazu. [...]

Ich möchte herzlich gern wissen, ob Euer Interesse an Dichtung und Literatur überhaupt weiter gewachsen ist oder abgenommen hat, und welche Bücher derzeit am meisten nach Euerm Geschmack sind. Wie findet Ihr Fielding, und muten Euch Hogarths Bilder nicht reichlich altmodisch an? Ihr seid ja kaum weiter als ich vom gesellschaftlichen Umgang entfernt, wenn Ihr bedenkt, daß der Mensch zu allen Zeiten immer nur in *einer* Gesellschaft leben kann. Ob er in den verschiedenen Zuständen der menschlichen Gesellschaft sein Glück zu finden vermag, hängt allein von seinen geistigen Kräften ab. Das heißt, Ihr könnt Euch einen römischen Triumphzug oder die Olympischen Spiele ebensogut wie ich vorstellen, aber wir können mit unseren leiblichen Augen immer nur die Sitten und Gebräuche eines Landes in einer bestimmten Epoche sehen – und dann sterben wir. Mir aber sind die längst vergangenen Bräuche und Eigenheiten, sei es der Babylonier oder der Baktrier, ebenso wirklich oder gar noch wirklicher als jene, in denen ich heutzutage lebe. Letzthin kreisen meine Gedanken um folgendes: Je mehr wir wissen, um so mehr entdecken wir das Unvermögen in der Welt, uns zufriedenzustellen – das ist eine alte Beobachtung; aber ich habe den Entschluß gefaßt, niemals etwas als gesichert hinzunehmen, sondern selbst noch die plattesten Sprichwörter auf ihre Wahrheit hin zu untersuchen. Dies aber ist wahr: Mrs. Tighe und Beattie haben mich einstmals in Entzücken versetzt, jetzt durchschaue ich sie und kann nichts an ihnen finden – höchstens Schwächen – und doch, wie viele sind noch immer von ihnen entzückt! Womöglich ergeht es einem höheren Wesen so mit Shakespeare, ob das sein kann? Nein – dieselbe Unzulänglichkeit finden wir auch (verzeih mir, kleine George, Du weißt, ich will Dich nicht mit den anderen in einen Topf werfen), von wenigen Ausnahmen abgesehen, bei den Frauen. Die Schneiderin, der Blaustrumpf und die reizendste Schwärmerin unterscheiden sich nur um winzige Grade und sind gleichermaßen lächerlich. Aber ich will nichts weiter dazu sagen. Ich könnte wohl allzu lästerlich daherreden – und, ehrlich gesagt, hab ich so wenig nachgedacht, daß ich eigentlich zu nichts so recht eine Meinung habe, außer zu Fragen des Geschmacks. Ich bin mir einer Wahrheit nie wirklich sicher, es sei denn, ich erkenne ganz klar ihre Schönheit – und selbst in dieser Wahrnehmungsfähigkeit fühle ich mich noch sehr unreif – und hoffe, sie wird wachsen. [...]

An Benjamin Robert Haydon

[8. März 1819]

Mein lieber Haydon,

Sie werden sich fragen, wo ich stecke und was ich treibe! Meistens stecke ich in Hampstead und treibe gar nichts, hab so eine Art cui bono Stimmung, nicht so ganz im Begriff, ein Epos zu schreiben. Doch Sie dürfen nicht glauben, ich hätte Sie vergessen. Nein, ich war so ungefähr jeden dritten Tag bei Abbey und bei den Anwälten. Lassen Sie mich doch bitte wissen, wie es Ihnen geht und in welcher Gemütsverfassung Sie sind.

Gestern im »Examiner« sind Sie großartig herausgekommen! Unter was für Kleingeistern wir doch leben! Neulich ging ich in eine Eisenwarenhandlung, da hab ich auch nichts anderes empfunden – ob Menschen oder Zinnkessel, das bleibt sich heutzutage ziemlich gleich. Sie lernen mit fünfunddreißig nicht mehr wie die kleinen Kinder, aber reden tun sie wie Zwanzigjährige. Gespräche nicht als Suche nach Erkenntnis, sondern als Effekthascherei.

In diesem Punkt gleichen sich zwei sonst so grundverschiedene Männer wie Wordsworth und Hunt. Einer meiner Freunde meinte neulich, wenn Lord Bacon heute in einer Runde eine Bemerkung fallenließe, würde die Unterhaltung sofort zum Stillstand kommen. Ich bin überzeugt, daß es so wäre, und deshalb bin ich zu dem Entschluß gekommen: niemals zu schreiben nur um des Schreibens willen oder um ein Gedicht gemacht zu haben, sondern stets nur aus dem Überströmen jedweder kleinen Erkenntnis oder Erfahrung, die ich womöglich in jahrelangem Nachdenken gewonnen habe. Andernfalls bleibe ich lieber stumm. Die Imagination, die ich habe, will ich entfalten, ganz und gar, weiß ich doch aus eigenem Erleben, welche Befriedigung darin liegt, große Konzepte zu haben, ohne die Mühsal des Sonetteschreibens. Ich will meine Liebe zum Dunkel nicht verderben, indem ich eine Ode auf die Finsternis schreibe!

Für meinen Lebensunterhalt, dafür will ich nicht schreiben, denn ich will nicht Mitläufer sein in jener vulgärsten aller Massen, dem Literatenvolk. Dessen bin ich mir ganz sicher, wenn ich mich so betrachte und mich sozusagen darin versuche, geistige Gewichte zu haben. Ich bin dreiundzwanzig, habe ein geringes Wissen und einen mittelmäßigen Verstand. Gewiß, im Taumel der Begeisterung bin ich zu ein paar guten Stellen verführt worden, aber das ist nicht das Eigentliche. [...]

An George und Georgiana Keats

[14. Februar – 3. Mai 1819]

[...] Heute morgen bin ich in einer Art lässigen und höchst gleichmütigen Stimmung: ich sehne mich nach ein oder zwei Strophen aus Thompsons »Schloß der Trägheit«. Alle meine

Leidenschaften schlafen, weil ich fast bis elf geschlummert und jede lebendige Faser an mir abgeschwächt habe zu einer angenehmen Empfindung ungefähr drei Grad diesseits der Ohnmacht. Hätte ich Perlenzähne und den Atem der Lilien, ich würde es Mattigkeit nennen – doch da ich es bin*, muß ich es wohl Faulheit heißen. In diesem Zustand der Verweichlichung sind die Fasern des Gehirns entspannt wie der restliche Körper, und das in solch heiterem Grad, daß die Freude kein verlockendes Äußeres und der Schmerz keinen unerträglich finsteren Blick mehr besitzen. Weder Poesie, Ehrgeiz noch Liebe zeigen irgendeine Regung ihrer Mienen, während sie an mir vorüberziehen: sie gleichen eher drei Figuren auf einer griechischen Vase – einem Mann und zwei Frauen – die in ihrer Verkleidung niemand außer mir zu unterscheiden vermöchte. Das ist das einzige Glück und ist einer der seltenen Fälle, in dem der Sieg über den Geist dem Körper zum Vorteil gereicht. Gerade erhielt ich eine Nachricht von Haslam, in welcher er schreibt, er erwarte, nachdem sein Vater schon seit geraumer Zeit ohne Besinnung war, nunmehr dessen Tod. Seine Mutter, schreibt er, trägt es mit Fassung. Morgen werd ich in die Stadt gehn, um ihn zu besuchen –. So ist die Welt: sehr viele glückliche Stunden können wir nicht erwarten; wie Wolken ballen Umstände sich dauernd zusammen und zerbersten. Noch während wir lachen, wird die Saat einer Kümmernis in das weite urbare Land der Ereignisse gestreut; während wir lachen, keimt sie, sprießt und trägt mit einem Mal eine giftige Frucht, die wir zu pflücken haben. So haben wir Muße, über das Unglück unserer Freunde zu räsonieren – unser eignes geht uns zu nah, um es in Worte zu fassen. Sehr wenige Menschen haben je eine völlige Selbstlosigkeit des Geistes erreicht, sehr wenige sind getragen worden von einem reinen Verlangen nach dem Wohl anderer. Den meisten Wohltätern der Menschheit wurde ihre Größe durch ein berechnendes Motiv getrübt: ein melodramatisches Schauspiel hat sie ver-

* insbesondere weil ich ein blaues Auge habe

zaubert. An der Art, wie ich Haslams Unglück empfinde, merke ich, wie weit entfernt von jedem niederen Grad an Selbstlosigkeit ich doch bin. Gleichwohl sollte dieses Gefühl bis zum äußersten gesteigert werden, da doch keine Gefahr besteht, daß es der Gemeinschaft je schaden könnte – zum Extrem getrieben, würde es das wohl. Andernfalls verlöre der Habicht sein Frühstück aus Rotkehlchen und das Rotkehlchen das seinige aus Würmern; der Löwe müßte genauso verhungern wie die Schwalbe. Die meisten Menschen machen ihren Weg mit dem gleichen Instinkt, mit dem gleichen von seinem Ziel nicht abrückenden Blick, der gleichen Lebensgier wie der Habicht. Der Habicht will ein Weibchen – genauso der Mann. Seht euch an, wie beide es anstellen und sich auf die gleiche Weise eines beschaffen. Beide wollen sie ein Nest und verschaffen sich eines auf die gleiche Weise; sie bekommen ihr Futter auf die gleiche Weise. Das edle Menschentier raucht zu seiner Unterhaltung Pfeife, der Habicht schwebt in den Wolken – das ist der einzige Unterschied ihrer Mußen. Das ist, was – für einen nachdenklichen Menschen – die Unterhaltsamkeit des Lebens ausmacht: Ich gehe durch die Felder und sehe ein Wiesel oder eine Feldmaus kurz aus dem trockenen Gras lugen – das Geschöpf hat ein Ziel, das seine Augen glänzen läßt. Ich gehe durch die Straßen einer Stadt und sehe einen Menschen vorübereilen – wohin? Das Geschöpf hat ein Ziel, das seine Augen glänzen läßt. Dann aber, wie Wordsworth sagt, »haben wir alle *ein* menschliches Herz«. – In der menschlichen Natur ist ein elektrisches Feuer, das sie reinigen will, so daß unter jenen Menschengeschöpfen beständig neuer Heldenmut geboren wird. Traurig ist, daß wir darüber staunen müssen – so wie wenn man eine Perle im Kehricht findet. Zweifellos hatten Tausende vollkommen unbekannter Leute ein vollkommen selbstloses Herz – mir aber fallen nur zwei ein: Sokrates und Jesus, ihre Lebensgeschichten beweisen es. Was ich Taylor vor kurzem in bezug auf Sokrates sagen hörte, das kann man auch von Jesus behaupten: er war ein solch großer Mensch, daß, obgleich er der Nachwelt nichts Selbstgeschriebenes hinterlassen hat, sein Denken, seine Aussprüche und seine Größe uns von anderen überliefert wurden. Beklagenswert ist nur, daß des letzteren Lebensgeschichte von Menschen geschrieben und abgeändert wurde, denen an frommen Lügen der Religion gelegen war. Und dennoch sehe ich durch all dies hindurch seinen Glanz. Gerade hier – obschon ich selbst den gleichen instinktiven Weg verfolge wie das in unserer Vorstellung am meisten menschliche Tier; obwohl ich jung aufs Geratewohl schreibe; mich abmühe um Fünkchen von Licht inmitten tiefster Finsternis; nicht weiß, wie es sich verhält mit irgendeiner Behauptung irgendeiner Meinung – kann ich hierin nicht doch frei von Sünde sein? Kann es nicht höhere Wesen geben, beglückt von jeder anmutigen, wenn auch instinktiven Haltung, in die mein Geist verfallen kann – so wie ich meine Freude habe an der Behendigkeit eines Wiesels oder der Scheu eines Rehs? Obwohl ein Streit auf der Straße eine häßliche Sache ist, sind die in ihm entfalteten Kräfte doch schön; noch der gewöhnlichste Mensch zeigt Anmut in einer Auseinandersetzung. Einem höheren Wesen erscheinen unsere Überlegungen vielleicht ähnlich gefärbt: obschon irrig, können sie doch schön sein. Und genau das ist, worin die Dichtung besteht; und wenn dem so ist, ist sie weniger schön als die Philosophie – aus dem gleichen Grund wie ein Adler weniger schön ist als eine Wahrheit. [...]

Dantes fünfter Gesang gefällt mir mehr und mehr; es ist der, in dem er auf Paolo und Francesca trifft. Ich hatte mehrere Tage in einer ziemlich niedergeschlagenen Verfassung verbracht und träumte dabei einmal, ich sei in jenem Höllenbezirk. Der Traum war eines der schönsten Erlebnisse, das ich je hatte: durch die, wie sie beschrieben wird, wirbelnde Atmosphäre schwebte ich dahin mit einem wunderschönen Wesen, auf dessen Lippen meine lagen – wie mir schien, eine Ewigkeit lang. Und inmitten all der Kälte und Finsternis dort war mir warm. Sogar blühende Baumwipfel schossen auf, und ab und an ruhten wir uns auf ihnen aus mit der Leichtigkeit einer

Wolke, bis der Wind uns wieder davonblies. Ich habe versucht, ein Sonett darauf zu schreiben – vierzehn Zeilen stehen da und enthalten doch nichts von dem, was ich empfand. O könnte ich es jede Nacht träumen! [...]

Kürzlich habe ich zwei ganz unterschiedliche Bücher gelesen: Robertsons »Amerika« und Voltaires »Jahrhundert Ludwigs des Vierzehnten«. Es ist wie Arm in Arm zwischen Pizarro und dem großen kleinen König zu gehen. In welch beklagenswerter Lage sehen wir in beiden Fällen die breite Masse des Volks: im ersteren, wo die Menschen in ihrem Denken scheinbar doch zur Ruhe hätten kommen können, weil ihre Sinne unverdorben sind, weil keine Zivilisation sie angreift und insbesondere weil sie der gegenseitigen Hilfe wie den gegenseitigen Verletzungen innerhalb einer Gemeinschaft sozusagen entfremdet sind und sie dadurch unmittelbarer unter dem Schutz der Vorsehung stehen – selbst dort hatte man Todesqualen schlimm wie oder schlimmer noch als Vögte, Schulden und das Elend eines zivilisierten Lebens zu ertragen. Das Ganze scheint darauf hinauszulaufen, daß der Mensch von Anbeginn an »ein ärmlich zweizinkig Geschöpf« ist, ausgeliefert derselben Unbill wie die Tiere des Walds, dazu bestimmt, Härten oder Ängste welcher Art auch zu erdulden. Wenn er auch Schritt für Schritt seine äußere Lage und Bequemlichkeit verbessert – auf jeder Stufe, jedem Absatz erwartet ihn doch eine neuerliche Reihe von Plagen: er ist sterblich, und noch immer steht über ihm ein Himmel mit seinen Sternen. Die packendste Frage, die wir uns stellen können, lautet: Bis zu welchem Grad glücklich läßt sich die Menschheit durch die beharrlichen Bemühungen eines so selten aufscheinenden Sokrates machen? Ich kann mir solch Glück bis zum Extrem gesteigert vorstellen – doch worin endet es unweigerlich? Im Tod. Und wer kann sich in diesem Fall mit dem Tod abfinden. – Die ganzen Sorgen des Lebens, die man nun über eine Reihe von Jahren hinweg wegsteckt, würden sich dann aufstauen für die letzten Tage im Leben eines Wesens, das, anstatt den Tod zu begrüßen, diese Welt verließe wie

Eva das Paradies. Tatsächlich aber glaube ich auch gar nicht an diese Art von Vervollkommnung – die Natur der Welt wird sie genausowenig zulassen wie die Bewohner der Welt, die ihr entsprechen. Laßt die Fische im Winter das Eis von den Flüssen wegphilosophieren, und sie werden immerfort herumspielen in der lauen Wonne des Sommers. Denkt an die Pole und die Wüsten Afrikas, an Strudel und Vulkane – *sie* laßt die Menschen beseitigen, und ich werde sagen, daß sie vielleicht zu irdischem Glück gelangen. Der Punkt, bis zu dem der Mensch kommen kann, liegt auf gleicher Höhe mit einem Parallelzustand in der unbeseelten Natur und nicht höher. Nehmen wir beispielsweise an, eine Rose habe Empfindungen; sie blüht an einem schönen Morgen, amüsiert sich. Da aber kommt kalter Wind, heiße Sonne – sie kann ihnen nicht entgehn, kann diesen Plagen nichts entgegensetzen, sie gehören zur Welt wie die Rose selbst. Ebensowenig kann der Mensch allem zum Trotz glücklich sein – die weltlichen Elemente nagen doch an seiner Natur. – Unter Irregeleiteten und Abergläubischen ist der übliche Beiname für diese Welt »ein Jammertal«, aus dem wir durch ein willkürliches Eingreifen Gottes erlöst und in den Himmel geführt würden. Welche begrenzte, kurzsichtige, beschränkte Vorstellung! Nennt die Welt, wenn ihr wollt, »das Tal der Seelenbildung« – dann werdet ihr auch den Sinn der Welt erkennen (ich spreche nun aufs Ehrfürchtigste von der menschlichen Natur, von der ich annehme, daß sie unsterblich ist, was ich wiederum voraussetze, um Euch einen Gedanken zu verdeutlichen, der mir einfiel zu ihr). Ich sage *Seelenbildung*, unterscheide also Seele und Intelligenz. Es mag Millionen von Intelligenzen oder auch Funken der Göttlichkeit geben – Seelen sind sie nicht, ehe sie nicht eine Identität erworben haben, ehe nicht jede persönlich sie selbst ist. Intelligenzen sind Atome erkennender Wahrnehmung – sie wissen und sehen und sind rein, kurz: sie sind Gott. Wie aber werden Seelen gebildet? Wie aber wird jenen Funken, die Gott sind, Identität verliehen werden, so daß jeder erst eine seiner individuellen Existenz entsprechende

Glückseligkeit besitzt? Wie anders als durch das Medium einer Welt wie dieser? Ich möchte diese Frage gern ausführlich betrachten, weil ich hinter ihr ein besseres Heilssystem als die christliche Religion sehe – oder eher noch ein System der Geist-Schöpfung. Zustande kommt letztere durch drei bedeutsame Stoffe, die eine Reihe von Jahren aufeinander einwirken. Diese drei Stoffe sind die *Intelligenz,* das *menschliche Herz,* (zum Unterschied von Intelligenz oder Geist) und die *Welt* oder der *Elementarraum,* der geeignet ist für das richtige Wirken von *Geist und Herz* aufeinander, um die *Seele* oder die *Intelligenz, die Identitätsvermögen besitzen soll,* zu formen. Ich kann schwerlich ausdrücken, was ich nur undeutlich erkenne – und doch glaube ich es zu erkennen. Damit Ihr klarer urteilen könnt, will ich es in eine möglichst einfache Form bringen: Nennen wir die *Welt* eine Schule, gegründet, um kleinen Kindern das Lesen beizubringen. Nennen wir das *menschliche Herz* die *Fibel,* die in dieser Schule benutzt wird, und nennen wir schließlich das *Kind, das lesen kann,* die *Seele,* gebildet durch jene *Schule* und ihre *Fibel.* Seht ihr nicht, wie notwendig eine Welt voller Leid und Bedrängnis ist, um eine Intelligenz zu schulen und zu einer Seele zu formen? Ein Ort, an dem das Herz fühlen und leiden muß auf tausenderlei Art! Und nicht bloß eine Fibel ist das Herz – es ist des Geistes Bibel, ist des Geistes Erfahrung, es ist die Brust, an der der Geist oder die Intelligenz seine Identität saugt. So verschiedenartig die Leben der Menschen sind, so verschiedenartig werden ihre Seelen, und so formt Gott individuelle Wesen, Seelen, Seelen mit Identität aus den Funken seines eigenen Seins. Dies erscheint mir die grobe Skizze eines Heilssystems, das unsere Vernunft und Menschenwürde nicht beleidigt. Ich bin überzeugt, daß so manche Schwierigkeiten, unter denen Christen sich abmühen, mit ihm verschwänden. Eine kommt mir auch sogleich in den Sinn: das Seelenheil der Kinder. In ihnen kehrt der Funke oder die Intelligenz zu Gott zurück – er hatte keine Zeit zu lernen oder verwandelt zu werden vom Herzen, dem Sitz der menschlichen Leidenschaften. – So recht verallgemeinernd vermutet man, die christliche Lehre sei den alten persischen und griechischen Philosophen nachgeahmt worden. Weshalb sollten sie jene Einfachheit dem allgemeinen Verständnis nicht noch verständlicher gemacht haben, indem sie in der gleichen Weise Mittler und Charaktere einführten wie in der heidnischen Mythologie Abstraktionen personifiziert wurden? Ich halte es ernstlich für wahrscheinlich, daß aus jenem System der Seelenbildung sämtliche faßbareren und persönlicheren Erlösungslehren hervorgingen, unter Zarathustriern, Christen und Hindus. Denn so wie ein Teil der menschlichen Gattung seinen gemeißelten Jupiter haben muß, so muß ein anderer Teil seinen faßbaren und mit Namen versehenen Mittler und Erlöser haben, seinen Christus, Oromanes oder Wischnu. Sollte, was ich gesagt habe, nicht deutlich genug sein – und ich befürchte es fast – dann will ich Euch zum Ausgangspunkt meiner Gedankenreihe zurückführen: Ich glaube, ich begann damit, zu betrachten, wie der Mensch durch die Umstände geformt wird – und was sind Umstände? – was anderes als Prüfsteine für sein Herz? – und was sind Prüfsteine? – was anderes als Prüfungen seines Herzens? – und was sind Prüfungen seines Herzens anderes als die Festiger und Umwandler seiner Natur? – und was ist seine umgewandelte Natur anderes als seine Seele? – und was war seine Seele, ehe sie auf die Welt kam und diesen Prüfungen, Umwandlungen und Vervollkommnungen ausgesetzt war? – Eine Intelligenz – ohne Identität – und wie kann jene Identität geformt werden? Durch das Medium des Herzens – und wie anders kann das Herz dieses Medium werden als in einer Welt der Umstände? […]

An Mary-Ann Jeffery

Wentworth Place – Hampstead – [31. Mai 1819]

[...] Bis jetzt habe ich mich kaum mehr um die Welt bekümmert als eine Fliege – meine Schwierigkeiten entsprangen alle der Einbildung. Über meinen Bruder George lief stets, was ich mit der Welt zu schaffen hatte. Jetzt merke ich, ich muß mich mit ihr herumschlagen, muß eine vorteilhafte Stellung einnehmen und anfangen zu kämpfen, muß wählen zwischen Verzweiflung und Energie. – Ich wähle letztere, auch wenn die Welt mir gegenüber einen quäkerischen Ausdruck angenommen hat, den ich früher für unmöglich hielt –

Nichts bringt je zurück, was sich verlor
An hellem Glanz im Gras und Herrlichkeit im Flor

Früher hielt ich das für den Traum eines Melancholikers –. [...]

An Mary-Ann Jeffery

Wentworth Place [9. Juni 1819]

[...] Ihr Rat, den Indienfahrer betreffend, ist ein sehr weiser Rat, denn er kommt mir eben recht, obwohl Sie in dem Punkt, daß er die geistigen Energien angreift, ein klein wenig im Irrtum sind: das wäre ganz im Gegenteil der denkbar beste Weg, dieselben zu stärken. Mit Menschen zusammen sein zu müssen, die sich nicht um einen kümmern, mit denen man keine Berührungspunkte hat, das zwingt den Geist, aus seinen eigenen Quellen zu schöpfen und erlaubt ihm, über die unterschiedlichen menschlichen Charaktere nachzusinnen und sie mit der Gelassenheit des Botanikers zu klassifizieren. So ein Indienfahrer ist eine kleine Welt. Einer der wesentlichen Gründe, weshalb die Engländer die größten Schriftsteller der Welt hervorgebracht haben, liegt darin, daß die englische Welt sie zu Lebzeiten schlecht behandelt und nach ihrem Tode gehätschelt hat. Im allgemeinen hat man sie auf die Seitenwege des Lebens abgedrängt, und sie haben die Fäulnis der Gesellschaft zu spüren bekommen. Sie wurden nicht wie Italiens Raphaele behandelt. Und wo ist der Engländer, und zugleich der Dichter, der anläßlich der Taufe eines der Pferde seines Helden ein grandioses Gelage gegeben hätte, wie etwa Boyardo es tat. Er besaß ein Schloß in den Apenninen. Er war ein adliger Romanzendichter, kein elender und erhabener Dichter des menschlichen Herzens. Shakespeares mittlere Lebensjahre waren ganz umwölkt, seine Tage waren nicht glücklicher als die eines Hamlet, der Shakespeare in seinem Alltagsleben vielleicht mehr ähnelt als irgendeine andere seiner Gestalten. Ben Jonson war ein gemeiner Soldat und focht in den Niederlanden im Angesicht zweier Heere Mann gegen Mann mit einem französischen Soldaten und erschlug ihn. Trotz alledem will ich nicht an Bord eines Indienfahrers gehen, mich nicht, nur um des Beispiels willen, kopfüber ins Dunkel stürzen: Ich ahne wohl, daß meine Berufung noch kommt, und das in hohem Maße. In letzter Zeit war ich sehr träge, sehr voll Widerwillen gegen das Schreiben, zum einen wegen des überwältigenden Eindrucks, den unsere toten Dichter auf mich gemacht haben, und zum anderen, weil meine Sucht nach Ruhm nicht mehr so stark ist. Ich hoffe, ich bin jetzt ein wenig mehr Philosoph als zuvor und folglich ein bißchen weniger verseschmiedendes Schoßhündchen. Ich habe nichts mehr in Druck gegeben, sonst hätte ich es Ihnen doch selbstverständlich geschickt. [...]

An Fanny Brawne

Shanklin, Insel Wight, Donnerstag [1. Juli 1819]

Meine liebste Lady,

ich bin froh, daß ich keine Gelegenheit fand, einen Brief abzuschicken, den ich Euch am Dienstagabend schrieb: Er glich allzusehr einem aus Rousseaus »Héloïse«. Heute morgen bin ich vernünftiger. Der Morgen ist für mich die einzig rechte Zeit, einem schönen Mädchen zu schreiben, das ich so sehr liebe. Denn in der Nacht, wenn der einsame Tag zu Ende ist und die einsame, stille musiklose Kammer meiner Rückkunft harrt wie eine Gruft, glaubt mir, da gewinnt meine Leidenschaft ganz und gar die Oberhand. Da möcht ich nicht, daß Ihr jene Rhapsodien sehen könntet, die ich bei mir nie und nimmer für möglich gehalten hätte und die ich bei anderen oft verlacht habe, denn ich befürchte, Ihr könntet mich sonst für allzu unglücklich halten oder gar für ein wenig verrückt. Jetzt sitze ich an einem sehr hübschen Landhausfenster mit Blick auf schönes, hügeliges Land, sehe das Meer ein klein wenig durchschimmern; es ist ein herrlicher Morgen. Wie federnd könnte mein Geist sein, wie glücklich könnte ich hier leben und Atem schöpfen und frei wie ein junger Hirsch an diesen schönen Küsten mich tummeln, bedrückte mich nicht die Erinnerung an Euch so schwer. Noch nie habe ich eine lange Reihe von Tagen ungetrübten Glücks erlebt: Immer hat der Tod oder die Krankheit eines nahen Menschen meine Stunden verdüstert, und nun, da solche Sorgen einmal nicht auf mir lasten, ist es, wie Ihr zugeben müßt, sehr arg, daß mich ein Schmerz anderer Art quälen soll. Fragt Euch selbst, meine Liebe, ob es nicht sehr grausam von Euch war, mich so zu fesseln und mir so die Freiheit zu rauben. Wollt Ihr mir das gestehen in dem Brief, den Ihr mir unverzüglich schreiben müßt, und alles tun, um mich zu trösten? Macht ihn opulent wie einen Mohntrunk, um mich zu betäuben. Schreibt nur die zartesten Worte, und küßt das Blatt, daß ich wenigstens meine

Lippen dorthin legen kann, wo die Euren gewesen sind. Ich selber weiß freilich nicht, wie ich meine Ergebenheit an eine so anmutige Gestalt zum Ausdruck bringen soll: Mir fehlt ein Wort, das »lichter« ist als »Licht«, ein Wort, das schöner ist als »schön«. Fast möchte ich mir wünschen, wir wären Schmetterlinge und unser Leben währte nur drei Sommertage lang. Drei solche Tage mit Euch könnte ich mit mehr Entzükken erfüllen als fünfzig gewöhnliche Jahre je zu geben vermöchten. [...]

An Fanny Brawne

8. Juli [1819]

[...] Warum soll ich nicht von Deiner Schönheit sprechen, wo ich Dich doch ohne sie niemals hätte lieben können. Ich kann mir für eine solche Liebe, wie ich sie für Dich empfinde, keinen anderen Anfang als die Schönheit vorstellen. Es mag eine Liebe geben, vor der ich, ohne jeden Hohn, die allergrößte Hochachtung habe und die ich bei anderen bewundere, doch hat diese nicht den Reichtum, die Üppigkeit, die vollkommene Gestalt, den Zauber der Liebe, die mein Herz begehrt. Drum laß mich von Deiner Schönheit reden, wenn ich mich damit auch selber in Gefahr bringe; wenn Du nämlich so grausam zu mir bist, ihre Macht auch anderswo zu versuchen. Du sagst, Du hättest Angst, ich könnte glauben, daß Du mich nicht liebst – indem Du so etwas sagst, steigerst Du noch mein Verlangen, Dir nah zu sein. Ich mache hier eifrig Gebrauch von meinen Talenten, nicht einen Tag lasse ich vergehen, ohne ein paar Blankverse zu schmieden oder ein paar Reime zusammenzukoppeln, und da muß ich gestehen, daß ich Dich (da wir einmal davon sprechen) nur um so mehr liebe, da ich glaube, daß ich Dir um meiner selbst willen gefallen habe und wegen nichts sonst. Ich habe Frauen getroffen, die, glaube ich, wahrhaftig gern ein Gedicht geheiratet und einen Roman zum Brautvater gehabt hätten. [...]

An John Hamilton Reynolds

[Insel Wight, 11. Juli 1819]

[...] Ich bin mit dem Akt fertig und in der Zeit vor Beginn des zweiten recht gut vorangekommen mit »Lamia«, denn ich habe den ersten Teil, der aus rund 400 Zeilen besteht, beendet. Ich hoffe zuversichtlich auf Erfolg, da ich jetzt bewußter denn je mein Vorgehen abwäge – sollte ich aber vor der Welt versagen, bin ich's auch so zufrieden. Und hier (denn ich weiß, Dir liegt mein Wohl am Herzen wie einem Bruder) kann ich nur wiederholen, was ich zu George sagte: so gern ich genösse, was das Leben an Annehmlichkeiten bereithält – ich bin in keinster Weise niedergeschlagen über andere Aussichten. Dafür habe ich zu viele nachdenkliche Tage verbracht und mir zu viele Nächte hindurch Vernunft gepredigt, und sie alle wären ja wirklich sinnlos, hätten sie mich nicht nach und nach gelehrt, die Angelegenheiten der Welt mit einer gesunden Nüchternheit zu betrachten. In der letzten Zeit habe ich mich gemausert: nicht in neue Federn und Flügel – die sind verschwunden, und an ihrer Stelle hoffe ich zwei ausdauernde sublunarische Beine zu erhalten. Ich habe mich verwandelt, aber nicht von einer Puppe in einen Schmetterling, sondern umgekehrt – habe zwei kleine Gucklöcher, durch die ich auf die Bühne der Welt schauen kann, und diese Welt habe ich seit unserer Ankunft hier fast vergessen. Wenn ich mich anfangs zum Schreiben hinsetzte, konnte ich die Notwendigkeit dazu kaum ernstnehmen – es erschien mir ein ganz wunderliches Unterfangen. Dasselbe Korn aber, das heute so schön ist, als hätte es gestern erst begonnen zu reifen, ist schon für den Markt bestimmt. Warum also sollte ich empfindlich sein. – [...]

An John Hamilton Reynolds

Winchester, [24. August 1819]

[...] Mit jedem Tag wächst meine Überzeugung, daß gutes Schreiben nächst gutem Handeln das höchste Ding auf Erden ist, und so wird mir das »Verlorene Paradies« zu einem noch größeren Wunder. Je mehr ich erkenne, was mein Fleiß mit der Zeit zu erreichen vermag, um so mehr schwillt mein Herz vor Stolz und Eigensinn. Ich weiß, ich habe es in der Hand, ein beliebter Schriftsteller zu werden – ich weiß, ich bin stark genug, das vergiftende Urteil des Publikums von mir zu weisen. Mein eigenes Wesen, von dessen Werden ich überzeugt bin, bedeutet mir mehr als all die Schatten in Männer- und Frauengestalt, die ein Königreich bevölkern. Die Seele ist eine Welt in sich und hat im eigenen Haus zu tun genug. Die Menschen, die ich kenne und die gleichsam ein Teil von mir geworden sind, könnte ich nicht missen, der Rest der Menschheit jedoch ist mir genauso unwirklich wie Miltons Hierarchien. Ich glaube, wenn mein Herz auf lange Dauer frei und gesund wäre und meine Lunge so stark wie die eines Ochsen, daß ich dem Ansturm extremer Gedanken und Gefühle gewachsen wäre, ohne müde zu werden, könnte ich mein Leben in fast völliger Einsamkeit zubringen, und sollte es achtzig Jahre währen. Aber ich fühle es, mein Körper ist zu schwach, um mich in die Höhe zu tragen; ich muß mich ständig bezähmen und muß trachten, nichts zu sein. Es wär umsonst, wollte ich versuchen, Ihnen vernünftiger zu schreiben: ich kann von nichts reden als von mir selbst, und was kann ich anderes sagen, als was ich empfinde? Wenn Sie meinen, Sie müßten mich wegen dieses Erregungszustands, in dem ich mich befinde, bedauern, so will ich die Flut Ihrer Gefühle in das rechte Flußbett lenken und erklären, daß dies der einzig geeignete Zustand für die beste Art von Dichtung ist – und das allein kümmert mich, allein dafür lebe ich. Verzeihen Sie, daß ich das Blatt nicht bis zum Ende vollschreibe, Briefe werden für mich so ermüdend, daß ich das nächste Mal, wenn ich von London wegfahre, alle bitten werde, sie mir zu erlassen. Vertrauen in meine Beständigkeit und der Verzicht auf meine Briefe, das wäre die höchste Gunstbezeigung, die ich mir vorstellen kann. [...]

An Charles Brown

[23. September 1819]

[...] Laß Dich durch mich nicht beunruhigen. Ich meine damit nicht, daß Du überhaupt nicht an mich denken sollst, aber beruhigt sein kannst, wenn Du an mich denkst – denn ich versichere Dir: ich bin soweit davon entfernt, unglücklich zu sein, wie nur möglich. Eingebildete Leiden haben mir stets mehr Qualen bereitet als wirkliche. Du weißt das nur zu gut. Wirkliche werden nie eine andere Wirkung auf mich haben als mich anzutreiben, von ihnen loszukommen oder sie zu umgehen. Das läßt sich leicht erklären. Unsere eingebildeten Schmerzen werden durch unsere Leidenschaften heraufbeschworen und durch leidenschaftliches Gefühl genährt; unsere wirklichen kommen von selbst, und ihnen stellt sich eine abstrakte Willensanstrengung entgegen. Wirkliche Leiden sind die Verdränger der Leidenschaft. Die eingebildeten nageln den Menschen als Leidenden fest, wie an ein Kreuz; die wirklichen spornen den Handelnden in ihm an. Ich wünschte, Du könntest mit einem Blick mein Herz für Dich ermessen. Einzig in einer hohen Stimmung kann ich dieses Wort ansonsten zu Papier bringen – nur im Gedicht. [...]

An George und Georgiana Keats

Winchester, Freitag [17.–27. September 1819]

[...] Die Welt hat mich nicht gut behandelt, und doch auch wieder unerhört gut. Ich kenne niemanden, dem sich so viele Geldbeutel öffnen würden wie mir – wenn ich nur meinen Nutzen daraus ziehen könnte, was ich aber nicht kann, weil die Besitzer dieser Geldbeutel allesamt nicht reich sind. Ich ertrage es gar nicht, lange bei Deiner momentanen Lage zu verweilen; wenn das Unglück so handgreiflich ist, sind wir schon froh, ihm und dem Gedanken daran entrinnen zu können. Ich kann mir nicht helfen, ich finde, dieser Mr. Audubon ist kein Ehrenmann. Warum ließ er Dich in dem Glauben, er sei ein vermögender Mann? Oder haben sich seine Verhältnisse so plötzlich geändert? Ehrlich gesagt, ich glaube nicht, daß Du der Welt gewachsen bist, jedenfalls nicht dem amerikanischen Sumpf. Aber, lieber Gott, wer kann diese Zufälle vorhersehen, Du hast Dein Bestes getan. Nimm die Sache so gelassen auf, wie Du es vermagst, und handle, auch wenn Du zuverlässig mit Hilfe aus England rechnen kannst, als ob keine Hilfe in Sicht wäre. Meine besteht, soviel ist gewiß, in einer leidlich gelungenen Tragödie – die mir mit Sicherheit ein Vermögen eingebracht hätte, wenn ich nicht, als ich eben damit zu Ende war, von Keans Absicht gehört hätte, nach Amerika zu gehen. Das war die schlechteste Nachricht, die mich erreichen konnte. Kein anderer Schauspieler als Kean kann die Hauptrolle übernehmen. Im Covent Garden würde sie höchstwahrscheinlich durchfallen. Wenn sie aber sogar dort Erfolg hätte, würde sie mich aus dem Sumpf ziehen. Ich meine den Sumpf eines schlechten Rufes, der immer mehr gegen mich ansteigt. Den Modeliteraten klingt mein Name vulgär, für die bin ich ein kleiner Weberjunge – eine Tragödie würde mich aus dieser Kalamität rausholen. Und eine Kalamität ist es, was unseren Geldbeutel betrifft. Aber sei Du nicht noch niedergeschlagener als ich; ich fühle, daß ich mit wirklichem

Unheil besser fertig werde als mit eingebildetem. Sobald ich merke, daß mich wieder einmal Wehleidigkeit überkommt, reiße ich mich hoch, wasche mich, ziehe mir ein sauberes Hemd an, bürste Haar und Kleider, binde mir ordentlich die Schuhbänder zu und putze mich ordentlich heraus, ganz so, als ob ich ausgehen wollte, und dann setze ich mich sauber und wohlig hin und schreibe. Das ist für mich die größte Erleichterung. Im übrigen gewöhne ich mich langsam auch daran, Sinnesfreuden zu entbehren. Mitten in der Welt lebe ich wie ein Eremit. Ich habe vergessen, wie man sich Kurzweil schafft und sich daran erfreut. Ich fühle in mir die Kraft, alles auszuhalten – jedes Elend, selbst Gefangenschaft, solange ich weder Weib noch Kinder habe. Du magst nun sagen, die Deinen seien Dein einziger Trost – es muß wohl so sein. [...]

Auf der nächsten Seite will ich ein bißchen über Politik sprechen. In jeder Epoche standen in England zwei- bis dreihundert Jahre lang Fragen von großem allgemeinem Interesse auf der Tagesordnung, so daß man, wie groß das Getöse auch sein mag, doch schwerlich irgendwelche grundlegenden Veränderungen in der Regierung vorhersagen kann, denn Tumulte dieser Art haben unser Land schon oft erschüttert. Alle zivilisierten Länder werden mit der Zeit immer aufgeklärter, und es sollte wohl ein steter Wandel zum Besseren stattfinden. Schau Dir dieses Land heute an und dann erinnere Dich nur der Zeiten, als der bloße Zweifel an der Gerechtigkeit eines im Zweikampf entschiedenen Streites als frevelhaft galt. Seither hat sich Schritt für Schritt alles gewandelt. Drei große Umwälzungen haben sich vollzogen: die erste zum Besseren, die zweite zum Schlechteren und die dritte wiederum zum Besseren. Die erste war die schrittweise Abschaffung der Adelstyrannei, als nämlich die Könige es nützlich fanden, das gemeine Volk zu beschwichtigen, seine Lage zu verbessern und ihm Gerechtigkeit widerfahren zu lassen. Eben zu der Zeit, als die Macht der Barone aufhörte und bevor die stehenden Heere zur Gefahr wurden, da gab es nur wenige Steuern, die Könige wurden vom Volk hoch über den Adel gestellt, und just dieses Volk hielt die Könige an der Kandare. Der Wandel zum Schlechteren in Europa bestand wiederum darin, daß allmählich in Vergessenheit geriet, daß die Könige eine Verpflichtung gegenüber der Menge haben. Es war Usus geworden, daß die Edelleute die unterwürfigen Diener der Könige waren. Da fingen die Könige an, den Adel als die Zierde ihrer Macht, als ihre Sklaven, das Volk indessen als ein Wesen zu betrachten, dessen ganzes Streben darauf gerichtet war, sie einzuschränken. Dann kam in allen Königreichen ein langer Kampf der Könige um die Aufhebung aller Privilegien des Volkes. Die Engländer waren das einzige Volk in Europa, das sich dagegen tüchtig zur Wehr setzte. Unter Heinrich VIII. waren sie Sklaven gewesen, aber unter William III. waren sie Freie, zu einer Zeit also, da die Franzosen unter Ludwig XIV. elende Sklaven waren. Das englische Beispiel und die liberalen Schriftsteller Frankreichs und Englands säten die Saat des Widerstandes gegen die Tyrannei – und die keimte im verborgenen, bis sie in der Französischen Revolution hervorbrach. Diese nahm einen unglücklichen Ausgang. Sie setzte dem raschen Voranschreiten des freien Denkens in England ein Ende und weckte an unserem Hofe die Hoffnung auf eine Rückkehr zum Despotismus des 16. Jahrhunderts. Man hat dieses Ereignis benutzt, um unsere Freiheit auf jede nur erdenkliche Weise zu untergraben. Man verbreitete eine abergläubische Furcht vor allem Neuen und Reformerischen. Gegenwärtig kämpft das englische Volk darum, diesen Aberglauben auszumerzen. Die Not hat es dazu aufgerüttelt. Vielleicht haben die derzeitigen Nöte dieser Nation in dem Punkt auch ihr Gutes, so furchtbar sie andererseits sind. Ich meine also, wie Du siehst, daß die Französische Revolution jener dritten Umwälzung, der Wende zum Besseren, ein zeitweiliges Ende bereitet hat. Nun ist sie wieder in Gang gekommen, und ich denke, sie wird zum Erfolg führen. Das ist kein Kampf zwischen Whigs und Tories, sondern zwischen Recht und Unrecht. Es gibt in England zur Zeit so gut wie keinen Parteiengeist. Die Mode ist, jeder wägt für sich allein ab, was Recht ist und was Unrecht. Ich weiß nur sehr wenig von diesen Dingen. Doch bin ich überzeugt, daß scheinbar geringfügige Ursachen große Veränderungen bewirken. Es gibt kleine Anzeichen, aus denen man schließen kann, wie die Dinge sich entwickeln werden. [...]

Du sprichst von Lord Byron und mir – zwischen uns beiden besteht ein wesentlicher Unterschied. Er beschreibt, was er sieht – ich beschreibe, was ich mir vorstelle. Meine Aufgabe ist die schwerste. Siehst Du den gewaltigen Unterschied? [...]

Das Schreiben hat gegenüber dem Reden den einen Nachteil: Man kann ein Blinzeln oder ein Nicken oder ein Schmunzeln oder ein Lippenkräuseln oder ein Lächeln – o gerechte Güte! nicht schreiben. Man kann nicht schriftlich den Finger an die Nase legen oder Dir gar in die Rippen stoßen oder Dich beim Knopf fassen, doch bei allen besonders lebendigen und spritzigen Stellen meines Briefes müßt Ihr Euch unbedingt vorstellen, ich sehe genauso aus, wie es die epischen Dichter beschreiben: bald hier, bald dort, bald den einen Fuß zur Zimmerdecke gekehrt, bald den anderen, bald die Feder hinterm Ohr, bald den Ellbogen im Munde. Oh, meine Freunde, Ihr verpaßt die Handlung, und Haltung ist alles, sagte schon Fusili, legte seinen Fuß an wie eine Muskete und schoß eine Schwalbe, die eben hinter seiner Schulter vorbeiflog. Und doch, besagte nicht das Wörtchen »nanu!«, »daß man den Finger an die Nase legt?« [...]

Seit damals, als Ihr mich verließet, habe ich mich, wie meine Freunde behaupten, völlig verändert – ich bin nicht mehr derselbe – in diesem Brief bin ich's vielleicht doch, weil man in einem Brief wieder der wird, der man war, als wir uns zuletzt sahen. Ich vermute, auch Ihr habt Euch verändert, jeder tut das. Alle sieben Jahre macht unser Körper eine vollkommene Erneuerung durch – nicht diese Hand war es, die sich vor sieben Jahren gegen Hammond zur Faust ballte. Wir sind wie die Gewandreliquien eines Heiligen, dasselbe und doch nicht dasselbe: Denn die emsigen Mönche flicken sie wieder und wieder, bis kein Fädchen mehr übrig ist von dem ursprünglichen Gewand, und trotzdem zeigen sie's immer noch als das Hemd des heiligen Antonius herum. Das ist auch der Grund, warum sich Menschen, die einstmals Busenfreunde waren, wenn sie eine Reihe von Jahren fern voneinander gelebt haben, kühl begegnen und keiner von beiden weiß, warum das so ist. Es ist einfach so, daß beide sich verändert haben. Bei Menschen, die miteinander leben, hat der eine eine sanfte formende und beeinflussende Macht über den anderen. Sie gleichen sich einander an. Es ist eine unangenehme Vorstellung, daß in sieben Jahren die gleichen Hände einander nicht mehr grüßen können. All das mag durch eine willkürliche und gewaltsame Anstrengung unseres Verstandes beidseitig verhindert werden. Manche meinen, ich hätte nicht mehr die dichterische Glut und das Feuer, das man mir einst nachsagte, vielleicht ist das wirklich wahr, doch hoffe ich, daß ich das ersetzen kann durch größere Gedankentiefe und Ruhe. Ich begnüge mich jetzt häufiger mit Lesen und Nachsinnen, doch zuweilen quälen mich ehrgeizige Gedanken. Ruhiger geht mein Puls, meine Verdauung ist auch besser geworden; ich versuche mich zu zwingen, mich nicht zermürbenden Grübeleien hinzugeben – bin kaum geneigt, selbst die besten Verse aufzuschreiben, wegen des Fiebers, das sie zurücklassen. Ich möchte ohne Fieber schreiben. Ich hoffe, eines Tages werde ich es können. [...]

In seinem Brief von gestern beklagte sich Brown auf das lebhafteste darüber, wie sehr sich Dilkes Haltung verändert hat. Er hat nur noch die »politische Gerechtigkeit« und seinen Jungen im Sinn. Und dabei ist doch die erste politische Pflicht, die ein Mann im Sinn haben sollte, das Glück seiner Freunde. Ich schrieb Brown ein paar Überlegungen zu diesem Thema und erklärte ihm, was ich von Dilkes Charakter halte. Was sich in folgender Quintessenz zusammenfassen läßt: Daß Dilke ein Mensch ist, der sich seiner persönlichen Identität nicht bewußt ist, solange er nicht über alles eine endgültige Meinung hat. Das einzige Mittel, den eigenen Verstand zu schärfen, ist aber, über nichts eine endgültige Meinung zu haben – seinen Geist als Durchfahrt für alle Gedanken offenzuhalten. Nicht nur für ein paar ausgesuchte. Menschen dieses Schlages sind nicht selten. Die halsstarrigen Streithammel, denen man immer wieder begegnet, sind vom selben Stamm. Nie gehen sie an eine Sache heran, die sie nicht vorher entschieden haben. Die wollen sie einem dann einhämmern, und wenn man den Spieß umdreht, denken sie immer noch, man ist im Unrecht. Dilke wird im ganzen Leben nicht die Wahrheit finden, weil er es fortwährend versucht. [...]

An Fanny Keats

Wentworth Place, Dienstag morgen [8. Februar 1820]

Meine liebe Fanny,

gestern abend hatte ich wieder leichtes Fieber, das zum Glück zurückging, und nun fühle ich mich recht wohl, wenn auch schwach wegen der geringen Menge an Nahrung, auf die ich mich beschränken muß. Ich bin sicher, eine Maus würde dabei verhungern. Gestern kam Mrs. Wylie. Ich habe ein sehr angenehmes Krankenzimmer. Man hat mir im vorderen Wohnzimmer, das zur Wiese hinausgeht, zu der auch – wie Du Dich sicherlich erinnerst – Mrs. Dilkes Fenster hinausgehen, auf dem Sofa ein Bett zurechtgemacht. Viel bequemer als so eine triste Stube im Obergeschoß, wo einem das Muster der Bettvorhänge auf die Nerven geht. Außerdem sehe ich alles, was passiert – zum Beispiel jetzt: wenn ich in meinem eigenen Zimmer gewesen wäre, hätte ich nicht sehen können, wie die Kohlen gebracht werden. Am Sonntag zwischen zwölf und eins gewahrte ich einen Krugjungen. Da dachte ich mir, das wird wohl das Ein-Uhr-Bier sein. Alte Frauen mit Spitzentüchern und roten Umhängen und schlichten Hauben sehe ich über die Heide schlurfen. Zigeuner, die auf Hasenfelle und Silberlöffel aus sind. Dann kommt ein Bursche mit einer hölzernen Uhr unterm Arm vorbei, die hundertmal und öfter schlägt. Dann kommt der alte französische Emigrant (der in Frankreich sehr vermögend war), die Hände auf dem Rücken verschränkt und das Gesicht voll politischer Ranküne. Dann kommt Mr. David Lewis, ein sehr gutmütiger, gutaussehender alter Herr, der sehr freundlich war zu Tom, George und mir. Und diese Burschen, die Maurer, laufen immer hin und her. Ich darf auch nicht die beiden alten Jungfern in Well Walk vergessen, die einen Schoßhund in der Mitte führen und ständig um ihn herum sind. Es ist eine fette kleine Bestie, die mit einem Stöckchen mit Elfenbeinspitze angestupst werden muß. Carlo, der Hund von unserer Nachbarin, Mrs. Brawne, und er treffen sich manchmal. Das Schoßhündchen hält Carlo für einen rechten Satansbraten, und seine beiden Frauchen sind derselben Meinung. Und dazu haben sie auch allen Grund – er würde sie alle über den Haufen rennen; einfach so zum Spaß. Ich werd ihm sagen, er soll sich mal die Fabel vom Knaben und den Fröschen durchlesen: obwohl er Zungen und Knochen ja lieber mag. […]

An Fanny Brawne

[Februar (?) 1820]

Meine liebe Fanny,

Deine Mutter soll nicht denken, Du könntest mir schaden, wenn Du abends schreibst. Aus irgendeinem Grunde war Dein Billett von gestern abend nicht so schön für mich wie die vorherigen. Ich möchte so gern, daß Du mich noch *Liebster* nennst. Dich glücklich und frohen Mutes zu wissen, ist mir ein großer Trost – laß mich dennoch glauben, daß Du nicht halb so glücklich bist, wie meine Genesung Dich machen würde. Ich gebe zu, ich bin nervös und halte mich vielleicht für kränker als ich bin. Wenn das so ist, mußt Du mir verzeihen und mich verwöhnen mit jener Zärtlichkeit, die Du mir in anderen Briefen bewiesen hast. Mein süßes Wesen, wenn ich zurückblicke auf die Schmerzen und Qualen, die ich um Dich gelitten habe seit dem Tage, als ich Dich verließ, um nach der Insel Wight zu gehen; die Verzückung, in der ich manche Tage zubrachte und dann wieder das Elend, staune ich nur um so mehr über die Schönheit, die den Zauber so glühend erhalten hat. Wenn ich Dir diese Zeilen hinüberschicke, werde ich im vorderen Wohnzimmer sein und aufpassen, ob Du Dich auf einen Augenblick im Garten zeigst. Ach, diese Krankheit steht wie eine Schranke zwischen Dir und mir! Selbst wenn es mir gut ginge – ich muß, so gut ich kann, zum Philosophen werden. Nun, da ich Gelegenheit hätte, bange, schlaflose Nächte kennenzulernen, erlebe ich, wie sich andere Gedanken einstellen und mich bedrängen. »Wenn ich sterben sollte«, sagte ich mir, »werde ich kein unsterbliches Werk hinterlassen, nichts, wodurch sich meine Freunde meiner voll Stolz erinnern könnten – aber ich habe das Prinzip der Schönheit in allen Dingen geliebt, und wenn ich genügend Zeit gehabt hätte, hätte ich mich wohl in Erinnerung gebracht.« Solche Gedanken kamen mir nur ganz von fern, als ich gesund war und jeder Herzschlag Dir galt – nun teilst Du mein ganzes Denken mit dieser (darf ich das sagen?) »letzten Schwäche edler Geister«. [...]

An Fanny Brawne

[März (?) 1820]

[...] Meine liebste Fanny, ich habe letzte Nacht gut geschlafen und fühle mich darum heute morgen nicht schlechter. Wenn ich mich nicht täusche, wird mir mit jedem Tag leichter auf der Brust. Je näher ein Rennpferd dem Ziel kommt, desto aufgeregter wird es, so fühle ich meine Ungeduld wachsen, während ich vor den Grenzen der Gesundheit ausharre. Vielleicht habe ich Deinetwegen meine Krankheit für schlimmer gehalten, als sie in Wirklichkeit ist: wie schrecklich war die Aussicht, in den Boden zu sinken anstatt in Deine Arme – der Unterschied ist höchst erstaunlich, Liebste. Der Tod muß zuletzt kommen; der Mensch muß sterben, wie Shallow sagt; doch bevor dies mein Schicksal ist, möchte ich gern versuchen, ob so ein süßes Geschöpf wie Du mir nicht noch größere Freuden zu geben vermag als Du sie mir schon gegeben hast. Laß mich noch ein paar mehr Jahre vor mir haben, und ich werde nicht sterben, ohne daß man meiner gedenkt. Paß auf Dich auf, Liebe, damit wir beide im Sommer wohlauf sind. Das Schreiben ermüdet mich durchaus nicht, ich muß doch nur hier und da ein paar Zeilen einsetzen, eine Arbeit, die einem auf die Nerven geht, wenn Körper und Geist bei Kräften sind, die mir aber gerade recht kommt, weil ich nichts weiter tun kann.

Von ganzem Herzen Dein
J. K. –

An Fanny Brawne

Dienstag morgen – [Mai (?) 1820]

Mein liebstes Mädchen,

ich schrieb Dir gestern einen Brief in der Annahme, ich würde Deine Mutter sehen. Ich will egoistisch genug sein, ihn Dir zu schicken, wenn ich auch weiß, er wird Dir ein wenig wehtun, denn ich möchte, daß Du begreifst, wie unglücklich ich aus Liebe zu Dir bin und wie ich Dich mit aller Macht dazu bringen will, Dein ganzes Herz mir zu geben, dessen ganzes Dasein von Dir abhängt. Du kannst keinen Schritt gehen noch einen Lidschlag tun, ohne daß es mir einen Stich ins Herz gibt. Ich begehre Dich. Denke an nichts als an mich! Leb nicht, als ob es mich gar nicht gäbe. Vergiß mich nicht. Aber habe ich denn ein Recht zu sagen, daß Du mich vergißt? Vielleicht denkst Du den ganzen Tag an mich? Habe ich denn ein Recht zu wollen, daß Du meinetwegen unglücklich bist? Du würdest mir verzeihen, daß ich es möchte, wenn Du wüßtest, wie ungeheuer leidenschaftlich es mich danach verlangt, von Dir geliebt zu werden. Und damit Du mich so lieben kannst, wie ich Dich liebe, darfst Du an keinen anderen als an mich denken und schon gar nicht solchen Satz schreiben. Gestern und heute früh hatte ich eine süße Vision: Ich sah Dich die ganze Zeit in Deinem Schäferinnenkostüm. Wie schmerzten meine Sinne! Wie ging mir das Herz davon auf! Wie waren meine Augen da voll Tränen! Wahrhaftig, ich glaube, eine wirkliche Liebe reicht aus, das weiteste Herz zu erfüllen. Daß Du allein in die Stadt gehst – es hat mir einen Schlag versetzt, als ich davon erfuhr, obwohl ich es ja erwartet habe. *Versprich mir, daß Du es eine Zeitlang sein läßt, bis es mir besser geht.* Versprich mir das, und bedecke das Papier über und über mit den zärtlichsten Namen. Wenn Du das nicht gutwillig tun kannst, sag es mir, meine Liebste – sag, was Du denkst – gib's zu, wenn Dein Herz zu sehr an der Welt hängt. Vielleicht kann ich Dich dann mit mehr Abstand sehen und bin nicht mehr imstande, so sehr von Dir Besitz zu ergreifen. Wenn Du einen Lieblingsvogel aus dem Käfig lassen müßtest, wie würdest Du ihn mit Blicken verzehren, solange er noch in Sicht wär; wär er dann außer Sichtweite, würdest Du Dich ein bißchen fassen. Wenn Du mir – sollte es an dem sein – gestehen wolltest, wie vieler Dinge Du außer mir bedarfst, dann werde ich vielleicht froher sein können, viel weniger gemartert. Ja, magst Du nun ausrufen, wie egoistisch, wie grausam, mich meine Jugend nicht genießen zu lassen! Zu wollen, daß ich unglücklich bin! Das mußt Du sein, wenn Du mich liebst – bei meiner Seele, ich kann mich mit nichts anderem bescheiden. Wenn Du Dich wirklich, wie man so sagt, auf einer Gesellschaft amüsieren, wenn Du den Leuten zulächeln kannst und Dir wünschst, sie sollen Dich *jetzt* bewundern, dann hast Du mich nie geliebt und wirst mich nie lieben. Für mich bedeutet Leben einzig und allein die Gewißheit Deiner Liebe – überzeuge mich davon, meine Süßeste. Wenn ich nicht irgendwie davon überzeugt werde, sterbe ich vor Seelenqual. Wenn wir lieben, dürfen wir nicht wie die anderen Männer und Frauen leben. Ich kann das Giftkraut Eisenhut der Modetorheiten, der Ziererei und des Klatsches nicht vertragen. Du mußt mein sein, um auf der Folterbank zu sterben, wenn ich es von Dir verlange. Ich will nicht behaupten, ich hätte mehr Gefühl als meine Mitmenschen – aber ich möchte, daß Du Dir meine Briefe, die sanften und die groben, ernsthaft noch einmal ansiehst und Dich fragst, ob der Mensch, der sie geschrieben hat, noch viel länger imstande sein wird, die Seelenqualen und die Ungewißheit auszuhalten, die zu bereiten Du auf besondere Weise geschaffen bist. – Meine körperliche Genesung nützt mir gar nichts, wenn Du mir nicht ganz und gar gehörst, sobald ich wieder wohlauf bin. Um Gottes willen, rette mich – oder sag mir, daß Dich meine Leidenschaft zu sehr erschreckt. Noch einmal: Gott segne Dich

J.K.

Nein, meine süße Fanny – ich habe unrecht. Ich will nicht, daß Du unglücklich bist und will es doch. Ich muß es wollen, solange es eine so süße Schönheit gibt – meine Liebste, mein Liebling! Leb wohl! Ich küsse Dich – o diese Qualen!

An Fanny Brawne

[Juni (?) 1820]

[...] Die Menschen sind rachsüchtig – achte nicht auf sie. Tu nichts als mich zu lieben – könnte ich dessen sicher sein, dann wären Leben und Gesundheit der Himmel für mich, und der Tod selbst wäre weniger schmerzvoll. Ich würde so gern an die Unsterblichkeit glauben – ich werde es nie schaffen, Dir ganz Lebwohl zu sagen. Ist mir bestimmt, hier glücklich zu sein mit Dir – wie kurz ist dann das längste Leben. Ich möchte an die Unsterblichkeit glauben – ich möchte für immer mit Dir leben. [...] Laß mich sicher sein, daß Du mein Herz und meine Seele bist, und ich könnte glücklicher sterben als andernfalls leben. Findest Du mich grausam, findest Du, daß ich Dich gekränkt habe – überdenk es noch einmal und schau mir ins Herz. Meine Liebe für Dich ist »wahr wie der Wahrheit Einfalt und einfältiger als ein Kind der Wahrheit«. Ich glaube, ich habe es bereits gesagt: Wie konnte ich Dich kränken wollen? Wie drohen, Dich zu verlassen? Doch nicht vor lauter Unmut über Dich, sondern vor lauter Erbärmlichkeit in mir selbst. [...]

An Fanny Brawne

Ich schreibe dies erst ganz zuletzt,
damit kein Aug es sehen kann.

[August (?) 1820]

Mein liebstes Mädchen,

ich wollte, Du könntest etwas erfinden, daß ich ohne Dich ganz froh sein kann. Mit jeder Stunde richtet sich all mein Sinnen nur immer mehr auf Dich. Alles andere schmeckt wie Spreu in meinem Munde. Es scheint mir beinahe unmöglich, nach Italien zu gehen. Tatsache ist, daß ich Dich nicht verlassen kann und keine Minute Zufriedenheit werde kosten können, bis es dem Schicksal gefällt, mich mit Dir für immer zusammenleben zu lassen. Aber in diesem Stil will ich nicht fortfahren. Ein gesunder Mensch wie Du kann sich die Schrecken nicht vorstellen, die Nerven und ein Gemüt wie das meine durchmachen. Welche Insel schlagen Deine Freunde vor, auf die wir uns zurückziehen sollen? Ich wäre glücklich, mit Dir allein dorthin zu gehen, aber in Gesellschaft, das würde ich ablehnen. Die Verleumdungen und Eifersüchtleien unter den neuen Kolonisten, die keinen anderen Zeitvertreib haben, sind unerträglich. Gestern besuchte mich Mr. Dilke und machte mir damit bei weitem mehr Kummer als Freude. Ich werde nie mehr in der Lage sein, die Gesellschaft der Leute zu ertragen, die sich in Elm Cottage und Wentworth Place zu treffen pflegten. Die letzten zwei Jahre schmecken mir wie Messing auf dem Gaumen. Wenn ich nicht mit Dir leben kann, will ich allein leben. Ich glaube nicht, daß meine Gesundheit sich sehr bessern wird, solange ich von Dir getrennt bin. Trotzdem bin ich nicht geneigt, Dich zu sehen – ich kann keine Lichtblitze ertragen, wenn ich hernach wieder in meine Düsternis zurückfalle. Ich bin jetzt nicht so unglücklich, wie ich wohl wäre, wenn ich Dich gestern gesehen hätte. Mit Dir glücklich zu sein, scheint so eine Unmöglichkeit! Dazu braucht es einen glücklicheren Stern als den meinen! Das wird nie sein. Ich füge eine Stelle aus einem Deiner Briefe bei und möchte gern, daß Du sie ein wenig änderst – Ich möchte (wenn Du so gut sein willst), daß Du mir die Sache nicht gar so kühl sagst. Wenn meine Gesundheit es erlaubte, könnte ich Dir ein Gedicht schreiben, das ich im Kopf habe, das Menschen, die in solcher Lage sind wie ich, ein Trost sein könnte. Ich würde jemanden darstellen, der, wie ich, einen Menschen liebt, der in solcher Freiheit lebt wie Du. Shakespeare bringt immer alles ganz souverän aufs Wesentliche. Hamlets Herz war von ebensolchem Elend erfüllt wie das meine, als er zu Ophelia sprach: »Geh in ein Kloster, geh, geh!« Wahrhaftig, am liebsten möchte ich die ganze Sache sofort aufgeben, ich würde gern sterben. Diese grausame Welt, der Du zulächelst, macht mich krank. Ich hasse die Männer und noch mehr die Frauen. Ich sehe für die Zukunft nichts als Dornen – ganz gleich, wo ich nächsten Winter bin, ob in Italien oder nirgendwo. Brown wird in Deiner Nähe sein mit seinen Unverschämtheiten – ich sehe keine Hoffnung, jemals zur Ruhe zu kommen. Nimm an, ich bin in Rom – ich würde Dich dort ja wie in einem Zauberspiegel sehen, wie Du zu jeder Tages- und

Nachtzeit in die Stadt gehst und wieder heimkehrst. Ich wollte, Du könntest mir ein wenig Vertrauen zur menschlichen Natur ins Herz träufeln. Ich kann keines aufbringen. Die Welt ist zu brutal für mich. Ich bin froh, daß es etwas wie das Grab gibt – ich weiß genau, ich werde nicht eher Ruhe finden, als bis ich dort bin. Das eine jedenfalls will ich mir gönnen, weder Dilke noch Brown noch einen ihrer Freunde jemals wiederzusehen. Ich wollte, ich läge voller Vertrauen in Deinen Armen oder der Blitz träfe mich.

Gott schütze Dich
J. K.

An Charles Brown

[14. August 1820]

Mein lieber Brown,

vielleicht haben Sie weder von *** noch von *** oder sonst irgendwie nicht erfahren, daß ein Anfall von Bluthusten nebst all seinen kräftezehrenden Folgen mich so lange gehindert hat, Ihnen zu schreiben. Nun habe ich Stoff für einen sehr langen Brief, aber nichts neues; ich muß also alles kurz machen. Ich werde ein Geständnis ablegen, und Sie sind aus mancherlei Gründen der einzige, dem ich's anvertrauen kann. Ein Winter in England würde mich umbringen, daran zweifle ich nicht mehr; ich habe deshalb beschlossen, nach Italien zu gehen, zu Lande oder zu Wasser. Nicht, daß ich mir noch viel davon verspreche – denn ich glaube, in mir ist ein kranker Kern, den man nicht so einfach herausziehen kann. *** Wenn ich sterben sollte *** Ich muß noch vor Ablauf eines Monats fort. Machen Sie sich meinetwegen keine Sorgen, mein lieber Brown. Sie müssen Ihre Zeit so gut und so glücklich ausfüllen, wie Sie können. Sie müssen meine Fehler so leicht wie möglich nehmen. Wieder gesund, will ich meine ganzen Briefschulden bei Ihnen abtragen *** [...].

An Percy Bysshe Shelley

Hampstead, den 16. August [1820]

Mein lieber Shelley,

ich bin Ihnen sehr dankbar, daß Sie mir – in fremdem Land und den Kopf ganz sicher über-, übervoll – einen solchen Brief schreiben, wie ich ihn hier vor mir habe. Sollte ich keinen Gebrauch von Ihrer Einladung machen, dann nur, weil mich ein Ereignis daran hindern könnte, das vorherzusagen mir das Herz schwermacht. Ohne Zweifel würde ein englischer Winter meinem Leben ein Ende setzen, und zwar durch gräßliches Siechtum, deshalb muß ich nach Italien, zu Land oder zu Wasser, wie ein Soldat gegen eine Batterie zu Felde zieht. Am schlimmsten steht es derzeit mit meinen Nerven, doch beruhigen sie sich bei dem Gedanken, daß mich, wie übel es auch kommen mag, nichts zwingen kann, so lange an einem Ort zu bleiben, bis ich die vier Pfosten eines Bettes zu hassen beginne. Ich freue mich, daß Ihnen mein armseliges Gedicht ein wenig gefällt, das ich, wenn ich könnte, nur zu gern ungeschrieben machen würde, käm's mir noch so wie ehedem auf meinen Ruf an. Durch Hunt bekam ich Ihre »Cenci«. Ich kann da nur das eine beurteilen, die poetische und dramatische Wirkung, die viele heutzutage als den Mammon ansehen. Ein modernes Werk, sagt man, müsse einen Zweck haben, der sein Gott sein kann – ein *Künstler* muß dem Mammon dienen – er muß »auf sich konzentriert« sein, vielleicht sogar selbstsüchtig. Sie werden mir gewiß verzeihen, wenn ich offen sage, Sie sollten Ihrer Großherzigkeit Zügel anlegen und mehr Künstler sein und »jede Fuge« Ihres Stoffs mit Gold ausfüllen. Der Gedanke an solche Beschränkung muß wie kalte Ketten auf Sie fallen, der Sie womöglich noch nie ein halbes Jahr lang mit gefalteten Schwingen dasaßen. Und sind dies nicht sonderbare Reden von dem Verfasser des »Endymion«, dessen Verstand einem durcheinander geratenen Kartenspiel glich – nun bin ich fein beisammen und nach den Augen sortiert. Meine Imagination ist ein Kloster, und ich bin der Mönch darin. Sie müssen sich meine Metap[hysik] allein erklären. Ich rechne jeden Tag mit dem Prometheus. Wäre mein Wunsch im Hinblick auf seine Wirksamkeit erfüllt worden, hätten Sie ihn noch im Manuskript oder wären eben erst dabei, den zweiten Akt zu vollenden. Ich erinnere mich, wie Sie mir damals in Hampstead Heath rieten, meine kränklichen Erstlinge nicht drucken zu lassen. Ich gebe Ihnen den Rat nun zurück. Die meisten Gedichte in dem Band, den ich Ihnen sende, wurden vor über zwei Jahren geschrieben und wären niemals an die Öffentlichkeit gelangt, hätte ich mir nicht finanziellen Gewinn davon versprochen. Sie sehen also, ich bin inzwischen durchaus geneigt, Ihren Rat anzunehmen. [...]

An Charles Brown

Samstag, [den 30.] September [1820].
»Maria Crowther«, vor Yarmouth, Insel Wight

[...] Ich möchte über Dinge schreiben, die mich nicht sehr aufregen – eines gibt es, das ich erwähnen muß, was hiermit geschehen ist. Selbst wenn mein Körper von allein wieder genesen würde, dies würde es verhindern. Das, wofür ich am allermeisten leben will, wird eine wesentliche Ursache für meinen Tod sein. Ich kann's nicht ändern. Wer kann's ändern? Wär ich gesund, es würde mich krank machen, und wie kann ich es in meinem Zustand ertragen? Ich möchte wohl meinen – Sie wissen, wovon ich rede – Sie wissen, was mir in den ersten Wochen meiner Krankheit in Ihrem Hause die größte Qual bereitet hat. Tag und Nacht wünsche ich mir, der Tod möge mich von diesen Qualen erlösen, und dann wieder wünsche ich den Tod weit fort, denn der Tod würde selbst diese Qualen noch auslöschen, die doch besser sind als nichts. Land und Meer, Schwäche und Verfall sind starke Trennkräfte, doch der Tod trennt für immer. Wenn der stechende Schmerz dieses Gedankens meinen Verstand ganz erreicht hat, dann kann ich sagen, daß die Bitterkeit des Todes vorüber ist. Oft sehne ich mich nach Ihnen, damit Sie mir die schönsten Erwartungen einreden. Ich denke, Sie werden, auch ohne daß ich es extra sage, Miss Brawne um meinetwillen ein Freund sein, wenn ich tot bin. Sie finden, sie hat viele Fehler – aber mir zuliebe sollten Sie meinen, sie hätte keinen einzigen. Wenn es irgend etwas gibt, sei es in Wort oder Tat, was Sie für sie tun können, so weiß ich, Sie werden es tun. Ich bin jetzt in einer Verfassung, wo die Frau als Frau nicht mehr Macht über mich hat als ein Stock oder ein Stein, und doch ist der Unterschied in meinen Gefühlen für Miss Brawne und für meine Schwester sehr erstaunlich. Das eine scheint das andere in einem unglaublichen Maße in sich aufzusaugen. Ich denke selten an meinen Bruder und meine Schwester in Amerika. Der Gedanke, Miss Brawne verlassen zu müssen, ist über alle Maßen furchtbar. Dieses Gefühl der Finsternis, das mich überkommt – immer und immer sehe ich ihre Gestalt, immer und immer entschwindet sie mir. Manche Sätze, die sie gewöhnlich zu mir sagte, als sie mich zuletzt in Wentworth Place pflegte, klingen mir noch im Ohr. Gibt es ein anderes Leben? Werde ich aufwachen und all das als Traum erkennen? Es muß eins geben, wir können nicht zu solchen Leiden geschaffen sein. […]

An Mrs. Samuel Brawne

24. [?] Oktober [1820]
Hafen von Neapel
zu Händen Giovannis

Meine liebe Mrs. Brawne,

einige wenige Worte mögen Ihnen sagen, wie unsere Überfahrt war und in welcher Lage wir uns befinden, und wenige Worte müssen es darum sein, weil das Gesundheitsamt unsere Briefe wegen der Quarantäne öffnet und ausräuchert. Wir müssen zehn Tage auf dem Schiff bleiben und sind im Moment zwischen lauter Schiffen eingekeilt. Die Seeluft hat mir ungefähr so viel genützt, wie stürmisches Wetter, schlechte Unterbringung und Verpflegung mir geschadet haben. Es geht mir also ungefähr genauso wie vorher. Grüßen Sie Fanny von Herzen von mir, und sagen Sie ihr, wenn ich mich besser fühle, gäb's hier im Hafen von Neapel genügend Stoff für einen ganzen Stapel Papier, aber er sieht aus wie ein Traum. – Jeder Mensch, der sein Boot rudern, umhergehen und reden kann, kommt mir im Verhältnis zu mir wie ein gänzlich anderes Wesen vor. Ich bin kaum von dieser Welt. [...] Es ist unmöglich, meinen Gesundheitszustand genau zu beschreiben – im Moment leide ich an schweren Verdauungsstörungen, was diesen Brief so unverdaulich macht. Ich möchte immer, Sie sollen sich meine Verfassung ein wenig schlimmer vorstellen als sie ist; da ich kein Sanguiniker bin, mag mir das wohl gelingen. Wenn ich nicht gesund werde, wird Ihre Trauer gelindert, wenn doch, wird Ihre Freude verdoppelt sein. Ich wage nicht, meine Gedanken an Fanny zu heften; ich habe nicht gewagt, an sie zu denken. So war denn der einzige Trost, der mir blieb, stundenlang daran zu denken, daß ich das Messer habe, das sie mir in einem silbernen Futteral gab, das Haar in einem Medaillon, das Notizbuch in einem Goldnetz – zeigen Sie ihr dies. Ich wage nicht, mehr zu sagen – doch Sie dürfen nicht denken, ich sei so krank, wie es aus diesem Briefe scheinen mag, wenn nämlich je ein Mensch ohne die Fähigkeit zu hoffen geboren wurde, dann bin ich es. Severn schreibt gerade an Haslam, und ich bat ihn eben, Haslam zu ersuchen, er möge Ihnen seinen Bericht über meinen Gesundheitszustand schicken. O was für einen Bericht könnte ich Ihnen vom Golf von Neapel geben, wenn ich mich noch einmal als Bürger dieser Welt fühlen könnte. Ich fühle, ein Geist in meinem Hirn könnt's recht gefällig zuwege bringen. O welch ein Elend ist es, einen zersplitterten Geist zu haben! Noch einmal meine lieben Grüße an Fanny – sagen Sie Tootts, ich wollte, ich könnte ihr einen Korb Trauben hochreichen – und sagen Sie Sam, die Burschen fangen hier mit einer Schnur so kleine Fische, fast wie Anchovis, und ziehen sie flink heraus. [...]

An Charles Brown

Rom, den 30. November 1820

Mein lieber Brown,

es ist mir das Schwerste auf der Welt, einen Brief zu schreiben. Mit meinem Magen ist es weiterhin so schlimm, daß ich fühle, wie er sich verschlechtert, sobald ich ein Buch aufschlage, doch geht es mir viel besser als in der Quarantäne. Dann habe ich Furcht davor, mich dem Für und Wider von Dingen auszusetzen, die mir in England interessant waren. Mir ist für gewöhnlich, als sei mein wirkliches Leben zu Ende, und ich führte ein postumes Dasein. [...] Einen Gedanken gibt es, stark genug, mich umzubringen: Es ging mir gut, ich war gesund, frisch etc. und ging mit ihr – und jetzt. – Das Wissen um den Gegensatz, das Gefühl von Licht und Schatten, all die Kenntnis (Ur-Ahnung), die nötig sind für ein Gedicht, sind der Genesung meines Magens höchst feindlich. Da, du Schurke, ich überlasse dich der Folter, aber Sie müssen Gebrauch machen von Ihrer Philosophie, wie ich Gebrauch mache von der meinen, wirklich – wie sollte ich sonst leben können? [...] Wenn ich genese, will ich mich mit aller Kraft bemühen, meine während der Krankheit begangenen Fehler wiedergutzumachen, und wenn nicht, so wird mir alle Schuld vergeben sein. Ich schreibe morgen oder übermorgen an ***. Ich will Mitte nächster Woche an *** schreiben. Severn geht es sehr gut, obgleich er solch ein langweiliges Leben hat an meiner Seite. Grüßen Sie alle Freunde von mir und sagen Sie ***, ich hätte London nicht verlassen, ohne mich von ihm zu verabschieden, wenn ich nicht so schwach gewesen wäre an Körper und Gemüt. Schreiben Sie George, sobald Sie diesen Brief erhalten haben, und sagen Sie ihm, wie es mir geht – soweit Sie es erraten können; und auch ein paar Zeilen an meine Schwester, die wie ein Geist durch meine Phantasie wandelt – sie ist Tom so ähnlich. Ich vermag selbst in einem Brief kaum, Ihnen Lebewohl zu sagen. Ich war schon immer ungeschickt im Verbeugen.

Gott segne Sie!
John Keats.

Anhang

Zu dieser Ausgabe

Der Übersetzung der Gedichte, Sonette, Oden, Dichtungen und des Dramenfragments liegt folgende Edition zugrunde: John Keats, *The Complete Poems*, hrsg. von John Barnard, 2. Aufl., Harmondsworth 1977. Ihr folgt auch der englische Text der vorliegenden Ausgabe. – Die Übersetzung der Briefe fußt auf: John Keats, *The Letters*, hrsg. von Maurice Buxton Forman, London 1931. – Mirko Bonné übersetzte die Briefe Keats' vom 10. Mai 1817, 23. Januar 1818, 22. (?) September 1818, 14. Februar – 3. Mai 1819, 31. Mai 1819, 11. Juli 1819, 23. September 1819 und Juni (?) 1820. Die übrigen Briefübersetzungen stammen von Christa Schuenke; der Abdruck der Briefe vom 22. November 1817, 19. Februar 1818, 13. März 1818, 9. April 1818, 3. Mai 1818, 21. bis 25. Mai 1818, 10. Juni 1818, 18. Juli 1818, 8. März 1819, 16. August 1820 und 30. November 1820 erfolgt mit Genehmigung der Matthes & Seitz Verlag GmbH, München. Die deutschen Fassungen wurden von der Übersetzerin noch einmal durchgesehen.

Nachbemerkung des Übersetzers

»Hier liegt einer, dessen Namen man mit Wasser schrieb«, lautet das in seinen Grabstein gemeißelte Vermächtnis John Keats'; der letzte, über ein nur fünfundzwanzig Jahre währendes Leben gebreitete Vers eines Dichters, dessen Werk und Selbstverständnis Ausdruck einer im Grunde bereits zutiefst modernen Zerrissenheit sind. Der aufs äußerste perfektionierten Struktur und Form seiner Lyrik, die in vielfältiger Weise noch einmal versucht, sämtliche englische Dichtungstraditionen aufzunehmen, steht die männliche Stimme eines Einzelnen entgegen, der sich nicht mehr abfinden will mit seinem »durch Reimwerk gefesselten Englisch«. Diesem aus »ehrfurchtsvoller Haltung« wie »fürchterlicher Spaltung, von der ein Abgrund bleibt«, resultierenden, für den heutigen Leser kaum mehr wahrnehmbaren ›Cockney‹ in Ausdruck und Vielfalt Rechnung zu tragen, war mein vorrangiges Ziel bei der Übersetzung und Auswahl des Keats'schen Werkes.

Somit versammelt vorliegende Ausgabe neben den berühmten Sonetten, Oden und Versdichtungen auch Gedichte, Epen und ein Dramenfragment, deren Form und Duktus zur Revision des Bilds vom schönheitsliebenden, tragisch in den Tod gesunknen Dichterjüngling Keats beitragen. Wie sehr sich John Keats um andere Ausdrucksformen bemühte, wie nah sein *wit* beispielsweise schon Nietzsche oder Rimbaud kam, mit welchem Humor dieser »fünf Fuß große Mister Junkets« durch sein puritanisch »glückliches England« geschritten sein muß, das machen erst seine Briefe vollständig deutlich.

Keats' Briefe, in der 1985 erstmals erschienenen Übersetzung von Christa Schuenke (John Keats, *Richtmaß des Schönen. Briefe*, Leipzig: Reclam), bilden das Fundament dieser Ausgabe. Mit ihr hoffen wir, eine zukünftig angemessenere, vielfältigere deutschsprachige Rezeption eröffnet und den mit Wasser geschriebenen Namen John Keats' auch in unserem Sprachraum behutsam lesbarer gemacht zu haben.

Mein besonderer Dank gilt der Kulturbehörde Hamburg, die mein Projekt mit einem Förderpreis und mehreren Stipendien unterstützt hat. Für ihre persönliche Hilfe bedanke ich mich herzlich bei Wolfgang Schömel, Karin von Schweder-Schreiner, Maria Poelchau, Hinrich Schmidt-Henkel, Oliver Platz, Matthias Göritz, Jürgen Abel,

Hans-Ulrich Möhring und Volker Ufertinger. Dietrich Klose und Dietmar Jaegle danke ich sehr für die redaktionelle Betreuung des Manuskripts im Reclam Verlag.

Lüneburg und Hamburg, 1995 *M. B.*

Anmerkungen

Folgende Siglen werden verwendet:
P John Keats: Poems. London 1817.
E John Keats: Endymion. A Poetical Romance. London 1818.
L John Keats: Lamia, Isabella, The Eve of St Agnes, and Other Poems. London 1820.

9 **Spenser-Imitation**

Entstanden 1814. Aufgenommen in P. Keats' ältestes erhaltenes Gedicht erinnert weniger an Spenser, dessen *The Faerie Queene* er nacheiferte, als an die Spenserianer des 18. Jahrhunderts wie James Thomson, James Beattie und Mary Tighe.

9,23 *Dido:* die Gründerin und Königin Karthagos, verbrannte sich selbst, nachdem Aeneas sie verlassen hatte.

11 **An die Hoffnung**

Entstanden Februar 1815. Aufgenommen in P.

11,13 *»Aug des Geistes«:* vgl. Shakespeare, *Hamlet* I,2,185.

15 **[Gebt mir Frauen, Schnupfkraut, Wein]**

Geschrieben zwischen Herbst 1815 und Juli 1816, während Keats Medizin studierte, auf den Heftumschlag eines Kommilitonen. Erstdruck 1883.

15 **An meinen Bruder George**

Entstanden in Margate, August 1816. Aufgenommen in P.

15,19 *goldne Leier:* das Symbol Apolls und der Dichtkunst.
15,31 *Libertas:* gemeint ist hier Leigh Hunt.
21,31 *Tafeln:* biegbare oder feste Schreibtafeln.
21,35 *Rotrock:* Soldat.

23 **Strophen**

Entstehungszeit unbekannt. Veröffentlicht 1914.

23,23 *Sankt Cupido:* Diesen ›Heiligen‹ hat Keats erfunden, um scherzhaft den ihm zu frommen Katholizismus zu verspotten.

25 Gereimte Zeilen in einem Brief, erhalten (von J. H. Reynolds) aus Oxford

Geschrieben im September 1817 in Oxford als Parodie auf den von Wordsworth mitunter gepflegten »Schulübungsstil« (M.B. Forman) voll gereimter Verknappungen. Veröffentlicht 1883.

27,1 *Vice:* (lat.) abwechselnd; (engl.) Laster.
27,6 *dominat:* (lat.) er herrscht.

27 [Im nacht-dunklen Dezember]

Entstanden 1817; veröffentlicht 1829. Vgl. dazu Keats' Idee von »negative capability« und »intensity«, wie sie z.B. im Brief an George und Thomas Keats vom 21.–27. Dezember 1817 zum Ausdruck kommt.

29 Apollo zu den Grazien

Geschrieben wahrscheinlich 1818 auf eine Arie aus Mozarts *Don Giovanni.* Erstdruck 1914.

31 [O werd nicht rot! O werd nicht rot!]

Geschrieben am 31. Januar 1818. Das Gedicht, aufgrund seiner sexuellen Andeutungen von Swinburne für nicht publikationsfähig erklärt, imitiert den Tonfall eines Rondeaus aus dem 17. Jahrhundert. Veröffentlicht 1883.

31,12 *O stöhn nicht so:* vgl. Shakespeare, *Viel Lärm um nichts* II,3 (Balthasars Lied).

33 [Klarett fort, Burgunder und Port]

Erhalten in einem Brief an John Hamilton Reynolds vom 31. Januar 1818. Strittig ist, ob der Text zusammen mit dem folgenden *(Dir Gott des Meridians)* ein einzelnes Gedicht bildet. Veröffentlicht 1848.

33,1 f. *Klarett … Hochheimer Keller:* dunkle Weine unterschiedlicher Art.
33,5 *Römer:* großes, bauchiges Weinglas.
33,9 *delphisch:* poetisch.
33,11 *Cajus:* Pseudonym von John Hamilton Reynolds.

33 [Dir Gott des Meridians]

Vgl. die Anm. zum vorhergehenden Text.

33,17 *Meridian:* hier: Mittag; angerufen wird Apoll, der Gott der Sonne und des Gesangs.

35 Robin Hood

Entstanden 1818. Aufgenommen in L. Vgl. dazu Keats' Ausführungen im Brief an Reynolds vom 3. Februar 1818.

37,3 f. *sieben Sterne, / Der Polarstrahl:* die Plejaden und der Polarstern.
37,12 *Weide Trent:* der Fluß bei Nottingham; im betrunkenen Zustand selbst für eine Flußaue gehalten.
37,15 *Morris:* ehemals besonders zu Maifesten beliebter »Mohrentanz«.
37,16 *Lied von Gamelyn:* früher Chaucer zugeschriebenes mittelalterliches Epos, erzählt die Geschichte eines unterdrückten Sohns, der im Wald »König der Entrechteten« wird.
37,18 *»im grünen Strauche«:* vgl. Chaucer, *The Canterbury Tales* (*The Friar's Tale*, Z. 88).
39,1 *Lincoln:* engl. Landstrich zwischen Trent und Humber.
39,8 *Sherwood:* ehemaliger Wald bei Nottingham, Stammsitz Robin Hoods und seiner Gefährten.

39 Zeilen auf die Meerfrauschenke

Geschrieben im Februar 1818 nach einem Besuch in der *Mermaid Tavern* in Cheapside, dem berühmten Treffpunkt elisabethanischer Dichter wie Shakespeare, Jonson, Beaumont und Fletcher. Aufgenommen in L.

39,17 *Kanariensekt:* sehr süßer Wein.
41,4 *Zodiakus:* der Tierkreis mit den zwölf Sternbildern.

41 Auszüge aus einer Oper

Entstanden wahrscheinlich im Februar 1818. Die im Titel erwähnte Oper könnte auf einen diesbezüglichen Plan gemeinsam mit Charles Brown hindeuten. Veröffentlicht 1848.

41,11 *olympische Zwölf:* die zwölf auf dem Olymp herrschenden Götter.
45,3–7 *Vielleicht … auf ihrer Hand:* Ironisierung von Shakespeares Sonett 130 (»My mistress' eyes are nothing like the sun«).
45,10 *Diana:* röm. Jagdgöttin, berühmt für ihre Schönheit.
45,11 *Juno:* röm. Göttin, als Gattin Jupiters Himmelskönigin.
45,12 *Lied:* Keats' erster Versuch in der Balladenform, auf den *Old Meg* und *La Belle Dame sans Merci* folgten.
47,5 *Zelter:* Paradepferd.

47 [Über den Hügel, über das Tal]

Erhalten in einem Brief an James Rice vom 23. März 1818. Erstdruck 1853.

47,15 *Dawlischen:* Dawlish, Ortschaft bei Teignmouth in Devon, die Keats zur Entstehungszeit des Gedichts besuchte.
47,29 *»Venus«:* hier umgangssprachl. für Prostituierte.

49 An J.H. Reynolds, Esq.

Geschrieben am 24. März 1818 in Devon. Die Epistel, verfaßt an einem einzigen Abend, nimmt insbesondere in Z. 67–105 wichtige Themen der reifen Poesie Keats' vorweg. Veröffentlicht (ohne die letzten vier Zeilen) 1848.

49,16 *Junius Brutus:* der Shakespeare-Darsteller Junius Brutus Booth.
51,1 *Märchenschloß:* die Beschreibung bezieht sich größtenteils auf Claude Lorrains gleichnamiges Gemälde in der Londoner National Gallery.
51,4 *Urganda:* Zauberin aus dem altspanischen Amadis-Roman.
51,21 *Lapplandhexe:* vgl. Milton, *Das verlorene Paradies* II, 664f.
53,11 *etwas stofflicher Erhabenheit:* vgl. Wordsworth, *Tintern Abbey* Z. 95ff.: »ein erhabner Sinn / Von etwas weit weit tiefer noch Durchsetztem, / Das wohnt im Licht der Sonnenuntergänge«.

55 [Süß, süß ist ein Auge, das grüßt]

Geschrieben am 28. Juni 1818 für George und Georgiana Keats. Veröffentlicht 1925.

55,28 *Komm ich zu euch:* Keats plante, ein Jahr in Amerika zu verbringen, wo Bruder und Schwägerin sich niedergelassen hatten.

57 [Old Meg, die war Zigeunerin]

Entstanden im Juli 1818. Publiziert 1838. Auf ihrer Wanderschaft durch Schottland erzählte Charles Brown Keats die Geschichte von Meg Merrilies aus Scotts Roman *Guy Mannering* (1814).

59 Ein Lied über mich selbst

Geschrieben im Juli 1818 für Fanny Keats während der Wanderung durch Schottland. Veröffentlicht 1883.

65,17 *fourscore:* altenglisches Maß, etwa »vier Stiegen« (= achtzig).

67 **[Willkommen Glück, willkommen Sorgen]**

Entstanden 1818. Erstdruck 1848. Zum Thema des Gedichts, dem »poetischen Charakter«, vgl. Keats' Brief an Richard Woodhouse vom 27. Oktober 1818. – Motto: Milton, *Das verlorene Paradies* II,898 bis 903.

67,25 *Momus':* Momus, röm. Gott des Scherzes und der Fröhlichkeit.

69 **[Wer ist Dichter? Wer hier, wer hier?]**

Vgl. die Anmerkungen zu vorhergehendem Gedicht, mit dem der Text vielfach in Verbindung gebracht wird, und Keats' Brief an Benjamin Bailey vom 22. November 1817.

69 **Phantasie**

Entstanden wahrscheinlich im Dezember 1818. Aufgenommen in L. Keats beschreibt das Gedicht in seinem Brief an George und Georgiana Keats vom 2. Januar 1819 als »eine Art Rondeau, die mir wohl lieb werden wird – die Idee drückt sich leichter, freudiger und freier in ihm aus als im Sonett«. Es stellt somit eine wichtige Übergangsform auf dem Weg vom Sonett zur späteren Odenstrophe dar.

73,29 *Ceres' Tochter:* Die Tochter der röm. Wachstumsgöttin ist Proserpina, Göttin der Unterwelt.
73,30 *Martergott:* Pluto oder Hades, Gott der Unterwelt.
73,34 *Hebe:* griech. Göttin der Jugend, Mundschenkin im Olymp.

75 **Lied des Märchenvogels**

Geschrieben wahrscheinlich im April 1819 für Charles Browns Märchensammlung *The Fairies Triumph.* Veröffentlicht 1838.

77 **La Belle Dame sans Merci. Eine Ballade**

Verfaßt am 21. April 1819. Veröffentlicht von Leigh Hunt im *Indicator* vom 10. Mai 1820 in einer teils eigenmächtig veränderten Fassung. Die zahlreichen Inspirationsquellen und Verweise des berühmten und unerschöpflichen Gedichts sind u. a. Alain Chartiers gleichnamige Ballade (1424), Spensers *The Faerie Queene*, Robert Burtons *Anatomy of Melancholy*, Careys Übertragung Dantes sowie die Volksballade *Thomas the Rhymer.*

77,21 *Ihr Haar war lang:* vgl. Coleridge, *The Rime of the Ancient Mariner*, Z. 190ff.: »Ihr Mund war rot, ihr Blick war frei, / Ihr Haar so gelb wie Gold – / Und ihre Haut war lepraweiß«.

79,15 *mit Küssen vier:* die Anzahl der Küsse beinhaltet sowohl erotische als auch Todessymbolik.

79,21 *Monarchen, Fürsten bleich:* vgl. *Ein Traum, nachdem ich Dantes Episode von Paolo und Francesca gelesen hatte,* Z. 12ff.

81 **[Zwei bis drei Vasen]**

Erhalten im Brief an Fanny Keats vom 1. Mai 1819. Erstdruck 1883.

81,27 *Sandy:* engl. Abk. von Alexander, Spitzname für einen Niederschotten.

81,28 *Emmi:* Omi, Tantchen.

81,30 *Mrs. – pst!:* gemeint ist Mrs. Abbey, die Frau von Keats' früherem Vormund.

83,6 *Bonnette:* Bonnett, eine französische Kappe oder Haube.

83 **[Wie kann ich die Erinnrung fort]**

Geschrieben im Oktober 1819, möglicherweise im Zusammenhang mit Keats' Brief an Fanny Brawne vom 13. Oktober: »Diesen Augenblick habe ich mich entschlossen, einige Verse ins Reine zu schreiben. [...] Ich muß Dir eine Zeile oder zwei schreiben und sehen, ob dies dazu beitragen wird, Dich aus meinem Sinn zu bringen, wenn auch für noch so kurze Zeit. [...] Ich war erstaunt, daß Menschen als Märtyrer für die Religion sterben können – ich schauderte davor. Ich schaudere nicht mehr – ich könnte zum Märtyrer werden für meine Religion – Liebe ist meine Religion – ich könnte dafür sterben. Ich könnte für Dich sterben. Mein Glaube ist Liebe, und Du bist meine einzige Lehre.« Veröffentlicht 1848.

83,18 *quergefärbter Spuk:* Keats wußte um den unterschiedlichen Reifegrad seiner Dichtung.

85,8 *dies verhaßte Land:* Keats bezieht sich auf die Schwierigkeiten seines Bruders in Amerika, dessen Landschaft als Gegensatz zu pastoraler Idylle dargestellt wird.

85,20 *die Natur, stets klar:* vgl. Pope, *An Essay on Man* I,294: »Eines ist klar: *was immer ist – 's ist recht.*«

85,31 *die Süße aller Qual:* vgl. *Willkommen Glück, willkommen Sorgen,* Z. 23.

87 **[Die Hand hier, lebenswarm und fähig jetzt]**

Für eine spätere Aufnahme in ein Gedicht oder Drama geschrieben wahrscheinlich im November oder Dezember 1819. Eventuell jedoch meint Keats im Brief an Fanny Brawne vom August (?) 1820 diesen

Text: »Wenn meine Gesundheit es erlaubte, könnte ich Dir ein Gedicht schreiben, das ich im Kopf habe.« Veröffentlicht 1848.

87,1–3 *Die Hand hier ... ihres Grabs:* vgl. *Der Fall des Hyperion* I,18.

89 Auf den Frieden

Entstanden im Frühjahr 1814 zur Feier des Ersten Pariser Friedens. Veröffentlicht 1905. Das unregelmäßige shakespearesche Sonett imitiert den Tonfall von Artikeln aus Leigh Hunts Magazin *Examiner.*

89,6 *Dreierkrone:* England, Schottland und Wales.
89,10 *Bergnymphe:* Europa, Schwester des Kadmos.
89,11 *Mit Englands Freude ... ein:* vgl. die Inschrift am Londoner Somerset House: »Europa Instaurata, Aupice Britanniae / Tyrannide Subversa, Vindice Libertatis«.

89 Geschrieben am Tag, als Mr. Leigh Hunt das Gefängnis verließ

Verfaßt am 2. Februar 1815. Aufgenommen in P. Wegen Majestätsbeleidigung hatte der Herausgeber des *Examiner* und spätere Freund und Förderer Keats' eine zweijährige Haftstrafe verbüßt.

89,23 *Lakai des Adels:* Stellvertretend für den Machtapparat verhöhnt der Text den Zellenwärter Hunts.

91 [O Einsamkeit! Hast du mich heimgesucht]

Geschrieben im Oktober 1815. Keats' erste Publikation erschien am 5. Mai 1816 im *Examiner.*

91,18 *gleichgesinnte Geister:* Keats und sein Bruder George oder G.F. Mathew, mit dem der Dichter zur Entstehungszeit des Texts einen Poesiezirkel bildete.

91 [Für einen, lange von der Stadt erdrückt]

Geschrieben im Juni 1816, wie der vorhergehende Text als Reaktion auf Enge und Niedergeschlagenheit während des Medizinstudiums in London. Aufgenommen in P.

91,19 *Für einen ... erdrückt:* vgl. Milton, *Das verlorene Paradies* IX,445 sowie Coleridge, *An die Nachtigall,* Z. 2.
91,28 *Philomelas:* Philomela, die Tochter des Königs von Athen, so berichtet der Mythos, wurde in eine Nachtigall verwandelt.

93 [O! wie ich's lieb, im Sommerabendschein]

Entstanden im Sommer 1816. Erstdruck 1848.

93,14 *Sidneys:* Sir Philip Sidney (1554–1586), Verfasser des Schäferromans *Arcadia*, Lyriker, Diplomat, Soldat.

93 An meinen Bruder George

Geschrieben in Margate im August 1816. Aufgenommen in P.

93,22 *der Bekränzten Glut:* gemeint sind die vom Abendrot ›geadelten‹ Wolken.
93,29 *Cynthia:* wie Phoebe, Luna und Diana ein von Keats auch in *Endymion* verwandter mythologischer Name des Mondes.

95 [Wie viele Barden vergolden die Zeit!]

Verfaßt wahrscheinlich im Oktober 1816. Die erste Zeile des englischen Originals befreit sich vom metrischen Maß des fünfhebigen Jambus, wie bereits Leigh Hunt in seiner Besprechung von P vermerkte.

95 Aufs erste Hineinschauen in Chapmans Homer

Geschrieben im Oktober 1816. Erschien erstmals im *Examiner* am 1. Dezember 1816 innerhalb Leigh Hunts Artikel *Young Poets.* Keats' erstes Gedicht von Rang bezieht sich auf George Chapmans (1559? bis 1634) Übersetzungen der *Ilias* (1611) und *Odyssee* (1615).

95,21 *Die goldnen Reiche:* gemeint ist das fantastische El Dorado, wahrscheinlich aber auch die vergoldeten Buchdeckel und -rücken.
97,1 *Astronom:* Als Auszeichnung während seiner Schulzeit erhielt Keats 1811 eine *Einführung in die Astronomie,* in der u. a. Herschels Entdeckung des Uranus (1781) beschrieben wird.
97,3 *Cortez:* Keats verwechselt hier wohl den Entdecker Mexikos mit demjenigen des Pazifiks, Balboa.
97,6 *Dariéns:* Darién, Landstrich und Bucht zwischen Panama und Kolumbien.

97 An eine junge Dame, die mir einen Lorbeerkranz sandte

Entstehungszeit unbekannt. Erstdruck 1848.

99 [Scharf wechseln Böen und wispern hier und dort]

Geschrieben im Oktober oder November 1816 nach einem Besuch in Hunts Cottage im Vale of Health, Hampstead. Aufgenommen in P.

99,12 *Lycidas:* Miltons 1637 auf einen ertrunkenen Freund verfaßte Elegie.

99,13 *Laura:* von Petrarca im *Canzoniere* verewigte Mädchengestalt. In Hunts Cottage befand sich ein Gemälde, welches das berühmte Liebespaar darstellte (vgl. auch *Schlaf und Dichtung*, Z. 389ff.).

99 **[An meine Brüder]**

Geschrieben am 18. November 1816 zu Tom Keats' 17. Geburtstag. Aufgenommen in P.

101 **Geschrieben aus Ekel vor volkstümlichem Aberglauben**

Entstanden am 22. Dezember 1816, einer Notiz von Tom Keats zufolge binnen 15 Minuten. Erstdruck 1876.

101,9 *Lydiens:* Lydien, reicher Staat der Antike an der Westküste Kleinasiens; vgl. Milton, *L'Allegro*, Z. 136.

103 **An G. A. W.**

Geschrieben im Dezember 1816, wahrscheinlich im Namen des Bruders, für Georgiana Augusta Wylie, die spätere Frau George Keats'. Aufgenommen in P.

103 **[Glücklich ist England! Mir wär es genug]**

Entstanden wahrscheinlich im Dezember 1816. Eines der berühmtesten Sonette Keats, in Thema und Tonfall stark Byron verpflichtet. Aufgenommen in P.

103,22 *Alpe:* im Singular auch bei Milton, *Das verlorene Paradies* II,620.

105 **[Nachdem von trübem Dunst die Flurn bedeckt]**

Datiert 31. Januar 1817. Erschienen im *Examiner* vom 23. Februar dieses Jahres, nachdem P bereits im Druck war.

105,9–14 *Und ruhiger … im Waldland:* vgl. die Herbstszenerie mit Keats großer Ode *An den Herbst.*

109,14 *eines Dichters Tod:* gemeint sein könnte der Dichter Thomas Chatterton, von dem Keats schrieb, er assoziiere stets den Herbst mit ihm.

105 An Leigh Hunt, Esq.

Entstanden als Zueignung wohl im Februar 1817. Aufgenommen in P.

105,20–23 *Kein Nymphenschwarm … im frühen Mai:* wahrscheinlich Darstellungen auf Nicolas Poussins Gemälde *Der Triumph Floras* nachempfunden; vgl. auch *Schlaf und Dichtung,* Z. 101–121.

107 Auf den Anblick der »Elgin Marbles«

Geschrieben vor dem 3. März 1817. Publiziert im *Examiner* vom 9. März 1817. Die Parthenon-Skulpturen der Athener Akropolis waren 1816 von Lord Elgin dem Britischen Museum übergeben worden.

107,15 *Riesigkeit:* das engl. »magnitude« bezeichnet u.a. auch eine astronomische Größenklasse.

107 [Auf eine Leander-Gemme, die Miss Reynolds, meine liebe Freundin, mir gab]

Geschrieben wahrscheinlich im März 1817, wie zahlreiche andere Gedichte für die mit Keats befreundeten Schwestern Reynolds. Erstdruck 1829.

107,16 *Gemme:* Stein mit vertieft oder erhaben geschnittenem Bild.

107,26–28 *Leander ist's … Heros Wange:* Leander, der Geliebte Heros, der Venuspriesterin zu Sestus, durchschwamm, um zu ihr zu kommen, den Hellespont und ertrank; Hero folgte ihm daraufhin in den Tod.

109 Auf das Meer

Entstanden im April 1817 auf der Insel Wight. Erstdruck im *Champion* vom 17. August 1817. Keats berichtet über die Entstehung des Gedichts in einem Brief an John Hamilton Reynolds vom 17. April 1817: »Weil ich nicht regelmäßig geschlafen hatte, war ich ziemlich *narvös [sic],* und die Stelle im Lear – ›Horcht! hört Ihr nicht die See?‹ – verfolgte mich aufs heftigste.«

109,4 f. *Spuk / Der Hekate:* griech. Göttin der Unterwelt, wurde bereits in der Antike mit dem (die Gezeiten beeinflussenden) Mond in Verbindung gebracht.

109 Auf das Sich-Hinsetzen, um nochmals »King Lear« zu lesen

Verfaßt am 22. Januar 1818. Erstdruck 1838. Keats bereitete *Endymion* zur Veröffentlichung vor und sann selbstkritisch nach über Unterschiede zwischen shakespearescher und »goldzüngiger« Dichtung.

109,19 *Federnsirene, Fernenkönigin:* Dichtung wird als Heldin im Stil Spensers dargestellt.
109,26 *Albions:* Albion, dichterischer Name für England.

111 [Wenn Furcht mir kommt, ich hörte auf zu sein]

Entstanden Ende Januar 1818. Erstdruck 1848. Das Gedicht markiert den Beginn von Keats' Präferenz der Sonettform Shakespeares vor derjenigen Petrarcas.

111,5 f. *auf der gestirnten ... hoher Kunst:* vgl. Keats Brief an John Hamilton Reynolds vom 19. Februar 1818: »eine himmlische Tapisserie [...], voll von Symbolen für sein geistiges Auge«.
111,9 *Geschöpf für eine Stunde Zeit:* vgl. die Anm. zum folgenden Sonett *An –*.

111 An –

Geschrieben am 4. Februar 1818. Erstdruck 1844. Das stark Shakespeare verpflichtete Gedicht richtet sich an eine junge Dame, die Keats im Sommer 1814 in den Londoner Vauxhall-Gärten gesehen hatte.

113 [Spenser! Jemandem, der dich heiß verehrt]

Verfaßt am 5. Februar 1818. Veröffentlicht 1848.

113,1 *Jemand ... heiß verehrt:* John Hamilton Reynolds.
113,5 *Elfendichter:* Eine Figur aus Spensers *The Faerie Queene* ist der »Elfenritter«.
113,7 *Phöbus:* die Sonne.

113 [O du, des Antlitz Winterwind gespürt]

Erhalten im Brief an John Hamilton Reynolds vom 19. Februar 1818. Veröffentlicht 1848. Das aus der imaginierten Sicht einer Drossel geschriebene Gedicht ist Keats' einziges reimloses Sonett.

115 Die menschlichen Jahreszeiten

Entstanden im März 1818 in Teignmouth. Erstdruck in Leigh Hunts *Literary Pocket Book* 1819. Vgl. Thema und Metaphorik von *An den Herbst* sowie Keats' Ausführungen zu Wirklichkeit und menschlichem Streben im Brief an Benjamin Bailey vom 13. März 1818.

115 An J.R.

Geschrieben im April 1818, als James Rice Keats in Teignmouth besuchte. Erstdruck 1848 (unter dem falschen Titel »An J.H. Reynolds«).

115,26 *Levante:* die um das östliche Mittelmeer gelegenen Länder.

117 An Homer

Entstanden wahrscheinlich im April 1818. Veröffentlicht 1848.

117,2 *Unwissenheit:* Keats konnte kein Griechisch, sondern las Homers Werke in der Übertragung Chapmans (vgl. sein Sonett *Aufs erste Hineinschauen in Chapmans Homer*).
117,3 *Kykladen:* griechische Inselgruppe in der südlichen Ägäis.
117,6 *doch riß der Vorhang:* vgl. Matthäus 27,51.
117,7–9 *Denn dir ... Pans dabei:* Homer wird als Dichter dargestellt, der mehr von der Natur als von Büchern inspiriert wurde.

117 Auf einen Besuch an Burns' Grab

Verfaßt am 1. Juli 1818 in Dumfries, wo der schottische Nationaldichter Robert Burns (1759–1796) begraben liegt. Erstdruck 1848. – Die Interpunktion des englischen Texts ist umstritten; Variante der Zeile 4: »I dreamèd long ago now new begun.«

117,23 *Saphirn ... im Raum:* vgl. *Ode an Psyche,* Z. 26.
117,24–28 *Bloß kalte Schönheit ... werfen!:* Die frühere Lesart (»endlos lang: / Denn wer schon weiß ... Drauf werfen?«) »macht Keats, dem es hier um Realität geht, zu einem, der Illusionen nachhängt« (G. Allott).
117,25 *Minos:* sagenhafter Herrscher von Kreta und Bezwinger des Minotaurus.

119 [Ein Leib von tausend Tagen Sterblichkeit]

Verfaßt am 11. Juli 1818 in Burns' Cottage zu Ayrshire, »bloß um ein paar Zeilen unter diesem Dach geschrieben zu haben« (Brief an John Hamilton Reynolds vom selben Tag). Erstdruck 1848.

119 Übersetzt aus dem Ronsard

Entstanden im September 1818. Veröffentlicht 1848. Das Fragment ist eine Übertragung von Pierre de Ronsards (1525–1585) *Nature ornant Cassandre,* dem zweiten Sonett der *Amours de Cassandre* (1552). R.M. Milnes (1848) fügte ein Couplet an: »So that her image in my soul upgrew, / The only thing adorable and true« (So ward ihr Bild in meiner Seele klar, / Als einziges verehrenswert und wahr).

121 [Was lachte ich heut nacht? Niemand der spricht]

Verfaßt vor dem 19. März 1819. Erstdruck 1848. In einem Brief an Bruder und Schwägerin kommentiert Keats das Sonett: »Es wurde aus keiner anderen Qual geschrieben als jener der Unwissenheit; mit keinem anderen Dürsten als jenem nach Erkenntnis, obgleich Gefühl und Leidenschaft mich die ersten Schritte in diese Richtung tun ließen. Sie vergingen, und ich schrieb mit dem Verstand, vielleicht auch – ich muß es gestehn – ein wenig mit dem Herzen.«

121,9 *Des Daeins Ziel:* vgl. Shakespeare, *Macbeth* IV,1,98 ff.
121,11 *scheiden diese Mitternacht:* vgl. *Ode an eine Nachtigall*, Z. 55 f.

121 [Das Haus der Trauer, von Mr. Scott verfaßt]

Entstanden wahrscheinlich im April 1819 als Parodie auf Wordsworths Sonett *Composed in the Valley near Dover.* Erstdruck 1936.

121,15 *Das Haus der Trauer:* Gedichtband von John Scott (1817).
121.16 *Magdalensermon:* »The Magdalen«, Hospital zu St. George's Fields, wo Prostituierte behandelt und ›kuriert‹ wurden.
121,22 *Groß Haydons Bild:* Benjamin Robert Haydon, Maler und zeitweiliger Freund Keats'; arbeitete gerade an seinem »Triumphalen Einzug Christi in Jerusalem«.

123 Ein Traum, nachdem ich Dantes Episode von Paolo und Francesca gelesen hatte

Geschrieben im April 1819. Erstdruck im *Indicator* vom 28. Juni 1820. Zur Entstehungszeit des Gedichts las Keats, in H. F. Careys Übersetzung (1805), Dantes *Inferno;* vgl. seine Ausführungen zu Traum und Sonett im Journalbrief an George und Georgiana Keats vom Februar/Mai 1819.

123,3 f. *Hermes ... Argus:* Die Göttin Juno ließ durch Argus, das hundertäugige Ungeheuer, Io, die Geliebte ihres Mannes, bewachen. Um Argus zu bezwingen, sandte Jupiter den Gott Hermes.
123,9 *Ida:* Berg bei Troja, heute Kas Dagh.
123,10 *Tempe:* sagenhaftes paradiesisches Tal am Fuß des Olymp.

123 [An den Schlaf]

Entstanden wahrscheinlich im April 1819. Erschienen 1838. Der Text stellt Keats' ersten konkreten Versuch dar, die Sonettform umzuwandeln in eine adäquate Odenstrophe (vgl. auch die Sonette *Wenn Reimwerk unser Englisch fesseln muß* und *Auf den Ruhm* sowie die *Ode an Psyche*).

123,22 *sänftigendst:* Das deutsche Wort folgt Keats' Neuschöpfung »soothest«.

125 [Wenn Reimwerk unser Englisch fesseln muß]

Entstanden im April 1819. Erstdruck 1848. Zu seinen Bemühungen um eine »bessere Sonettstrophe« (vgl. Anm. zu *An den Schlaf*) schreibt Keats an Bruder und Schwägerin: »Die gültige [petrarchische] ist der Sprache ob ihrer klauenhaften Reime nicht allzu angemessen; die andere [shakespearesche] erscheint zu elegisch, und das Couplet am Schluß hat nur selten einen angenehmen Effekt.«

125,2 *Andromeda:* Zur Besänftigung eines Meerungeheuers bzw. Neptuns Zorn wurde Andromeda nackt an einen Felsen gefesselt. Perseus befreite und heiratete sie.

125 Auf den Ruhm

Verfaßt am 30. April 1819. Veröffentlicht 1848. Ein weiteres Experiment mit der Sonettform (s. Anm. zu den beiden vorhergehenden Texten).

127 [Der Tag ist fort, mit aller Süße fort!]

Entstanden wahrscheinlich am 10. Oktober 1819. Erstdruck 1838.

127,8 *Wärme, Weiße, Paradies:* vgl. das Sonett *Ich fleh dich an um Gnade, Mitleid, Liebe!*

127,13 *Amors Meßbuch:* vgl. die Gedichte *Wie kann ich die Erinnrung fort*, Z. 25 f. und *An Fanny*, Z. 50–53.

127 [Ich fleh dich an um Gnade, Mitleid, Liebe! –]

Geschrieben wahrscheinlich im Oktober 1819. Am 19. Oktober schrieb Keats an Fanny Brawne: »Ich muß mich mit Ketten belasten. Ich sollte den Würfel auf Liebe oder Tod werfen – zu nichts anderem habe ich Geduld.« Erstdruck 1848.

129 [Glänzender Stern! wär ich doch stet wie du –]

Wahrscheinlich im Oktober oder November 1819 entstanden, nicht, wie lange angenommen, während der Überfahrt nach Italien im Herbst 1820. Veröffentlicht 1838. Die Bezüge und Anspielungen dieses wie die Essenz aus Keats' Schaffen anmutenden Texts sind vielfältig; vgl. u.a. Z. 1–4 mit der Beschreibung Windermeres im Brief an Thomas Keats vom 25. Juni 1818: »[Die Anblicke] lassen einen die Unterschiede im Leben vergessen: Alter und Jugend, Armut und Reichtum, und erheben die sinnliche Anschauung gewissermaßen zu einem Polarstern, der niemals aufhören kann, offenen Auges und standhaft über den Wundern der erhabenen Macht zu stehen.« (Vgl. auch Wordsworth, *The Excursion*, IV,691 ff.)

129,4 *Einsiedler:* vgl. *Der St.-Agnes-Abend*, Z. 277.
129,10 *Gebettet … Brust:* vgl. das Gedicht *Wie kann ich die Erinnrung fort*, Z. 48 f. und das Sonett *Ich fleh dich an*, Z. 8.

131 Ode an den Mai. Fragment

Verfaßt am 1. Mai 1818, erhalten im Brief an John Hamilton Reynolds vom 3. Mai 1818. Das an Horaz' Rhythmik geschulte und in einzelnen Passagen noch Wordsworth verpflichtete Fragment gilt als Wendepunkt in Keats' Schaffen, der auf den maskulinen, energischen Tonfall der reiferen Werke vorausweist. Erstdruck 1848.

131,6 *Bajä:* Seestadt nahe Rom.
131,8 *älterm Sizilianisch:* die Sprache des syrakusischen Idyllendichters Theokrit (um 300–260 v. Chr.).

131 Ode an Psyche

Entstanden Ende April 1819. Aufgenommen in L. Keats beschreibt das Gedicht als »das erste und einzige, für das ich selbst gelinde Schmerzen auf mich genommen habe. Größtenteils habe ich meine Verse eilig hingeworfen – diese sind mit Muße entstanden. […] Ihr müßt wissen, daß Psyche nicht als Göttin betrachtet wurde vor der Zeit Apuleius des Platonikers, der nach der augustäischen Epoche lebte, daher wurde der Göttin auch nicht mit jener antiken Inbrunst gehuldigt und geopfert […] Mein Glaube ist zu orthodox, als daß ich eine heidnische Göttin so vernachlässigt sehen könnte.« (Journalbrief an George und Georgiana Keats vom Februar/Mai 1819) Außer William Adlingtons elisabethanischer Apuleius-Übertragung beeinflußten die Handlung der Ode Spensers *Faerie Queene* und Mary Tighes *Psyche*. Zur Strophenstruktur vgl. die Anm. zum Sonett *An den Schlaf*.

131,24 *Flügel:* Psyche, die menschliche Seele, wurde dargestellt als Vogel (Z. 22) oder Schmetterling (vgl. *Ode an die Melancholie*, Z. 6f.).

133,11 *Flügelknaben:* Cupido, der Liebesgott und Sohn der Venus, wurde ausgesandt, um Psyche zu bestrafen, verliebte sich jedoch in sie.

133,15 *verschwundnen Göttermacht:* Die Olympier sind verschwunden, da Psyche sie an Schönheit übertrifft (vgl. *Hyperion* II, 228f.)

133,16 *Phöbes Stern:* der Mond, kontrastiert mit Z. 27 »Hesp'rus«, d.h. der Venus als Abendstern.

135,7–19 *Ja, ich will ... Phantasie erdächt:* vgl. die geistige Landschaft mit der Panopferstätte in *Endymion* I,63–106.

135,24 *Für heiße Liebe:* offen bleibt, ob Psyche auf Eros wartet oder umgekehrt.

135 Ode auf eine griechische Urne

Entstanden im Mai 1819. Erstdruck 1820. Keats' berühmtestes und am häufigsten interpretiertes Gedicht bezieht sich nicht auf ein einzelnes antikes Schmuckgefäß, in großen Teilen jedoch auf die Sosibios-Vase; Darstellungen auf den *Elgin Marbles* sowie zeitgenössische Reproduktionen klassischer Motive kommen hinzu; vgl. außerdem Wordsworths Sonett *Upon a Sight of a Beautiful Picture* sowie Keats' frühere Verarbeitungen von antiken Opferritualen u.a. in seinem Gedicht *An J. H. Reynolds, Esq.*, Z. 20f.

135,25 *griechische Urne:* Keats war sich bewußt, daß griechische Urnen dazu dienten, die Asche der Toten aufzubewahren, vgl. *Endymion* III, 431f.: »Weshalb die Not, / Urnen voll Tränen, als wärst kalt du, tot.«

137,6 *Bacchanal:* ausschweifendes Fest zu Ehren Bacchus'.

139,16 *aus dem Denken schreckt:* vgl. die gleiche Formulierung im Gedicht *An J. H. Reynolds*, Z. 77 sowie der *Ode an eine Nachtigall*, Z. 34.

139,17 *kaltes Hirtenspiel:* vgl. die »kalte Schönheit« im Sonett *Auf einen Besuch an Burns' Grab*.

139,21 f. *»Schönheit ... reicht«:* Die Mehrdeutigkeit des Gedichts kulminiert in der ungewissen Setzung der Anführungszeichen (andere Lesart: »Schönheit ist Wahrheit, Wahrheit schön« – soviel / [...]). Es muß letztendlich offen bleiben, ob die beiden Schlußverse von der Urne, vom Dichter oder, aufgeteilt, von beiden gesprochen werden; offen bleibt auch, an wen sie sich richten, an die Menschen, die Urne oder die Gestalten auf der Urne. Vgl. hierzu auch Keats' Brief an Benjamin Bailey vom 22. November 1817.

139 Ode an eine Nachtigall

Datiert Mai 1819. Erstdruck Juli 1819. Am Beispiel einer einzelnen, im Verlauf des Texts mythisch transformierten Nachtigall behandelt diese längste der sechs großen Oden (wie auch die *Ode auf eine griechische Urne*) u.a. die Frage nach Wesen und Grenzen künstlerischer Betrachtung. Neben Wordsworth und Coleridges *To the Nightingale* haben v.a. William Hazlitts (1778–1830) Vorlesungen über englische Dichtung, die Keats selbst besuchte, den Text entscheidend beeinflußt.

139,25–28 *Mein Herz ... sinken würd:* vgl. Horaz, *Epoden* XIV,1–4.
141,13 *Hippokrene:* sprechender Musenquell der Sage.
141,19 *Sich auflösen, verschwinden:* vgl. *Endymion* I,97–100.
141,24 *verfällt:* vgl. Wordsworth, *The Excursion* IV,760: »Derweil man alt wird, schwindet, und verfällt«.
143,3 *Parderwagen:* von Leoparden gezogenes Gefährt.
143,28 *wie köstlich Sterben ist:* vgl. *Ode auf die Melancholie,* Z. 18.
145,3 *Geschlecht:* vgl. Wordsworth, *The Excursion* IV,761 f.: »Und zahllose Geschlechter dieser Menschheit / Vergehn; und keine Spur bleibt, wo sie schritten«.
145,7 *Ruth:* vgl. das alttestamentarische Buch Ruth II,1–3.
147,10 *Zauberfenster:* vgl. das »Märchenschloß« im Gedicht *An J. H. Reynolds, Esq.,* Z. 50.
145,21, f. *War es Vision? ... schlafe ich?:* vgl. Shakespear, *Die lustigen Weiber von Windsor* III,5,123 f.: »Ist das Erscheinung? Ist's ein Traum? Schlaf ich?«

145 Ode auf die Melancholie

Verfaßt wahrscheinlich im Mai 1819. Aufgenommen in L. In Anlehnung an Robert Burtons *Anatomie der Melancholie* untersucht das Gedicht die Beziehungen zwischen Schwermut und Freude, Schönheit und Vergänglichkeit; es wurde irrtümlich für weniger komplex gehalten und v.a. aufgrund seiner (vorgeblich) makabren Metaphorik kritisiert. Die folgende ursprüngliche Eröffnungsstrophe hat Keats selbst gestrichen: »Baust du auch eine Barke aus Gebein, / Stellst Galgen geisterhaft als Masten auf, / Nähst Kredos um zu Segeln, daß Gegrein / Sie bläht, mit Blutflecken und Schaudern drauf; / Und steuert dich ein Drachenschwanz am Heck, / Den, zwar lang abgetrennt, doch Schmerz noch bäumt, / Scherst du Medusas Totenschädel kahl / Für langes Tauwerk, es hat keinen Zweck, / Suchst du Melancholie – selbst wenn sie träumt / An einem Strand im trüben Lethetal.« Vgl. die Metaphorik des Gedichts auch mit *Willkommen Glück, willkommen Sorgen.*

145,26–147,1 *Eisenhut / Nachtschatten / Eibenbeern:* giftige Pflanzen und Früchte.

147,2 *Totenuhr und Totenkopf:* ein auch im Sargholz lebender Klopfkäfer bzw. ein Schmetterling mit schädelähnlicher Zeichnung auf dem Rücken.

147,3 *Klagepsyche:* Psyche wurde u.a. als Schmetterling dargestellt.

147,315–17 *Und zeigt die Herrin ... Augen vor:* vgl. *Lamia* II,64–77.

147,28 *Trophäen:* Antike Tempel waren behängt mit Siegestrophäen; vgl. auch Shakespeares Sonett 31, Z. 9f.: »Lebendger Liebe Grab bist du erbaut, / Prangst mit Trophäen meiner toten Lieben«.

149 **Ode auf die Lässigkeit**

Verfaßt wahrscheinlich Ende Mai/Anfang Juni 1819 (vgl. den Brief an Sarah Jeffery vom 9. Juni: »In letzter Zeit war ich sehr träge«). Erstdruck 1848. Keats schrieb diese am stärksten autobiographisch geprägte Ode nach dem Durchgehen älterer Aufzeichnungen, darunter sein Journalbrief an Bruder und Schwägerin von Februar/Mai 1819: »Weder Poesie, Ehrgeiz noch Liebe zeigen irgendeine Regung ihrer Mienen, während sie an mir vorüberziehen.« Gehalt und Struktur schließen an die früheren Oden an, vgl. aber auch das Sonett *Auf den Ruhm.* – Motto: Matthäus 6,28.

149,13 *Phidias' Künsten:* Phidias (um 490–448 v. Chr.), griechischer Bildhauer, Schöpfer u.a. der »Elgin Marbles«.

151,10 *dieser kurze Fieberstich:* vgl. Shakespeare, *Macbeth* III,2,23: »Sanft schläft er nach des Lebens Fieberschauern«; der Bezug legt nahe, daß Keats bei »Liebe«, »Ehrgeiz« und »Poesie« auch an die drei Hexen aus »Macbeth« dachte.

153,4 f. *Denn ich will ... Farce!:* eine Reaktion auf die herabwürdigende Ablehnung v.a. der *Poems* in verschiedenen konservativen Blättern (vgl. hierzu Keats' Brief an James Augustus Hessey vom 8. Oktober 1818).

153 An den Herbst

Entstanden wahrscheinlich am 19. September 1819 in Winchester. Aufgenommen in L. Bei der Betrachtung eines Herbsttags gelangt die letzte der großen Oden zur reinen Form des »Aufgehens, Steigens und Untergehens ihrer Bildwelt, natürlich und glanzvoll wie die Sonne« (A. Ward). Anklänge gibt es an Thomas Chattertons *Aella*, Coleridges *Frost at Midnight* und an Verse Wordsworths, vgl. aber auch Keats' Sonett *Nachdem von trübem Dunst* sowie Keats' Brief an John Hamilton Reynolds vom 21. September 1819: »Wie schön die Jahreszeit jetzt ist – wie fein die Luft. Voll leichter Herbheit. Wirklich, ohne Scherz, keusches Wetter, Dianahimmel – nie zuvor habe ich Stoppelfelder so sehr gemocht wie gerade jetzt. Ja, viel mehr als das frostige Grün des Frühlings. Irgendwie sieht ein Stoppelfeld warm aus, genauso wie manche Bilder warm aussehen.«

153,4 *Busenfreundin:* In Verbindung mit den Personifizierungen der zweiten Strophe, die Darstellungen der römischen Fruchtbarkeitsgöttin Ceres aufgreifen, erscheint der Herbst entgegen der Tradition in weiblicher Gestalt.

155,22 *Busch-Heimchen:* In dieser ›Verbindung‹ von Buschgrillen und Heimchen sind Sommer und Winter gleichzeitig präsent (vgl. das Sonett *Auf Grashüpfer und Heimchen*).

157 An Fanny

Verfaßt wahrscheinlich im Februar 1820, kurz nach der ersten Lungenblutung (vgl. Zeittafel). Erstdruck 1848. Zur Entstehungszeit des Gedichts war Keats bereits stark geschwächt und pflegebedürftig; Fanny Brawne lebte gemeinsam mit ihrer Mutter im selben Haus und hatte Keats' Angebot, das Verlöbnis zu lösen, abgelehnt. Vgl. auch Keats' Briefe an Fanny Brawne vom Februar bis August 1820.

157,5 *Dreifuß:* dreifüßiger Stuhl, auf dem Pythia, die Priesterin zu Delphi, die Sprüche des Orakels verkündete.

161,4–6 *der Heilgen Liebe Stuhl / Abendmahl:* vgl. die erotisch-religiöse Metaphorik im Sonett *Der Tag ist fort!*

165 Schlaf und Dichtung

Geschrieben von Oktober bis Dezember 1816, größtenteils in Leigh Hunts Cottage im Valley of Health, Hampstead. Das Epos greift Themen aus der Epistel *An meinen Bruder George* auf und weist in Anliegen und Ausdruck bereits auf die reiferen Werke voraus. Der Abriß der künstlerischen Entwicklung in Z. 96–154 erinnert an Wordsworth' *Tintern Abbey;* vgl. aber auch Keats' »Gleichnis vom menschlichen Leben« als einem »großen Haus mit vielen Gemächern« (Brief an John Hamilton Reynolds vom 3. Mai 1818). Keats kurzer Überblick der englischen Dichtungsgeschichte in Z. 162–229 zeigt seine eindeutige Präferenz elisabethanischer und Dichter des siebzehnten Jahrhunderts (Z. 171–180). *Schlaf und Dichtung* fand Aufnahme in P. – Das Motto stammt aus dem altenglischen Epos *The Floure and the Leafe,* Z. 17 bis 21, das heute nicht mehr als Werk Chaucers gilt.

165,15 *Cordelias Gesicht:* Cordelia, eine der drei Töchter des König Lear.

167,11 f. *Phantasien … Kamin:* vgl. *An die Hoffnung* sowie *An meine Brüder.*

167,14 *Mäander:* altgriech. Name des Flusses Menderes in Westanatolien.

167,28 *Montmorencis Sturzwand:* Montmorenci: wasserfallreicher Fluß in der kanadischen Provinz Quebec.

169,5 *Stengeln:* Stengel: aus der Luft betrachtete Bäume.

170,34 *Stäbe Jakobs:* vgl. 1. Mose 30,37–42.

171,2 *Leierspieler:* Apoll.

171,6 *Boileau:* Nicolas Boileau-Despréaux (1636–1711), französischer Dichter und Kritiker, stellte in seiner *Art poétique* Gesetze und Grundsätze literarischen Schaffens auf.

171,35 *Polyphemen:* nach Polyphem, dem einäugigen Riesen der Odysseus-Sage.

172,12 *der Poesie … ein Freund:* vgl. *Ode auf eine griechische Urne,* Z. 48.

172,15 *Paphos:* im Altertum blühende Stadt auf Zypern.

175,16 *Im Haus des Dichters:* Beschreibung der Bibliothek von Hunts Cottage mit seinen Reproduktionen von Gemälden Poussins, Claude Lorrains und Tizians.

176,7 *Sapphos edle Züge:* Bezug genommen wird auf eine Büste der griechischen Dichterin.

176,11 *Alfreds des Großen:* Alfred der Große (849–901), König von Wessex, brach die Übermacht der dänischen Wikinger in England und förderte die altenglische Literatur.

176,13 *Kosciuszkos:* Tadeusz Kosciuszko (1746–1817), polnischer Feldherr, kämpfte gegen die Teilung Polens und im Unabhängigkeitskrieg auf amerikanischer Seite.

176,15 f. *Petrarca / Lauras:* vgl. das Sonett *Scharf wechseln Böen* und die dazugehörige Anm.

177 **Endymion. Eine poetische Romanze**

Entstanden von April bis November 1817. Erschienen im Mai 1818. Keats kannte den Mythos von dem Hirtenkönig, in den sich die Mondgöttin verliebt, aus Lemprières *Classical Dictionary* (1788); beeinflußt wurde er überdies durch Spences *Polymetis*, Draytons *Man in the Moone*, Lylys *Endimion* sowie Ovids *Metamorphosen*. *Endymion* entstand im Wettstreit mit Shelley – beide Dichter sollten ein Werk von über 4000 Zeilen im Herbst 1817 fertiggestellt haben (vgl. I,49–57) – und wurde v. a. von konservativen Blättern als Ableger der »Cockney-School« um Leigh Hunt polemisch angegriffen. Keats selbst beschrieb die Dichtung in einem bereits entschärften Vorwort als »nicht von solcher Vollkommenheit, daß ihr Gedrucktwerden sich rechtfertigen ließe [...]: die Fundamente sind zu sandig. Sollte dies Junge wegsterben, so hat es seine Gründe. [...] Natürlich schreibe ich dies nicht mit dem leisesten Hauch der Absicht, Kritik vorwegzunehmen, sondern allein aus meinem Wunsch heraus, Menschen versöhnlich zu stimmen, die zu sehen fähig sind und sehen mit einem andächtigen Aug, zur Ehre der englischen Literatur. Die Vorstellungskraft eines Knaben ist gesund wie die reife Vorstellungskraft eines Mannes gesund ist; es gibt jedoch einen Lebensabschnitt dazwischen, in welchem die Seele sich in der Gärung befindet, der Charakter unentschieden ist, der Lebensweg ungewiß, der Ehrgeiz kurzsichtig: daher rühren Süßlichkeit und all die tausend Bitterkeiten, die jene Menschen, von denen ich spreche, notwendigerweise schmecken müssen, gehen sie die folgenden Seiten durch.« – Motto: Shakespeares Sonett 17, Z. 12.

179,5 *Latmos Felsenhänge:* Latmos: Berg in Kleinasien, in der Sage die Heimat Endymions.
180,20 *Ganymed:* der schöne Mundschenk des Zeus.
181,3–183,10 *O du, des mächtiger ... Berg dir an:* die »Hymne an Pan« gilt durch ihren Ausdruck und die Struktur als wichtiger Schritt hin zu den großen Oden des Spätwerks.
181,7 *Dryas:* Baumnymphe.
181,15 f. *Syrinx' ... Liebeswahn:* die Nymphe verwandelte sich auf der Flucht vor Pan in ein Schilfrohr.
183,9 *Päan:* feierliches Dank- oder Preislied.
183,14 *ionische Delphine:* Delphine im Ionischen Meer, das zwischen Griechenland und Unteritalien liegt.
183,22 *Thermopylaens:* Thermopylae: Engpaß in Mittelgriechenland, 480 v. Chr.; Ort der Niederlage des Leonidas gegen Xerxes.

184,7 *Marmormensch ... Arabiens alte Mär:* vgl. den versteinerten Prinzen der *Märchen aus 1001 Nacht.*
184,32 *Schwesterliebe:* Die Figur der Peona, die Endymion beigesellte Schwester, belegt Keats' Bestreben, die klassische Mythologie zu vermenschlichen.
188,31 *Des Morpheus Quelle:* Morpheus: griechischer Gott des Schlafes.
189,21 *Essenz:* Übersetzung von engl. »essence« (Sein, Wesen); Keats war ausgebildeter Apotheker und nutzte Metaphern aus dem Bereich der Chemie (vgl. seinen Brief an Benjamin Bailey vom 22. November 1817).
190,6 *Ich-auslöschender:* vgl. die *Ode an eine Nachtigall,* Z. 21, 72.
191,9 f. *Winzigkeiten ... Gedanken-Fliegen:* vgl. Shakespeare, *Romeo und Julia,* I,4,58 f.
192,6–8 *Versenken ... Rand der Welt:* vgl. das Sonett *Wenn Furcht mir kommt.*
193,13 *Hellas' großem Admiral:* Themistokles, dessen Flotte 480 v. Chr. bei Salamis die Perser schlug.
193,17–22 *Julia / Hero / Imogen / Pastorella:* die Heldinnen aus Shakespeares *Romeo and Juliet,* Marlowes *Hero and Leander,* Shakespeares *Cymbeline* und Spensers *The Faerie Queene.*
196,5 f. *durch Nesseln ... Feuer zieht:* vgl. Shakespeare, *König Lear* III, 4,50 ff.
198,3 *in des Kariers Ohr:* d. h. in Endymions Ohr; der Berg Latmos liegt in Karien.
200,3 *hesperisch:* nach Hesperus, dem Abendstern.
200,5 f. *Wohligkeit ... geseufztes Glück:* vgl. *Ode auf die Lässigkeit,* Z. 16–18.
200,15–23 *O mein Herz ... wahren Müßiggang:* Endymion rätselt, ob die unbekannte Geliebte eine der Horen (Z. 688), eine der Plejaden (Z. 689 f.), eine Seenymphe (Z. 690 f.) oder eine Gehilfin Dianas (Z. 692 ff.) ist.
200,25 *Auroras:* Aurora: römische Göttin der Morgenröte.
201,21 *Minervas:* Minerva: römische Göttin der Künste.
202,1 *Empyriums:* Empyrium: Götterhimmel.
203,26–204,13 *Manch einer ... ihr Ziel:* Attacke gegen die Tory-Regierung u. a. reaktionäre Regime gemäß Leigh Hunts Artikeln im *Examiner.*
203,32 f. *Fuchsfackeln ... Hoffnungen:* vgl. Buch der Richter 15,4–5.
204,3 *Volk im Purpurkleid:* der Klerus.
204,34 *holde Schwester:* Diana, der Mond.

205,26 *lenzt's:* lenzen: seemännisch für »vor dem Sturm laufen«.
205,27 *Tellus':* Tellus: die Urgöttin der Erde.
206,26–28 *glänzendhellem Wesen ... Natur:* vgl. das Sonett *Glänzender Stern!*, Z. 1,10–12.
207,17–29 *Zu verweben ... Meers um mich:* illustrierendes Beispiel für eine »Gemeinschaft mit Essenz«.
208,10–16 *grüne Flut ... gellen:* vgl. Shakespeare, *Der Sturm* I,2,3–9.
210,29 *Memphis / Babylon / Ninive:* drei antike, für ihre Pracht berühmte Städte.
211,30 *Äolus:* griechischer Gott der Winde.
212,11–30 *Blast leise ... zu hörn:* vgl. die *Ode auf eine griechische Urne*, Z. 11–14.
212,18 *Kythere:* Venus, die nach Hesiod nahe Kythera dem Meer entstieg.
213,20 *Von Osten kam erhabnes Singen:* der erhabene hebräische Stil der Bibel.
213,21 *Neun:* die neun Musen.
213,25 *Ausonia:* der klassische Name Italiens, das erst mit Vergil, später mit Dante zu ›sprechen‹ begann.
214,10–218,23 *»O Sorgen ... Dunkelheit.«:* Keats kommentiert das »kleine Lied« im Brief an Benjamin Bailey vom 22. November 1817 gemeinsam mit seinen »Lieblingsideen« aus dem »ersten Buch« des *Endymion*.
215,18 *In Wasserlilien:* vgl. Milton, *Lycidas*, Z. 150.
216,15 *Silen:* der trunkene greise Begleiter des Bacchus.
217,22 *Einhorn:* gemeint ist das Nashorn.
217,23 *Osiris':* Osiris: ägyptischer Fruchtbarkeits- und Totengott.
217,31 *Brahma:* das All-Eine im hinduistischen Glauben.
219,34–220,2 *Er, der ... schmolz:* Ikarus.
220,18 *dädalisch:* Spenser wie auch Shelley benutzen das engl. »daedal« im Sinne von »kunstfertig, geübt«.
221,10 *Es liegt eine Höhle:* vgl. die Beschreibung der »Höhle der Verschwiegenheit« mit der *Ode auf die Melancholie*.
221,34 *Semele:* die Mutter des Bacchus.
223,23 *Umschlungen sterben:* vgl. die *Ode an eine Nachtigall*, Z. 55.
224,3 *Rhadamanthus:* Sohn Jupiters, einer der Höllenrichter.
224,6 f. *Bei Greis Saturnus ... durchkrampft:* vgl. *Hyperion* I,89–94.

225 **Hyperion. Ein Fragment**

Geschrieben von September bis Dezember 1818. Aufgenommen in L. Das Epos orientierte sich ursprünglich vom Umfang her an Miltons *Verlorenem Paradies,* dem es auch stilistisch und metaphorisch so stark verpflichtet ist, daß Keats es v.a. deshalb im April 1819 aufgab. Die Rahmenhandlung schildert den Machtverlust der Titanen zugunsten der Olympier: kraft »ewigen Gesetzes« wird Saturn von Jupiter, Hyperion vom neuen Sonnengott Apoll abgelöst. Hesiods *Theogonie,* Hyginus' *Fabulae* sowie Dantes *Göttliche Komödie* komplettierten Keats' mythologische Quellen (s. Anm. zu *Endymion*). Keats selbst vergleicht *Endymion* und *Hyperion* in seinem Brief an Benjamin Robert Haydon vom 23. Januar 1818.

226,2 *Ixions Rad:* Ixion wurde von Jupiter an ein ewig sich drehendes Rad gefesselt.

226,6–8 *dies Antlitz … gemacht:* vgl. *Der Fall des Hyperion* I,256ff.

227,33–228,4 *Sieh auf … Kraft her:* vgl. Shakespeare, *King Lear* I,4,226ff.

229,13 *Die drei Rebellen:* Saturns Söhne Jupiter, Neptun und Pluto, die das Reich des Vaters unter sich aufteilten.

229,33 *sog ein noch Weihrauch:* vgl. Milton, *Das verlorene Paradies* X, 272f.

231,12 *Horen:* in der griechischen Mythologie ursprünglich Personifikationen der Jahreszeiten.

232,35 *Breitgürtige Koluren:* durch die Himmelspole gelegte Kreise.

233,1 *Nadir:* in der Astronomie der dem Zenit gegenüberliegende Punkt an der Himmelskugel.

233,32 *Coelus:* auch Uranus, der griechische Himmelsgott und Vater der Titanen.

233,36 *Mächtepaar:* Coelus und Tellus, die Erdgöttin.

235,15 *Kybele:* Göttermutter, oft gleichgesetzt mit Tellus.

235,30 *Gyges:* Keats' Umgang mit mythologischen Namen ist recht frei; Gyges – wie auch manch anderer der im folgenden genannten – gehört nicht zu den Titanen.

237,2 *Oxus:* Fluß östlich des Kaspischen Meers.

237,16 *Gorgonen:* drei weibliche Ungeheuer, deren Blicke versteinerten.

240,4 *sein Haar nicht triefend:* Okeanus' Haar ist trocken, da es seines Elements, des Wassers, beraubt ist.

240,15 *Wir fallen durch Naturgesetz:* Okeanus' Rede illustriert im folgenden u.a. Keats' Ansicht, daß sowohl persönliche Entwicklung als auch Geschichte im allgemeinen dem Gesetz des Fortschritts unterliegen. Vgl. Apollos »Vergöttlichung« (III,113–120), die Ausführungen zu individuellem Wissen in *Schlaf und Dichtung*, Z. 101 bis 121, und den Brief an John Hamilton Reynolds vom 3. Mai 1818.

241,30 *den jungen Gott der Meere:* Neptun, der Nachfolger des Okeanus.

243,20 *›Apoll! junger Apoll!‹:* vgl. das Gedicht *Apollo zu den Grazien.*

244,34 *das beschwingte Ding / Sieg:* die Siegesgöttin wird mit Flügeln dargestellt.

245,32/34 *Des Memnonbilds / Memnons Harfe:* Memnon, dem Sohn Auroras wurde bei Theben ein riesiges Steinbildnis errichtet, das der Sage nach zu jedem Sonnenaufgang feierliche Töne von sich gab.

246,26/28 *Delph'sche Harfe / Dor'sche Flöte:* Instrumente, die von Apolls anbrechender Herrschaft künden.

247,12 *Gigant der Sonne:* Hyperion.

248,23 f. *Macht, / Die Throne … verließ:* Mnemosyne, die Göttin des Gedächtnisses, hat die Titanen um Apollos willen verlassen.

249,29–31 *als hätt ich … jetzt unsterblich:* vgl. *Ode an eine Nachtigall,* Z. 2–4.

249,35 *Bald griff ihn wilde Regung:* vgl. Apollos Vergöttlichung mit Lamias ›Verweiblichung‹ (*Lamia,* Z. 146–168).

251 Der St.-Agnes-Abend

Verfaßt im Januar und Februar 1819, überarbeitet im September. Aufgenommen in L. Aufgrund seiner offensichtlich erotisch-religiösen Bildersprache (v. a. in Z. 314–322) war das Epos einst heftig umstritten. So mußte Keats auf Drängen seines Verlegers Taylor die folgende (nach Strophe VI eingefügte) »für Damen ungeeignete« Strophe wieder streichen: »Ihr zukünftiger Herr erschien ihr da / Und brächte opfernd – noch im Traum diesmal – / Köstliche Speisen ihren Lippen nah: / Daß Wurst, Wein, süßer Rahm wie Früchte prall / Am Gaumen sie berühre, überall / Geschmack – zu hören wär Musik, zu sehn / Noch mehr Genuß, in blendendhellem Schwall / Fast fühlbar. Wach dann wieder aufzustehn, / Am keuschen Morgen warm, nicht weinend Magdalen!« Die Liebesgeschichte von Porphyro und Madeleine fragt u. a. nach Wesen und Verhältnis von Vorstellungskraft und Verblendung; eingebettet ist sie in eine Szenerie, mit der sich Keats bewußt in die Tradition mittelalterlicher Dichtung stellt. Darüber hinaus verarbeitete er u. a. Shakespeares *Romeo und Julia,* Boccaccios *Decame-*

ron und Burtons *Anatomie der Melancholie.* Keats selbst empfand das »kleine Gedicht« als zu genüßlich und sentimental und plante das Drama *König Stephen* als Gegenentwurf. – Die hl. Agnes (griech. ›die Keusche‹) ist Schutzpatronin der Jungfräulichkeit. Am St.-Agnes-Abend, der Nacht zum 21. Januar, erscheint der Überlieferung zufolge der fastenden und in sich gehenden Jungfrau ihr künftiger Gatte.

251,7 *Fürbitters:* Fürbitter: ein für Gebete bezahlter Bettler oder Kirchendiener.
255,8–10 *beim heilgen Webstuhl ... Wolle drehn:* Gehuldigt wird der hl. Agnes alljährlich in der gleichnamigen römischen Basilika; Nonnen spinnen dort die Wolle zweier geweihter Lämmer zu Garn.
257,10 *Merlin ... die Schuld beglich:* Merlin hatte seine Zauberkraft von einem väterlichen Dämon erhalten; als er sie in liebender Verblendung Nimue offenbarte, vernichtete sie ihn damit.
258,19 f. *zungenlos ... die Nachtigall:* Philomele wurde von Tereus geschändet und der Zunge beraubt; die Götter verwandelten sie daraufhin in eine Nachtigall.
260,15 *Jett:* Pechkohle.
261,7 f. *Nun sei ... erwacht:* vgl. das Sonett *Glänzender Stern!*, Z. 1–4.
261,25 *Lied der Provence:* vgl. *La Belle Dame sans Merci* u. Anm.
263,22 *343: Elfenwind des Märchenlands:* vgl. *La Belle Dame sans Merci*, Z. 29 und *Ode an eine Nachtigall*, Z. 70, 74.
264,27 *Angela starb alt:* In Keats' überarbeiteter Fassung hieß es: »Angela trat ab / Gelähmt vom Schlagfluß; sein Gesicht entstellt, / Halb stöhnend und halb lächelnd, aber starb / Der Fürbitter und sank kurz keuchend steif ins Grab.«

265 **Der St.-Markus-Abend**

Entstanden im Februar 1819. Erstdruck 1848. Das unvollendete Epos ist inhaltlich eng verbunden mit *Der St.-Agnes-Abend*, seine v. a. Thomas Chattertons *Aella* nachempfundene Atmosphäre komprimiert nicht minder mittelalterliche Wirklichkeit, Traum und religiöse Verblendung. Den Rahmen hierzu bildet der in Yorkshire verbreitete Brauch, sich über drei Jahre hinweg jeweils am Abend des 24. April in der Kirchenhalle zu versammeln; der Legende zufolge erscheinen dort die Geister jener Einwohner, die im darauffolgenden Jahr sterben.

265,23 *Auf den ... Orgeln bliesen:* vgl. die Beschreibung Korinths in *Lamia* I, 352–361.
265,25 *Bertha:* Name der Heldin in Chattertons *Aella*.

265,30 *Himmelssternen:* Hier und in den folgenden acht Versen schildert Keats Details, die er an den Glasfenstern der StanstedKapelle bei Bedhampton gesehen hatte.
266,1 *Aarons Brustschild:* vgl. 2. Mose 28,15–30.
266,1 f. *Leuchtern ... beschrieben:* vgl. Offenbarung des Johannes 1,12 bis 20.
265,3 *seinem Flügel:* Sinnbild des hl. Markus ist ein geflügelter Löwe.
266,4 *Bundeslade ... Cherubim:* vgl. Hebräer 9,4–5.
266,6 *goldne Mäuse:* vgl. 1. Samuel 6,1–5.
266,12 *Sykomorn:* Sykomoren: Bergahornbäume.
267,13 *Lima-Mäuse:* gemeint sind wohl Gespenster- oder Koboldmakis, eine Lemurenaffenart (engl. »lemur mice«).
267,14 *Avadavat:* Amadavat: indischer Singvogel.
267,14 *fußlose Trauben ... Paradies:* Der Legende nach kann der Paradiesvogel nicht landen – er ist »fußlos«.
267,19 *Pik-Dame:* die Todeskarte.
267,32 *Also von träumen ... vnd leben:* Keats imitiert hier Chaucer im Stil Chattertons.
267,35 *lailachklaid:* Leilachkleid: Totenhemd aus Leinen.
268,10 *Sankt Ciciliens:* die hl. Cäcilie, Schutzpatronin der Musik.
268,17 *Venedig:* der hl. Markus ist der Schutzpatron Venedigs.

269 **Lamia**

Geschrieben von Juli bis September 1819 auf der Insel Wight und in Winchester, überarbeitet im darauffolgenden März. Aufgenommen in L. Die Geschichte Lamias, der häßlich-schönen, ihre Kinder verschlingenden Schlangenfrau, las Keats in Lemprières *Classical Dictionary* und hat sie für seine Zwecke umgewandelt; Quellen für die Hermes-Episode (I,1–145) waren v.a. Ovids *Metamorphosen* und Marlowes *Hero und Leander.* Klarheit und Objektivität, die er in *Endymion* und *Der St.-Agnes-Abend* vermißte, hoffte Keats mit *Lamia* zu erlangen; in einem Brief schrieb er: »Ich bin sicher, daß [die Dichtung] ein gewisses Feuer erfüllt, welches die Leute irgendwie packen muß. Gib ihnen schöne oder unschöne Empfindungen – was sie wollen, sind Empfindungen, welcher Art sie auch sind.«

269,3–8 *Zu einer Zeit ... Primelauen:* Darstellungen der Vertreibung klassisch-mythologischer Figuren durch die Gestalten der englischen Volkssage waren zu Keats' Zeit weit verbreitet.
269,5 *Oberons:* Oberon, Elfenkönig in Shakespeares *Ein Sommernachtstraum,* ursprünglich Gestalt eines altfranzösischen Epos.

269,18 *Tritonen:* Triton: eine griechische Meergottheit, halb Mensch, halb Delphin.

270,26 *Ariadnes Kranz:* Bacchus schenkte Ariadne einen Kranz aus sieben Sternen.

270,31 *Wie um … weint:* Pluto entführte Proserpina aus Sizilien in die Unterwelt, wo sie Königin wurde; in anderen Darstellungen verwandelt Jupiter sie in eine Schlange.

271,11 *Phöbus' hellem Speer:* Phöbus Speer: die Strahlen der Sonne.

271,15 *Lethes Stern:* Zu den zahlreichen Aufgaben des Götterboten gehörte es auch, die Geister der Toten bis zu Charons Fähre über die Lethe zu geleiten.

273,6 *Nicht blaß wie sterbliche Verliebte:* vgl. die *Ode auf eine griechische Urne*, Z. 25–30.

273,8 *Elfenblut:* vgl. die *Ode an eine Nachtigall*, Z. 73 f.

273,35 *Kenchreä:* Hafen des antiken Korinth.

274,2 *Peräa:* der Stadt Korinth vorgelagerte Hügelkette.

274,5 *Kleonä:* Dorf südlich von Korinth.

275,17 *Ägina:* Insel zwischen Peloponnes und Attika.

278,13 *Peris:* zum Guten strebende feenhafte Wesen in der altpersischen Mythologie.

278,17 *Pyrrhas Kieseln:* Pyrrha, gemeinsam mit Deukalion Überlebende einer Sintflut, warf die orakelhaft verheißenen Kieselsteine über ihre Schultern und ›säte‹ so die neuen Menschen.

279,26 *Apollonius:* Apollonius von Tyana, Philosoph der pythagoreischen Schule, lebte im ersten Jahrhundert n. Chr.

281,1–10 *Seit an Seit … sichtbar bliebe:* vgl. die *Ode an Psyche*, Z. 9–20.

282,21–26 *Auch fand … dunkle Venen:* vgl. die *Ode auf die Melancholie*, Z. 18–20.

286,9–30 *Weich glitt … umflochten:* In einer früheren Fassung kontrastierte Keats Opulenz und tumbe Trunkenheit beim Hochzeitsgelage satirischer: »Weich die Musik, die Tische hell entbrannt / Unter dem unsichtbaren Fahnenband / Des Zaubers; aufgestellt in Doppelreihn, / Schien jeder ein verschneites Beet zu sein, / Sprechende Blumen schmückend an den Wegen, / Die lachten, redeten nach warmem Regen; / Und packte süßer Appetit den Sinn, / Ergoß sich Wein und schnitt man Fleisch hauchdünn. / Weich die Musik, der flache Teller sang, / Geküßt vom leeren Krug – und neuer Klang: / Flink räumten Diener ab – »Zum Wohl, ihr Leute«, / Schrien einer – zwei – schon leert, als wär er Beute, / Ein Gierhals einen Becher Helikon. / Zu schnell, zu schnell schlüpft sein Genuß davon. / »Woher kommt die Musik?« fragt eine Schöne. / »Ja, Schatz, woher nur? Hat die Luft hier Töne?« / »Puh!« wispert einer, »Mmh!« des Gierhals Gaumen, / Schon formt sein fetter Mund ein Tuch für seinen Daumen.«

286,27 *weiden-goldnen Körben:* aus den golden glänzenden Zweigen des Weidenbaums geflochtene Körbe.

286,34 *Natterzungen:* Farnpflanzen.

287,2 *Thyrsus:* der efeu- und weinlaubumrankte Stab des Bacchus.

287,5–7 *Flieht nicht ... ein Regenbogen:* vgl. Keats' Artikel über den Shakespeare-Darsteller Kean im *Champion* vom 21. Dezember 1817: »Erfreut uns ein wenig in unserer mangelhaften Zeit! – denn das Poetische lebt allein in Büchern noch – vertrieben von der Heide ist der Kobold, und der Regenbogen ist all seiner Geheimnisse beraubt!« (Vgl. auch die Briefe an Benjamin Bailey vom 13. März 1818 und an John Hamilton Reynolds vom 3. Mai 1818 sowie *Schlaf und Dichtung,* Z. 101–121.

288,31 *Sein Dämonauge:* zum Rollentausch zwischen Apollonius und Lamia vgl. u. a. I,56.

290 **Der Fall des Hyperion. Ein Traum**

Verfaßt von Juli bis September 1819, u. a. auf der Insel Wight. Erstdruck 1856. Die Wiederaufnahme des im April aufgegebenen Hyperion-Komplexes sucht die Strukturen von *Hyperion, Der St.-Agnes-Abend* und *Lamia* zu verbinden. Die Frage nach dem Wesen von Dichtung und Dichter, die Dialektik zwischen Traum und Wirklichkeit sowie verstärktes Angehen der Leidensproblematik sollten das ohnehin mächtige Vorhaben *Hyperion* ergänzen. Das Epos belegt deutlich Keats fortgesetzte Milton- v. a. aber Dante-Lektüre (vgl. den Brief an John Hamilton Reynolds vom 24. August 1819). In einem Brief an Reynolds vom September 1819 erläutert Keats den Grund für den neuerlichen Abbruch des Werks: »Ich habe Hyperion aufgegeben: Es waren zuviel Miltonsche Inversionen darin. Miltonsche Verse kann man nicht anders schreiben als in einer kunstfertigen oder besser gesagt künstlerischen Stimmung. Ich möchte mich anderen Empfindungen hingeben. Das Englische sollte mehr gepflegt werden.« Im Herbst 1819 brach überdies die Lungentuberkulose des Dichters offen aus.

292,5 *Verfehl:* deutsche Nachbildung der Keatsschen Prägung »faulture« (»fault«/»failure«).

292,10 *von Motten ... nicht zu fressen:* vgl. Matthäus 6,20.

292,18 *bossierte Dach:* bossieren: behauen.

293,3 *Majas Weihrauch:* Duft wie von Maienblumen; vgl. auch die *Ode an den Mai* und *An Leigh Hunt*, Esq., Z. 7–8.

293,35 f. *Wie holde Engel ... flogen:* vgl. Jakobs Himmelsleiter, 1. Mose 28,12.

294,1 *behörnten Schrein:* Antike Altäre waren oftmals mit Hörnern verziert.

294,12 *Leid der Welt:* vgl. *Schlaf und Dichtung*, Z. 122–125.

295,31 *in einem Anfall Pythias:* Die Priesterin des Apollo-Schreins zu Delphi verkündete die Sprüche des Orakels sozusagen in Trance.

295,35–296,1 *Spottlyristen ... mieser Dichtkunst:* vgl. Keats' frühere Attacke auf die zeitgenössische Dichtung in *Schlaf und Dichtung*, Z. 231–235.

296,24 *Monetas:* Moneta, Beiname der römischen Himmelsgöttin Juno.

303,9 *Vorraum dieses Traums:* vgl. den Brief an John Hamilton Reynolds vom 3. Mai 1818, in dem Keats sein »Gleichnis vom menschlichen Leben« als einem »großen Haus mit vielen Gemächern« entwirft.

309 **König Stephen. Ein Fragment einer Tragödie**

Geschrieben wahrscheinlich von August bis November 1819. Erstdruck 1848. Im Gegensatz zu dem abgeschlossenen Fünfakter *Otho the Great*, den Keats nach Plänen und Vorstellungen seines Freunds Brown lediglich ausformulierte, gilt das *King Stephen*-Fragment als eigenständiger Versuch des Dichters, ein Drama shakespearescher Prägung zu schreiben: »mein größter Ehrgeiz – wenn ich einmal ehrgeizig bin« (Brief an John Taylor vom 17. November 1819). Die Rahmenhandlung bildet die Thronfolgeschlacht um Lincoln im Jahr 1141. Stephen von Blois (auch Boulogne), seit dem Tod Heinrichs I. im Jahre 1135 Träger der englischen Krone, unterliegt – nach deren Landung in England – Mathilde (Maud), der Tochter Heinrichs. Nach Mathildes Sieg über Stephen folgen Bürgerkrieg und Jahre der Anarchie. 1154 trat Stephen zugunsten Heinrichs II. ab.

309,16 *Gloucester:* Robert von Gloucester, Halbbruder Mauds, durchbrach gemeinsam mit Ranulf von Chester die Belagerung Lincolns durch Stephens Heer.

310,1 f. *De Redvers ... Baldwin sich fürchtet:* Keats verwechselt Baldwin de Redvers, der auf Seiten Mauds stand, mit Baldwin Fitz-Gilbert, einem Anführer des königlichen Heers.

311,16 *Der Herzog der Bretagne:* Alan, der Anführer der mit den Königstruppen verbündeten bretonischen Streitmacht.

311,17 *Wales' Beaglen:* nimmt Bezug auf die englische Spürhundrasse Beagle; das unabhängige Fürstentum Wales unterstützte Maud im Kampf gegen Stephen.
311,23 *Pallas ... Ilions:* Pallas ist ein Beiname Athenes, der griechischen Schutzgöttin des Kampfes, Ilion ein anderer Name Trojas.
313,5 *Bellonas:* Bellona: die römische Kriegsgöttin.
313,14 *Pylos ... Nestors Bart:* Nestor, König von Pylos, überlebte als einer der griechischen Anführer den Trojanischen Krieg.
315,5 *Boulogne:* Stephen war vermählt mit der Tochter des Grafen von Boulogne.
317,7 *Dezember wird Juni sein:* vgl. Shakespeare, *Richard III.* I,1,1 f.: »Nun ward der Winter unsers Mißvergnügens / Glorreicher Sommer durch die Sonne Yorks«.

319 **Briefe**

321,23–27 *Igel sollen ... Schoß der Zeit:* beide Zitate aus Shakespeares *Der Sturm* I,2.
322,5–8 *Ein edles Herz ... schaffen will:* Spenser, *The Faerie Queene* I,5,1–4.
322,24 *Mein Gedicht:* gemeint ist *Endymion*, an dem Keats in Margate zu arbeiten begonnen hatte.
323,13–19 *Mag Ruhm ... Zukunft:* Shakespeare, *Liebes Leid und Lust* I,1.
323,27 f. *Rechnungspestilenz:* Der Maler Haydon war ständig in Geldschwierigkeiten.
324,6 f. *einer, Fenchel ... Handwerk:* Shakespeare, *König Lear* IV,6.
324,11 *Mäusen gleich:* Shakespeare, *König Lear* IV,6.
325,9 *Alfred:* Der Angelsachsenkönig Alfred der Große verband militärische Machtfülle mit herausragender Kulturleistung (vgl. *Schlaf und Dichtung*, Z. 385–389 und Anm.).
327,26 *keinen Lorbeerkranz:* Nach Erscheinen von Keats' erstem Gedichtband hatte Leigh Hunt dem Verfasser einen Lorbeerkranz aufgesetzt, worauf Keats zwei Sonette schrieb (vgl. *An eine junge Dame*).
330,34 *das muß Wahrheit sein:* vgl. die *Ode auf eine griechische Urne*, Z. 49 f. und Anm.
331,1 *durch ihre Sublimierung:* Keats greift einerseits zurück auf die für die englische Romantik grundlegende Schrift von Edmund Burke *A Philosophical Inquiry into the Origins of our Ideas of the Sublime and the Beautiful* (1756), andererseits verwendet er seine Kenntnisse aus der zeitgenössischen Chemie und Physiologie, in

der die Sublimation und Ätherisierung fester Stoffe eine wichtige Rolle spielten. Vgl. das Gedicht *Wer ist Dichter?*

331,3 *aus dem kleinen Lied: Endymion* IV,146–290.

331,6 *Adams Traum:* vgl. Milton, *Das verlorene Paradies* VIII,460 bis VIII,490; Adam erlebt im Traum, wie Gott aus seiner Rippe Eva erschafft; als er erwacht, findet er Eva lebendig vor sich.

333,24 *»Christus wird von den Juden verleugnet«:* Gemälde von Benjamin West (1738–1820); der Amerikaner West war – als Nachfolger Joshua Reynolds – seit 1792 Präsident der Royal Academy.

333,28 *Hill:* Thomas Hill, ein reicher Kunstsammler und Mitherausgeber der Zeitschrift *The Monthly Mirror.*

333,28 *Kingston:* John Kingston war stellvertretender Aufseher der Stempelbehörde und damit unmittelbarer Vorgesetzter Wordsworths, der als Stempelbeamter im Staatsdienst beschäftigt war.

333,29 *du Bois:* Edward Du Bois, Mitherausgeber des *Monthly Mirror* und Beiträger des radikaleren *Morning Chronicle.*

336,11 *Ihre Mahlzeit Haselnüsse:* Reynolds hatte zwei Robin-Hood-Sonette geschickt – gewissermaßen aus dem Sherwood-Forest und seinen Haselnußbüschen.

337,24 *mit Esau ziehen:* In 1. Mose wird erzählt, wie Esau, der Sohn Isaaks, von seinem Zwillingsbruder Jakob um das Erstgeburtsrecht betrogen wird.

337,26 *»schönäugige Bachstelzen«:* Zitat aus einem Gedicht Leigh Hunts (*The Nymphs* II,70).

337,27 *»Cherub Kontemplation«:* Milton, *Il Penseroso,* Z. 54.

337,28 f. *»Matthew … in der Hand«:* Wordsworth, *The Two April Mornings,* Z. 59 f.

337,29 f. *Jacques »hingestreckt an einer Eiche:* Figur und Zitat aus Shakespeares *Wie es Euch gefällt* (II,1).

338,7 *»Childe Harold«:* Byrons vierter Gesang von *Ritter Harolds Pilgerfahrt* erschien im April 1818.

338,20 f. *zu »allen zweiunddreißig Palästen«:* vermutlich die 32 »Orte der Freude« nach der Lehre Buddhas.

338,27 f. *»einen öden Winkel«:* Shakespeare, *Der Sturm* I,1.

338,28 f. *»zieht's rund … einen Gürtel«:* Shakespeare, *Ein Sommernachtstraum* II,1.

339,2 f. *»am Geist und Puls des Guten«:* Wordsworth, *The Old Cumberland Beggar,* Z. 77.

342,5 f. *»Oh! Eine Feuermuse … stiege!«:* Shakespeare, *Heinrich V.,* Prolog.

343,8 f. *»zu heiligen … betrachtet:* vgl. Shelley, *Hymn to Intellectual Beauty*, Z. 13–15.
344,11 *»Seht … hausen!«:* Shakespeare, *Heinrich VI.*, 3. Teil, V,1.
345,18 *»Leimruten … Flügel«:* vgl. Shakespeare, *Heinrich VI.*,2. Teil, III,3.
346,17 *Last des Mysteriums:* vgl. Wordsworth, *Tintern Abbey*, Z. 38.
346,22 *10000 Klafter tief:* vgl. Milton, *Das verlorene Paradies* II,934.
346,24 *eines flügellosen Geschöpfes:* vgl. Shakespeare, *König Lear* III,4.
346,34 f. *»die unsres Fleisches Erbteil«:* Shakespeare, *Hamlet* III,1.
347,29 *»Wissen ist Leid«:* vgl. Byron, *Manfred* I,1.
348,19 f. *Patmore / Coleman / Gray / Gay / Little:* mehr oder minder bedeutende englische Dichter (Little war ein Pseudonym für Thomas Moore).
348,23 *»von Gray … zu Shakespeare«:* Persiflage einer Zeile aus Popes *Essay on Man* IV,380: »From grave to gay, from lively to severe« (»Von ernst zu froh, von munter zu bedrückt«).
348,36 *Hogarth:* William Hogarth (1697–1764), berühmter Maler und Kupferstecher, fertigte u. a. Porträts beliebter Shakespeare-Darsteller an.
350,25 *»Comus«:* Maskenspiel Miltons, 1634 vor höfischem Publikum aufgeführt.
350,25 f. *der Scheiterhaufen in Smithfield:* In Smithfield, unmittelbar vor den östlichen Stadttoren Londons, wurden im 15. und 16. Jh. »Ketzer« öffentlich verbrannt.
351,16 *Moores Geschenk:* vermutlich ein Exemplar seines Werkes *The Fudge Family in Paris* (1818).
353,4 *Oxforder Zeitung:* Bailey hatte in der *Oxford University & City Harald and Midland County Chronicle* Besprechungen von *Endymion* veröffentlicht.
353,18 f. *weil Frauen Krebs bekommen:* vgl. Keats' Brief an Bailey vom 23. Januar 1818.
354,2 f. *»sonderlicher als Frauenliebe«:* 2. Samuel 1,26.
355,4 *Parenthese:* Wortspiel mit »parents« (Eltern) und »thesis« (Gebot).
355,9–11 *in greifbaren Dingen … die es nicht sind:* vgl. Keats' Einteilung der »übersinnlichen Dinge« im Brief an Benjamin Bailey vom 13. März 1818.
356,28 *»schwanger geht« mit Menschenliebe:* vgl. Spenser, *The Faerie Queene* I,5,1 f.
358,10 *Little Britain:* Straße im Londoner Osten, in der die Wohnung der Reynolds lag.

359,27 f. *»mit nach rückwärts ... Zauber bannen«:* Milton, *Comus*, Z. 817.

360,2 f. *Mr. John Keats, fünf Fuß hoch:* von Hunt verliehener Spitzname; Keats maß weniger als 1,60 m.

360,26–28 *vom Hängen ... beinahe ertrunken bin:* nach dem englischen Sprichwort: »Wem es bestimmt ist, gehängt zu werden, der kann nicht ertrinken.«

361,8 *Gestalt einer Frau:* gemeint ist Fanny Brawne; Keats verliebte sich in die Achtzehnjährige kurz nach seiner Rückkehr aus Schottland.

362,32 *»genus irritabile«:* (lat.) das reizbare Geschlecht (vgl. Horaz, *Epistulae* II,2,102).

363,10 *eine Sache für sich und steht allein:* vgl. Shakespeare, *Troilus und Cressida* I,2. Vgl. auch die Anm. zum Gedicht *Willkommen Glück, willkommen Sorgen.*

365,17 *Sir F. Burdett:* Sir Frances Burdett (1770–1844), ein bekannter Reformer unter den englischen Aristokraten, der mit den sogenannten Radikalen um Leigh Hunt in Verbindung stand.

365,21 f. *Algernon Sidney:* Sidney (1622–1683) war einer der herausragenden aristokratischen Republikaner.

365,29 f. *Justitian:* eigtl. Justinian: oströmischer Kaiser (527–565), ließ das römische Recht im *Corpus iuris civilis* aufzeichnen.

365,32 f. *Hog ... Lord Bacon:* Sir Frances Bacon (1561–1626), englischer Staatsmann und Philosoph, war u.a. Lordkanzler. Keats spielt mit der Bedeutung der englischen Namen »hog« (Schwein) und »bacon« (Speck).

366,8 f. *Zar Alexander:* Alexander I. erweiterte nach den Napoleonischen Kriegen mit Hilfe von Bildungs- und Verwaltungsreformen, durch Stärkung des Absolutismus und Kriege beträchtlich die Grenzen Rußlands.

366,9 *Diokletian:* römischer Kaiser von 284–305 n. Chr., ordnete Heer und Verwaltung neu zur Tetrarchie.

366,19 f. *Godwinschen Perfektibilitätsprinzips:* William Godwin (1756–1836), Moralphilosoph und Schriftsteller, entwickelte die Idee von der absoluten Vervollkommnungsfähigkeit durch Bildung bei Abwesenheit von Besitz und staatlichem Zwang.

366,27 *den beiden Sidneys:* neben Algernon Sidney (s.o.) wohl Sir Philip Sidney (1554–1585), Staatsmann am elisabethanischen Hof, Dichter und Verfasser u.a. der *Defense of Poesie.*

366,33 *Birkbecks Geist:* Morris Birkbeck (1764–1825) spekulierte mit angekauftem Siedlerland in Amerika; Keats' Verleger Taylor und Hessey hatten seine *Letters from Illinois* veröffentlicht.

367,26 f. *»rauscht ... Purpur herein«:* Milton, *Il Penseroso,* 97 f.

367,30 f. *»Verlorne Seele ... harre der Überfahrt«:* vgl. Shakespeare, *Troilus und Cressida* III,2.

368,30 f. *»solchen Wahnsinn ... weinen«:* vgl. Shakespeare, *Maß für Maß* II,2.

369,22 f. *Fertigstellung Ihres Bildes:* gemeint ist Haydons Gemälde »Triumphaler Einzug Christi in Jerusalem«; vgl. das Sonett *Das Haus der Trauer,* Z. 8 und Anm.

374,21 *cui bono:* (lat.): wem nützt es?

375,19 *Ode auf die Finsternis:* vgl. das Sonett *Was lachte ich heut nacht?*

375,32 *Thomsons:* James Thomson (1700–1748), von Keats hochgeschätzter englischer Dichter, in seinem berühmten Epos *The Seasons* Wegbereiter der neueren Naturlyrik.

377,26 *»haben wir alle* ein *menschliches Herz«:* vgl. Wordsworth, *The Old Cumberland Beggar* I,153.

379,6 *Robertsons »Amerika«:* William Robertson (1721–1793), als Historiker Verfasser einer *Geschichte von Amerika.*

379,7 f. *Pizarro:* Francisco Pizarro (1478–1541), spanischer Konquistador, eroberte das Inkareich in Peru.

379,20 *»ein ärmlich ... Geschöpf«:* Shakespeare, *König Lear* III,4.

383,12 f. *Nichts bringt ... im Flor:* Wordsworth, *Ode: Intimations of Immortality,* Z. 181 f.

383,17 *Indienfahrer:* Auf der Suche nach Gelderwerb hatte Keats erwogen, als Schiffsarzt auf einem Indienfahrer anzuheuern.

384,7 *Boyardo:* Matteo Maria Bojardo (1434–1494), italienischer Dichter, schrieb u.a. *Der verliebte Orlando* (1495). Angeblich fiel Bojardo der Name für seinen Helden Rodamonte während eines Ausritts ein, worauf er begeistert nach Hause ritt und seinen Leuten befahl, die Glocken läuten zu lassen.

384,14 *Jonson:* Ben Jonson (1572–1637), neben Shakespeare und Marlowe der bedeutendste elisabethanische Dichter. Vgl. auch die Anm. zur *Ode auf die Lässigkeit.*

385,6 *Rousseaus »Heloise«:* Jean-Jacques Rousseau (1712–1778) läßt in seinem Roman *Julie ou La Nouvelle Héloïse* (1761) den Helden leidenschaftlich schmachtende Briefe schreiben.

388,17 f. *Miltons Hierarchien:* Zur Entstehungszeit des Briefes setzte sich Keats verstärkt mit dem mythologischen und historischen Gehalt von Miltons *Verlorenem Paradies* auseinander.

390,11 *Mr. Audubon:* John James Audubon (1785–1851), Naturforscher; verkaufte George Keats ein Boot mit Waren, das – wie Audubon wußte – längst gesunken war.
391,1–7 *Sobald ich merke ... und schreibe:* vgl. Sterne, *Tristram Shandy* IX,13.
392,33 f. *Whigs und Tories:* die beiden herrschenden Parteien zu Keats' Zeit, deren Vertreter entsprechend dem bis 1832 geltenden Parlamentswahlsystem fast ausschließlich dem Adel angehörten.
393,14 *gar in die Rippen stoßen:* vgl. Shakespeare, *Othello* I,2.
393,21 f. *Fusili:* Johann Heinrich Füßli (1741–1825), Schweizer Maler, nannte sich in England Henry Fuseli (auch Fusely); »Haltung ist alles« war ein oft von ihm gebrauchter Ausdruck. Keats spielt mit den Worten »Füsilieren«, »Fuß«, »Muskete«.
393,33 *Hammond:* Thomas Hammond war der Wundarzt und Apotheker, bei dem Keats in die Lehre ging und mit dem er sich Ende 1813 überwarf.
396,18 f. *Zungen und Knochen:* vgl. Shakespeare, *Ein Sommernachtstraum* IV,1.
397,23 f. *»letzten Schwäche edler Geister«:* Milton, *Lycidas,* Z. 71.
398,5 *Shallow:* vgl. Shakespeare, *Heinrich IV,* 2. Teil, III,2.
402,27 *»Geh in ein Kloster ... geh!«:* Shakespeare, *Hamlet* III, 1.
404,28 *»jede Fuge«:* vgl. Spenser, *The Faerie Queene* II,7.
405,2 *Metap[hysik]:* im Original abgekürzt, entweder »Metaphysik« oder »Metaphorik«.
405,3 *Prometheus:* Shelleys *Prometheus Unbound,* von Shelley im gemeinsamen Verlag Ollier veröffentlicht und Keats versprochen; freilich schwingt auch der an einen Felsen geschmiedete Titan selbst in Keats' Worten mit.
405,9 *Band:* Keats' zweiter Gedichtband *Lamia, Isabella, The Eve of St Agnes, and other Poems,* erschien Ende Juni 1820.
408,10/12 *Tootts / Sam:* Tootts war der Spitzname von Fanny Brawnes jüngerer Schwester Margaret, Sam derjenige von Fannys Bruder.

Zeittafel

1795 29. oder 31. Oktober: John Keats wird im Haus der Eltern Thomas und Frances Keats, den *Swan and Hoop*-Mietställen im Londoner Vorort Finsbury, geboren.

1797 28. Februar: Geburt des Bruders George.

1799 18. November: Geburt des Bruders Tom.

1803 3. Juni: Geburt der Schwester Fanny. August: Keats besucht die Schule in Enfield; Beginn der Freundschaft mit Charles Cowden Clarke.

1804 16. April: Tod des Vaters nach einem Reitunfall. Juni: Keats' Mutter heiratet erneut und gibt die Kinder zu den Großeltern nach Enfield.

1805 8. März: Tod des Großvaters. Mit der Großmutter Umzug nach Edmonton.

1807 Rückkehr der Mutter.

1809 Die Mutter, Frances Keats, erkrankt, Keats pflegt sie.

1810 März: Frances Keats stirbt an Lungentuberkulose. Juli: J. N. Sandall und R. Abbey werden zu Vormündern der Keats-Kinder bestimmt.

1811 Sommer: Keats verläßt die Schule und beginnt eine Ausbildung zum Wundarzt. Prosaübersetzung von Vergils *Aeneis.*

1813 Erste Lektüre von Spensers *The Faerie Queene;* Keats liest regelmäßig Leigh Hunts liberales Magazin *Examiner.*

1814 Erste Gedichte (*Imitation of Spenser, To Lord Byron* u. a.) Dezember: Tod der Großmutter.

1815 Schwärmerischer Poesiezirkel mit George Felton Mathew. 2. Februar: Sonett auf die Entlassung Hunts aus dem Gefängnis. 1. Oktober: Immatrikulation an den

United Hospitals of Guy's and St. Thomas's in London. 29. Oktober: Erfolgreiche Bewerbung um die Stellung eines Assistenzwundarztes.

1816 Mai: Hunt veröffentlicht Keats' *O Solitude!* im *Examiner.* Bekanntschaft mit Joseph Severn. Juli: Keats besteht die Prüfung zum Apothekerdoktor. August: Aufenthalt mit Bruder Tom in Margate. Oktober: Die Sonette *How many bards!* und *On First Looking into Chapmans Homer* entstehen. Durch Clarke Bekanntschaft mit Leigh Hunt, Benjamin Robert Haydon und John Hamilton Reynolds; Bruch mit Mathew. November: Mit den Brüdern Umzug nach Cheapside. Dezember: Fertigstellung von *Sleep and Poetry.* Hunt zitiert *How many bards!* in seinem Artikel »Young Poets«. Bekanntschaft mit Shelley. Abbruch der Studien und Entschluß, Dichter zu werden.

1817 März: Keats sieht die *Elgin Marbles* im Britischen Museum. Der erste Gedichtband, *Poems,* erscheint bei Ollier in London. Umzug mit den Brüdern nach Hampstead. April bis August: Buch I und II von *Endymion* entstehen während Aufenthalten in Carisbrooke, Margate, Canterbury, Hastings. Freundschaften mit Benjamin Bailey, Charles Brown, Charles Dilke. September: Mit Dilke in Oxford; *Endymion,* Buch III. Oktober: Keats erkrankt und nimmt deswegen Quecksilber. November: Abschluß des *Endymion* in Burford Bridge. Keats schreibt Theaterkritiken und definiert in einem Brief an die Brüder Schlüsselbegriffe seines Dichtungsverständnisses (»intensity«, »negative capability«).

1818 Januar bis Februar: Keats trifft Wordsworth und besucht Hazlitts Vorlesungen über englische Dichter. Überarbeitung des *Endymion.* März bis April: Mit dem schwerkranken Tom in Teignmouth. *Endymion* erscheint bei Taylor and Hessey, London. Mai: Brief an Reynolds mit dem *»Gleichnis vom menschlichen Le-*

ben« als einem *»großen Haus mit vielen Gemächern«*. Juni: George wandert aus nach Amerika. Juni bis August: Wanderung mit Brown durch Schottland und Irland; Heimkehr aufgrund schwerer Erkältung. August bis September: Keats pflegt Tom in Hampstead, lernt Fanny Brawne kennen. In der konservativen Presse stoßen die *Poems* und der *Endymion* auf entschiedene Ablehnung. Beginn der Arbeit an *Hyperion*. 1. Dezember: Tom stirbt an Lungentuberkulose. Keats zieht mit Brown nach Wentworth Place, Hampstead.

1819 Januar bis Februar: Reisen nach Sussex und Hampshire. *The Eve of St Agnes* und *The Eve of St Mark* entstehen. März/April: Keats gibt *Hyperion* auf. Fanny Brawne mietet sich in Wentworth Place ein. April bis Mai: Brief an George mit dem Entwurf der Welt als *»Tal der Seelenbildung«*; Keats schreibt *La Belle Dame sans Merci* und die großen Oden (*Ode an Psyche, Ode auf eine griechische Urne, Ode an eine Nachtigall, Ode auf die Melancholie, Ode auf die Lässigkeit*). Inoffizielle Verlobung mit Fanny Brawne. Geldschwierigkeiten; Plan, Schiffsarzt zu werden. Juni bis September: Aufenthalte in Shanklin und Winchester; schreibt *Lamia*, gemeinsam mit Brown *Otho the Great*, das zweite Hyperion-Fragment und *An den Herbst*. Erste Anzeichen von Tuberkulose. Oktober bis Dezember: *König Stephen* entsteht. Offizielle Verlobung mit Fanny Brawne. Labiler Gesundheitszustand, Depressionen.

1820 Januar: George auf Kapitalsuche in England. *Otho the Great* wird nicht aufgeführt. Februar: Erste Lungenblutung, Bettruhe für den Rest des Monats. März: Überarbeitet *Lamia*. April: Umzug nach Kentish Town. Hunt veröffentlicht *La Belle Dame sans Merci* im *Indicator*. Juni: Zweite Hämorrhagie; Keats zieht zu Hunt. Juli: der Band *Lamia, Isabella, The Eve of St Agnes, and other Poems* erscheint bei Taylor and Hessey und wird positiv aufgenommen. Ärztliche Empfehlung einer Kur in Italien; Shelley lädt Keats ein, den Winter über zu ihm nach Pisa zu kommen. Keats zieht zu den Brawnes nach Wentworth Place. September: segelt mit Severn an Bord der »Maria Crowther« nach Italien. Oktober: Zehntägige Quarantäne im Hafen von Neapel. 15. November: Ankunft in Rom, er wohnt Piazza di Spagna Nr. 26. 30. November: Keats schreibt den letzten Brief an Brown.

1821 23. Februar: Keats stirbt gegen 23 Uhr. 26. Februar: Bestattung auf dem Protestantischen Friedhof in Rom.

Nachwort

Keats im Urteil der Nachwelt

Wenn man in der ersten Hälfte unseres Jahrhunderts einen Kenner der englischen Poesie nach dem größten lyrischen Dichter seit Milton gefragt hätte, wäre einem mit großer Wahrscheinlichkeit John Keats genannt worden. Alle einschlägigen Anthologien räumten seinen Gedichten einen breiten Raum ein, die angelsächsische Keatsforschung war aktiv und fruchtbar, und die deutsche Vorstellung von ›Lyrik‹ – die ja keineswegs mit dem Bedeutungsumfang des englischen Wortes *poetry* deckungsgleich ist – machte es auch den deutschen Liebhabern von Gedichten leicht, in Keats geradezu den Prototyp des Lyrikers zu sehen. Zweifellos trug die ergreifende Biographie des frühverstorbenen Romantikers nicht wenig zu seiner Beliebtheit bei, doch auch unsentimentale und realistische Leser konnten, wenn sie sich auf seine besten Texte einließen, oft zum ersten Mal in ihrem Leben die beglückende Wirkung vollendeter Poesie erleben.

Schon 1976 mußte freilich Helmut Viebrock, der deutsche Anglist, der sich am intensivsten mit Keats befaßt hat, nicht ohne leises Bedauern feststellen, daß »sich das Interesse der Forscher« nun stärker »an dem revolutionären Visionär Blake, dem poetologischen Theoretiker Coleridge, dem politischen Aktivisten Byron und dem Sozialutopisten Shelley entzündet« hatte.[1]

Die ›Übersättigung‹ durch Keats, die Viebrock bei Kritikern und Lesern registrierte, war natürlich zeit- und ursachengleich mit dem Generationsbruch in der Nachkriegszeit, den man als »neue Aufklärung«, als 68er Revolte und (speziell in der Kunst- und Literaturauffassung) als Paradigmenwechsel bezeichnet hat – von einem (angeblich) verengten und

1 Helmut Viebrock, *John Keats*, Darmstadt 1977 (Erträge der Forschung, 67), S. I.

unwissenschaftlichen, vorwiegend idealistischen und ästhetischen zu einem rationalistisch-theoriebewußten und (angeblich) methodisch sauberen Literaturbegriff, der sich freilich nur allzuoft als militant ideologisiert erwies. Was dabei auf der Strecke blieb, waren die emotionalen und sinnlichen *valeurs* von Lyrik, und speziell der Art von Lyrik, bei der die Schönheit sowohl Hauptcharakteristikum der Form als auch thematischer Kern der Aussage ist. Und dies ist bei Keats der Fall.[2]

Es hieße freilich die Fülle dessen, was er dichterisch zum Ausdruck brachte, ungebührlich verengen, wollte man in ihm nur einen Schönheitspriester des *l'art pour l'art* und des Elfenbeinturms sehen, wenn man ihn auch mit einem gewissen Recht als den Vater dieser späteren Tendenzen gesehen hat. Abgesehen davon, daß Dichtung, die ja mit Sprache und damit mit Bedeutungen arbeitet, nie gänzlich »dehumanisiert« werden kann[3], d.h. nie ganz den Bezug zu jenen Phänomenen der Wirklichkeit auszuschalten vermag, die sich aus der Kommunikation oder Konfrontation des Dichters mit der Welt ergeben – abgesehen von dieser Grundtatsache gilt für Keats: Sein Sensualismus transferiert soviel reale ›Welt‹ in die Lyrik, daß diese nie zum bloßen Formenspiel wird; und sein Werk trägt zudem so viele Spuren des Leidensdrucks, den diesem Dichter sein Festhalten an dem Ideal der Schönheit inmitten einer ihn gar nicht mit Schönheit verwöhnenden Existenz verursachte, daß von einem Abgehobensein in eine rein ästhetische Sphäre nicht die Rede sein kann.

Keats ist nicht etwa deshalb zu einem Stammvater der Dichtung der Schönheit im 19. und 20. Jahrhundert geworden, weil er den Ausschluß der Kontingenz, der Gefährdung aller menschlichen Existenz, aus dem Material der Lyrik ge-

2 Es gibt viele Belege dafür, von der Anfangszeile des *Endymion* (1817): »A thing of beauty is a joy for ever: / Its loveliness increases; it will never / Pass into nothingness« bis zu dem Brief an Fanny Brawne vom Februar 1820, in dem Keats schreibt: »I habe lov'd the principle of beauty in all things«.

3 Vgl. Michael Hamburger, *Wahrheit und Poesie*, Frankfurt a. M. 1985, S. 49.

fordert oder praktiziert hätte. Er wurde sich vielmehr – neben der Beseligung dieser Existenz durch das Erleben des Schönen – auch der tiefen Fragwürdigkeit des Schönheitskultes angesichts der Schattenseiten der *condition humaine* und des sozialen Daseins immer mehr bewußt, und er hat sein Wissen an alle schönheitssüchtigen Poeten der Nachwelt vererbt, gleich ob sie dieser Erkenntnis in ihren Werken Rechnung trugen oder durch deren emphatische Verleugnung im Werk ihren *mauvaise foi* zu unterdrücken suchten.

Was Keats von den anderen Romantikern seiner Generation abgrenzt und ihren Glauben dämpft, daß die Poesie als »etwas Göttliches ... emporsteige, um Licht und Feuer aus jenen ewigen Regionen herabzuholen, zu welchen der eulenflügelige Verstand nicht einmal aufzufliegen wagt«[4], ist seine wachsende Skepsis gegenüber allen metaphysischen und auch ethischen Legitimationen des Schönen, das zugleich Wahrheit sei. Zwar ersehnte er eine philosophische Beglaubigung des transzendenten Status der Schönheit mit gleicher Inständigkeit wie der naturoptimistische Wordsworth, der spekulative Coleridge und der dichtungsgläubige Shelley, und er entwarf auch – vor allem in seiner »poetischen Romanze« *Endymion* und in seinen Briefen – gelegentlich »systems of salvation« (Heilssysteme). Aber er brachte einer metaphysischen und moralischen Nobilitierung des Schönheitsideals immer starke Zweifel entgegen.[5] Damit ist er (neben Byron) der sich selbst gegenüber aufrichtigste der englischen Romantiker, der selbstkritischste und – abgesehen von seinen tragischen äußeren Lebensumständen – derjenige, der die Tragik romantischen Künstlertums in den nur gut vier Jahren seines Schaffens wahrscheinlich intensiver erfah-

4 Percy Bysshe Shelley, *A Defence of Poetry*, London 1840.

5 Vgl. etwa die Unterscheidung zwischen dem genialen Menschen und dem Machtmenschen im Brief an Benjamin Bailey vom 22. November 1817, die Bemerkungen über den »poetischen Charakter«, der kein Selbst habe, im Brief an Richard Woodhouse vom 27. Oktober 1818 oder die Thematisierung der fragwürdigen Doppelnatur der Schönheit in der Verserzählung *Lamia*.

ren hat als der weltschmerzbedrückte, aber vitale Publikumsliebling Byron, der am Leid der politischen Realitäten schwer tragende, aber freiheitsberauschte Shelley oder die beiden das Austrocknen ihrer Dichtergabe lange überlebenden Dichterfreunde Wordsworth und Coleridge.

Die Lebensumstände

Keats' kurzes Leben[6] war von vielen Heimsuchungen überschattet. – Am 31. Oktober 1795 als Sohn eines Mietstallbesitzers im Londoner Vorort Finsbury geboren, verbrachte er seine frühe Kindheit in einem nicht gerade unterprivilegierten, aber doch recht ungeistigen Milieu. Nach dem Verlust des Vaters, der 1804 tödlich verunglückte, und nach der raschen Wiederverheiratung der Mutter mit einem zweifelhaften Ehrenmann, den sie auch bald wieder verließ, so wie sie vier Monate nach dem Tod ihres ersten Mannes um des zweiten willen ihre vier Kinder verlassen hatte, war John Keats eigentlich fast immer abhängig von Verwandten, Vormündern oder Freunden. Dies war, was die Freunde betrifft, freilich ein Gewinn für ihn. Denn während der Vormund Richard Abbey Keats und seine Geschwister in der Berufswahl und -ausbildung autoritär beeinflußte und ihr Erbe zum Teil veruntreute, gaben ihm die Freunde die Chance, seinen Bildungshunger zu stillen und seinen Bekanntenkreis so zu erweitern, daß er mit namhaften Künstlern wie dem Maler Benjamin Robert Haydon und führenden Autoren der liberalen Intellektuellenschicht wie Leigh Hunt, William Wordsworth, William Hazlitt, Charles Lamb, William Godwin und Percy Bysshe Shelley in Kontakt kam.

Einer seiner engeren Freunde, Charles Armitage Brown,

6 Von den vielen Biographien – vgl. dazu die Bibliographie bei Viebrock (s. Anm. 1), S. 20–22 – erwies sich für die Zwecke dieser Einführung als besonders hilfreich, da betont sachlich: Walter Jackson Bate, *Keats*, Cambridge (Mass.) 1963.

half Keats mehrmals finanziell und ließ ihn ein Jahr in seinem Appartement in Wentworth Place, Hampstead (heute ein Keats-Museum) wohnen. Ein anderer, der Maler Joseph Severn, der Keats einige Male porträtiert hat, reiste im September 1820 mit dem bereits todkranken Dichter nach Rom und pflegte ihn dort in einem Haus an der Spanischen Treppe (heute ebenfalls eine Keats-Gedenkstätte) bis zu seinem frühen Ende.[7]

Einen besonders großen – wenn auch etwas fragwürdigen – Anteil an Keats' Entwicklung als Dichter hatte der elf Jahre ältere Poet und ›Radikale‹ Leigh Hunt.[8] Dessen Vorbild bestärkte den jungen Keats in seinem 1816 (nach der Beendigung seiner Lehre als Apotheker und Wundarzt) gefaßten Entschluß, Dichter zu werden. Auch festigten Hunts liberale Ideen und Aktivitäten in seinem jungen Bewunderer die politischen Überzeugungen, die er schon in seiner Schulausbildung von dem progressiven Sohn des Schulleiters, seinem Freund Charles Cowden Clarke, empfangen hatte – neben vielen literarischen Anregungen und der Begeisterung für die Antike und die Elisabethaner. Hunts Einfluß ist in den frühen dichterischen Versuchen Keats' und auch in seinem ersten großen Erzählgedicht *Endymion* überall zu spüren, und dieser Einfluß hat Keats nicht nur bei den Tory-Kritikern geschadet, für die Hunt aus politischen Gründen inakzeptabel war[9], sondern er hat ihn auch ästhetisch in eine Richtung gedrängt, von der er sich erst langsam befreien mußte: mangelnde sprachliche und metrische Zucht, kleinliche Detail-

7 Weitere enge Freunde, denen Keats viel verdankte, waren Benjamin Bailey, Charles Wentworth Dilke, William Haslam, Richard Woodhouse und John Hamilton Reynolds.

8 Einen guten Überblick über die politischen Gruppierungen der Zeit gibt Malcolm Kelsall, *Byron's Politics*, Brighton (Suss.) / Totowa (N.Y.) 1987.

9 Der im konservativen *Blackwood's Magazine* im Rahmen einer Serie »Über die Cockney-Schule in der Dichtung« im August 1818 erschienene Artikel über Keats war so vernichtend und böswillig, daß sich Shelley veranlaßt sah, den frühen Tod seines Dichterfreundes auf diesen Verriß zurückzuführen (siehe Shelleys Elegie auf den Tod von Keats: *Adonais*, Str. 36 und Vorwort).

freudigkeit und die Tendenz, »[to make] fine things petty and beautiful things hateful«, wie er in einer sehr kritischen Briefstelle über Hunt schrieb[10].

Ein junger Mann, mit dem so viele geistig regsame und kreative Menschen Freundschaft schließen, muß entweder besonders begabt oder besonders attraktiv sein. John Keats war beides. Seine Schulkameraden bescheinigten ihm in späteren Zeugnissen Mut, Feinfühligkeit, Mitleidsfähigkeit und Großzügigkeit, freilich auch einen etwas hitzigen Charakter[11]. Dazu war er offenherzig, ritterlich und gelegentlich bis zur Kampfbereitschaft erregt, wenn er Zeuge von Ungehörigkeiten oder Ungerechtigkeit wurde.

Es ist eine besondere Grausamkeit des Schicksals, daß dieser gut aussehende und geniale Jüngling 1819 im Alter von nur vierundzwanzig Jahren von der Tuberkulose heimgesucht wurde, der auch sein Bruder Thomas ein Jahr zuvor neunzehnjährig erlegen war, bis zuletzt gepflegt von seinem Bruder John.

Über Keats' äußeren Lebenslauf ist wenig nachzutragen: zweimal besuchte er die Isle of Wight, nach der Publikation seines ersten Gedichtbandes 1817 und im Sommer seines »fruchtbaren Jahres« 1819; 1818 wanderte er durch Schottland, was womöglich zum Ausbruch der tödlichen Krankheit ebenso beitrug wie die Pflege des Bruders; quälend war die Geschichte der Liebe des bereits mit häufigen Rachenschmerzen geplagten und bald ernstlich erkrankenden Keats zu der achtzehnjährigen Fanny Brawne. Keats' Liebesbriefe an Fanny, die er seit dem Sommer 1819 und dann vor allem aus Rom schrieb, wohin er sich im Herbst 1820 vor dem rauhen englischen Winter geflüchtet hatte und wo er auch starb, sind erschütternde Dokumente dieses Dichterlebens, das am 23. Februar 1821 erlosch. Keats ist auf dem protestantischen Friedhof in Rom begraben.

10 Brief an Georg und Georgiana Keats vom 16. Dezember 1818 – 4. Januar 1819.

11 Vgl. Bate (s. Anm. 6), S. 17f.

Die dichterischen Anfänge

Die wesentliche dichterische Produktion von Keats konzentriert sich auf die Jahre 1817 bis 1819. Was (seit 1815) vorausging und zum Teil in seine erste Veröffentlichung, den im März 1817 erschienenen Band *Poems* Eingang fand, ist ungleich in der Qualität und oft unsicher in der ohnehin lockeren und assoziativen Gedankenführung, der stilistischen Ausrichtung und der Gattungsorientierung. Da, wo Keats ansetzt zu erzählen – und Erzählen in Versen war seit Scotts und Byrons Versromanzen die große Mode geworden[12] –, scheitert er an einem offensichtlichen Mangel an narrativen Einfällen ebenso wie an der Exuberanz der alles überwuchernden, mit allen Sinnen erfaßten Bilddetails. Die Vorbilder – Spenser, verschiedene vorromantische und spätklassizistische Dichtungsmodelle sowie die Zeitgenossen Thomas Moore und (vor allem) Leigh Hunt – sind leicht auszumachen. Eine etwas süßliche pubertäre Erotik, für die – neben des Dichters Jugend – ebenfalls Hunt und Moore mitverantwortlich sind, ist heute schwer erträglich und schadete auch zu Keats' Lebzeiten seiner Reputation bei den Kritikern, zumal diese erotischen Fantasien auch noch in dem 1817 begonnenen und im Frühjahr 1818 publizierten *»long Poem« Endymion* gelegentlich die Wirkung schmälern[13].

Dennoch, der Band *Poems* von 1817 ist aus mehreren Gründen aufschlußreich:

1. In den zwei längeren, den Band einrahmenden Gedichten *I stood tip-toe upon a little hill* und *Sleep and Poetry* tastet sich Keats auf dem Weg über Naturbilder, antike Mythen und

12 Vgl. dazu Hermann Fischer, *Die romantische Verserzählung in England*, Tübingen 1964; engl. Neuausg.: H.F.: *Romantic Verse Narrative*, Cambridge 1991.

13 Daß solche Einwände nicht nur auf die Prüderie der Zeitgenossen zurückzuführen sind, sondern auch heute ihre Berechtigung haben, weist John Barnard nach in: »*Endymion*: ›Pretty Paganism‹ and ›Purgatory Blind‹«, in: Hermione de Almeida (Hrsg.), *Critical Essays on John Keats*, Boston (Mass.) 1990, S. 47–67.

frühere Dichterschicksale an eine Bestimmung des Wesens, des Ursprungs und der Funktion von Dichtung heran[14]. Daraus entsteht sicher noch keine kohärente Dichtungstheorie, wie Keats ja zeitlebens gegenüber rational erfaßbaren Systemen mißtrauisch war[15] – trotz der schon erwähnten »systems of salvation«, die er entwarf, und so sehr er auch seine mangelnde philosophische Schulung bedauerte.[16] Das geistige Fundament des Klassizismus ist jedenfalls verlassen[17] und wird auch an einer Stelle polemisch abgewertet[18].

2. Während sich in den beiden eben genannten Gedichten und in den Spenser-Imitationen der Sensualismus ankündigt, der für Keats' Lyrik bis zum Ende, bis zur Ode *To Autumn* vom September 1819 so charakteristisch werden sollte, reflektieren die drei Episteln (an zwei Freunde und an den Bruder George) einerseits den sich festigenden Entschluß, sein Leben dem Dichterberuf zu widmen, andererseits aber auch die Selbstzweifel, die dieser Entschluß auslöste und die in Keats immer wieder aufsteigen sollten.

3. In *I stood tip-toe* und *Sleep and Poetry* finden sich immer wieder Ansätze zu einer Art des Verständnisses und Ge-

14 »[...] the end and aim of poetry«, *Sleep and Poetry*, Z. 293.

15 Vgl. seine Briefe an George und Thomas Keats vom 21.Dezember 1817 (Kritik an Coleridges theoretisierendem Zerdenken aller Geheimnisse) und an James Rice vom 24.März 1818 (über die Unmöglichkeit, den Drang nach Spekulationen über Jenseitiges in Zaum zu halten). Ähnlich die wichtige Stelle über das Wissen im ersten Drittel des Briefes an John Hamilton Reynolds vom 3.Mai 1818. Vgl. auch den Brief an George und Thomas Keats vom 23.Januar 1818 (über das graduelle Reifen der Denkfähigkeit) und *Lamia* II,229.

16 Vgl. dazu die Verweise unter dem Stichwort »Philosophy: growing interest of K. in« im Index von Bate (s. Anm. 6).

17 Daß dies bei Keats das ständige Interesse an verstechnischer Systematik nicht ausschloß, hat W. J. Bate in seiner Keats-Biographie von 1963 und schon früher in *The Stylistic Development of John Keats*, London 1945 (Neuaufl. 1958) nachgewiesen, Keats' »Wortschreinerei« untersuchte M.R. Ridley in *Keats' Craftsmanship*, Oxford 1933 (Neuaufl. 1962 und 1963).

18 *Sleep and Poetry*, Z. 181–206. Diese Stelle mit ihrem Angriff auf die Schule von Boileau und (implizit) Pope löste Byrons Abneigung gegen Keats' Dichtungen aus.

brauchs der Stoffe der antiken Mythologie, welche die Wohlmeinenden unter den Zeitgenossen später anläßlich der längeren Dichtungen *Endymion* und *Hyperion* als eine sehr originelle Leistung hervorhoben. Die mythologischen Gestalten, vor allem solche, mit denen Keats durch Ovid und Apuleius, aber auch durch das Antikenlexikon von Lemprière[19] vertraut war, sind keine ornamentalen Versatzstücke aus einer toten Kulturepoche, sondern erhalten eine neue Aktualität, die ihnen aus zwei Wurzeln zukommt: aus einer Wiedergewinnung ihrer Naturgöttlichkeit im Sinne von Wordsworths großer Mythenpassage im vierten Buch seiner *Excursion*[20] (die Keats kannte) und aus einer Psychologisierung der Göttergestalten, die diese für das Symbolisieren menschlicher Belange geeignet macht[21]. Vor allem in *I stood tip-toe* begegnet man bereits Mythenmotiven,[22] die Keats in *Endymion* für die Gesamtsymbolik dieser Dichtung nutzte.

4. An den – einschließlich des Widmungssonetts an Leigh Hunt – siebzehn Sonetten des Bandes, die fast alle 1816 entstanden waren, kann man, obwohl sie zum Teil reine Etüden in dieser Gedichtform sind, erkennen, wie Keats schon in seinen Anfängen sich anhand der vorgegebenen Form die Fähigkeit zu strukturieren erarbeiten wollte, eine Fähigkeit, die später zum Gelingen der großen Oden wesentlich beitrug.

19 Lemprière, *Bibliotheca Classica, or a Classical Dictionary, containing a full account of all the Proper Names mentioned in Ancient Authors*, Reading 1788.

20 Erschienen 1814. Die Stelle umfaßt Z. 631–762 im 4. Buch.

21 Der bedeutende Kritiker der *Edinburgh Review* Francis Jeffrey hob diese Errungenschaft in seiner Rezension von *Endymion* und *Lamia* im August 1820 besonders hervor, und Byron beugte sich dessen Urteil, als er in *Don Juan* XI, Str. LX schrieb: »Er [Keats] konnte ohne Griechisch so erhaben / Von Göttern reden (oder lernt' es endlich) / Wie einst die Götter selbst geredet haben«.

22 S. Z. 47–52 (über Apollo), Z. 155–162 (über die Welt Pans und Floras), Z. 113–140 und Z. 181–242 (über die Mondgöttin Cynthia und die Wunderwirkung ihrer Hochzeitsnacht mit Endymion). Z. 141–150 deuten schon die Thematik der späteren *Ode an Psyche* an.

Mit welchem Erfolg er dies tat, läßt sich an dem besten Gedicht des ganzen Bandes ablesen, dem Sonett *On first looking into Chapman's Homer*, das bereits weltliterarischen Rang hat und völlig frei ist von der ›Vulgarität‹ des kleinbürgerlichen Geschmacks von Hunt[23].

5. Die wenigen Stellen, in denen sich Keats zu politischen Themen äußert[24], sind so allgemein gehalten, daß sie bereits seine Abneigung gegen alle Tendenzdichtung erkennen lassen.[25]

Der Qualitätssprung von den *Poems* von 1817 zu der bedeutenden Lyrik des Jahres 1819 wird nur erklärlich, wenn man sich auf ein genaueres Studium sowohl der dazwischenliegenden Briefe als auch der längeren Erzähldichtungen einläßt. Freilich ist dies hier nur in einer Zusammenfassung möglich.

Die Briefe als Schlüssel zu Keats' Gedankenwelt

Der junge Keats erlangte seine geistige Reife in den Jahren nach dem Wiener Kongreß, in denen die junge Intellektuellengeneration auf das Wiedererstarken der alten Gewalten in Europa – Dynastien, Kirche, einengende Verwaltungs- und Überwachungsapparate – mit Enttäuschung und innerer Entfremdung reagierte. Als Schüler der Clarkes in Enfield und als naturwissenschaftlich ausgebildeter Lehrling im Guy's Hospital nahm Keats wie selbstverständlich den Skeptizismus und Agnostizismus[26] der ›radikal-liberalen‹ Kreise um

23 Vgl. Viebrock (s. Anm. 1), S. 2 und den dortigen Hinweis auf John Bayleys Vortrag *Keats and Reality* von 1962.

24 Vgl. die Sonette *Written on the day that Mr. Leigh Hunt left Prison* und *To Kosciusko* sowie einige Passagen in den Versepisteln. Auch *Endymion* II,1–22 ist ein politisches Glaubensbekenntnis.

25 »Wir hassen Dichtung mit handgreiflicher Tendenz« schrieb er in einem Brief an John Hamilton Reynolds vom 3. Februar 1818.

26 Besonders instruktiv ist hierzu: Stuart M. Sperry, *Keats the Poet*, Princeton 1973.

die Brüder John und Leigh Hunt an, ohne daß ihm zugleich – so wie Wordsworth, Coleridge, Shelley und auch Byron – die Alternative einer traditionellen philosophischen Universitätsausbildung zuteil wurde. Diese Ausgangslage erklärt die sensualistische und naturalistische Komponente vieler seiner Dichtungen, ihre auf Sinneserfahrung gegründete Ding- und Detailfreudigkeit. Und ebenso erklärt sie die – meist recht flach verallgemeinernden – antikirchlichen Äußerungen in manchen frühen Gedichten und Briefen[27]. Sie macht aber auch sein Ungenügen an dem Perfektibilitätswahn und dem oberflächlichen Hedonismus vieler seiner liberalen Zeitgenossen verständlich: Dieser wahrhaft »romantische« Dichter konnte sich nicht in dem »philosophischen Küchengarten« der agnostischen Mentalität seiner Umgebung zur Ruhe setzen, denn »der geistige Landhausbesitzer weiß um die *terra semi-incognita* des Überwirklichen«[28] – seine Sehnsucht nach einer tieferen Sinngebung der Existenz ist daher unabweisbar.

Wie Shelley erhoffte Keats sich diese Sinngebung wohl letzten Endes von der Poesie.[29] Aber sein ganzes kurzes Leben war überschattet von Zweifeln an einer so hohen Leistungsfähigkeit der Dichtung[30], von der Unsicherheit, wie

27 Vgl. dazu Bate (s. Anm. 6), S. 132ff., S. 217 und – zur späteren Einstellung zur Religion – S. 688ff.

28 Brief an John Rice vom 24. März 1818.

29 Diese Hoffnung läßt sich von den Anfängen über *Endymion* bis zu der *Ode to a Grecian Urn* und zu der Abbruchstelle des *Hyperion*-Fragmentes immer wieder ausmachen. Die wichtigsten Briefstellen dazu finden sich in seinen Briefen an Reynolds vom 3. Mai 1818 und an George und Georgiana Keats vom 21. April 1819.

30 Werke über diesen Zweifel sind *Lamia*, *La Belle Dame Sans Merci* und *The Fall of Hyperion*. Eine Briefstelle sei wörtlich zitiert: »Ich bin manchmal so ungeheuer skeptisch, daß ich denke, die Poesie selbst sei ein bloßes Irrlicht, dazu da, jeden, der zufällig seines Funkelns ansichtig wird, zu amüsieren« (an Bailey am 13. März 1818); vgl. auch den Brief an George und Georgiana Keats vom 19. März 1819 über den Widerstreit von Intensität *(energy)* und Wahrheit in der Dichtkunst.

eine solche Dichtung auszusehen hätte[31] und ob er selber ausersehen sei, ein wahrer Dichter zu werden[32].

Wie Leigh Hunt war Keats fasziniert von der sinnlichen Schönheit, aber er erkannte mehr und mehr nicht nur die Gefahr des Eskapismus, die in jeder »Ding-Dichtung« liegt, sondern auch das Illusionäre und moralisch Gefährliche eines Schönheitskultes ohne ethische und metaphysische Bezüge – also einer Wirkungspoetik, bei der einzig die Intensität Gradmesser des poetischen Wertes ist.

Wie Byron war Keats zu scharfsichtig, zu gut mit dem Leid vertraut und zu sehr auf reale politische Reform ausgerichtet, als daß er sich mit dem romantischen Traum vom Ideal, das durch die subjektive Einbildungskraft der Dichter zu erreichen ist, hätte zufrieden geben können. Aber andererseits wäre Byrons Zynismus und spontaner Aktionismus (als Selbstschutz der verwundeten Seele) keine praktikable Lösung für Keats gewesen: dazu war seine Schönheitssehnsucht zu stark und dazu war sie auch zu sehr mit dem Gedanken an das Große, das Erhabene und einen höheren Sinn des leidvollen Lebens verwoben.[33]

Die Briefe belegen, neben der Dankesschuld an seine großen Zeitgenossen, deren er sich immer bewußt war, seine entschiedene Abwendung von allen seine Individualität erdrückenden Einflüssen: von Wordsworths »egotistical sublime«,[34] von Coleridges bohrendem Analysieren aller metaphysischen

31 Vgl. die Briefe an George und Thomas Keats vom 21. Dezember 1817 (Intensität als Gradmesser; die negative Fähigkeit des Dichters), an Reynolds vom 3. Februar 1818 (Unaufdringlichkeit der Dichtung), an John Taylor vom 27. Februar 1818 (Axiome zur Dichtung) und an George und Georgiana Keats vom 18. Februar 1819 (Kritik an Byron).

32 Breite Ausführungen zu diesen Zweifeln bei Bate (s. Anm. 6), Kap. 5–7. Vgl. auch Canto I der Traumvision *Der Fall Hyperions*.

33 Hier waren die Freundschaft mit dem religiös überzeugten B. R. Haydon, die Lektüre von Chapmans Homerübersetzung, Shakespeares *König Lear* und der Anblick der von Lord Elgin nach England gebrachten Parthenonskulpturen, die 1816 im Britischen Museum aufgestellt worden waren, entscheidende Erlebnisse.

34 Brief an Woodhouse vom 27. Oktober 1818.

Geheimnisse,[35] von Hunts »self delusions«,[36] von Byrons nacktem Realismus,[37] Zynismus,[38] und extrovertiertem Posieren[39] und von den menschheitsbeglückenden Höhenflügen der Fantasie Shelleys, dem er aus Rom vier Wochen vor seinem Tod eine weise Beschränkung auf sein Künstlertum empfahl[40].

Weniger offensichtlich als diese Distanzierungen ist das Reifen einer systematischen Welt- und Dichtungsauffassung bei Keats. Ein so junger Mensch, dessen Lebensumstände eine nähere Berührung mit philosophischen Systemen nicht ermöglichten und der auch von seiner Mentalität her zu sensibel und zu ›romantisch‹ war, um eine kohärente Poetologie auszubilden, mußte mit Zweifeln und Unentschlossenheiten leben. Die Briefe enthalten viele Zeugnisse davon. Glänzend (und oft apodiktisch) formulierte Axiome stehen da neben Eingeständnissen der eigenen Unsicherheit – so etwa in dem oft zitierten Brief an Reynolds vom 3. Mai 1818 über das Leben als ein großes Haus mit vielen Zimmern, in dem die Türen aus dem zweiten Zimmer, der »Chamber of Maiden Thought«, alle in dunkle Gänge hinausführen – »we see not the ballance of good and evil. We are in a Mist ... We feel the 'burden of the Mystery'[41]« oder in dem Brief an den Bruder George in Amerika vom 19. März 1819, in dem Keats nach längerem Hin- und Herwenden der Frage, ob der Mensch eher ein von Instinkten gelenktes Geschöpf wie die Tiere sei oder selbstlos handeln könne wie Sokrates und Christus, von

35 Brief an George und Thomas Keats vom 21. Dezember 1817.

36 Briefe an Haydon vom 10.–11. Mai 1817 und an George und Thomas Keats vom 17. Dezember 1818.

37 Brief an George und Georgiana Keats vom 18. September 1819.

38 Keats gab noch auf der Seereise nach Rom im September 1820 seiner Empörung über die Schiffbruchschilderung in Byrons *Don Juan*, Canto II Ausdruck.

39 Vgl. Anm. 32.

40 Brief vom 16. August 1820. Vgl. den Brief an Bailey vom 8. Oktober 1817.

41 Keats zitiert hier Wordsworths *Lines composed a few miles above Tintern Abbey*, Z. 38.

sich sagt: »I myself am pursueing the same instinctive course as the veriest human animal you can think of – I am however young – straining at particles of light in the midst of a great darkness«.

Der Konflikt zwischen einer Faszination durch das Natürliche – Instinkt, Energie, animalische Kraft, Machttrieb, aber auch Trägheit[42] und passives Entgegennehmen der Inspiration, die nur dann etwas tauge, wenn sie dem Dichter »natürlich zufließe« – einerseits und den moralisch als verpflichtend erkannten Forderungen der Vernunft nach »Selbstlosigkeit«[43] andererseits wird für Keats geradezu identisch mit dem Konflikt zwischen Poesie und Moralphilosophie.

Eine lange Erörterung dieses seines Kernthemas enthält der schon erwähnte Brief an George und Georgiana Keats vom 19. März 1819. Keats reklamiert hier für sich zwar die Gabe der Selbsterkenntnis, nicht aber die Fähigkeit zu philosophischem Denken. Und indem er sein Nichtwissen eingesteht, läßt er seine Spekulationen fallen mit der Bemerkung, daß einzig die Erfahrung zähle: »Nothing ever becomes real till it is experienced«. Wie wenig ihm aber diese Reduzierung des Problems auf die bloße Empirie seine gedankliche Beunruhigung abnehmen kann, verrät das nun in den Brief aufgenommene Sonett *Why did I laugh to-night?*, das nicht nur die »Agonie seines Nichtwissens«[44] widerspiegelt, sondern mit dem Gedanken an die Unabweisbarkeit des Todes als der intensivsten Erfahrung die ganze Diskussion in einem agnostischen Schauer abbrechen läßt.[45]

42 Vgl. die *Ode on Indolence* vom Frühjahr 1819 und dazu eine direkt auf sie vorbereitende Stelle im Brief an George und Georgiana Keats vom 19. März / April 1819; ebenso die am 30. April 1819 an Bruder und Schwägerin gesandten Sonette *On Fame* und *To Sleep*.

43 Brief an George und Georgiana Keats vom 19. März 1819.

44 »[...] it was written with no Agony but that of ignorance« heißt es in dem zitierten Brief.

45 Vgl. auch die Versepistel »To John Hamilton Reynolds« vom 25. März 1818, deren zweite Hälfte (Z. 67–109) ähnliche Gedanken enthält, und das Sonett »When I have fears« vom Januar 1818.

Endymion – »Prüfstein der Erfindungsgabe«[46]

Im *Endymion* war der Erweis und das Erlebnis der Identität von Ideal und Wirklichkeit wohl das ursprüngliche Ziel der Anlage von – vage allegorischer – Handlung und Gedankenführung: die »fellowship with essence«[47], das heißt die »sort of onenesst«[48], die in »a kind of Pleasure Thermometer«[49] über die Stufen Freundschaft und Liebe erreicht wird, bedeutet die »chief intensity«, die zugleich die Wahrheit der höchsten Liebe[50] ist, und von dieser geht, wie von der Brautnacht Cynthias in *I stood tip-toe*, Segen für die ganze Erde aus[51]. Doch schon während der Abfassung scheint Keats der Glauben an diese glatte Lösung zweifelhaft geworden zu sein. Die Intensität des Leidens an dem Konflikt zwischen irdischer und göttlicher Schönheit – verkörpert durch die beiden Geliebten Endymions, das indische Mädchen und die Göttin Phoebe/Cynthia – ebenso wie die Fragwürdigkeit der geistigen und moralischen Nobilitierung der sinnlichen Liebe ließen den Dichter zunächst die »identitätsphilosophische« Lösung – die beiden Damen erweisen sich als ein und dieselbe Person – im vierten Buch überlang hinausschieben und dann in den 25 Schlußzeilen der langen Dichtung allzu rasch präsentieren, worauf er die beiden Liebenden schnell in ungreifbare Fernen entrückt[52].

46 Vgl. den Brief an Bailey vom 8. Oktober 1817.
47 *Endymion* I,778.
48 Ebd. I,796.
49 Brief an John Taylor vom 30. Januar 1818.
50 Vgl. Brief an John Taylor vom 30. Januar 1818 und *Endymion* I,800.
51 *Endymion* I,832–842.
52 Ebd. IV,977–1003.

Die drei romantischen Verserzählungen und die Ballade von *La Belle Dame sans Merci*

In *Isabella or the Pot of Basil*, entstanden im März/April 1818, einer Nachdichtung von Boccaccios *Decamerone*-Novelle IV,5, und auch in *The Eve of St Agnes*, entstanden im Januar 1819, einer ›mittelalterlichen‹ Romanze eigner Erfindung, verzichtet Keats auf greifbar allegorische Elemente, wenn auch die Liebesvereinigung in dem späteren Werk[53] von zumindest einem Kritiker als eine symbolische Inszenierung von Ideen, die Keats in seinen Briefen geäußert hatte, gedeutet worden ist – Ideen über die Authentizität der Imagination und über die Überlegenheit der *sensations* über das Wahrheitsstreben: die Sinnesempfindungen seien eine Vorahnung und Vorankündigung künftiger Wirklichkeit – das was wir auf Erden Glück nennen, werde sich in einem künftigen Glück »in a finer tone«[54] wiederholen. – Keats hielt nicht allzuviel von diesen beiden Verserzählungen. Wenn er freilich *Isabella* als »too smokeable« und zu sehr von »inexperience of life, and simplicity of knowledge« zeugend abtat und an dem *St. Agnes-Abend* den gleichen Fehler entdeckte, »only not so glaring«[55], – so heißt das nicht, daß er aus der Erfahrung mit den beiden Romanzen nicht viel gelernt hätte. Die Meisterlichkeit seiner Verssprache ist unbestreitbar, die suggestive Erfassung von Sinneseindrücken und Atmosphäre hat dem späteren 19. Jahrhundert besonders diese Dichtungen teuer gemacht, und die Farbnuancierung in *The Eve of St Agnes* wollte Keats noch im November 1819 als Drapierung für ein neues Poem mit mehr Charakterzeichnung und Gefühl wie-

53 *Eve of St Agnes*, Str. 36.

54 Brief an Bailey vom 22. November 1817. – Der genannte Kritiker ist Earl R. Wasserman, vgl. E. R. W.: *The Finer Tone: Keats' Major Poems*, Baltimore 1935; von seiner »symbolischen« Deutung abweichende Interpretationen gaben Jack Stillinger, *The Hoodwinking of Madeline and other Essays*, University of Illinois Press 1971, und Christopher Ricks, *Keats and Embarrassment*, Oxford 1974.

55 Brief an Woodhouse vom 21. September 1819.

derverwenden[56]. Seine Selbstkritik läßt aber erkennen, daß er diese beiden Romanzen des Jahres 1818 kaum für die Behandlung seiner Zentralproblematik bestimmt hatte, so sehr sie auch von einigen seiner anderen Themen gespeist sein mögen. Aber sie machten ihn reif für die großen Dichtungen seines *annus mirabilis* 1819.

Die von Hunts Stilsünden völlig freie[57] brillante Verserzählung *Lamia* und die ungemein kunstvolle Ballade *La Belle Dame sans Merci* führen die Thematik des *Endymion* weiter, indem sie die dort erzwungene Lösung radikal in Frage stellen: Der Liebhaber des schönen Doppelwesens Lamia, Lycius, stirbt, als ihm der nüchterne Blick des Philosophen Apollonius die unter der Schönheit verborgene Schlangennatur der Geliebten offenbart; und der Ritter, den La Belle Dame Sans Merci in ihre Zaubergrotte gelockt hat, sieht dort die Todverfallenenheit der Schönheitssucher, d.h. der Opfer der dämonischen Ekstase der »chief intensity«, und er erwacht »Alone and palely loitering« auf dem kalten Hügelabhang, in einer verwelkten Welt ohne Vogelsang.

Die fünf großen Oden: »rounded perfection and felicity of loveliness«[58]

Diese berühmten Gedichte tun, was Keats im August 1820 seinem Dichterkollegen Shelley für dessen Schaffen empfahl: sie befrachten »every rift of [their] subject with ore«[59]. Keine der zahllosen Interpretationen schöpft sie aus, keine kann ihre Schönheit, ihre gedankliche Dichte und formale Perfektion hinreichend erklären. Es ist aber vielleicht sinnvoll, hier eine Verbindung herzustellen zwischen der Gedankenwelt, die

56 Brief an John Taylor vom 17. November 1819.
57 Keats hatte seine Reimpaartechnik an Drydens Vorbild geschult.
58 Matthew Arnold, »Keats«, in: M.A.: *Essays in Criticism. Second series*, London 1888.
59 Brief an Shelley vom 16. August 1820.

bisher aus den Briefen und früheren Versdichtungen herausdestilliert wurden, und diesen fünf Oden.

Die *Ode to a Nightingale* dramatisiert die Problematik der Imagination: das Crescendo der rauschhaft erlebten Annäherung der Fantasie an den Vogel – Symbol zeitenthobener Schönheit – fällt in sich zusammen im Erwachen aus dieser »selbstauflösenden«[60] Ekstase und klingt aus in ratloser Ernüchterung. Die Ode ist damit eine noch reichere und diesmal rein lyrische Wiederholung der Thematik der fast gleichzeitig entstandenen Ballade von *La Belle Dame Sans Merci.* Wie dort wird das Symbol der Faszination aller Kritik enthoben und die Problematik der romantischen ›Sympathie mit dem Tod‹[61] einzig dem Schauenden und Lauschenden, d.h. dem lyrischen Ich zugeordnet.

Die *Ode to a Grecian Urn* ist eine Frucht jener Begeisterung für die Kunst der griechischen Antike, die in Keats schon im März 1817 durch Haydon und durch die Parthenonskulpturen ausgelöst worden war.[62] Sie ist aber auch als eine Summe seiner Kunstanschauung berühmt geworden. Freilich hat man sie oft als das Credo eines *l'art pour l'art*-Künstlers mißverstanden – zu Unrecht, denn der Keats des Frühjahrs 1819 ist nicht mehr der Jüngling, der am 22. November 1817 an Bailey geschrieben hatte: »What the imagination seizes as Beauty must be truth«. Der berühmte Schluß der Ode

'Beauty is truth, truth beauty‹ – that is all
Ye know on earth, and all ye need to know'

scheint zwar ein nahezu identisches Bekenntnis des Dichters zu sein, doch hier spricht nicht, wie in jenem Brief, Keats, sondern die Urne selbst. Was sie sagt, ist das, was das Kunstwerk – »a friend to man« – einzig uns zu sagen vermag, und das ist fürwahr eine menschenfreundliche Botschaft,

60 *Endymion* I,788: »enthralments / Far more self-destroying«.
61 Thomas Mann nannte die Sympathie mit dem Tod in seinen *Betrachtungen eines Unpolitischen* »Formel und Grundbestimmung aller Romantik«.
62 Vgl. Anm. 34.

»sweeter« als die zeitunterworfenen Melodien der Musik, süßer auch als die von subjektivem Verstehen (und Mißverstehen!) abhängigen, artikulierten und dadurch begrenzten Sprachmitteilungen der Dichtung. Diese Süßigkeit und immerwährende Schönheit, und nicht der ›narrative‹ Inhalt der dargestellten Szenen, ist das Glück und die Wahrheit, welche die Urne spenden kann, das, was uns aus ihr entgegenleuchtet – mehr kann sie nicht geben. Alle Fragen, die an sie gestellt werden (in den Strophen I und IV) prallen an ihrer marmornen Stille ab, alle Erklärungen jener Vorgänge aus einer längst vergangenen Zeit, die ihre Oberfläche schmücken, bleibt sie schuldig. Ihre Wahrheit ist nicht die Wahrheit der Menschen, deren Leben in der Zeit verläuft, ihre Schönheit ist nicht die vergängliche Schönheit der Natur. Die dargestellten Szenen haben keinen Vorgangs- und Verlaufscharakter und es mangelt ihnen deshalb »for ever« die Erfüllung, die Reife, das Vergehen. Ihre Melodien bleiben ungehört, der Ansatz zum Kuß ist erstarrt in der »Cold Pastoral« der stummen, nur mit sich selbst gefüllten Form, »All breathing human passion far above«.

Die *Ode on Melancholy* stellt neben dieses ›reine‹, ästhetisch distanzierte Glück der Urne den melancholisch schmerzlichen Genuß menschlicher, d.h. vergänglicher Wonnen. Die dem Welken ausgesetzte Naturschönheit und die durch Zwist bedrohte Liebe haben jenen oxymoronischen Charakter allen irdischen Glücks, den Keats seit seinen dichterischen Anfängen so oft in sprachliche Formeln gebannt hatte[63].

Die *Ode to Psyche,* die früheste der fünf Oden[64], hat als einzige noch die traditionelle Epiphanie[65] einer – wenn auch erst im Hellenismus literarisch gezeugten – wirklichen Gott-

63 Z.B. »balmy pain« in *I stood tip-toe*, Z. 162; vgl. auch *Endymion* II,1, II,346 bis 372 und VI,146–290; ferner *On sitting down to read King Lear once again*, Z. 8; *Isabella* XIII, *Hyperion* II,288, *Ode to Psyche* Z. 52 und *Ode on Melancholy*, passim, und dazu das verwandte Sonett *Bright Star*.

64 Sie entstand im April 1819.

65 Vgl. Kurt Schlüter, *Die englische Ode*, Bonn 1964.

heit zum Gegenstand. Dabei wird freilich die antike Quelle, die *Amor und Psyche*-Erzählung des Apuleius, gedanklich vertieft. In der letzten Strophe gibt der Dichter den Numina (Psyche = Seele, Amor = Liebe) nicht nur den reichen Bedeutungsgehalt, den er für diese Begriffe in seinen Briefen und Dichtungen bisher entfaltet hatte, sondern verspricht auch, ihnen in seinen Gedanken ein Sanktuarium zu errichten, in dem ihrer Vereinigung – die bei Apuleius erst durch ein Machtwort Jupiters möglich wird – nichts mehr im Wege steht (die Ode selbst ist bereits dieses Sanktuarium).

Epiphanien sind freilich auch die anderen vier Oden. In allen begegnet das lyrische Ich etwas Wesenhaftem oder Symbolischem, von dem es angerührt wird wie von der Erscheinung eines Numen, in einem »greeting of the spirit«[66] aus der »*terra semi-incognita*«[67] des Überwirklichen. Bei der sprachlich schönsten der Oden, *To Autumn*, ist, wie Leonard Unger gezeigt hat,[68] der Gegenstand – die Evokation des Herbstes in herrlichen Naturbildern bis hin zu einer diskreten Personifikation in der Strophe II – vollkommen identisch mit dem Thema, einem ganz unpathetischen Akzeptieren der Vergänglichkeit, des Abschieds und Sterbens als eines integralen Bestandteils des Naturprozesses: wie der Frühling hat auch der Herbst seine Musik (III), wie der vollreife Sommer (I) hat er seine Fruchtgaben und Blumen (II).

Einverständnis mit der Kontingenz als einer Grundbedingung irdischen Glücks – das war das Resultat des durch die paar fruchtbaren Jahre ausgetragenen Konflikts in Keats' Denken, des Konflikts zwischen einem konsequenten Naturalismus und einem geistig zu gewinnenden »*system of salvation*«. In *To Autumn* ist jene Identität der beiden Pole, die im *Endymion* postuliert, aber nicht überzeugend realisiert worden war, auf einer höheren Ebene verwirklicht.

66 Brief an Bailey vom 13. März 1818.

67 Brief an Rice vom 24. März 1818.

68 Leonard Unger, »Keats and the Music of Autumn«, in: John Fraser (Hrsg.): *Keats: The Odes. A Casebook*, London/Basingstoke 1971.

Das »Vale of Soul-making« und die *Hyperion*-Dichtungen

Den entscheidenden Schritt zu dieser Synthese belegt der Brief an George und Georgiana Keats vom 21. April 1819, geschrieben in dem Monat also, in dem die großen Odendichtungen begonnen wurden. Es ist wohl kein Zufall, daß ein Zitat aus Shakespeares *König Lear* – seit langem ein Katalysator für Keats' feinste Gedanken – in der Nähe steht. Hier kommt er – nach einem radikalen In-Frage-Stellen der Möglichkeit menschlichen Glücks angesichts der destruktiven Naturgewalten und der Todverfallenheit des Menschen – zu der Einsicht, die Welt sei nicht ein Jammertal, das der transzendenten Erlösung bedarf, sondern ein »Tal der Seelenwerdung«. Dieses »soul-making« ist eine Schulung für den göttlichen Funken der Intelligenz in uns; dabei ist das Herz die Fibel und die Welt voller Leid und Bedrängnis die Schule. Wer in der Fibel des fühlenden und leidenden Herzens zu lesen gelernt hat, erlangt seine Identität, wird zu einer Seele.

Das Werk, in dem Keats diese Seelenwerdung (unter Verwendung eines mythologischen Stoffes) aus der individualethischen Begrenztheit einer Art Frühexistentialismus herausführen und auf eine Kunstphilosophie und Politik umfassende Ebene emporheben wollte, war *Hyperion.* Er hatte die Verserzählung bereits im Sommer 1818 in Angriff genommen, im April 1819 jedoch als Fragment nach 1527 Zeilen abgebrochen. Im Spätsommer 1819 nahm Keats den Stoff in einer stark veränderten Fassung unter dem Titel *The Fall of Hyperion: A Dream* wieder auf, stellte das Unternehmen jedoch abermals nach über 500 Zeilen endgültig ein.

Die frühere Fassung kombiniert zwei Komplexe:

Der erste ist die nur tragisch zu behandelnde Erkenntnis, daß »jeder Fortschritt zugleich Verlust bedeutet und daß es keine kreative Fortentwicklung geben kann, ohne daß das Vorhergehende schmerzhaft, obwohl oft ohne eigene Schuld, zerstört wird.«[69] Dieses Thema, in den Jahren nach Napoleons Sturz von großer politischer Aktualität, ist eingekleidet in die Erzählung von der Ablösung des Goldenen Zeitalters der Titanen durch die Herrschaft der olympischen Götter. Es wirft, in Form der Beratung der Titanen in Buch II, mehrere Fragen auf: Fragen nach Gewalt und Gewaltlosigkeit, Herrschaftsberechtigung des höheren, »Selbst-losen« Wissens und der damit einhergehenden überlegenen Schönheit, nach Leiden und Dulden, Gut und Böse.

Der zweite Themenkomplex ist die ›Seelenwerdung‹. In der früheren Fassung ist sie an dem jungen Gott Apollo exemplifiziert, in der späteren wird sie dem Erzähler-Ich, also dem Dichter zugeteilt: Apollo hat fern von den an ihrem bevorstehenden Sturz aus ihrer bisherigen pastoralen Unschuld und Unwissenheit leidenden Titanen als schönheitstrunkener Träumer gelebt, aber an dieser isolierten Existenz kein Genügen mehr gefunden. Da erscheint ihm Mnemosyne, die Göttin der Geschichte, und er liest in ihren Augen die ganze Tragik des Weltprozesses[70]. Darüber wird er zum Gott oder, wie Keats es in einem charakteristischen Paradoxon ausdrückt, er »stirbt ins Leben«[71]. Damit hat er jene Seelenwerdung erlangt, die ihn sowohl zum Gott der neuen Herrschaft als auch zum tragischen Dichter befähigt: sein »knowledge enormous«[72] gibt ihm jene höchste Schönheit, welcher – nach der Erkenntnis des Meergottes Oceanus – die höchste Macht gebührt[73].

Im *Fall of Hyperion* ist dieser große Entwurf dadurch, daß anstatt des Gottes Apollo das Ich des Dichters in einer Traum-im-Traum-Struktur der »Last des Weltmysteriums«[74] und dem »ungeheueren Wissen« ausgesetzt wird, einerseits

69 M.H. Abrams, *Natural Supernaturalism*, Toronto 1971, S. 126.

70 *Hyperion* II,114ff.

71 Ebd. III,125–136: »liker still to one who should with fierce convulse / Die into life«.

72 Ebd. III,113.

73 Ebd. II,229.

74 Den Ausdruck »the burthen of the mystery« aus Wordsworths Gedicht *Tintern Abbey* hat Keats wiederholt in seinen Briefen zitiert.

erzähltechnisch und gedanklich komplizierter geworden, andererseits aber wird hier die politische Thematik der Machtbefähigung hinter die Frage nach einer humanen Poetik zurückgedrängt.

Es gibt viele Mutmaßungen über die Gründe für das Abbrechen dieses umfassenden, wahrhaft »epischen« Projekts[75]. Die wahrscheinlichsten Thesen sind, daß Keats mit dem, was er niederschrieb, alles gesagt hatte, was er sagen wollte und konnte; daß die Titelgestalt Hyperion, deren Aufbruch zur Aktion das ganze erste Buch der Erstfassung einnimmt, nach der Vergöttlichung Apollos keine Funktion mehr haben konnte; und daß Keats' Kraft wegen seiner fortschreitenden Krankheit dem riesigen Vorhaben nicht mehr gewachsen war[76].

Er hat nach dem September 1819 nichts mehr von Bedeutung geschrieben[77]. Aber auch wenn sein im Alter von vierundzwanzig Jahren nach unsäglichem körperlichem und seelischem Leiden zu Ende gegangenes Leben Fragment geblieben ist, so ist es ein Fragment von der Art seiner *Hyperion*-Dichtung: alles, was er der Menschheit sagen konnte, war gesagt.

75 Daß Keats sich stark an Miltons *Paradise Lost* orientierte, ist offensichtlich.

76 Keats selbst gab Reynolds in seinem Brief vom 21. September 1819 als Grund an, das Miltonsche Vorbild für seine Dichtung sei zu übermächtig geworden.

77 Seine Dramenversuche vom Sommer 1819 und eine Satire vom Herbst desselben Jahres, *The Cap and Bells*, sind selbstauferlegte Pflichtarbeiten, die nichts mit Keats eigentlichen Themen zu tun haben.

Verzeichnis der englischen und deutschen Gedichtüberschriften- und anfänge

Verzeichnis der Briefe